LAW AS INSTITUTION

Law and Philosophy Library

VOLUME 90

For further volumes:
http://www.springer.com/series/6210

LAW AS INSTITUTION

by

Massimo La Torre

"Magna Graecia" University of Catanzaro, Italy
University of Hull, United Kingdom

Springer

Prof. Massimo La Torre
Università degli Studi "Magna Graecia" di Catanzaro
88100 Catanzaro, Italy
and
The University of Hull
Hull HU6 7RX, United Kingdom
M.La-Torre@hull.ac.uk

ISSN 1572-4395
ISBN 978-1-4020-6606-1 e-ISBN 978-1-4020-6607-8
DOI 10.1007/978-1-4020-6607-8
Springer Dordrecht Heidelberg London New York

Library of Congress Control Number: 2010927688

Printed on acid-free paper

Springer is part of Springer Science+Business Media (www.springer.com)

I wish to dedicate this book to my sister,
Adriana La Torre

Preface

This book – which is the result of several years of research, discussion, writing and re-writing – consists of three parts and eight chapters. The first part is given by the two first chapters introducing the issue of validity and facticity in law. The second part (Chapters 3, 4 and 5) is the core of this study and tries to present a theory based on a specific view about language and social practice. The third part deal with the issue of value judgments and views about morality and consists of Chapters 6 and 7. Chapter 8 should finally serve as epilogue.

In the first chapter a discussion is started about the relationship between law and power, seen as a presupposition for an assessment of the nature of law. As a matter of fact, as has been remarked, "general theories of law struggle to do justice to the multiple dualities of the law".[1] Indeed, law has a "dual nature": it is a fact, but it also a norm, a sort of ideal entity. Law is sanction, but it is also discourse. It is effectivity, or facticity, but it is also a vehicle of principles among which the central one is justice. But this duality is not only a phenomenological, or a matter of justification and implementation as two separate moments. It is an ontological quality too, and it is there from the beginning, from the moment where law "springs" as a distinct experience and practice. Here we are then confronted with the question of power.

Law without power (some would say without "sanction" or "force") is not even conceivable or definable, This is so because law is a portion of reality which at the same time produces reality (conducts). Law is the power of doing things that "hold" in society. But at the same time this power should not exceed given limits and has to follow certain criteria, and the law is there to check power, to constrain it. Power and law are thus inextricably related. This is the reason why legal theory and philosophy are first of all theories about the relationship between law and power. So that there are theories which defend the primacy of law over power, and other ones which reverse the role of law, and consider this as instrumental to power. In Chapter 1 the former are played against the latter, to consider their relative merits and deficiencies. Legal positivism and natural law are here really the issue, the one stressing facticity, the other appealing to ideality. Constitutionalism and the rule of law in this sense indeed are a development of the modern natural law tradition.

[1] J. Raz, *Between Authority and Interpretation*, Oxford 2009, p. 1.

Chapter 2 concludes the first part of the book by considering an alternative view about the relationship between power and law. Here the main approach discussed is Hans Kelsen's "pure theory". As a matter of fact, Kelsen presents his own theory as a solution to the controversy, in so far as power is reconceptualised as an order of rules, a legal order, or more simply as "law". In this sense, the opposition between law and power dissolves. However, such dissolution is only apparent, since on the one side the law is conceived as based on coercion and facticity and on the other hand whatever effective law is ennobled as "valid" system of law.

In the second part of the book there is a shift towards a consideration of the law as a phenomenon possibly concerned with language. Once traditional explanatory strategies are seen as unsatisfactory, and nevertheless law is accepted as being a social fact, there is the possibility of addressing this fact as somehow analogically linked with a system of language. This is attempted in Chapters 3 and 4. Here there is first an analysis of theories of linguistic meaning, their limits and merits and their possible consequences for the explanation of human action and for the concept of law. Several theories of meaning are assessed and finally the so-called use theory is outlined as the most convincing (though with some important caveats) and as the closest to the legal point of view. Actually the use theory thinks of "use" in terms very similar to legal notion of "custom" or "customary law". For the use theory in a sense language is the same as "customary law". However, "custom" here is not mere regularity, but eminently a normative game and a special room for action, a play of giving and asking for reasons. Recent developments in philosophy and in philosophy of law, especially rational pragmatism, discourse theory and inferentialism, seem to largely support this view.

Once assessed the "use theory" as the most reliable approach to language meaning, in Chapter 4 there is the attempt to build a bridge between such theory and the traditional institutionalist theories of law. These are reviewed and then supplemented through the neo-institutionalism more recently defended by Neil MacCormick and Ota Weinberger. Neo-institutionalism is then shown to be the most promising approach to cope with the ontology of law, though some reform in the standard theory is proposed to render more plausible and less circular the definition given of what an "institution" means and is. In particular, constitutive rules or "declarations" cannot kept outside an institutionalist perspective, though they cannot be said to produce directly "institutional facts" or better the scope of action which the "institution" consists of. They are rather "conditions" to be prescribed in understanding and performing a piece of conduct. This is why a definition of "institution" is advanced whereby constitutive rules are integrated with a notion of efficacy and effective performance.

Chapter 5 resumes the discussion of the relationship between law and power, while power is now conceptualized through the notion of institution. Kelsen's solution thus appears more promising, if however power is no longer related to facticity or coercion or sanction, but rather to institutional facts and institutions.

The third part of the book develops and tries to make explicit the normative side of the idea of law as institution. Here in Chapter 6 there is first a summing up of meaning theories and of their implications for a conception of normative language. Special attention is devoted to the "speech acts" theory. After that in Chapter 7 an attempt is made to apply the results obtained in Chapters 3 and 6 to meta-ethics and the study of morality and moral sentences. Meta-ethical doctrines are reviewed and criticized by focusing then to the issue of universalizability. At the end of the chapter a definition of the moral point of view is advanced. In this chapter – which is of special importance to the argument of my research – moral doctrines are assessed at the meta-theoretical level and a particular attention is given to "discourse theory" approaches.

The "institution" of institutionalist doctrines usually claims to be self-sufficient. This in the book is seen as a deficiency. The law in particular has an ideal side which a Wittgensteinian notion of institutional fact seems not to be able to grasp. However, Wittgenstein himself by referring when speaking of an institution to its "Witz", its "point" or "sense", points out that we need a content and ideal side. This need to be explicitly thematized, and this is Chapter 7's main task.

Finally, Chapter 8 concludes summing up what the neo-institutionalist approach defended would imply as for the relationship between law and morality. Here different approaches are reviewed and discussed. The outcome is a partial endorsement of a discourse theory approach. Institutionalism, old and new, to make sense of the ideal side of law, of its dual nature, cannot maintain morality outside the precinct of legal practice. In this sense, institutionalism – to be faithful to its own notion of institution – cannot keep faith to legal positivism. Institutionalism needs – this might be a conclusion – morality and a theory of morality to render justice to the concept of law we adopt from the internal point of view. But the morality theory searched for cannot be a Platonist one, distant from practice, and imposed upon it, or even one that could believe to derive practice from one or a few basic principles in a logicist mood. Law's own ontology (and practice) is normative and therefore requires to be explained an idealist perspective as well. A moderate meta-ethical cognitivism will be the way out from the realist dumbness of legal positivism. And a moderate cognitivism rooted in the pragmatics of legal discourse will have as a consequence a defence of a moderate connection between law and morality: a connection more "practical" than just "conceptual".

In short, this book springs from the need to go beyond Neil MacCormick's and Ota Weinberger's institutional theory of law. The need is to trace back the lines of the theoretical tradition of legal institutionalism, to see how much of it has stood the test of time and more modern developments in legal theory, and link these "residues" (which are considerable) with a new version of legal institutionalism that has been gaining ground in recent years. In this book I try to link together those two formidable pieces of research, the "old" and the "new" institutionalism, and to render their philosophical bases explicit, specifically as far as the philosophy of language is concerned. In this area my aim is to outline the connections between theory of meaning, theory of the norm and theory of legal validity. To this end I put to the test some of the most debated theories of meaning, reaching the conclusion that institutionalist legal theory can be better "founded" if an equally institutionalist theory of language (a "use theory") is adopted.

The stimulating character of neo-institutionalism derives – I believe – from the fact that it makes possible to adopt an institutional perspective without having to accept the heavy holistic and essentialist presuppositions which were at the bottom of the "old" institutionalism. It accepts, for instance, the concept of a "rule", and makes it rather a constitutive element of institutions. And by introducing the idea of "rule" into the walls of "institutions" it render these permeable to individual reflection and criticism. Rules, as matter of fact, whenever they are not conceived as mere regularities or scientific laws, imply what Hart calls a "reflective attitude"; and reflection cannot but be exercised by individuals. Neo-institutionalism thus allows for individualism, which is the starting point of modernity and of what Jürgen Habermas calls "post-conventional morality". Here, therefore, institutions are not meant to resuscitate the socialization of the "ancient" passing through the integration of individuals in a community supposedly primordial and the adhesion to effective models of action considered as fully constitutive of individual ethical conduct.

Nor would the new kind of institutionalism I defends follow any dream of ontological excellence of collective social entities, though ascribing to the institution a proper existential dimension. Between organicism (and the celebration of *Volksgeist*) and empiricist reductionism (and the acknowledgment only of "brute facts") it marks a third way. In particular, challenging and extremely promising is the possibility offered by neo-institutionalism of connecting a notion of institution with a moderately cognitivist approach to ethics, so to avoid the strong moralism and objectivism usually connected to institutionalist views, such as those for instance of Georges Renard, Rudolf Smend or Arnold Gehlen. This actually is my main objective in this book: to conjugate an institutional legal theory with a (moderate) cognitivist meta-ethics, to land into a procedural and deliberative concept of political action.

Indeed, I seek principally to fill an embarrassing gap: the lack in of a definition of "institution". Once in possession of this concept, it is then applied to the thorny topic of the binding force of law, a point that institutionalists have largely neglected. Eventually, my claim is that the notion of institution prepares the ground for a redefinition of the concept of power. To do so it is obviously necessary to take a third factor into account as well as law and power: "society".

It is important to stress that my legal theoretical project needs a cognitivist meta-ethics as a preparation to his conclusive step: a reassessment of the disputed relationship between law and morality. Here it is made clear how institutionalism does not preclude a reflective and critical morality and thus both connects and separates the legal and the moral domain. On the other side the concept of law I develop from an institutional perspective, rejecting as this does the imperativist background and the prescritivism present even in recent more refined versions of normativism (such as those by Kelsen, Ross and Hart), leaves open the field for an antiauthoritarian and deliberative conception of the body politic. For instance, a prescriptivist theory of law cannot solve the dramatic contradiction between a rule which grants rights (freedoms and powers in the end) and the same rule seen as essentially imperative and hence as a restriction of human capacities of agency.

Rights have been the other recurrent subject in my research. In my book *Disavventure del diritto soggettivo* (Giuffrè, Milano 1996) I strongly criticized the reductionist strategy of conceiving rights as a mirror of commands and obligations. My attempt there was to re-conceptualise rights first as thick concepts which cannot be submitted to an empiricist and logicist treatment such as the one proposed by Alf Ross in his famous "Tû-Tû" article. Rights are not vehicles to be taken to any destination. There is in them a thick cultural and political core. Moreover, they are mostly powers, not pale reflexes of other more fundamental deontic operators. The triad of traditional deontic operators cannot – this was my claim – offer an intelligent account of rights' conceptual structure. Rights indeed have a permanent problem with legal positivism which tries to tame them through a reductionist strategy. On the contrary, institutionalism, especially in the shape given to it in this book, focussing on constitutive rules as the basic rules of a legal system and, moreover, having of the rule a concept of a device that enlarges and does not reduce human chances of action, can perfectly accept rights as products of normative propositions. To take rights seriously, to calmly accept their particular ontology and their intricate logical structure, another, different theory of law is needed: this – I believe – is neo-institutionalism.

This work bases and is a development of my *Norme, istituzioni, valori* (Laterza, Bari 1999). It re-elaborates on this previous monograph, trying to make of my theoretical proposal a more integrated and convincing case. And it would not have been conceived and carried on without the inspiring research project of two masters of legal theory, Professors Ota Weinberger and Neil MacCormick, who have both sadly passed away last year. I learned so much from them and I owe such a lot to their intelligence, scholarship and friendship that they may be said in a sense sort of co-authors of my work. The following pages are also meant as a tribute to the memory of these two great scholars.

Contents

Part I
Law and Power

Chapter 1
Two Opposing Conceptions

1.1 Preliminary

There is a direct connection between law and politics in so far as legal actions and decisions contribute to collective practice.[1] Controversy governs the nature of this connection however. In legal and political theory, two chief ways of understanding the relationship between law and power traditionally emerge. According to the first conception, more widespread (particularly in the modern epoch), law is an expression of power, its instrument and issue. According to the second, less widespread, conception, law is the source of, or prerequisite for, or limit on power. This opposition is well recognized by many of the more aware writers on legal theory.

Hans Kelsen, for instance, in his *Der soziologische und der juristische Staatsbegriff*, considers a series of legal doctrines according to whether they posit the State as prerequisite (*Voraussetzung*) for law or vice versa. Norberto Bobbio, dealing specifically with the relation between the two concepts of power and law, said the following: "The general theories of law and State can be differentiated into two great categories according to whether they assert the primacy of power over norm, or conversely of norm over power".[2] I shall seek below to illustrate some examples of these two divergent ways of conceiving the relationship between law and power. I make no claims to completeness or even adequacy in my treatment of the theme, aiming more to introduce arguments and lead up to considerations relevant for a critique of the prescriptivist conception of law. What interests me here is not so much a classification of ways of conceiving the relation between law and

---

[1] C. S. Nino, *Derecho, moral y política. Una revisión de la teoría general del derecho*, Barcelona 1994, pp. 147–148.

[2] N. Bobbio, *Kelsen e il potere giuridico*, in *Ricerche politiche*, ed. by M. Bovero, Milano 1982, p. 3. Cf. also H. J. Wolff, *Verwaltungsrecht*, 8th ed., vol. 1, München 1971, § 25, where the German scholar refers to the constant dualism of *veritas* and *auctoritas* or of *ratio* and *voluntas*. Western legal reasoning reformulates the opposition between law and power in terms of two distinct but also competing principles that derive from "legal sources", but are both extra-legislative and beyond custom.

M. La Torre, *Law as Institution*, Law and Philosophy Library 90,
DOI 10.1007/978-1-4020-6607-8_1, © Springer Science+Business Media B.V. 2010

power as the preliminaries for singling out one particular way of conceiving the phenomenon of law for discussion.

The point is not to provide the solution to a "chicken-and-egg" problem (which came first?), but to conceptualize a tension that is always present in legal experience. This tension is that between the unavailability and the instrumentalization of the law by the holders of political power, and by subjects capable of exercising pressures of various types, as holders of extra-legal, material or psychological, force. All this obviously involves referring back to the structure of legal argumentation, and specifically to what is to be regarded as a legally valid argument. Accordingly, the question of the relationship between law and power is by no means otiose, or a simply a matter of sterile academic debate.

The opposition mentioned above between two views of the relationship between law and power runs through the whole history of political and legal thought. Classical Greek thought gives us illustrious examples of each conception. The Sophists' thought generally asserts that the law is a means for the stronger to dominate the weaker. Nonetheless, in *Gorgias* Plato makes Kallikles say that the positive laws are a creation of the weaker to neutralize the natural superiority of the stronger.[3] Pericles, in Xenophon's *Memorabilia*, maintains that law is everything that the sovereign power has laid down as obligatory: "All that the sovereign in a polity prescribes by deliberating what ought to be done, all that is called law"[4] and there is the well-known "argument of Thrasymachus" in the first book of Plato's *Republic*, according to which positive law and justice coincide with the interest of the stronger.[5]

The Sophists' "realistic" approach was opposed by Stoic thought, which instead generally upheld the primacy of law over power. This conception was taken over into Roman political and legal thought, largely influenced by Stoicism. A noted example is Cicero's work, according to which law as positive command is merely a "popular" or "vulgar" notion,[6] while there is a true law, that is right reason, conform to nature, grasped by everyone, permanent, eternal: "est quidem vera lex recta ratio naturae congruens, diffusa in omnes, constans, sempiterna".[7] Aristotle, who like the Sophists upheld a realist conception and therefore distanced himself from the Stoics' rationalistic natural-law approach, based nonetheless political power, the constitution of a people, its *politeia*, on the existence of a body of laws. In a famous passage, the Stagirite says this: "Where the laws have no authority, there is no constitution. The law ought to be supreme over all, and the magistracies should judge of particulars, and only this should be considered a constitution".[8]

---

[3] See *Gorgia*, 483b.

[4] *Memorabilia*, II, 43–44. Cf. P. Koller, *Theorie des Rechts. Eine Einführung*, 2nd ed., Wien 1997, pp. 38ff.

[5] See *Res publica*, 338c.

[6] See *De Legibus*, I, vi, 19.

[7] *De Re Publica*, III, xxii, 33.

[8] *Politics*, ed. by S. Everson, English trans. by J. Barnes, Cambridge 1988, 1292a, pp. 32–35.

In the Middle Ages the opposition is represented on one side by the Thomist doctrine, for which the *lex aeterna* is eminently rational, and not arbitrary, will. On the other side, we find the highly voluntaristic Occamist doctrine for which the moral law is above any criterion of rationality and consists in the pure command of God. Occam holds that evil is nothing but conduct contrary to what one is obliged to comply with (the formula taken up by Hobbes). Obviously, in both doctrines the relationship between law and power is reinterpreted in ethical and theological terms as the relation existing between the just (law in the ethical sense) and divine activity (power in the theological sense).

According to Aquinas, the just (which is the rational) in a certain sense preexists the divine power, or better, the divine will cannot wish anything but the just (rational). According to Occam, by contrast, the just is the product of the arbitrary divine will. The two formulae lead to two distinct outcomes. The first asserts, in line with Occam's commentary on Peter Lombard's *Sentences*, that if God had prescribed theft and murder, the acts denoted by these terms would cease to be thefts and murders, since their meaning is not absolutely given, but is rather the outcome of divine intelligence and resolve, "quia ista nomina significant tales actus non absolute: sed connotando vel dando intelligere, quod faciens tales actus per praeceptum divinum obligatur ad oppositum".[9] On the other hand, Gabriel Biel, taking up an expression of Gregory of Rimini's, maintains that an action which is just according to reason is so, even if God does not exist or does not wish it (which actually are both said an absurd assumption): "Nam si per impossibile Deus non esset, qui est ratio divina, aut ratio illa divina esset errans, adhuc si quis ageret contra rectam rationem angelicam, vel humanam, aut aliam aliquam, si qua esset, peccaret".[10] This indeed is a formulation that paves the way to the later modern natural law based more on human (individual) rights than on divine authority.

As far as legal theory in the strictest sense is concerned, the contrast in the Middle Ages is between a conception that picks up Ulpian's fragment in the Digest, according to which what is liked by the king that is law, *quod principi placuit legis habet vigorem*, and hence the imperial tradition of a power above its own law, and those viewes that give expression to the typically feudal need to limit central power. The latter line of thought was particularly lively in England, given the particular historical and social situation in that country. Rudolph von Gneist, in his classic study on English administrative law, cites an old maxim of the English courts that is revelatory of the Anglo-Saxon way of understanding the relationship between law and power and according to which law is the greatest patrimony and inheritance of kings and the one over which the sime title of king is based: "La loi est le plus haute inheritance, que le roy ad; car par la ley il meme et tautes ses sujets sont rules, et si la ley ne fuit, nul roy, et nul inheritance sera".[11] And Bracton, the great theorist of English

---

[9]Cited from the appendix to G. Fassò, *La legge della ragione*, Bologna 1966, p. 276.

[10]G. Fassò, *Op. cit.*, pp. 283–284.

[11]See R. von Gneist, *Englisches Verwaltungsrecht*, vol. 1, Berlin 1897, p. 454.

medieval constitutionalism, asserted: "The king must not be under man but under God and the law because law makes the king".[12]

1.2 The Law as Expression of Power. "Analytical Jurisprudence" and Legal Positivism

1.2.1 The modern era opened with a fierce, somewhat dark vision of the legal phenomenon: "Recht ist Gewalt", law is violence – as Martin Luther said.[13] As a result of the legitimacy crisis of that era, provoked by religion wars and the discovery of cultural pluralism, there was a growing tendency to sceptical views and a multiplication of doctrines that detached law from normative ideas and in the end reduced it to basic material force. Law is here seen as a product of power and not vice versa. One of the most authoritative upholders of the doctrine that law is based on power in the early modern period – as is well known – is Thomas Hobbes. He takes up the Occamist view that evil is equivalent to what is prohibited by God's will, and applies it to ethics and to law. The just and the unjust are for Hobbes exclusively determined by the commands or prohibitions of whoever holds supreme power in a community. "Accordingly", we read in *De Cive*, "it belongs to the same chief power to make some common rules for all men, and to declare them publicly, by which every man may know what may be called his, what another's, what just, what good, what evil; that is summarily, what is to be done, what to be avoided in our common course of life".[14]

The civil laws, which for Hobbes define the just and the unjust, are conceived of as commands of the supreme power. Thus, ethics is subordinate to positive law, and this to political power. "Those rules and measures are usually called civil laws, or the laws of the city, as being the commands of him who hath the supreme power in the city. And the *civil laws* (what we may define them) are nothing else but *laws of the State*, because they are the commands of whoever in the State holds the supreme power. And the civil laws (to define them) are nothing but the commands of him who hath the chief authority in the city, for direction of the future actions of his citizens".[15] The definition given in *Leviathan* does not vary greatly from the one in *De Cive*: "Civil Law, is to every Subject, those Rules, which the Commonwealth hath Commanded him, by Word, Writing, or other sufficient Sign of the Will, to make use of, for the Distinction of Right, and Wrong; that is to say, of what is contrary, and what is not contrary, to the Rule".[16] Similarly, in *Behemoth* we read

---

[12] H. Bracton, *De legibus et consuetudinibus Angliae*, vol. 2, ed. by G. E. Woodbine, 1968, p. 33.

[13] M. Luther, *Tischreden*, ed. by K. Aland, Stuttgart 1981, p. 207 (§ 497).

[14] T. Hobbes, *De Cive*, VI, 9, in *English Works of Thomas Hobbes*, ed. by Sir William Molesworth, vol. 2, Aalen 1966, p. 77.

[15] Ibid.

[16] T. Hobbes, *Leviathan*, ed. by C. B. Macpherson, Harmondsworth 1982, Part II, Chapter XXVI, p. 312.

the following: "Every law is a command that imposes doing, or abstaining from doing, something".[17]

This way of conceiving of the relationship between law and political power has two further effects as far as the theory of power is concerned. For saying that positive law, the *civil* law, is the command of the holder of supreme power means asserting a conception of that power as above the law it promulgates. "Above", in this context, means "not bound by". The power is not bound by the law it promulgates; it is above it. "Whence it is plain, that the city", it is said in *De Cive*, "is not tied to the civil laws; for the civil laws are the laws of the city, by which, if she were engaged, she should be engaged to herself".[18] "Whoever holds the supreme power is not bound by the civil laws (which would mean be bound by himself), nor obliged to any citizen".[19] The same concept is expressed still more clearly in *Leviathan:* "The Soveraign of a Commonwealth, be it an assembly, or one Man, is not subject to the Civill Lawes. For having power to make, and repeale Lawes, he may when he pleaseth, free himselfe from that subjection, by repealing those Lawes that trouble him, and making of new".[20]

Asserting that law is the command of a sovereign power has a further effect on the idea of power that is adopted when drawing the distinction between it and law (and asserting its superiority). Power, in this case, cannot but be seen as power of coercion, force or violence. If the law is command, such a command, in order to be obeyed, cannot depend on respect for a body of norms (which would also be commands), but rather, on the capacity to impose itself on its addressee, that is, on the force that accompanies it.

The Hobbesian doctrine was adopted almost in toto by legal positivism. The link with Hobbes is particularly direct, for obvious reasons, in John Austin, the founder of "analytical jurisprudence", the British, utilitarian and empiricist, version of the legal positivism that had taken over the European continent following the French revolution. The way from Hobbes to Austin goes via Blackstone, the author of the monumental *Commentaries* on the English laws, and via Bentham, who despite his enlightened background and political radicalism developed a vaguely "realistic" and positive conception of law. Blackstone, for instance, writes: "The law, in its most general and comprehensive sense, signifies a rule of action [. . .] And it is that rule of action, which is prescribed by some superior and which the inferior is bound to obey".[21] And for Bentham, the law is "an assemblage of signs declarative of a volition conceived or adopted by the *sovereign* in a state, concerning the conduct to

[17] T. Hobbes, *Behemoth*, ed. by F. Tönnies, London 1969, p. 50.

[18] T. Hobbes, *De Cive*, VI, 14, p. 83.

[19] Ibid. See also *De Cive*, XIII, 4.

[20] T. Hobbes, *Leviathan*, ed. by C. B. Macpherson, Part II, Chapter XXVI, p. 313.

[21] W. Blackstone, *Commentaries on the Laws of England*, facsimile of the First Edition of 1765–1769, vol. 1, *Of the Rights of Persons* (1765), with an Introduction by S. N. Katz, Chicago and London 1979, p. 38.

be observed in a certain *case* by a certain person or class of persons, who in the case in question are or are supposed to be subject to his power".[22]

John Austin puts forward Hobbes' theory of law again, in its essential features. These may be reduced to four main assumptions: (a) positive law is a command; (b) a command is the expression of a desire (to be accomplished by someone different from the issuer of the command), accompanied by the threat of some ill (or sanction) should the addressee of the command not wish to submit to the will (or desire) of the issuer; (c) law is the command of a political superior directed to a political inferior, or of a politically sovereign entity (which does not recognize any higher authority); (d) sovereign power is not bound by its own laws (commands), it is *legibus solutus*. Each of these assumptions is contained in Austin's best-known work, *The Province of Jurisprudence Determined* (1832). Regarding this, it should be recalled that the English lawyer distinguishes, as we know, between two chief types of law, those "properly" and those "improperly" called such. He further distinguishes laws according to the following four categories: (1) divine laws, (2) positive laws, (3) rules of positive morality, and (4) laws in a metaphorical sense. Austin states that only "the divine laws and the positive laws are properly so called",[23] since only "the laws proper, or properly so called, are commands".[24]

As far as the nature of the command is concerned, as an expression of will accompanied by the threat of a sanction, Austin asserts that "it is the power and purpose of inflicting an eventual evil [. . .] which gives to the expression of a wish the name of command".[25] (Thus, the elements accompanying the command are for Austin above all desire, then the threat of sanction, and finally the manifestation of desire). "The ideas or notions comprehended by the term *command*," he writes, "are the following. 1. The wish or desire conceived by a rational being, that another rational being shall do or forbear. 2. An evil to proceed from the former, and to be incurred by the latter, in case the latter comply not the wish. 3. An expression or intimation of the wish by words or other signs".[26]

But command is not enough for there to be law; the command must come from the sovereign power of an independent political community. In a general sense, Austin notes that the very concept of command refers to a relationship of superior to inferior. "It appears, then, that the term *superiority* (like the terms *duty* and sanctions) is implied by the term *command*. For superiority is the power of enforcing compliance with a wish: and the expression or intimation of a wish, with the power and the purpose of enforcing it, are the constituent elements of a command".[27] The concept of "sovereign" is, however, more restricted than that of "political superior";

---

[22] J. Bentham, *The Limits of Jurisprudence Defined*, New York 1945, p. 88.

[23] J. Austin, *The Province of Jurisprudence Determined*, ed. by W. E. Rumble, Cambridge 1995, p. 10.

[24] Ibid.

[25] Ibid., p. 24.

[26] Ibid.

[27] Ibid., p. 30.

the sovereign power is that "political superior" which has no other "political superior" above it. In that case, the society over which the sovereign power is exercised will be called politically independent.

Custom or "habit" is then introduced to account for the stability of power in a political community – a reference which seems to mitigate, and to conflict with, the centrality of will and threat in articulating power relations. Obedience to be political should not be punctual, but rather "habitual". "Unless habitual obedience – thus says Austin – be rendered by the bulk of its members, and be rendered by the bulk of its members to *one and the same* superior the given society is either in a state of nature, or is split into two or more independent political societies".[28] However, it is not clear how a social habit could have arisen from a practice of commands which is not yet upheld by customary obedience, being such custom what makes effective that practice on a larger (social) scale.

In any case here law and sovereignty are seen as inextricably interwoven: "every positive law, or every law simply and strictly called, is set, directly or circuitously by a sovereign person or body, to a member or members of the independent political society wherein that person or body is sovereign or supreme".[29] But not every command emanating from the sovereign constitutes a law. This is the case only for a command that has as its object a *class* of actions (positive or negative), that is, is *general*. The "occasional" or "particular" command does not give us a rule of law. "But, as contradistinguished or opposed to an occasional or particular command, a law is a command which obliges a person or persons, and obliges *generally* to acts or forbearances of a class".[30] This is also a more or less explicit affirmation that the command, to be valid as law, must not be exhausted in a single moment, or be effective for a specific occasion, but must have duration and stability in time.

Finally, there is the illimitability of the sovereign power, its position above the law it promulgates. "Now it follows from the essential difference of a positive law and from the nature of sovereignty and independent political society, that the power of a monarch properly so called, or the power of a sovereign number in its collegiate and sovereign capacity, is incapable of legal limitation".[31] For Austin, the sovereign may not only change the law at whim, but is in no way subordinate to the law while it is in force. "The immediate author of a law of the kind, or any of the sovereign successors to that immediate author, may abrogate the law at pleasure. And though the law not abrogated, the sovereign for the time being not constrained to observe it by a legal or political sanction. For if the sovereign for the time being were legally bound to observe it, that present sovereign would be in a state of subjection to a higher or superior sovereign".[32]

---

[28] Ibid., p. 169. Emphasis in original.

[29] Ibid., p. 212.

[30] Ibid., p. 29.

[31] Ibid., p., 212.

[32] Ibid.

In Austin's thought too, as in Hobbes', what underlies the view of a political power completely "different" from the law, and which it uses as its *instrumentum regni*, is the "realistic" conception of power as strength, force, violence. One passage in Austin is significant in this regard: "But taken with the meaning wherein here understand it, the term *superiority* signifies *might*: the power of affecting others with evil or pain, and of forcing them, through fear of that evil, to fashion their conduct to one's wishes".[33]

1.2.2 The conception of law as expression of political power is common to the whole field of legal positivism. In Germany in particular, a large part of the legal doctrine of the nineteenth century took up this conception, though with differing nuances. These varied essentially along a range of positions at the extremes of which were on one hand those who welcomed the assumption of the illimitability of sovereign power by legal means, and on the other those who instead theorized the so-called "self-limitation" of the State. However, both these positions concurred at the descriptive level in locating political power prior to and above the legal system. Good examples of these two different positions are, in the field of public law, Conrad Bornhak's and Georg Jellinek's respectively.

Bornhak's thought (along with Max Seydel, one of the exponents of the so-called *Herrschertheorie*[34]) largely follows the same theoretical path as Hobbes and Austin: the State is dominion, and law is the expression of that dominion, which is legally unlimited and unlimitable, since were it somehow limited or limitable it would cease to be dominion, that is, supreme power in a certain territorial area. "The State", writes Bornhak, "is dominion [*Herrschaft*]. This means nothing other than that the State dominates, is the subject of dominion [*Subjekt der Herrschaft*]. For the moment, there is no need to consider further how that dominion should or may be organized. Here it is sufficient to note that the State is the subject of dominion, and hence the starting point for all public law, founded on dominion [...] The State's dominion is legally unlimited and unlimitable [*rechtlich unbeschränkt und unbeschränkbar*]".[35] "For any limitation presupposes a force [*Macht*] that can limit the State and hence is superior to it. Such a superior power [*Gewalt*] is, however, irreconcilable with the independence conceptually [*begrifflich*] necessary to the State power [*Staatsgewalt*]".[36]

The Hobbesian inspiration becomes still clearer at the point where Bornhak asserts, following the English philosopher, that every State is automatically (conceptually) absolute. This, he clarifies, does not always correspond with practice, since sometimes the State does not have enough force to accomplish what is theoretically (legally) possible for it. "The State is accordingly absolute from intrinsic necessity, whatever be its constitutional form. The facts, however, may not correspond with this legal absolutism. The weakness of State power may prevent the

[33] Ibid., p. 30. Emphasis in original.

[34] See M. Seydel, *Grundzüge einer allgemeinen Staatslehre*, Würzburg 1873, especially pp. 1–18.

[35] C. Bornhak, *Allgemeine Staatslehre*, Berlin 1896, p. 9.

[36] Ibid., p. 11.

State from doing what is legally permitted".[37] It should however be mentioned that for Bornhak, who does not, as we have seen, accept legal limits to the State's power, political power may be subject to constraints of an ethical nature. "But", he writes, "even for the State which has no limits on its force, there exist the limits of the moral order [*der sittlichen Ordnung*], which it cannot cross with impunity".[38]

The doctrine of Georg Jellinek (not to be confused with his son Walter, like him an outstanding public lawyer) has greatly influenced theories of public law not only in the Germanic cultural arena but also in Italy and France. As well as Vittorio Emanuele Orlando in Italy, a great French public-law figure took up the lines of Jellinek's conception of law: Carré de Malberg. Jellinek's constitutional theory, as we know, is based on the concept of the State's self-obligation (*Selbstverpflichtung*); only through that self-limitation does it become a "State of Law". But the State is seen by Jellinek as fundamentally once again an absolute sovereign power. It is in virtue of this absoluteness that the State power, in his view, creates the legal order. "But", writes Jellinek, "the supporter of the public legal order is the State itself, and in fact is exclusively the sovereign State the creator of its own order. Now the State, which determines itself and establishes its own order with full formal freedom, *is not subject to any higher power*".[39]

The State, according to Jellinek, becomes a legal order by setting a limit de jure on its own sovereignty, which de facto remains absolute. "It is only insofar as the State conceives itself as legally limited that it becomes a subject of rights. An agent which in no way is a subject of duties, constitutes a subject of power, not a subject of rights. The concept of right already contains that restriction".[40] Since Jellinek maintains that every legal order is a relation between persons, and is thus an upholder of the so-called "relational theory" of law,[41] the State, for this Austrian public lawyer, creates law only insofar as it acknowledges that others have a subjectivity in some way analogous (but not equal) to its own. "The State", he says, "considered in itself, as de facto power, transforms itself by recognizing the personality of the subjects into a legally limited power. In this form its de facto power, established and limited by its own legal order, acquires the character of legal power; its interests take on the character of legal interests".[42]

As Léon Duguit notes,[43] Jellinek's theory of the State's self-limitation has a precedent in the thought of Jhering as expressed in the latter's *Der Zweck im Recht*. For the idea of law that Jhering develops, particularly after moving away from his original positions (those of "Pandectistics"), is markedly imperativist in character.

---

[37] Ibid.

[38] Ibid., pp. 11–12.

[39] G. Jellinek, *System der subjektiven öffentlichen Rechten*, 2nd ed., Tübingen 1919, p. 10. Italics mine.

[40] Ibid., p. 195.

[41] See S. Cotta, *Prospettive filosofiche del diritto*, 3rd revised and expanded ed., Turin 1979, pp. 8ff.

[42] G. Jellinek, *System der subjektiven öffenlichen Rechten*, p. 194.

[43] See L. Duguit, *L'Etat, le droit objectif et la loi positive*, vol. 1, Paris 1901, pp. 107ff.

He identifies the norm with an imperative coming from the State power.[44] And he adds: "From this point of view, all law presents itself as the coercive system brought about by the State, as the coercive apparatus organized and directed by the State power".[45]

For Jhering, as for Austin, not every imperative emanating from State power is, however, a norm of law, but only those imperatives that have an abstract and general nature. "But not all the legal imperatives of State power", writes the German jurist, "are legal norms; indeed, we must distinguish between concrete and abstract imperatives, since only the latter are legal norms".[46] Moreover, in Jhering's view, in order for law to reach its fullest expression, the legal norms (that is, the abstract imperatives of State power) must be valid bilaterally, that is, must also bind the State power. "In promulgating the legal norm, the State power may propose to bind through it only the addressees, but not itself, thus reserving the right to decide the individual case according to discretion. However, the State power may promulgate a norm in the intention – and even the explicit affirmation – that it wishes to bind itself too. Only in this way, if this assurance is actually respected, does law reach its perfect form: that is, the certainty that the norm laid down must necessarily be applied".[47] The prescriptive nature of these last statements by Jhering is clear enough. This is why Carré de Malberg, while attributing scientific value to Jellinek's theory, stresses the essentially political intent, in his view, of this first elaboration by Jhering of the theory of the State's self-limitation.[48]

1.3 The Supremacy of the Law. Natural Law, Constitutionalism, the Rule of Law

1.3.1 At the origins of the conception that sets law at the foundation of political power, just as for the opposite theory, we find, in the early modern period, the work of an English thinker. This time it is John Locke. In this philosopher's thought the relation between the phenomena of law and of politics is particularly well-articulated.

(i) Firstly, we find in Locke the assertion of a natural law that governs all human actions, and hence also the actions of political power. "The law of nature", writes Locke "stands as an eternal rule to all men, *legislators* as well as others. The *rules* that they make for other men actions must, as well as their own and other men

[44] See R. von Jhering, *Der Zweck im Recht*, vol. 1, Hildesheim 1970, p. 260.

[45] Ibid., p. 261.

[46] Ibid., p. 263.

[47] Ibid., pp. 263–264.

[48] See R. Carré de Malberg, *Contribution à la théorie générale de l'Etat*, vol. 1, Paris 1920, pp. 231–232.

actions, be conformable to the law of nature, i.e. to the will of God, of which that is a declaration".[49]

(ii) As far as the positive laws are concerned, these for Locke mark the passage from the state of nature to civil society (political power is, for Locke, above all the power to make laws) and are expressions of the opinion and the will of the whole society. Were that not so, in the English philosopher's view, we would be in the presence no longer of a law but of an arbitrary act of power. "Nor can any edict of any body else, in what form soever conceived, or by what power soever backed, have the force and obligation of a *law*, which has not its *sanctions from* that *legislative* which the public has chosen and appointed. For without this the law could not have that, which is absolutely necessary to its being a *law, the consent of the society*, over whom no body can have a power to make laws, but by their own consent, and by authority received by them".[50] Locke cites Hooker, who in his *Laws of Ecclesiastical Polity* had maintained that "those, then, are not laws save what the public approval has rendered such" and that "laws therefore humane, of what kind soever, are available by consent".[51]

(iii) Finally, in Locke's work there is the affirmation that political power must be exercised through law, this being understood as a formal, certain and public act. "Whatever form the common-wealth is under", he writes, "the ruling power ought to govern by *declared* and *received laws*, and not by extemporary dictates and undetermined resolutions".[52]

In the first of these different ways of thinking about the relationship between law and power, we are in the presence of classical natural-law theory. In the second, we have before us a formulation that brings together elements of the democratic theory regarding the origin and exercise of political power with a highly prescriptive connotation, and hints at a "sociological" theory of power (anticipating Hume's ideas on the matter) for which power is founded (and not *must* be founded; the intent here is descriptive) on the consent of the associated. One may find grounds in this anticipation of sociological theory for upholding a different version of the relations between law and power, which sees the two terms as overlapping. This is not on the side of power (according to which law is power) as some radical asserters of legal positivism maintain, but on the side of law (according to which power is law), as

---

[49] J. Locke, *Second Treatise on Government*, XI, 136, in *Two Treatises of Government*, ed. by P. Laslett, Cambridge 1988, p. 358. "What for Locke renders the state of nature unacceptable," writes Norberto Bobbio, "is not the fact that there are no laws (the state of nature is the one in which the natural laws prevail), but the fact that, when a natural law is violated, there is no suitable body to secure respect for it or punish the culprit" (N. Bobbio, *Locke e il diritto naturale*, Torino 1963, p. 210).

[50] J. Locke, *Second Treatise of Government*, XI, 134, p. 356. Emphasis in original. On Locke's contractual theory there are interesting observations by P. Koller, *Neue Theorien des Sozialkontrakts*, Berlin 1987, pp. 19ff.

[51] J. Locke, *Second Treatise on Government*, XI, 134, p. 356.

[52] Ibid., XI, 137, p. 360. Emphasis in original.

may be derived from the anthropological studies that conceive society in terms of a normative system (the reference being to the work of scholars like Marcel Mauss, Claude Levy-Strauss, Marshall Sahlins).

The third way is a formulation that may be called "formal law", seeing in the form of the law as abstract, general, certain and public a barrier to the arbitrariness of power. One of the most convinced upholders of this mode of thought three centuries later was Franz Neumann. Locke does not, however, believe that the form of law as such is the sole and most effective guarantee against the excesses of political power.

In the English philosopher's thought, the law is strongly tied to the popular will and is never seen as a purely formal fact. The formalities associated with the law (that it is public, for instance) have, in Locke's view, the object of maintaining the contact between the rule and the popular will. In consequence it is the fact that the law derives from the people that is the guarantee of its legality, not mere respect for some procedures occurring exclusively within the political apparatus (as maintained in the doctrines of the *Rechtsstaat*): that is, in the fact that the political system does not, at institutional level, break off contact with society, but continues to be determined by it. For Locke, then, who affirms (descriptively and prescriptively) that law is the basis for power, "tyranny is the exercise of power beyond right"[53] and "there is tyranny when the governour, however intituled, makes not the law, but his will".[54]

It may, schematically, be said that in Locke the three principal variants of the theory setting the phenomenon of law before and above that of politics are present. (i) In the first, the law is essentially natural law. (ii) In the second, law is the fundamental law laid down by the popular will (constitution), to which all the other legal and political acts must conform. (iii) In the third variant, finally, law is a formal rule, characterized by generality, abstractness, certainty and public in nature. It is general in that it is directed to the generality of citizens. It is abstract, as promulgated to regulate and sanction a case conceived in abstract terms and not a specific event (for instance, murder "in the abstract", not the murder of a plumber or of Mr. Smith "concretely"). It is *certain*, since the political power (a) cannot modify the norm at pleasure through a material act of will but can do so only by respecting definite procedures; (b) cannot itself evade respect for the norm, and must while it is in force observe and apply it. Finally it is *public* insofar as the norm is made known to the generality of citizens through appropriate procedures, so that it is possible for every citizen to be aware of it (in which case alone, on this theory, the maxim *ignorantia legis non excusat* is justified). Of these three versions of the thesis of the superiority of law over power, particularly representative versions can be found in the theories of (i) William Godwin, (ii) Thomas Paine, and (iii) Franz Neumann.

1.3.2 Godwin, in his monumental *Enquiry concerning Political Justice*, criticizes, inter alia, the assumption, common to the absolutist and the democratic theories (to Hobbes and to Rousseau, for instance) that the sovereign's will is omnipotent. Against this conception, Godwin appeals to a natural law that finds its source in a

[53] Ibid., XVIII, 199, p. 398.
[54] Ibid.

space beyond manipulation by any human entity: this space, for Godwin, is reason. "It cannot be too strongly inculcated", he writes, "that societies and communities of men are in no case empowered to establish absurdity and injustice; that the voice of the people is not, as has sometimes been ridiculously asserted, 'the voice of truth and of God'; and that universal consent cannot convert the unjust to the just".[55] "If a congregation of men", he continues, "agree universally to cut off their right hand, to shut their ears upon free inquiry, or to affirm two upon a particular occasion to be sixteen, in all these cases they are wrong, and ought unequivocally to be censured for usurping an authority that does not belong to them. They ought to be told, 'gentlemen, you are not, as in the intoxication of power you have been led to imagine, omnipotent; there is a authority greater than yours, to which you are bound assiduously to conform yourselves'".[56]

It follows in Godwin's view that the legislator (whoever this be) does not really *produce* the law, but somehow *interprets* it; it interprets a law given to him, and cannot create it. "The most crowed forum", he writes "or the most venerable senate, cannot make one proposition to be a rule of justice that was not substantially so previously to their decision. They can only interpret and announce that law which derives its real validity from a higher and less mutable authority".[57]

A different accent we find in Thomas Paine's political theory, this is the expression of the ideological ferment that prepared and followed the two great democratic revolutions, the American and the French. Paine's theoretical thinking turns round the notion of constitution. For Paine, as for the American and French revolutionaries, the constitution (seen as the product of the popular will) is the basis for political power, so that a power without constitution is declared undoubtedly illegal. "A constitution", writes Paine, "is not the act of a government, but of a people that constitutes a government; and a government without a constitution is power without a right".[58]

Paine distinguishes constituent power (which resides in the people) and constituted power (which is government). The constitution is the act whereby the people gives itself its own norms and establishes the powers of its representatives. These (who together form the government) cannot in any way modify the norms laid down in the constitution. "Every society and association that is established", he writes, "has first agreed upon a number of original articles, digested into form, which are its officers, whose powers and authorities are described in that Constitution, and the Government of that society. Those officers, by whatever name they are called, have no authority to add to, alter, or abridge the original articles".[59]

1.3.3 The legal thought of Franz Neumann, a German social-democratic jurist, takes as its chief object the transformation of the functions of law first in the regime he

---

[55] W. Godwin, *Enquiry Concerning Political Justice and Its Influence on Modern Morals and Happiness*, ed. by I. Kramnick, Harmondsworth 1976, Book II, Chapter V, p. 196.

[56] Ibid., p. 197.

[57] Ibid.

[58] T. Paine, *Rights of Man*, London 1969, Part II, Chapter IV, p. 182.

[59] Ibid., p. 190.

terms "monopolistic capitalism" (which he believes he sees in Weimar Germany) and then in the National Socialist regime. In both regimes, but much more under Nazi dominion, Neumann points to the decline of the traditional, liberal and positive, conception of law. This is in his view marked by three chief features: (a) the formulation of the law must be general, (b) this generality must be specific, that is, must refer to definite facts and not to moral criteria as, in his view, is the case with the so-called *Generalklauseln*,[60] (c) must not be retroactive.[61] Only in the presence of these requirements can one, for Neumann, speak of law in the proper sense.

Preliminarily, he distinguishes between "technical norms" and "laws". The former are culturally indifferent, neutral, and proper to any social system that applies the division of labour. "Any society based on a division of labour will necessarily produce competencies, jurisdictions, regularities, which give the appearance of a functioning legal system [...] But they are, in the words of my later teacher E. Mayer, 'culturally indifferent rules' of a predominantly technical character. They may acquire political or economic relevance at any moment (for instance, traffic rules may play a considerable role in the economic struggle between the railroad and the automobile), but in normal cases they are culturally neutral".[62] The technical norms, according to this view, do not form a juridical system, insofar as they do not constitute laws in a strict sense.

According to Neumann, laws can be distinguished by whether they are the exclusive product of the sovereign will, or else the combined product of that will and of reason. This gives us two notions of (objective) law, a "political" and a "rational" one. "Two notions of law", he writes, "must be distinguished, a political and a rational notion. In a political sense, law is every measure of a sovereign power, regardless of its form or content [...] The law is then will and nothing else. The rational concept of law, on the other hand, is determined by its form and content, not by its origin. Not every act of the sovereign is law. Law in this sense is a norm, comprehensible by reason, open to theoretical understanding, and containing an ethical postulate, primarily that of equality. Law is reason and will".[63] But for Neumann, only the "rational" type of law is law in the proper sense. Equally, for him, only the State of law is a State in the proper sense.

The law in the proper sense, endowed with its three characteristic features (mentioned above) that serve to make it "rational", thus constitutes a barrier or a limit, to the arbitrariness of sovereign power, just by virtue of its intrinsic rationality. "The

---

[60]On which see G. Teubner, *Standards und Direktiven in Generalklauseln*, Frankfurt am Main 1971.

[61]See F. Neumann, *The Challenge in the Function of Law in Modern Society*, in Id., *The Democratic and the Authoritarian State*, ed. by H. Marcuse, New York 1964, especially pp. 29–30.

[62]F. Neumann, *Behemoth. The Structure and Practice of National Socialism, 1933–1944*, New York 1944, p. 440.

[63]Ibid.

rational law, he says, at bottom, serves also to protect the weak".[64] It should be stressed that here the rationality of law is identified with the formal structure of the norm that renders foreseeable and calculable both the consequences deriving from transgression and the conduct required of members of society if they wish to secure a legally relevant end. "The reasonableness of law is no longer determined by the rationality of the society in which the law operates, as in Thomist natural law, but by its formal structure. The reasonableness thus becomes rationality, but a rationality which is formal and technical at the same time, that is, foreseeable and calculable".[65]

In consequence, the National Socialist regime, according to Neumann, cannot be defined as a "State" in the proper sense. Following from this conclusion the title he gives his book dedicated to the Hitler regime is significant: *Behemoth*, which in the Hobbesian terminology adopted by Neumann, is used in opposition to *Leviathan* (which indicates a politically and legally ordered system), to denote a situation of anarchy and illegality, and thus of arbitrariness, once the law is seen as the essential condition of social order and of protection of the individual against the excesses of political power. Accordingly, "If the general law is the basic form of right, if law is not only voluntas but also *ratio*, then we must deny the existence of law in the fascist state".[66] Where the norm is a mere expression of political power, that is, is not clad in the general and abstract form that would make it a law, one cannot speak of a legal system. "Does such a system deserve the name of law?" wonders Neumann in connection with the Nazi system. "Yes, if law is merely the will of sovereign; definitely not, if law, unlike the sovereign's command, must be rational either in for or in content".[67]

---

[64] Ibid., p. 447.

[65] Ibid., p. 441. It may be interesting to recall that this is the theoretical point around which the debate between Ernst Forsthoff and Wolfgang Abendroth revolved in Federal Germany in the 1960s. The question at issue was how to found the legitimacy of the social State that was taking shape with the new German Federal constitution (*Grundgesetz*) of 1948. Forsthoff trusted the virtues of general, abstract law, holding that this had intrinsic legitimating potential, and accordingly recommended that the measures of the social State should be channeled into the forms of law in the formal-liberal sense. Abendroth turned, in order to find guarantees of the legitimacy of law, to the subjects and procedures for promulgating the law, not to its logical properties. In relation to this see what Habermas has to say in his *Law and Morality*, in *Tanner Lectures on Human Values*, vol. 8, Salt Lake City 1988, pp. 217ff.

[66] F. Neumann, *Behemoth*, p. 451. See also F. Neumann, *The Rule of Law. Political Theory and the Legal System in Modern Society*, Leamington Spa 1986, p. 298: "Law does not exist in Germany, because law is now exclusively a technique of transforming the political will of the Leader into constitutional reality. Law is nothing but an *arcanum dominationis*".

[67] F. Neumann, *Behemoth*, p. 458. On this position of Neumann's, see W. Luthardt, *Unrechtstaat oder Doppelstaat? Kritischtheoretische Reflektionen über die Struktur des Nationalsozialismus aus der Sicht demokratischer Sozialisten*, in *Recht, Rechtsphilosophie und Nationalsozialismus*, ed. by H. Rotthleuthner, Wiesbaden 1983, pp. 197ff.

1.4 Power as Expression of Law. Léon Michoud and Hugo Krabbe

1.4.1 As far as strictly legal, and specifically public law, doctrines are concerned, it is not easy to find jurists who venture to assert the supremacy of law over what Germanic doctrine last century called *Herrschaft*.[68] It is particularly hard after the codifications and the birth of so-called legal positivism, which defined itself as the conception that posits the statute (act of State) as the sole form of law.[69] And it is still harder in German-speaking countries or Italy, the countries where legal positivism was cultivated, particularly as far as public law goes. Of two examples I have managed to find and will set out below of jurists that do not in their doctrinal thinking keep to the "realist" dogma[70] of legal positivism, one is a French scholar, and the other a Dutch professor: Léon Michoud and Hugo Krabbe.

At the start of his treatment of "rights of public power belonging to the State", in the second volume of his work on legal personality,[71] Michoud draws the distinction between the sovereignty of the prince or the people and sovereignty of the State,[72] taking up an idea of Georg Jellinek's. "But the idea of the sovereignty of the prince", he says "and that of the sovereignty of the people are political ideas, having as their consequence a certain distribution of powers in the body politic. The idea of sovereignty of the *State*, on the contrary, is an idea of a purely legal nature that may fit with any distribution of powers".[73] The idea of "sovereignty of the State" does not imply any particular political constitution. "It is capable of fitting both with the concentration of powers in the hands of one man or an assembly, and with their separation among different bodies, some of which (like the king in certain monarchies, like voters with us) may even be regarded as having rights to being

---

[68] As regards this, some notes by Hugo Krabbe are interesting: "The State's power, according to Mamenbrecher, is irresistible, untouchable, sacred; Otto Mayer speaks of the 'unconditional dominance of State authority', of the 'capacity of the State for legally predominating will'; Jellinek of the 'unconditional assertion of its own will in relation to others'; Laband of dominion [*Herrschaft*] as the 'specific privilege of the State'" (H. Krabbe, *Die moderne Staatsidee*, 2nd ed., Den Haag 1919, p. 6. In this connection cf. also H. Krabbe, *Die Lehre der Rechtssouveränität. Beitrag zur Staatslehre*, Groningen 1906, pp. 2–3).

[69] A well-known example of this way of conceiving of the law is Vittorio Emanuele Orlando's: "In an advanced State, the chief source of law is the statute, that is, the declaration of a legal norm made with outward signs and endowed with absolute imperium by the competent authority of the State" (V. E. Orlando, *Principi di diritto costituzionale*, 5th ed., Florence 1909, p. 50, emphasis in original).

[70] The "realism" of which the positive-law doctrine is so proud refers not so much to the concept of "reality" but rather "royalty", if it is true, as it is, that it amounts to reproposing the ancient maxim *rex facit legem*.

[71] L. Michoud, *La théorie de la responsabilitè morale et son application au droit français*, 2nd ed., vol. 2, Paris 1924.

[72] On this point see the observations by Otto Hintze, in O. Hintze, *Wesen und Wandlung des modernen Staats*, Berlin 1931, pp. 8–9.

[73] L. Michoud, *Op. cit.*, pp. 53–54.

such bodies. In consequence, it does not exclude any form of government; it is not a political theory in the proper sense of the term".[74] The meaning of the idea of "sovereignty of the State" is, according to Michoud, that the sovereignty lies not in the hands of a particular holder, even be that the people, but in that of the national collectivity in general.

The consequence of the notion of sovereignty of the State is, in Michoud's view, that the holder of power does not exercise it on his own behalf but in the more general name and interest of the collectivity. This implies a limitation on the prerogatives of the holder of power, whoever that be. "In the theory of sovereignty of the State", he writes, "the limitation comes naturally from the idea that this holder exercises a power conferred on him solely in the interest of the collectivity, from which it follows that this exercise becomes illegitimate from the moment he loses sight of that interest. His right, however exalted and even unique, does not go beyond that".[75]

In any case, whoever (physical person, group or institution) exercises power, that is, issues laws, is, for Michoud, nothing but an *organ* of the national collectivity. The right to make laws that this organ has does not belong to it, but to the collectivity.[76] The organ is subordinate to that right, even if this is not accompanied by any specific sanction in the event of a breach. The fact that the organ of the national collectivity is de facto sovereign, in the sense that it does not have above it any other organ capable of imposing its own decisions, does not mean that this organ is also sovereign de jure.

At this point we must ask what content Michoud attributes to the notion of (objective) law. This does not, in his view, coincide with the law laid down by organs of the State. There is a law that precedes and is beyond the action of the State. "The notion of law is, in fact", he writes, "by no means identical with the notion of *law promulgated by the organs of the State*. There were legal relations among men and rules for governing them before States were constituted, in primitive patriarchal societies, in groups like the clan and the horde. Even after the constitution of States, for long the law continued to be expressed in customs without State intervention. These two observations suffice to show that the idea of law is independent of the idea of State, and that the former is antecedent to the latter".[77] Accordingly, since the law is prior and superior to the State, the role of the latter, that is, of the legislative power, is, for this French lawyer, chiefly that of registering the rules already operative in the social fabric.

---

[74]Ibid., p. 54.

[75]Ibid., p. 55.

[76]It is just to avoid these possible implications of the doctrine that conceives of legislative power as a mere "organ" of the State and hence, at least ideally, subordinate to it, that some Nazi legal doctrine decisively rules out the possibility of the Führer's being an "organ" (in the legal sense). In this connection, see what was written by one of the most radical Nazi jurists, R. Höhn, *Rechtsgemeinschaft und Volksgemeinschaft*, Hamburg 1935, pp. 10–11, and pp. 75–77.

[77]L. Michoud, *Op. cit.*, p. 56.

Thus far, Michoud has theorized two types of limitation on the full deployment of political power. The first limitation lies in the impersonal nature of the holder of political power, the national collectivity. This is seen as obliging the material holder of power to act within the framework of the collectivity's interests. The first limit would, then, be the general interest, which should represent the aim of political action. The second limitation, related to the first, lies in the fact that the material holder of political power (king, elective assembly, or even popular meetings) is not also its legal bearer. This bearer is always, according to the French jurist, the collectivity as a whole. Accordingly, the organ that exercises the political power and promulgates the laws must express those norms and values that already prevail within the collectivity of which it is, thus, the "organ": the representative, the spokesman, the expression. This second limit, accordingly, lies in the relation of representation that exists between the collectivity and its organs.

Michoud further identifies a third limit, set by a natural law superior to the norms expressed by the popular consciousness. Natural law here seems to refer to strong normative criteria to be found through moral reasoning. In the case of a clash between natural law and social consciousness the former would prevail as it is ranked superior in the hierarchy. "We accept", he writes, "that above the very limit resulting from the social awareness of the group there is another limit, of an entirely ideal nature, namely that of natural law, and that this limit is imposed not only on the group's organs but even on the group itself should it decide otherwise through its organs".[78] Like many thinkers who set law above political power, Michoud goes as far as accepting the right to resist those political actions, (those laws) issued in flagrant violation of right (the whole set of norms expressed by the social consciousness). "The theory we have formulated", he writes, "has the consequence of showing that the legislature de facto depends on the social group whose representative it is, and that the de facto resistance of that group may invalidate its decision".[79]

1.4.2 As mentioned above, another legal doctrine that unties law from political power and makes the latter depend on the former is that of the Dutch author Hugo Krabbe. In opposition to the theory of "State sovereignty" common to much thinking in positive law (Krabbe refers specifically to Gerber, Laband, Georg Jellinek, and Otto Mayer) he sets up a theory of the "sovereignty of law". For the former, law is held to derive its origin from the original power attributed to the State. "The doctrine of the sovereignty of the State", writes the Dutch scholar, "derives every authority in the society, from the State. The State is the person with authority, the source of all power, a phenomenon of natural and original power. This point of view has the necessary consequence that the law too derives its authority from the State, and sometimes also its content".[80]

For the theory of the sovereignty of law that he forcefully asserts, the relationship between law and State is supposed to be contrary to the theory of State sovereignty.

---

[78] Ibid., pp. 57–58.

[79] Ibid., p. 57.

[80] H. Krabbe, *Die Lehre der Rechtssouveränität*, p. 5.

It is no longer the power of the State, conceived of as original, that produces law, but the law that attributes power and authority to the State. Not only is the power of the State, in Krabbe's view, in some way produced by law, but the law conditions and constantly upholds the activity of political power. Political power, that is, once "created" by the law, cannot free itself from it. The law upholds the State's activity, both through ordinary laws and through laws specifically promulgated to regulate the action of State organs.

To support the thesis of the sovereignty of law, Krabbe begins with the theory of the *Rechtsstaat*, although he does regard it as unsatisfactory. This theory recognizes as sovereign authority the power of law, but does not, according to Krabbe, draw from this the ultimate conclusions, confining itself to maintaining that the State's activity coincides with laws without going further and asserting the subordination of the State to law.[81]

The theories of the *Rechtsstaat* are unsatisfactory, in Krabbe's view, because they maintain what he calls the *Obrigkeitsidee*, that is, the idea of a sovereign political authority that draws its supremacy from sources other than law. For instance, he reproaches Georg Jellinek for not succeeding in freeing himself, in formulating his theses of the "self-limitation of the State", from the age-old tradition that sees the State's origins in personal power, the will of a sovereign (seen as a physical person, whether an individual or some other entity of mysterious origin). Krabbe, in short, accuses the public-law doctrine dominant at the time he wrote, of not succeeding in overcoming the personality-based conception of the State rooted in the ancient patrimonial States.

Krabbe several times asserts that his theory, far from being merely prescriptive, instead describes the reality of contemporary legal phenomena. He seeks clearly to distinguish law and justice: "As in the doctrine of law, so also in the doctrine of the sovereignty of law the concepts of *law* and of *justice* should be carefully distinguished".[82] His "doctrine of the sovereignty of law" is, according to him, founded on actually recording the developments of the modern shape of the State. The modern State can no longer, in his view, be identified with the figure, however preeminent, of a king, emperor, prince or sovereign, nor can political and legal action, in the modern State, be said to emanate from the will of a particular individual. The State is today impersonal, and as such, therefore, borne upon law. This is in particular due to the rise of the parliamentary State, since in a parliamentary system political will becomes abstract. Because of shifting majorities, it can no longer be attributed to particular individuals. "The will of the old historical subject of authority", Krabbe writes, "is no longer binding in itself; the assent of parliament is needed. In parliament, however, it is enough to have the assent of a changing majority, made up at one time of some persons, at other times others; accordingly, at least the exercise of the authority falling to parliament is no longer in the hands of particular persons".[83]

---

[81] See H. Krabbe, *Die moderne Staatsidee*, p. 2.

[82] Ibid., p. 40.

[83] Ibid., p. 7.

Consequently, in Krabbe's view, if the law (which is now a measure promulgated by parliament) can no longer be referred to a definite subject but instead to an entity whose composition is mutable, the norm becomes abstract and can no longer find its foundation in a manifestation of will. This new foundation of the law that takes over with the rise of the parliamentary regime derives, according to Krabbe, from the legal awareness of a people. The fact that parliament is elected means that this institution must be seen as the organ of the popular consciousness, so that the law finds its original source of production in that consciousness. "Thus there appears on the horizon" writes the Dutch jurist, "an entirely new foundation of the rule of the law. It is not the will of an authority, present only in the imagination, but the legal awareness of the people that attributes to the law its binding force; the *statute* is then valid only thanks to the *law* expressed in it".[84] Krabbe, as we see, distinguishes very clearly between statute (*Gesetz*) and law (*Recht*). The former is promulgated by the legislator, the second is the product of the people's legal awareness. The two legal phenomena are not however individually independent: the statute is valid only insofar as it reflects the law or is an expression of it.

To further develop his concept of the phenomenon of law, Krabbe again starts from a critique of voluntarist theory. He identifies two principal forms of such theories: (a) the validity of law is derived from an original power of supremacy, what Krabbe calls *Obrigkeitsgewalt*, (b) the law's validity is derived from the will of the members. Krabbe criticizes both of these theories; the former "because in reality there is no authority, no subject with the right to command".[85] The latter he claims takes no account of the function of law, which is to direct the will of the associated, such that law cannot coincide with their will. Krabbe does not accept this second theory "because the law, which aims to subject human will, cannot derive its validity from that very will".[86] Moreover, both the voluntarist theories in one way or another fail to lay the necessary stress on the objectivity of the law. The theory that derives the validity of law from the will of individuals ends by expelling every element of objectivity from the concept of law. Instead, the theory that derives the validity of law from the will of the authority (*Obrigkeit*) obsessively rigidifies the objectivity of law, to such a point that it becomes totally independent of popular sentiment.

What, then, is the conception of law developed by Hugo Krabbe? This can be understood on the basis of the two assumptions necessary according to the Dutch jurist to make it possible to speak of the law's validity. The first is that the law owes its validity to a power that is beyond human will and accordingly possesses an objectivity of its own in relation to that will. The law "owes its validity to a power that is objective in relation to that will".[87] The second assumption is that the content of the norm is related to the spiritual nature of man, given that it is aimed at determining human conduct. For Krabbe, there are two further elements producing

[84]Ibid., pp. 7–8. Emphasis in original.

[85]Ibid., p. 47.

[86]Ibid.

[87]Ibid., p. 48.

the validity of law apart from the two assumptions just mentioned: a material and a formal one.

The material element consists in the fact that the law is an expression of the legal awareness of men: the "doctrine of the sovereignty of law", writes Krabbe, "rises from the field of autonomy. The binding nature of law is to be found in people's legal awareness [*im Rechtsbewußtsein der Menschen*]".[88] The formal element consists in the law's intrinsic capacity as such to bind the individuals it addresses. "The bindingness of legal norms results from the fact that they are *legal* norms[. . .]. The bindingness does not need to be conferred solely form the outside, nor would this be possible, since there does not exist any other source of power [*eine andere Gewaltsquelle*]".[89] The definition of valid law given by Krabbe is accordingly as follows: "Valid law is, then, any general or particular norm, written or not, which is rooted [*wurzelt*] in the legal feeling or legal awareness of man".[90]

It follows from this conception that political power comes only through the mediation of law. The power of command is bound up with the capacity to produce law, but in such a way that it is the law that determines the command, not vice versa. "It follows from this", writes Krabbe, "that a binding command may be given only through the production of *law*. If the production of law is assigned to any person whatever, then, he contemporaneously receives the right to command, but always in the sense that the command issued is a consequence of the law that he (that person) produces. He does not separately hold the right of command, so that a norm could sometimes be binding and sometimes not. The norm he produces may command or forbid, but cannot, at pleasure, command and forbid, or else not command or forbid. It is in law and only in law that power [*Gewalt*] lies; and vice versa, a duty of obedience may be founded only upon law".[91]

If the law does not coincide with political power, it is then, according to Krabbe, conceivable for a measure of political power to be anti-legal, that is, for a statute not to be law. "A statute which is not setted on this foundations (the legal feeling or awareness of people) is *not* law, it lacks validity, even if it is voluntarily or compulsory observed. There is also the possibility to recognize that there may be legal provisions which lack the character of being a legal norm".[92] The element of coercion, the fact that a norm is de facto coercively imposed on the members of society, does not, according to Krabbe, tell us anything about its legal nature. The coercion serves only to *maintain* the norm, but cannot produce it, that is, attribute to it the value of a legal provision.[93]

---

[88] H. Krabbe, *Die Lehre der Rechtssouveränität*, p. 187.

[89] Ibid., pp. 187–188. Emphasis in original.

[90] H. Krabbe, *Die moderne Staatsidee*, p. 41.

[91] H. Krabbe, *Die Lehre der Rechtssouveränität*, p. 188. Emphasis in original.

[92] H. Krabbe, *Die moderne Staatsidee*, p. 50. Emphasis in original.

[93] Ibid., p. 51.

Chapter 2
The Normativist View

2.1 Preliminary

The dilemma traditionally afflicting the theory of law is due to its falling into one of the two following categories: (i) radical "realism" subordinating the reasons of law to the requirements of power, or else reducing the validity of norms to their "facticity"; (ii) radical "normativism" that cages the violence political power uses in a web of rules, or else excludes the relevance of consideration of the "effectiveness" of norms. The way out seems to be suggested by those who in a certain way and a certain sense interpret the one phenomenon (power) in terms of the other (law), or even vice versa. For this "third" way the two terms of the opposition are seen as ultimately equivalent or homologous. The opposition turns out on this view to be as it were the effect of an optical illusion: law and power are no longer anything but two faces of the same phenomenon, only artificially separated, and played off one against the other.

The relation between law and power may be developed at both a descriptive level and an eminently normative level. In the first case what interests us is the *reality* of phenomena, and their corresponding conceptualization. Whoever works on this level will pursue sociological research, or else attempt a structural analysis of normative systems from a legal theory perspective. In the second case what is of interest is the *foundation*, the *justification* or the *axiological validity* of these phenomena. Here a more properly philosophical view will prevail, and considerations of an eminently ethical nature cannot be avoided. In the first case one deals with questions like, "Is political power a social entity independent of or prior to forms of legal regulation, or to social norms actually in force?", or like: "Are legal norms in some sense constitutive of political power?". In the second case one will ask questions like: "Is it just for the law to be in the sway of political power?", or "What are the reasons that justify obedience to political power?". In this chapter, the level I intend to advance on is the former, specifically from the viewpoint of legal theory. One cannot however be unaware that the two types of research are mutually interdependent. The "third way" between radical realism and radical normativism will therefore be considered while maintaining considerable distance from moral philosophy.

M. La Torre, *Law as Institution*, Law and Philosophy Library 90,
DOI 10.1007/978-1-4020-6607-8_2, © Springer Science+Business Media B.V. 2010

2.2 Power Conceived of as Law: Hans Kelsen

As is well known, Hans Kelsen superimposed and identified the two concepts of law (legal order) and of State. In so doing he moved from a radical distinction between "is", *Sein*, and "ought", *Sollen*. The State, like the law, is, in his view, located in the area of *Sollen*. "The 'ought' terminology", writes Kelsen, "thus guarantees the purity of the science dealing with the State (or with law) as one with an object distinct from nature".[1] In relation to this, Kelsen criticizes Georg Jellinek's so-called *Zwei-Seiten-Theorie*. Jellinek, in his monumental *Allgemeine Staatslehre*, had divided the doctrine of the State into a "social doctrine" (whose methodology is closer to that of the empirical sciences) and a "legal doctrine" (understood as "normative" science), considering that the same object (the State) can be studied both from the normative viewpoint (typical of the legal sciences) and from the causal one (typical of the natural sciences).[2]

For Jellinek there are two concepts of State – the sociological and the legal. The sociological one which is prior to the legal one is as follows: " The State is an associative unity of sedentary human beings endowed with original supremacy power [*Herrschermacht*]".[3] Whereas according to the legal one; "The State [. . .] is the institution of a sedentary people, that is, a territorial institution endowed with an original supremacy power".[4] The difference between the two concepts resides essentially in the fact that the sociological one does not mention "people", but human beings. The State is qualified as *Verbandseinheit*, association, not as *Körperschaft*, corporation or institution or else legal person. As a "legal concept" (*Rechtsbegriff*) the state is conceived in terms of an institutional organization of people, resident permanently in a certain territory, endowed with "originary power of rule" (*ursprüngliche Herrschermacht*), which is a property also mentioned by the sociological concept. He sets out the doctrine of the "three elements" of the State: people, territory and sovereignty. But people, territory and "Herrschermacht" are all empirical concepts such as to denote an entity subject to the laws of physical causality. According to this perspective the juridicization of the notion of the State remains incomplete, in so far as it refers to its character as "embodiment" as *Körperschaft*.

By contrast with Jellinek, Kelsen instead considers that the essence of the State is purely normative. For the State, argues Kelsen, does not exist as a natural entity: "The State is not a visible or tangible body".[5] It is manifested through human behaviour that is regarded as actions of the State, or "imputed" to the State. But

---

[1] H. Kelsen, *Der soziologische und der juristische Staatsbegriff. Kritische Untersuchung des Verhältnisses von Staat und Recht*, 2nd ed., Tübingen 1928, p. 77.

[2] See G. Jellinek, *Allgemeine Staatslehre*, Berlin 1900, pp. 9ff., 25ff. and 47ff. Jellinek nonetheless distinguishes the social sciences from the natural sciences by arguing that the former are, as it were, individualizing (ibid., pp. 25–27).

[3] G. Jellinek, *Allgemeine Staatslehre*, p. 173.

[4] Ibid., p. 183.

[5] H. Kelsen, *General Theory of Law and the State*, English trans. by A. Wedberg, Cambridge, MA 1945, p. 191.

what does it mean that behaviour is "imputed" to the State, that is, to an entity that is not present in the physical world? Firstly, it is possible to impute or ascribe behaviour to a subject – asserts Kelsen – only where there are norms that constitute those acriptions. For ascription is a quite different operation from the empirical observation of an event through which one may assert some causal chain.

Imputing or attributing behaviour means attributing it to a particular subject not by asserting or describing a particular causal link, but according to a system of norms. Imputation is accordingly an eminently normative or juridical operation. "To impute a human action to the State" writes Kelsen, "as to an invisible person, is to relate a human action as the action of a State organ to the unity of the order which stipulates this action. The State as a person is nothing but the personification of this unity".[6] The State, accordingly, is a *purely* normative or legal concept, or as Kelsen puts it, "there is no sociological concept of the State different from the concept of legal order".[7]

However, asserting that the essence of the State is normative does not, for Kelsen, mean eliminating from it the element of coercion. In connection with his conception of the State, he stresses that it follows in the wake of the dominant doctrine, the Gerber-Laband-Jellinek line that sees the State essentially as a coercive apparatus.[8] He underlines that his theory, nonetheless, differs from traditional doctrine because in the former the element of coercion is considered not in its material aspect, but as a specific aspect of the normative order. The State is therefore, for the "pure theory", a system of rules that have as their content coercion (a sanction): "The State is a coercive order. For the specifically 'political' element of this organization consists in the coercion excercised by man against man, regulated by this order".[9]

Kelsen rejects the conception that sets the sovereign above the legal order, in both the German *Herrschertheorie* version and the English-speaking one of *Analytical Jurisprudence*.[10] This rejection goes hand in hand with that of the imperativist conception of law that sees it as a mere command or political decision. "The fact that one man *dominates* others, that is, that one's will becomes the reason for the other's will, cannot characterize the State; instead, what does is the fact that there is a stable order according to which one must command and the other must obey. Only this order establishes [*begründet*] the unity of the many relations of dominance that present themselves to a merely empirical observation".[11]

The conception that sees the aspect of dominance or the figure of the sovereign as a characteristic feature of the State reproduces in Kelsen's view the confusion

---

[6] Ibid., p. 192.

[7] Ibid.

[8] See *ibid*.

[9] H. Kelsen, *The Pure Theory of Law*, English trans. by M. Knight, Berkely, CA and Los Angeles, CA 1967, p. 286.

[10] On the differences, as far as the conception of the State is concerned, between "pure theory" and "analytical theory of law", see H. Kelsen, *The Pure Theory of Law and Analytical Jurisprudence*, in *Harvard Law Review*, vol. 55, 1941.

[11] H. Kelsen, *Der soziologische und juristische Staatsbegriff*, p. 83. Emphasis in original.

between the two distinct levels of *Sein* and *Sollen*. The coercive element, typical of the State, cannot be grasped outside the normative level, on the level of "being", as Austin does. His conception of the sovereign, writes Kelsen, "is sociological or political",[12] but should be assigned to the area of *Sollen*, as constituting the typical content of the norms of the legal system. "In the conceptual definition of the State", writes Kelsen, "it is important that the aspect of coercion [*Zwangsmoment*] be grasped in this unequivocal determinacy; as content of the normative order, and not be substituted – as the dominant doctrine that slips over onto the level of being [*die in die Seinsebene ausgleitende herrschende Lehre*] tends to do – by the unclear aspect of 'dominion' [*Herrschaft*] in the sense of a motivation".[13]

It may be said that Kelsen assigns the State, the political order *par excellence*, to the level of law, because he is moved by the requirement for coherence of his theoretical construction, centered round the rigid distinction between "is" and "ought", where the "ought" involved, as far as law is concerned, is quite distinct from the ethical or political one, and is the "specific being of law".[14] If we were to conceive of the State and law as distinct entities, one would be entirely material, at a natural and social level and accordingly governed by laws of a causal type (in Kelsen nature and society are often identified, specifically as regards the type of law that governs what happens in them[15]). The other would be entirely normative and located exclusively on a legal level; we would be compelled – as is done by Georg Jellinek – to split legal knowledge in two. This is because by accepting the distinction between State and law founded on ontological bases, we would make law derive from an ontological level that is foreign to it, given that the object of our consideration is positive State law, that is, the law issued or produced by the State.[16]

But if the source of law, (here the State) is something outside it, if *Sollen* refers for its existence to *Sein*, then the normative level and the natural-social level cannot be distinguished with the clearness Kelsen proposes. If the State (conceived of as a natural and social entity) produces law (a normative entity), the phenomenon of law cannot be isolated exclusively in the area of *Sollen*, and on the other hand the knowledge of law cannot come solely as a normative science, but also (and above all) as a social or natural (causal) science. One could then no longer maintain the "purity" of legal method and science (that is, its normative methodological monism). In consideration of all this, Kelsen's conclusion is that "law can come only from law

---

[12] H. Kelsen, *The Pure Theory of Law and Analitical Jurisprudence*, p. 64.

[13] H. Kelsen, *Der soziologische und juristische Staatsbegriff*, p. 83.

[14] Ibid., p. 80.

[15] It is not sufficiently clear whether for Kelsen the social dimension ought to be assimilated to the natural, causal one, and hence sociology to an empirical causal science. Even if he often seems decisively to assert this assimilation, there are nonetheless places in his work in which society is seen as a normative dimension, a world of *Sollen* and not of *Sein*, and in consequence social science is conceived of as a normative science. See e.g. H. Kelsen, *Der Staat als Integration. Eine prinzipielle Auseinandersetzung*, Wien 1930, pp. 6–7.

[16] On this, cf. H. Kelsen, *Vorrede zur zweiten Auflage*, in H. Kelsen, *Der soziologische und juristische Staatsbegriff*, p. v.

[*Recht kann nur aus Recht werden*]" and hence that "the State must be conceived of as a legal order".[17]

The criticism that Kelsen develops against, say, the theses of Krabbe, who also tends more or less to identify the phenomena of law and sovereignty, is based just on the fact that the Dutch jurist still maintains the distinction between State and law, and by so doing falls into a theory of the State that is full of internal contradictions. "Although", writes Kelsen of Hugo Krabbe, "he subsequently expanded this thesis into the formula 'that the authority of the State is nothing other than the authority of the law', he nonetheless maintains that the State has an independent existence in relation to the law; he is accordingly precluded from seeing the identity of the State order and the legal order – which alone allows a non-contradictory theory of the State –".[18] While Krabbe postulates the identity of State and law as a political ideal to which reality may possibly not correspond, for Kelsen the identity of State and law is a factual datum, or an epistemological assumption, always present in the history of legal and political formations. According to Kelsen, the limit of Krabbe's theory lies chiefly in the fact that he (Krabbe) conceives "the identification of State and law not as a logical and epistemological problem, but as a political postulate, which may either be realized or not in the historical process".[19]

Kelsen's conception that identifies State and law on the level of the normative order seems to bring about the reduction of political power to a legal phenomenon, to the norm, and hence – as Noberto Bobbio maintains – to giving expression in the context of the general theory of law to the ancient ideal of government by laws (by contrast with government by men) or of the State based on rule of law (in contrast with the State's right). Bobbio draws an opposition between the legal positivist tradition on the one hand and the doctrine of the rule of law on the other. "The two limiting concepts", he writes, "of legal positivism and the rule-of-law doctrine respectively are the *summa potestas* or sovereignty and the fundamental norm".[20] The two concepts of "sovereignty" and "fundamental norm" both have the function of closing the "system". However, one ("sovereignty"), according to Bobbio, serves to close a system founded on the supremacy of power over law, while the other (Kelsen's *Grundnorm*) serves the symmetrically opposite purpose of closing a system founded on the supremacy of law over power.

One could doubt that the "fundamental norm" in the *Pure Theory of Law* is outside of and opposed to the legal, positivist tradition. One could further believe that as far as Kelsen's doctrine is concerned, one ought to speak not so much of reducing power to law but the other way round, the reduction of law to power. Consider Kelsen's critique of the theory of the *Rechtsstaat* and the so-called *Selbstverpflichtungslehre*. The Austrian jurist maintains that from a strictly legal viewpoint it is meaningless to raise the problem that occupies Georg Jellinek's work,

---

17 H. Kelsen, *Der soziologische und juristische Staatsbegriff*, p. 133.

18 Ibid., p. 185.

19 Ibid.

20 N. Bobbio, *Dal potere al diritto e viceversa*, in *Rivista di filosofia*, 1981, p. 356.

and in general theoreticians of the State based on rule of law, of whether or not there is a norm that binds the activity of the sovereign or the State organs. In fact, according to Kelsen, who here again develops with extreme consistency typical theories of legal positivism, the norm is per se always binding, since otherwise one could not call it a norm. Where it is possible for the sovereign or the organ not to keep to the preexisting norm, one must then regard as being in force a norm that so regulates the modification of norms, that is, attributes to the sovereign or the organ the power to amend the preexisting norm.[21]

According to Kelsen, it is not possible to conceive of a State not bound by its own order (that is, the law), since this order is, for the Austrian jurist, the State itself. Thus the compound "*Rechtsstaat*" is pleonastic, since every State is as such a "Rechtsstaat". "There cannot therefore be", writes Kelsen, "any State not bound by its own order, free in relation to it, insofar the idea of a State bound by its order, freed from hypostatization, has a meaning, because the State is this order itself, cannot *be* anything but *order*, and the idea of a State liberated from 'its' order is a contradiction in terms. Since then this order can be only the legal order, no State is conceivable other than the Rechtsstaat, and the word *Rechsstaat* is a pleonasm".[22]

From the viewpoint of legal positivism, which recognizes the legal character of the valid norm whatever be its content, and that validity is connected with respect for certain formalities and the fact that the norm is issued by a given subject (sovereign or organ), even a despotic regime may be a "State of law". "As negation of the State of law", writes Kelsen, "is specifically considered the absolute monarchy, despotism. Even this has a specific order, and is conceivable only as a specific order. The rule that coercion is to be exercised only when commanded by the despot and in the way he wants is just as much a rule of *law* as the one that coercion is to be exercised whenever decided by the popular assembly and in the way it wants. Both are, from the viewpoint of the concept of positive law, *equivalent* original hypotheses".[23]

In relation to this, to better understand the meaning of Kelsen's identification of State and law, it is necessary to mention the way Kelsen resolves the question of a "wrongful act of State[*Staatsunrecht*]". Kelsen denies that there can be any such thing as a wrongful act of State. The State, which is nothing but the personification of law, can never have attributed to it a wrongful act, because of the fact that "the subject of the wrongful act [*das Unrechtssubjekt*] can never be at the same time the subject of law [*das Rechtssubjekt*]".[24]

What lies behind Kelsen's consistently normativistic construction doesn't seem to be the ideal of the supremacy of the norm over power, but more the recognition that every power, insofar as it exercises effective coercive action over its subjects,

[21] See H. Kelsen, *Op. ult. cit.*, p. 186.

[22] Ibid., p. 187. My emphasis.

[23] Ibid., My emphasis.

[24] Ibid., p. 136.

is a legal order.[25] This is because the content of the basic norm is not, for Kelsen, a behaviour of the members of society (which is instead the object of kind of secondary norm derived by arguing *a contrario* from the primary one), but a sanction, that is, a coercive act of the State. In Kelsen's doctrine the sanction does not lie *outside* the legal order that lays down the behaviour of the members of society. It does not have the subsidiary function of ensuring compliance with the prescribed conduct, and is not the object of the norms commonly called "secondary", as is the case for the traditional doctrine. For Kelsen the sanction is to be located within the primary legal norm, since, as we have said, in Kelsen's system the former (sanction) is the object of the latter (norm). In this way the scope of intervention by the State, conceived of as the apparatus of coercion, is located within the area of law. "Thus", he writes, "it is theoretically unacceptable to identify, apart from an order containing norms that provide for the sanction, a system of legal norms that lay down the human conduct that avoid the sanction, and assert the former as the coercive apparatus of the State and the latter as the law in the proper and strict sense".[26]

In Kelsen's definition of the law as a *Zwangsordnung*, what qualifies the law as such is not so much the normative element (the *Ordnung*) as the element of force, of coercion (the *Zwang*). "What distinguishes the legal order from all the other social orders", he writes, "is the fact that it regulates human behaviour through a specific technique. If we ignore this specific element of law, if we do not conceive of the law as a specific social technique, if we define the law simply as order or organization, and not as a *coercive* order (or organization), then we lose the possibility of distinguishing law from other social phenomena, we identify law with society".[27] On this point, on the intrinsically coercive nature of law, Kelsen develops his critique of the thesis of Eugen Ehrlich, who maintained that coerciveness is not an essential feature of law, while nonetheless maintaining the normative nature of the phenomenon of law.[28]

Summarizing, we may say that Kelsen's doctrine of the identity of law (legal order) and State (political power) is possible through two parallel processes of superposition of two concepts. There is a first superposition of "law" and "State" on the level of "law": the State is conceived of as an order, as a set of norms, that is, as a phenomenon of law. The two concepts (State and law) are both brought within the category of normative phenomena, which is, in Kelsen's view, the one typical of law. "As soon as the State is recognized as a unity of orders [*Ordnungseinheit*], as a norm, there is", writes Kelsen, "no possibility of counterposing it as association

[25]"Political power", writes Kelsen, "is the efficacy of the coercive order recognized as law" (H. Kelsen, *General Theory of Law and the State*, p. 191). But who is the author of this recognition? And what does "recognition" mean in this context? One might well ask. And supposing an order were effective irrespective of its "recognition" on the part of the great mass of members of society?

[26]H. Kelsen, *Der soziologische und juristische Staatsbegriff*, p. 88.

[27]H. Kelsen, *General Theory of Law and the State*, p. 26. My emphasis.

[28]On this see ibid., pp. 24–28.

[*Verband*] to law as norm. State and law both fall within the same category of normative order".[29]

However, were the identity of State and law to come about solely through their both being normative phenomena, they could not be distinguished from other phenomena which while being normative are not legal.[30] In the last analysis, they would end up being confused with society which is also an order of human behaviour. What distinguishes law from other normative phenomena (like ethics or religion for instance) is, according to Kelsen, the fact that the law has as its object an act of force, the sanction or coercion.

At the level of coercion (typical of the State), comes the second superposition of the concepts of State and law made by Kelsen. The concepts are identified because both denote orders that rest on the use of force, on the specific "social technique" that is coercion. It is only at this level, the one that according to Kelsen qualifies the phenomenon of law as such (distinguishing it from other normative phenomena), the level of power (or force, or coercion), that the final identification of the two concepts comes about. This is explicitly stated in Kelsen's work, and he acknowledges his debt to traditional legal doctrines. "And if the essence of legal norm", he writes, "is seen in its coercive nature, then law and the State are in the same way coercive orders in the sense of a system of coercion".[31] It does not accordingly seem overly unplausible to conclude that the identification of law and State made by Kelsen comes about on the side of the State (or of political power). In this sense, it may perhaps be said that Kelsen's doctrine is a variant of the traditional theses that subordinate the phenomenon of law to the activity of power.

Note that for Kelsen the State is not a particular type of legal order, a species of the genus "law". The State, in Kelsen's theory, is the legal order *par excellence*; it is the same thing as the legal order. According to Kelsen the two concepts of State and of legal order totally coincide and are interchangeable. Obviously, in asserting this thesis, Kelsen has to face an objection that might seem insurmountable: where is the State in a society which though possessing a legal system does not display any institution characterized by the monopoly of power that Kelsen assumes as the distinctive feature of the State? The Austrian jurist, to overcome this objection, is compelled to apply even to so-called primitive societies a conceptual grid modelled on the figure of the modern State, in particular the concept of "organ", obviously requiring some conceptual stretching. For instance, according to Kelsen, in a society in which the principle of private vendetta applies, the "avenger" is acting as "organ" of society itself. "In the primitive society the legal order in principle delegates the act of coercion to the very person who has been hurt in his interests (protected by law). He then acts as the 'organ' of the coercive order (blood vendetta)".[32] Thus, an injured person taking revenge in primitive society is seen as the organ of a coercive

---

[29] H. Kelsen, *Der soziologische und juristische Staatsbegriff*, pp. 86–87.

[30] See H. Kelsen, *General Theory of the Law and the State*, p. 28.

[31] H. Kelsen, *Der soziologische und juristische Staatsbegriff*, p. 87.

[32] Ibid., p. 90.

apparatus which is already a kind of State and differs from the modern State only in respect of the greater specialization of tasks present in the latter.

For Kelsen then, as is argued in the first edition of *Reine Rechtslehre* of 1934, probably the work most representative of his thought, law cannot exist without power or force, that is without the presence of force in its most elementary manifestations involving coercion or violence. Law nonetheless is not to be identified with force or violence: "Law is a particular order (or organization) of force [*eine bestimmte Ordnung (oder Organisation) der Macht*]".[33] Law has force as an object and it regulates and organizes it according to a formula that remains ambiguous. Kelsen's normative solution, as will be shown by its development of decisionistic ideas that seek to deny any action of logic within the sphere of legal reasoning,[34] is little more than a compromise.

2.3 Law, Command, Norm

Which of the two classical conceptions of the relations between law and power is more satisfactory? The one that reduces the law to an instrument of power, or the other that sees the law as an entity that precedes and in some sense determines political phenomena? One must indeed say that usually both conceptions are set on different levels: the former is generally presented as a descriptive theory of a state of things as it is, and the second instead as a prescriptive or ideal theory of a state of affairs as they ought to be. However, at the level of description of actual reality, both conceptions are in my view unsatisfactory. The conception that sets law before and above political power errs as it is too "idealistic". The other, the conception that sets political power before and above law, errs as too "realistic". For the one presupposes an entirely ideal entity that can actually at least limit the material activity of power and its deployment of force. The other ultimately reduces the political relation to a mere power relation, a command/obedience relation mostly modelled according to a cause/effect dynamics.

Let us briefly consider the theory of law as limit on or prerequisite of power. This ends up by maintaining that the norm as such, the form of law, is able to set an arduous if not insurmountable obstacle to the sovereign's arbitrariness. The idealism of this conception is evident, since it considers that a material force can be limited or arrested in its movements by something (the law), conceived of in absolutely abstract terms (in the least abstract case as procedural form; in the most abstract case as "justice").

Those who like Franz Neumann maintain that the law (as *form of law*) prevents arbitrariness of political power, and in essence reproposes the theory of the State's "self-limitation" should be reminded of two things. On the one hand that the political power can always formalize its own will, and its own arbitrariness. As has been

---

[33] H. Kelsen, *Reine Rechtslehre*, 1st ed., Wien 1934, p. 70.

[34] See H. Kelsen, *Allgemeine Theorie der Normen*, Wien 1978.

remarked, "by contrast with the common injustice repressed by the laws, political injustice is essentially legalized injustice". "As supreme legislator, even the most unjust tyrant or most authoritarian despot is, when he wishes, able to respect the limit of strict legality".[35]

On the other hand, speaking of the State's "self-limitation" means relying on the benevolence of the sovereign himself, who can and will (but might also not wish to) put certain limits on his own power. Moreover, this theory is infected by a conceptual circularity it cannot escape. The law (understood as positive law) is, it is asserted, a limit on the activity of the State itself, so that the passive subject of the limitation is also its active subject. This vicious circle is set up at the point when the law is identified with the positive law, and the latter with the law promulgated by the State. "We are now", as Bertrand de Jouvenel stresses, "going round in a vicious circle! Political authority should be just; it needs, that is to say, to act in conformity with the law. But the epitome of the rules is given out by political authority itself. Therefore the authority which makes laws is, by definition, always just". "Laws are the only source of the law. Therefore, whatever is in a law is law, and there can be no remedy against the laws. Accept it, and to seek in law a bulwark against power becomes pure illusion. The law is, as the jurists put it, 'positive'".[36]

The theory of the State's "self-limitation" can escape the vicious circle by laying down the distinction between the law and statute. This operation has two outcomes. The first is to presuppose an ideal law above the law of the State. This is the natural-law outcome recommended by de Jouvenel, who, however, cannot avoid the objection of idealism, considering that this ideal law is "presupposed" and not laid down (however that might come about).

The second way out might be to get rid of the legal positivist principle of the unity and uniqueness of the legal order (in a given territory). One might then consider need for or the existence of several legal systems that mutually influence (and limit) each other. But these other (objective) systems different from the State's, if they are neither "ideal" or "natural", are accordingly "laid down". And if they are laid down, this is (not always intentionally or deliberately[37]) done by some social group that is beyond State control, by some other institution. That means that the second way out of the distinction between law and State consists in the pluralist conception of society, that is, a conception that sees (or hopes to) several powers operating within the social space. In this sense, then, the theory that asserts that the law sets limits to the activity of political power (specifically the State) ends up with a theory asserting the need for or existence of a plurality of powers mutually limiting and balancing each other, and thus insists on the unavoidable overlap of law and power, rather than on their separation.

---

[35] Both quotations from R. De Stefano, *L'accettazione della legge*, Reggio Calabria 1977, p. 76.

[36] Both quotations from B. de Jouvenel, *On Power*, English trans. by J. F. Huntington, Boston, MA 1969, 3rd ed., the first from pp. 302–303, the second from p. 303.

[37] On this point see F. A. Hayek, *The Results of Human Action but not of Human Design*, in Id., *Studies in Philosophy, Politics and Economics*, London 1967, pp. 96ff.

Let us now consider the conception that makes law subservient to power. This too separates the normative level (law) from the material one (power). In some imperativist versions, the normative plan is denied and resolved into the material one of force. These are in general the ones that interpret the law as the political superior's command to the political inferior. This very reduction of the normative level to the material one constitutes the extreme example of what I earlier called the "error" of overrealism. This consists in explicitly or implicitly placing social and essentially human reality on the same level as physical phenomena, and in applying to the world of social and human phenomena the model of causal explanation typical of the physical sciences. Social phenomena, according to this view, are regarded as the outcome of the action of a series of physical forces connected with each other through binding relations of cause and effect. Thus, the command is held to be the cause, and obedience to the command the effect. Or better, the cause is seen as consisting in the threat of sanction that accompanies the command (explicitly or implicitly), and obedience to result from fear of the penalty that is the effect of the threat. This is broadly the pattern employed by Bentham and John Austin. In more recent times, to justify this model, recourse has been made to anthropology based on the model of Pavlovian-Skinnerian learning through stimulus and response.

Moreover, this conception that defines the law as command and accordingly as a relation existing essentially between two or more individuals, in any case as an *interpersonal* relation, is forced to presuppose that society consists basically of interindividual relations, voluntary and coercive. It is accordingly an atomized space, a sort of "exploded diagram". This is very far from the reality of social formations, which are instead characterized by the *impersonality* of their fundamental and constitutive relations (consider only the language of a society, which cannot be defined as a "convention", if by this is meant a voluntary, conscious agreement among a definite number of parties[38] still less as a unilateral decision[39]).

The imperativist conceptions, Austin's for instance, in assuming that society consists only of more or less personal relations, ignore the specific dimensions of society (the specifically social one of the phenomena of collective life), and build their theses on a void. Against imperativism one may further adduce the criticisms traditionally made of voluntarist theories of the phenomenon of law. How is it possible for the law to apply even after the death of the person whose will it is held to be? Is it possible for the legislator to want that conduct permanently? How is it possible to apply law even to those who do not know it or understand it and are incapable of understanding it, as the principle *ignorantia legis non excusat* asserts? How is it possible still to speak of will in the psychological sense in relation to measures issued by collective deliberative bodies like parliamentary assemblies, or even the central

---

[38] Here I would refer to K. R. Popper, *On the Theory of Objective Mind*, in Id., *Objective Knowledge. An Evolutionary Approach*, Rev. ed., Oxford 1986, pp. 159–160.

[39] As we know, this is Humpty Dumpty's conception (see L. Carrol., *Through the Looking Glass and what Alice Found There*, London 1979, p. 79); for a critique see A. Flew, *Thinking about Thinking. (Or, Do I sincerely want to be right)* 5th ed., Glasgow 1985, pp. 76–77.

committee of a party, where the decision results from a majority combination of the various individual wills?

However, not just imperativist theories (meaning those that define law as command) but also those theories that in general speak of law as an expression of power (even though defining the law as norm or rule) in my view run into the "error" of overrealism. For these theories this error is the outcome of the conception that force produces law, even if the two phenomena are not made to coincide. For these theoreticians (Marx and Soviet jurists, for instance) the law is one of the many *instrumenta regni* that political power uses to impose itself and perpetuate itself within the social body. For them too, then, the distinction between legal activity and political activity diminishes to the point of disappearing: legal activity is always political activity. This is crudely put by Max Stirner: "The State practices 'violence', and it calls its violence 'law'; that of the individual, 'crime'".[40]

What objections can be raised against this way of understanding the law, which sees it as the product or expression of power? Some have been mentioned. It seems that the two following should attentively be considered: on the one hand, this conception does not take account of the normal unfolding of life in a society, and correspondingly of situations of aggression towards the social bond. On the other, it does not take account of one fact, which the wisdom of the ancient Romans caught in the maxim: *nemo ad facere cogi potest*, nobody can be compelled to a doing, in so far as a doing presupposes will and intention, and these are never fully causally predetermined.

Whoever maintains that the law is an expression of power is unable or ill at ease to draw a qualitative distinction between the act of a bandit ordering an unfortunate to hand over his purse, and the norm prescribing that anyone who steals will be punished by imprisonment of, say, between 3 and 7 years. If anything, a quantitative distinction is drawn in terms of the intensity, duration and legitimacy of the power that the agent (bandit or state functionary) is able to deploy. This means that the distinguishing criterion between legal commands and non-legal commands is made to lie in the effectiveness, duration and legitimacy of the coercion exercised over a particular subject. A legal act would then be an effective, lasting and legitimate coercive act. Violence nonetheless remains the "core" of the act. Here, however, imperativist legal thought reveals its distance from common sense, for which the difference between an act of violence and a norm, between the highwayman and the ordinary citizen, is somehow immediate and intuitive.

It might be objected that the parallel is not to be drawn between the citizen and the highwayman, but between the highwayman and the State official, as imperativist theories in general do. I believe instead that the two subjects to be compared are not

---

[40] M. Stirner, *The Ego and Its Own*, ed. by D. Leopold, Cambridge 1995, p. 176. Stirner has a drastically voluntaristic and imperativistic conception of law. He certainly reduces law to command: "People are at pains to distinguish *law* from arbitrary *orders*, from an ordinance: the former comes from a duly entitled authority. But a law over humane action (ethical law, state law, etc.) is always a *declaration of will*, and so an order" (M. Stirner, *The Ego and Its Own*, p. 174).

the robber and the policeman, an operation that suits those who see the law as command (but isolated from the general context of social behaviour). The comparison in my view should be drawn between those who conform, act in compliance with the norms of a given community, and those who instead break these norms by violently attacking the social normality. In other words, the opposition between the highwayman and the man in the street refers to the one between peace and war. Those who maintain that the law is command and that it is essentially an arbitrary and violent act, or that the law is political and that politics is violence, cannot distinguish – within a given social group – a state of peace from a state of war. If anything, peace will be seen by them as an appendix to war, or else war as an appendix to peace, the only difference between the two states consisting in the fact that in war the violence is declared and explicit, while in peace the violence is latent and masked by law. Karl von Clausewitz brings out this way of thinking with his famous phrase that "war is merely the continuation of policy by other means".[41] War is seen by the Prussian general as a continuation of politics by other means, and the mirror image of this is Lenin's inverted version of the proposition: politics as continuation of war by other means.

On this point of view that strictly links war and politics – which is one of the outcomes of the conception of power as violence – peace and war are in some sense interchangeable conditions, since both of these states are seen as the terrain of politics, which is conceived of essentially as a manifestation of violence. This amounts to maintaining that it is violence and force that govern the life of man and of society. Here once again the imperativist viewpoint, or "realism" (in the sense of "political realism") betrays its remoteness from common sense, for which peace and war are quite distinct conditions. On the other hand, it shows a deep misunderstanding of the mechanism that holds society together. War (and in particularly civil war) is the greatest possible antisocial manifestation, the mortal struggle among men in place of the communication and exchange that constitute the normal nature of the social bond. This coincides with peace, security, order, without which social life becomes impossible, and the individual's existence is precarious.

It is not true, as the imperativist theorists manage to maintain (think of Marx, Lenin or Stirner), that peace and war are equivalent. Peace is the absence of war. This means that society (which can only exist if its members are at peace with each other) is governed by the absence of violence, or its limitation.[42] But if this is so, then the law cannot be conceived of in terms of command (or, which amounts to the same thing, as an arbitrary and violent act). This clearly emerges in a legal phenomenon that remains the fundamental one once one stops arguing in the narrow terms of legal positivism and recognizes as the area in which the phenomenon of law is manifested the whole territory of society, not just the area of typical institutional

[41] K. von Clausewitz, *On War*, English trans. by M. Howard and P. Paret, Princeton, NJ 1976, p. 87.

[42] On war as antithesis of law and in general on the possible relations between war and law, cf. N. Bobbio, *Diritto e guerra*, in N. Bobbio, *Il problema della guerra e le vie della pace*, Bologna 1979, pp. 97ff.

mechanisms of the State (courtrooms, bureaucrats' offices, jails and barracks). This phenomenon, still fundamental today for the functioning of the legal order, is custom. It lies at the very core of society: the social bond is in fact largely not voluntary, but customary. How, then, can an extremely voluntarist and constructivist[43] theory like imperativism manage to explain, the phenomenon of custom and its "constitutive" action in relation to the legal order? Custom is mostly taken the emergence of convergent schemes of conduct or a "habit of obedience", a habit that can obviously be referred to a command one is brought "customarily" to obey. Convergence of conduct indeed here is referred back to an attitude of deference towards power and to a practice of obeying. This *habit of obedience* to which Bentham and Austin in particular refer to expain law and its rules is not by itself a source of law (which remains command and thus the will of a "political superior"). This *habit* explains only the reason why the command is usually obeyed; a reason identified not in recognition of the command's legitimacy but in an unreflective attitude of obedience created over centuries of threats and privations associated with executing the orders of a political superior. More than a "reason" there is instead a "motive", where the former (the reason) is presented with propositional content and comes to form part of practical reasoning, while the latter (the motive) is not presented as a statement (though it can always be expressed as such) and instead constitutes more an element in some causal chain.

The other objection to an imperativist conception of law is the one that may be summarized as it was mentioned before – in the Latin maxim *nemo ad facere cogi potest*: no one can be constrained to do something. If this is so, obedience to a command is always to some extent voluntary. But if obedience is not a mechanical fact, not a mere *pati*, and instead requires a share of will and awareness, this means that the effectiveness of the command, but also and particularly the possibility of the command's being conceived as such by its addressee, depend on some form, however minimal, of "consent" on the part of the latter. And they also involve referencc to his moral responsibility.

It is no mere chance that some analytical reconstructions of the concept of power base it not so much on the possibility of getting something done as on that of stopping something being done. For instance, according to Felix Oppenheim, a thinker of a neopositivist background whom we might assign to the realistic tendency in conceptions of power, the latter is, as far as power exercised over third parties is concerned, eminently *power to stop something being done*. "To have power", he writes, "is to be capable of exercizing power, that is, to be able to subject others to one's control or to limit their freedom".[44] And the American philosopher consequently gives the following definition of power: "Y exercises power over X with respect to his not doing *x* if X does not or cannot do *x* or would be penalized if he did as a result of some power act *y* of Y".[45] Power here is seen eminently as negative

---

[43]Cf. F. A. Hayek, *Rechtsordnung und Handelsordnung*, Karlsruhe 1967.

[44]F. E. Oppenheim, *Dimensions of Freedom*, New York, NY 1961, p. 100.

[45]Ibid., p. 91.

power, power to prevent an action, or as punitive power, power to inflict a sanction, but not as positive power, power to bring about conduct.

Whoever commands, indeed, presupposes a form of "consent" from the subject to whom the command is addressed. This "consent" is exercised in at least two ways. Firstly, obedience to the command is, as we have said, a voluntary act, not a mere *pati*, or a submission to absolute compulsion (as that of natural laws might be). Command is not physical determination of conduct but rather its prescription. Command is not torture: the tortured is not "commanded". It has equally to refer back to an element of autonomy on the part of the commanded, no less than when establishing if this is the best way to carry out the command. There is a context in which the command is applied that is not totally under the control of the one who issued the command, and that can't be understood with mere reference to the propositional content of the command. A command rests on an element, however minimal, of autonomy and free valuation by the subject of the command. No command is ever able to fully direct the will which it is addressed to; it can only make the will assume a special disposition. It cannot more than that because it just aims to the command's successful execution. A minimum of personal initiative should be presupposed when executing a command, because there is no number of commands that could cover all variables of time, place and persons possible when executing the command. In this sense, there is always a reasoned obedience and not a perfect concretisation of a command.

Secondly, the subject consents to a *particular individual's* producing the command. Otherwise that particular statement, through which the command is expressed, would be perceived as something different, as the request for a favour, say, or as advice, or else as a threat. Think, for instance, of the statement "the door needs to be shut", which if uttered by a subject in the context of a group consisting of several individuals is perceived as a command only by those members of the group who recognize the utterer's authority to give them commands. By the others the statement is perceived as the non-imperative expression of a necessity or desire. This second point is very well grasped by one Nazi theorist of law, Ernst Forsthoff, who in his book *Der totale Staat*, a prefiguration of the totalitarian regime of National Socialism, nonetheless refuses to fully adopt the decisionist theory of law, arguing as follows. "Any command, however", Forsthoff writes, "presupposes a higher rank that confers legitimacy on the command, irrespective of the personal qualities of the superior. A non-commissioned officer commands not because he is necessarily the bravest soldier (though he ought to be), but in virtue of the rank he holds".[46] The issuing of a command is thus according to Forsthoff not founded on nothing, or on mere physical superiority, but on some preexisting normative order.

It is interesting to note that even in one of the most tenacious upholders of the imperativist theory we find, and relatively explicitly, an awareness of the consensual basis on which command rests. On the question of voluntariness as a requirement for

[46] E. Forsthoff, *Der totale Staat*, 2nd ed., Hamburg 1933, p. 34.

obedience, it may be recalled that Hobbes clearly distinguished *pati*, which is involuntarily and necessarily submitting to coercive action manifested, for instance, in an execution, when the condemned person suffers death, and *facere* (or *non facere*), which is in any case a voluntary act even when it constitutes the object of a command that is obeyed. "When a thief hath broken the laws", writes Hobbes, "and according to the law is therefore executed, can any man understand that this suffering of his is in obedience to the law? Every law is a command *to do*, or *to forbear*: neither of these is fulfilled by suffering. If any suffering can be called obedience, it must be such as is voluntary; for no involuntary action can be counted a submission to the law".[47]

On the second point, the recognition of the authority of the issuer of the command by his addressee, it may be recalled that for Hobbes not every command constitutes a law, but only a command coming from whoever the command's addressee has previously recognized as having the authority to command. "And the first it is manifest, that law in general, is not counsel, but command; but only of him, whose command is addressed to one formerly obliged to obey him".[48] Here the concept of law as a set of commands more or less explicitley refers to a normativist view of the phenomenon of law. Hobbes asserts that not every command constitutes a legal provision, but only a command issued by a person to whom the command's addressee is already previously bound. The command is accordingly law if there is "something" outside it that qualifies as law the relationship between "addressee" and "commander", that is, "something" that makes the addressee of the command recognize the latter as law, and obey it. This "something", outside the command and preceding it, can only be given by a norm or a set of norms.

The conviction that command is at the origin of law, that is of "ought", has been defined by Neil MacCormick as the "imperativist fallacy". What leads MacCormick to this conclusion is above all the fact, similar to the one mentioned above by Hobbes, that in order to constitute a legal provision the command has to presuppose "something" outside it. We shall here summarize MacCormick's arguments in this regard.

A command falls within the category of acts through which a person A intends a person B to carry out action X. For this category includes other acts than command, like advice, prayer or request. In all these cases the linguistic utterance may be the same (say, "do not smoke"), so we cannot from this alone deduce the actual nature of the act, whether it is, say, a command, advice or request. This leads MacCormick to maintain that the feature that makes a linguistic utterance a command does not lie in that utterance, or is not deducible from the structure or mood (the imperative, say) of the utterance. The feature that makes an utterance a command is outside the utterance itself. This amounts to saying that the command is a command because it presupposes "something" that is not a command. "What is next required", MacCormick goes on, "is to find the element which distinguishes order

[47] T. Hobbes, *Behemoth*, ed. by F. Tönnies, p. 50.

[48] T. Hobbes, *Leviathan*, ed. by C. B. Macpherson, Part I, Chapter 26, p. 312.

and commands from other acts, such as requests, which also involve the intention to be understood as intending to get the addressee to do some act. The key to this is the fact that somebody who commands is necessarily calling for *obedience* on the part of his addressee, whereas to make a request is to appeal to the kindness of courtesy of the other. To 'call for obedience', in the sense here intended, involves asserting one's superiority over another. There are certain relationships, relationships of superiority and inferiority, which may exist between persons, such that the inferior is in one sense or another required to comply with the expressed wishes of other in relation to his conduct. One person is properly said to obey another if he complies with the other's expressed wishes, willingly or unwillingly, in recognition that he is required to do so in virtue of their relationship".[49]

The "key" then, to understanding the difference between commands and acts like requests or prayers lies in the relation existing between utterer and addressee of the linguistic statement in question. In order for there to be command, and not for instance advice, there has to be a relation of superiority between the two subjects. "Commanding", writes MacCormick, "is only appropriate in a context of superiority, whereas requesting is appropriate (though not only appropriate) between people who acknowledge each other as equals, provided that they are on friendly or at least courteous terms with each other".[50] This superiority may, according to MacCormick, be based either on physical force or on a body of rules shared by utterer and addressee of the linguistic statement, who attributes superiority (in a social rather than physical sense) to the utterer. Nonetheless, according to MacCormick – though somehow in contradiction with what he previously said – a command is possible even in a context in which there is no relation of superiority at all between utterer and addressee of the linguistic statement considered. This would, say, be the case where someone sitting at a restaurant table said to another, sitting at another table, "pass me the salt". This is less true between Italians. An Italian would in fact be unlikely to use the second person singular of the imperative in order to approach a stranger (in Italian) in the situation described above. An Italian would use the polite form ("Could you give me the salt?", or "Would you give me the salt?", "Could you pass me the salt?"), probably accompanied by a "please"; which in itself reveals, I feel, that we are in the presence not of a command, but of a request.

MacCormick, then, considers that in order for there to be a command the qualifying feature is above all the utterer's intention and *then* the context in which the utterance is made (the relation between utterer and addressee). "Our conclusion", he writes, "calls for the amendment of Bentham's definition ('A parole expression of the will of a superior is a command'); a command is an utterance which the speaker intends his addressee to take as expressing a will that the addressee do some act in

---

[49]N. MacCormick, *Legal Obligation and the Imperative Fallacy*, in *Oxford Essays in Jurisprudence*, Second Series, ed. by A. W. B. Simpson, Oxford 1973, p. 106.

[50]Ibid.

recognition of the speaker's superiority".[51] But MacCormick immediately adds: "A command is sincere and appropriate ('felicitous') only if the commander does wish to get the deed done and only if he is in fact superior to his addressee in respect of the act commanded".[52] A command is thus "happy" (using John Langshaw Austin's terminology[53]) only if the utterer is indeed in a position of superiority in relation to the addressee. The utterer's intention accordingly does not tell us whether we are in the presence of a genuine command or, say, the expression of an egocentric or simply impolite person (consider the example of the salt mentioned above).

Not every utterance of what "ought to be" is a command, but only one implying a relationship of superiority between utterer and addressee: this is MacCormick's conclusion. This conclusion might be flanked by another: the command is not one based on a relation of physical superiority, but only one based on a relation of *social* primacy. But one is socially superior because the norms of a society assign a certain rank. The (political) command accordingly refers to a normative system in force.

If the command (at least a political one) presupposes in order to be operative a norm or body of norms, then the following conclusion may be drawn. (i) The law (the norm) cannot be derived from a command or, as Neil MacCormick writes, "'ought' is no more derivable from 'shall' that from 'is'".[54] (ii) The political command, far from being a manifestation of material force, is overwhelmingly a normative phenomenon, that is, legal *lato sensu*. Political power, the power to determine the social conduct of a community, cannot in consequence be defined as the power of command, still less as mere de facto power. It is so intimately bound up with normative phenomena that it can be explained only in terms of norms. But if political power can be explained only as being fixed by norms, it becomes impossible to explain the norms as the product of power. Accordingly, any theory seeking to define law as expression or manifestation or instrument of power (whether political or merely physical) is revealed as fallacious.

2.4 Normative Order, Political Power, Dominion

Indeed an interesting way of expressing the relation between law and power is the one that seeks to render the two terms identical. In Kelsen, as we saw earlier, this identification comes about more at the level of power (seen as force and coercion) than at the normative level. Nonetheless, Kelsen's thoughts on the matter offer lots

[51] Ibid., p. 108. My emphasis.

[52] Ibid., pp. 108–109.

[53] Cfr. J. L. Austin, *How to do Things with Words*, 2nd ed., ed. by J. O. Urmson and M. Sbisà, Oxford 1982, pp. 12ff.

[54] N. MacCormick, *Op. cit.*, p. 112.

of hints that may lead us to conclusions other than the one he seems to reach. For he strongly brings out the ideological aspect of the dynamics of political phenomena.

In spite of his political "realism", Kelsen, when he describes the manifestation of political phenomena, always stresses that it is individuals' ideological representations that are the motor or raw material that keeps political power going. In 1922, in words he was to repeat almost verbatim 20 years later in the *General Theory of Law and State*, he wrote: "One tends to say that the 'State' is guns and bayonets, means of production etc. This is, however, to forget that all these are only inanimate, indifferent things, and only the use made of them by men is decisive. Machines and machine guns come into consideration in the social context only in connection with human actions. The rule or norm for these human actions is the ultimate decisive instance on which all that depends".[55]

Political power, according to Kelsen, is not a thing, a material entity, nor a relation of merely physical forces. "Any 'power' [*Macht*] does not lie in the existence of these things, of this scaffold or these 'machine guns', but *only and exclusively* in the fact that the men that use the scaffolds and machine guns may be motivated by norms that are valid for them and that in their entirety, as a coercive order, constitute the State or the law. But if all the social 'power' lies in the motivating force [*in der motivierenden Kraft*] of certain normative representations [*Normvorstellungen*], then it is simply senseless to represent the State as power lying 'behind' the legal norms in order to make them effective".[56] According to Kelsen mere force cannot in itself constitute a political order. This is in his view fundamentally an idea, the representation of an order. Men who occupy public offices, he adds, are seen as "organs" of a collectivity, or of a generally valid coercive order. Were that not so, and the subject accordingly fell under men who held public power not as "organs" of a system but as holders of power through violence and thus fell under not a system but men, in that case one could not speak of a State but only of a situation of

---

[55] H. Kelsen, *Der soziologische und juristische Staatsbegriff*, p. 89. Cfr. H. Kelsen, *General Theory of Law and State*, English trans. by A. Wedberg, New York, NY 1973, pp. 190–191: "'Power' is not prisons and electric chairs, machine guns and cannons; 'power' is not any kind of substance or entity hidden behind the social order. Political power is the efficacy of the coercive order recognized as law".

[56] H. Kelsen, *Der soziologische und juristische Staatsbegriff*, p. 89, my emphasis. Kelsen could thus have subscribed to the following considerations by Cornelius Castoriadis: "Behind the monopoly of legitimate violence lies the monopoly of the legitimate word; the latter is in turn constituted by the monopoly of valid meaning. The master of meaning reigns over the master of violence. The voice of violence can ring out only in the havoc of the collapse of the edifice of instituted meanings. And in order for violence to intervene, it is further necessary for the word – the injunction of existing power – to conserve its power over 'groups of armed men'. The fourth company of the Pavlovsky regiment, his majesty's bodyguard, and the Semenovsky regiment were the most solid pillars of the Tsar's throne – until those days of 26 and 27 February 1917 when they fraternized with the crowd and turned their arms against their officers. The world's most powerful army will not protect you if it is not loyal to you – and the ultimate foundation of its loyalty is the imaginary belief in your imaginary legitimacy" (C. Castoriadis, *Pouvoir, politique, autonomie*, in Id., *Le monde morcelé*, Paris 1990, p. 123).

naked violence. Kelsen's conclusion is that the State, the political order, is nothing other than an idea, the *representation* of an order.[57]

However, this conception of political and legal phenomena, which would seem to be entirely concentrated on recognition of the normative aspect of social phenomena, makes a twofold concession to imperativist and realist thought. One strong concession to voluntarist and imperativist conceptions is made when he asserts that the norm is the meaning of an act of will,[58] essentially sharing Walter Dubislav's thesis that "there is no imperative without imperator" (*kein Imperativ ohne Imperator*).[59] There is a concession to a form of "political realism" when Kelsen specifies that the object of the legal norm is the sanction, and thus identifies normative order and coercive order, *Gesamtheit* and *Zwangsordnung*.

Against the voluntarist theses of the "mature" Kelsen one may however raise most of the objections often brought against imperativism.[60] However, criticisms in the legal philosophical literature of the theory setting the phenomenon of coercion and sanction at the centre of law are less frequent. Here I am concerned not so much with recalling that there is a considerable number of legal norms that do not provide for sanctions or are not accompanied by sanctions, as with pointing out that treating an event as a sanction cannot be done independently of one or more norms that attribute to that event the quality of being a sanction. "Human behaviour", writes Kelsen, "can be considered as a delict only if a positive legal norm attaches a sanction as a consequence to his behaviour as a condition".[61] From this assumption it seems possible to derive the position that the sanction, as coercive act, is something that is such irrespective of the fact of its being described as a sanction and of its attribution by a norm to a particular piece of conduct treated per se (irrespective of the sanction) as wrongful. The sanction would in this view take the shape of *any* coercive act provided for by the State and associated with some human behaviour, which would become "wrongful" only in virtue of that attribution.

As we know, for Kelsen behaviour is "wrongful" not as being violation of conduct prescribed by a norm, but only as being the condition for application of a sanction. In this particular theory of legal norms, there is first of all the sanction and then the wrongful behaviour, which is wrongful insofar as it is against it that the sanction is directed. The sanction cannot accordingly be defined as the harm laid

[57] On the importance of the psychological element in the area of legal phenomena, Kelsen lingers again in speaking of the reasons for compliance with norms. Cf. e.g. H. Kelsen, *The Pure Theory of Law*, pp. 31–32.

[58] Cf. H. Kelsen, *Op. ult. cit.*, pp. 3ff.

[59] In this connection see O. Weinberger, *Der Begriff der Sanktion und seine Rolle in der Normenlogik*, in *Grundprobleme der deontischen Logik*, ed. by H. Lenk, Pullach bei München 1974, p. 105.

[60] There is strong criticism of voluntarism by the "early" Kelsen: see H. Kelsen, *Hauptprobleme der Staatsrechtslehre entwickelt aus der Lehre vom Rechtssatze*, 2nd ed., Tübingen 1923, pp. 97ff. and 189ff. For some traditional sound arguments against voluntarist theories see e.g. A. Falzea, *Introduzione alle scienze giuridiche*, Part One, *Il concetto di diritto*, Milano 1975, p. 96.

[61] H. Kelsen, *General Theory of Law and the State*, p. 53.

down for the case of non-compliance with conduct prescribed by a norm, since here the conduct prescribed by the norm is derived *a contrario* from the conduct that constitutes the condition for application of the sanction. The sanction is an event that is to be described as such (as sanction) irrespective of breach of a precept. In the traditional doctrine for which the distinction between primary norm (that prescribes a certain conduct) and secondary norm (that prescribes a sanction) applies, the sanction can be defined as the harm associated with a wrongful act where the wrongful conduct comes about as violation of the prescribed conduct and can be defined and ascertained irrespective of its being associated with a sanction. This is true even in the paradoxical case that no sanction is associated with it. In Kelsen's doctrine, by contrast, it is the definition of wrongfulness that it depends on attribution of a sanction to a particular conduct (which is then wrongful). In short, while in the traditional doctrine the definition of an act as a sanction depends on the norm that attributes a particular harm to an event already treated as wrongful, in Kelsen's doctrine the definition of an act as a sanction depends not so much on a norm as on the intrinsic nature of the act, that is, its coercive nature. This emerges clearly from, say, Kelsen's distinction between "independent norms" and "non-independent norms".

Kelsen further recognizes within an order the existence of norms that do not provide for any sanction, but he terms them "non-independent" norms and links them to some norm that does lay down a sanction. "If a legal system, such as a statute passed by parliament", he writes, "contains one norm that prescribes a non observance of the first, then the first norm is not an independent norm, but fundamentally tied to the second".[62] But if there are different types of norms – and this seems here to be recognized by Kelsen – and not all of them provide for a sanction, how can we manage to recognize a particular act as a sanction, unless by recourse to features extrinsic to the fact that this act is prescribed by a norm? The sanction, in order to be recognized as such, cannot here make reference to a normative criterion, but only to a material or empirical criterion. On this view, then, it will be possible to describe an act as a sanction irrespective of the existence of a norm or of a normative order. Or again, utilizing a terminology Kelsen does not use, one might then say that the sanction is a "brute fact", not an "institutional fact".[63] This, however, leads to paradoxical consequences, unacceptable to any jurist, and moreover encroaches on the "purity" of legal science advocated by Kelsen.

Consider the following norm x, valid and effective in many modern legal orders: "anyone with an income must pay the State a certain sum of money in proportion to that income". It is certain that paying the sum of money to the State constitutes harm to those who must do so. It is also certain that the norm x considered has a similar

[62] H. Kelsen, *The Pure Theory of Law*, p. 55. This centrality of sanction in Kelsen's legal theory makes an intelligent commentator say that "the pure theory seems merely to develop and refine themes from Austin" (M. Barberis, *Il diritto come discorso e come comportamento. Trenta lezioni di filosofia del diritto*, Torino 1990, p. 184).

[63] On this distinction, cf. J. Searle, *Speech Acts. An Essay in the Philosophy of Language*, Cambridge 1969.

structure to the norm y of equal validity and effectiveness in many modern legal orders, "whoever parks a car in front of an entry marked 'No Parking' must pay the State a sum of money". From norm y, however, it follows that it is forbidden to park a car before an entry marked "No Parking". Yet both types of conduct (having an income and parking a car before an entry marked "No Parking") are associated with the same outcome, paying the State a certain sum of money. However, the outcome is the same only if regarded from an "external" viewpoint as "brute fact", but no longer if regarded from an internal viewpoint, as an "institutional fact".[64] With reference to the normative order the payment of money to the State is in the case of norm x a tax, and only in the case of norm y a *sanction* (a fine). A coercive act, which in itself from the "external" viewpoint is only a "brute fact", may from the "internal" viewpoint act as an "institutional fact", in very different and indeed opposite ways. Consider the brute fact of a person's being chained, which may constitute arrest or kidnapping, or violent death for one human being caused by another, which may be either capital punishment or murder.

The conclusions to draw at this point are two: it is not possible to define the concept of sanction by purely empirical criteria; the concept of sanction refers to a norm of conduct the breach of which is the condition for the sanction.[65] The legal norm cannot accordingly be defined in terms of (through) the sanction; on the contrary, it is the sanction that can be defined only in terms of (through) the norm.

Moreover, if we conceive of the sanction in purely material or empirical terms, as for instance a harm or damage of an economic or physical or even moral nature, and we assume that the object of the legal norms is exclusively, or even only mainly, the inflicting of such damage or harm, the definition of the norm and ascertaining of its existence will depend on extranormative elements (material or empirical). This amounts to maintaining that legal science as normative knowledge (whatever that means) is not sufficient in itself, and requires subsidiary elements of empirical knowledge. If however this conclusion is accepted, one can no longer defend the thesis, so dear to Kelsen, of the "purity" of legal science.

However, despite the limits and the imperativist and "realistic" concessions in Kelsen's doctrine, it seems to me that in order to understand the relation between law and power and ultimately explain these two phenomena, the path taken by Kelsen, namely identifying the two phenomena, is the one to pursue to the end. With one warning: one needs to avoid the doctrine of coerciveness as the characteristic feature of the phenomenon of law, and not to isolate law within the walls of the construction, in any case historically recent, of the State.

Taking the viewpoint of anthropology, which has dealt most with the existing relation between nature and society, or as it is often put, between nature and "culture", society turns out to be not an entity of a physical nature, "brute facts", but

---

[64] Cf. A. Ross, *Directives and Norms*, London 1968, p. 87: "Not any disagreeable reaction is a sanction. The notion of a sanction is intimately connected with the feeling of disapproval. A merely external record of behaviour must lead to unacceptable results".

[65] Cf. O. Weinberger, *Op. cit.*, p. 93 and p. 108.

the product of the collective representations of the individuals making up the society, that is, a set of "institutional facts".[66] Thanks to language and its capacity for evoking that which is not present to the senses through the relation of meaning, man becomes an *animal symbolicum*.[67] Human conduct is no longer constituted through a chain of stimuli and responses and by conditioned reflex, but filters instincts and the stimuli arriving from the senses through the symbolic screen consisting of language, its concepts and the meanings rooted in it. Consider, for instance, the elementary (but not exclusively "brute") fact that food, before being eaten by man, is in general cooked, by contrast with what happens among animals, and cooked differently by each society. Human behaviour, if the "culturalist" theory is accepted, is not determined purely mechanically or instinctively, but also symbolically. But "symbolically determined" is equivalent to "normatively determined". The symbol is something which stays for something else; its logical structure could be said to be the following: "x stays for x". The symbol does not determine anything with causal binding force, but only is an ascription of a sense or status to something in the world and this happens through a system of references, meanings, that may however be broken or violated.

Without going too far into the area of anthropology or human ethnology, it might, after due consideration, be maintained that typically human conduct has at least two features: it is in some sense free of instinctual determination; it is intentional. This brings about a considerable indeterminacy in the trajectories of human action, certainly more than with animal behaviour. This indeterminacy obviously makes the human being's response to the various situations he has to react to and the constitution of his own trajectory of action harder. Humans cope with this indeterminacy by creating preconstituted models of action and ideas of action. In order to act, man, once instinctual determination has weakened, needs rules of conduct. These are in turn based on *ideas* of conduct. That means on conceptions of the way man ought to act, on *Weltanschauungen*. Man, that is, acts in accordance with what he thinks is the way he acts (or ought to). Human action is thus determined by rules of conduct that correspond to certain concepts (not only of action, but also concerning the very "being" of the subject). The Sicilian peasant killed his adulterous wife because there was an "unwritten" social rule prescribing the punishment of death for betrayal, and this rule was founded on a certain image and "concept" of being a "man" (specifically the so-called "man of honour").

As has been argued, "there is an enormously large number of kinds of behaviours in which the possession of certain concepts is a presupposition of the performance: these concepts are thus integral to performances of these kinds".[68] This obviously applies not to all human conduct, but only to typically human (and social) conduct.

[66] Cf. N. MacCormick, *Law as Institutional Fact*, in N. MacCormick and O. Weinberger, *An Institutional Theory of Law*, Dordrecht 1985.

[67] Cf. E. Cassirer, *Essay on Man. An Introduction to a Philosophy of Human Culture*, Garden City, NY 1953, p. 44.

[68] A. Flew, *Thinking about Social Thinking. The Philosophy of the Social Sciences*, Oxford 1985, pp. 24–25.

In this sense, then, the norm (or symbol) is constitutive of social being. If this is so, at a basic level law (understood in the broadest sense as system of rules) and society coincide. This had in any case been seen (though immediately rejected) by Kelsen in his polemic against Eugen Ehrlich, when he accused the latter of dissolving the difference between legal order and social order by denying that coerciveness is the characteristic feature of law. On the other hand for Kelsen – with some reservations[69] – law and society are both "orders of human conduct" and hence normative phenomena.[70]

When, however, starting from the assumption of the symbolic nature of human behaviour it may be asserted that law and society coincide, this means something different from what Kelsen maintains when he claims that law and society belong to the same category of "order". If, at this point, we speak of "law", what we are saying is that the general symbolic network that constitutes as "typically human" the behaviour of man is equivalent to that of "normative phenomena", and so we use the term "law" in a very general sense. On the other hand, when we say that society is constituted through a network of symbols (norms), we are not here yet thinking of the particular order of a society (its political and legal institutions), but of the basic fact of its existence, of its possibility of existence, of an original "normative stratum", which results essentially from language. On this first "state", or thanks to this first constitutive normative level, it is possible to construct a social order in the strict sense, of customs, usages, habits and principles that are socially shared.

But if social conduct rests on norms (linguistic first of all, and social in the strict sense thereafter), there cannot be a phenomenon of political power that does not rest on such norms. In this sense, law (understood as a normative phenomenon in the broad sense) and political power (understood as running a community's affairs) end up coinciding. However, there remains on the one hand to define what is law in the strict sense, and on the other to draw the distinction between the intrinsically political nature of the social order (to which I have related the concept of political power) and the phenomena of political hierarchy that I propose to define as *dominion*.

---

[69] Sometimes Kelsen seems to equate the sphere of society with that of nature, regarding only legal phenomena as normative ones. Cf. e.g. the last section of the first chapter in H. Kelsen, *Reiner Rechtslehre*, 1st ed., p. 9: "Indem man das Recht als Norm bestimmt und die Rechtswissenschaft (die eine von der Funktion der rechtssetzenden und rechtsanwendenden Organe verschiedene Funktion ist) auf die Erkenntnis von Normen beschränkt, grenzt man das Recht gegen die Natur und die Rechtswissenschaft als Normwissenschaft gegen alle anderen Wissenschaften ab, die auf kausal-gesetzliche Erklärung natürlicher Vorgänge abzielen". See also H. Kelsen, *The Pure Theory of Law*, p. 89: "Psychology, ethnology, history, sociology are disciplines that gave human behaviour as their object so far as it is determined by causal laws, which means, so far as it occurs in the realm of nature or natural reality". For the Austrian jurist sociology, then, does not have any different epistemological status from that attributed to the natural sciences. On the other hand, however, Kelsen introduces the category of "normative social sciences", among which he includes ethics, theology and legal science, but not sociology.

[70] See, e.g. H. Kelsen, *Causality and Imputations*, in Id., *The Pure Theory of Law*, pp. 76ff., where Kelsen seems to adopt the thesis that upholds that "the dualism of nature as causal order and society as normative order".

To explain the formation of *dominion*, which in general takes shape in a series of relations between political superior and political inferior, I can no longer refer to situations of purely physical constraint, once the thesis of the normative nature of the social being is accepted. I believe that there is dominion where the "institutional norms" (in the strict sense) – a third "stratum" after the "primary" one of language and the "secondary" one of social customs – which explicitly and formally regulate social conduct (and thus constitute law in the strict sense) are hypostatized and beyond the disposal of the members of society.

As far as the basic norms of being in society (language) and that of the social order (customs) go, it should be said that these norms are always the product of man, and therefore to a certain extent arbitrary and haphazard, and never the result of objective forces (whatever might be a supposed consistent nature of man, or internal dynamics of living systems and social systems). However, it is clear that these norms, though a product of human activity, are so unconsciously or unintentionally. They are, as Hayek says, following the result of human action but not of human design.[71]

Society as social being and as order is by no means, contrary to what some natural law proponents supposed, the result of a *pactum unionis*, that is, a conscious, voluntary decision by the members of that society. In relation to this, I find Hume's position more convincing: he, though not denying that the consent of the members plays a certain part in the constitution and maintenance of the social order, stresses the largely spontaneous nature of human associations and notes that force is frequently at the origin of the various political regimes.

In Hume's thought two conceptions of political power overlap. One recognizes the role played by consensus and opinion and connects with these the effectiveness of coercive acts of authority and the stability of the political order; the other instead sets force at the basis of the phenomenon of law. "The force", writes Hume, "which now prevails, and which is founded on fleets and armies, is plainly political, and derived from authority, the effect of established government. A man's natural force consists only in the vigour of his limbs, and the firmness of his courage; which could never subject multitudes to the command of one. Nothing but their own consent, and their sense of the advantages resulting from peace and order, could have had that influence".[72] Recall also his well-known statement: "It is, therefore, on opinion only that government is founded; and this maxim extends to the most despotic and most military governments, as well as to the most free and most popular".[73]

As we know, Hume identifies two chief types of opinion: (a) opinion of interest and (b) opinion of right. The latter is in turn distinguished into (i) opinion of right to power and (ii) opinion of right to property. The first type of opinion, that of *interest*, consists in the sense of the general advantage which is reached from government.

---

[71]See F. A. Hayek, *The Results of Human Action but not of Human Design*.

[72]D. Hume, *Essays Moral Political and Literary*, ed. by H. Green and T. H. Grose, vol. 1, London 1882, p. 445.

[73]Ibid., p. 110.

It comes down to a prudential calculation. *The opinion of right to power* is the conviction that the holders of power in the prevailing political regime have a right to hold that power.

However, to the contractualists who maintain not only the "historical" hypothesis of the "original contract", that civil society arose from an agreement among its members, but also the theoretical hypothesis of the contract as justificatory foundation of the prevailing political system, Hume objects that nowhere does political power justify what it does in virtue of a contractual relation between subject and sovereign. "But would these reasoners look abroad into the world", writes Hume, "they would meet with nothing that, in the least, corresponds to their ideas, or can warrant so refined and philosophical a system. On the contrary, we find everywhere princes who claim their subjects as their property, and assert their independent right of sovereignty, from conquest or succession. We find also everywhere subjects who acknowledge this right in their prince, and suppose themselves born under obligations of obedience to a certain sovereign, as much as under the ties of reference and duty to certain parents. These connections are always conceived to be equally independent of our consent, in Persia and China, in France and Spain, and even in Holland and England, wherever the doctrines above mentioned have not been carefully inculcated".[74]

But even the hypothesis of the "original contract" is, according to Hume, unsatisfactory. "Almost all the governments which exist at present, or of which there remains any record in history, have been founded originally, either on usurpation or conquest, or both, without any pretence of a fair consent or voluntary subjection of the people".[75] Behind this last statement by Hume, in clear contradiction with the idea previously expressed by him that it is opinion that constitutes political power, there is, I believe, a pessimistic view of history. "The face of the earth is continually changing", he writes, "by the increase of small kingdoms into great empires, by the dissolution of great empires into smaller kingdoms, by the planting of colonies, by the migration of tribes. Is there anything discoverable in all these events but force and violence? Where is the mutual agreement or voluntary association so much talked of?"[76]

To Hume's criticisms of contractualism, its supporters might however reply by referring to a distinction very dear to the Scottish philosopher: between "is" and "ought". The contractualist might reply to Hume's criticisms that his doctrine is purely normative, is made up of prescriptive statements, whereas Hume's realism is a descriptive theory, a sociological theory *ante litteram*. The contractualist's intention, contrary to Hume's, is not to *explain* but to *justify* a certain political regime.[77] However, Hume's "realistic" theory might be opposed by the arguments developed by the "normativist" Hume, in particular the one that holds that the force involved

---

[74]Ibid., p. 446.

[75]Ibid., p. 447.

[76]Ibid.

[77]In this connection see P. Koller, *Neue Theorien des Sozialkontrakts*, pp. 12ff.

in the formation of political regimes is not the physical force of an individual but the organized force of a group, which in order to constitute itself needs its members to share common principles and rules.

Hume in fact distinguishes consent from what he, as we have seen, calls "opinion". "Suppose again", he writes, "their native king restored, by means of an army, which he levies in foreign countries: they receive him with joy and exultation, and show plainly with what reluctance they have submitted to any other yoke. I may now ask, upon what foundations the prince's title stands? Not on popular consent surely: for though the people willingly acquiesce in his authority, they never imagine that their consent made him sovereign. They consent, because they apprehend him to be already by birth, their legitimate sovereign".[78] What, then, determines the obedience of the subject is not pure and simple consent in itself constituting the foundation of sovereignty, but the opinion that particular sovereign is legitimate, because certain rules and principles are shared regarding the formation of sovereign power, in this case regarding the succession of the legitimate prince. To be sure, in this case too there is consent, but it is not the absolutely original consent of the contractualists, the sole source of which is reason, but a consent motivated by the recognition of certain common principles, opinions and rules. These are, for Hume, largely the product of custom and usage to which time has attributed the sanction of "justice"; they are, to use Hayek's expression, the product of human action but not of human "design".

Society is indeed the outcome of processes largely beyond human will, which yet have their roots in the minds and actions of individuals. At the institutional level, the typically legal and political one of norms laid down to regulate the affairs of the members of the given social group, there may be at least two possibilities. The first is that the "institutional" norms too are the *unconscious* result of the activity of the group's members. In this case, which is in general that of the so-called primitive societies, these norms are not subject to argument since there is no awareness of their existence as human rules (and not as divine or natural laws). They are hypostatized, so that the intrinsic political nature of society becomes in the end something that could be called "dominion", a political rule not open to public discussion and deliberation. The second possibility is that those norms be *consciously* and explicitly laid down by the community members. In order here for there to be a situation of "dominion" (that is, ultimately, of subjection of a "political inferior" to a "political superior"), it is not so much the content of the norms that has to be considered as their relation to the members. If these are subject to discussion and modification, if, that is, the community maintains its control over its creations, there is nothing but the maintenance of the collective cause, that is, politics in its most genuine sense. Otherwise, if the community cannot openly and publicly discuss nor expressly amend its norms, then we have, adapting the Marxian terminology, *alienation*, whereby the product of man (in this case not a good but a norm) is removed from his power of disposal (in this case not to "use", but to discuss and the

---

[78] D. Hume, *Op. ult. cit.*, p. 453.

amend this human product). This is what would constitute the political phenomenon that we have called "dominion". The "dominion", accordingly, far from being the "producer" of the legal norms (as "political realism" asserts), is their "product", where, for various reasons, these norms are regarded as not subject to discussion or amendment by the community.

Paradoxically in relation to the traditional terminology,[79] if "government of laws" is considered as opposed to "government of men", as a political system in which the norms are always in any case outside the awareness and will of the members, then this "government by laws" amounts to a situation of political oppression and not a regime of liberty. "Government of men", in turn, if conceived of as a political system in which the norms are always "at the disposal" of the members to change them, that is, can always be criticized and discussed by them, would then constitute not a despotic regime, but the "open society" whose possibility we have begun to envisage only with "modernity".

2.5 Autonomy, Heteronomy, Ideology

While Franz Neumann's theory is more a doctrine of the rationality of the general law and of the State based on rule of law, Thomas Paine's is one of the most significant expressions of modern constitutionalism, that is, the conception that lays down the principle of the primacy of laws or the law over political power. Law, on this conception, is a limit on the exercise of power. For constitutionalism "a political power is 'limited' when the activity characteristic of it, that of issuing commands in the form of norms whose effectiveness is ultimately based on coercion, is in turn regulated by higher norms that lay down bounds as to what can be imposed by power through coercive norms".[80] In this case one of two things must be true: either the higher norms that "limit" political power arc the expression of another power (in contradiction with the theory that conceives of the modern State as an entity holding the monopoly of political power); or else these higher laws are in some way an expression of the same power that they limit (and this is the well-known theory of Georg Jellinek and others of the State's "self-limitation"). But in this last case the self-limitation (which may cohabit with a conception of the State as monopoly of force) is in any case exposed to the arbitrariness of political power. What guarantees do we have that the power that "limits itself" may not stop wanting to do so? Were

[79] Cf. N. Bobbio, *La teoria dello Stato e del potere*, in *Max Weber e l'analisi del mondo moderno*, Torino 1981, p. 236. The traditional political theory made the equation good government equals impersonal power and bad government equals personal power. "Personal power par excellence" writes Bobbio, "is the tyrant's" (ibid.). Yet the entirely modern experience of bureaucratic and totalitarian regimes seems to refute the thesis that the impersonality of power is a characteristic of free political regimes. Hannah Arendt very appropriately defines the bureaucratic political form (which is very far from constituting a model of free society) as "the rule of nobody" (H. Arendt, *Eichmann in Jerusalem. A Report on the Banality of Evil*, Harmondsworth 1983, p. 289).

[80] M. Bovero, *Introduzione*, in *Ricerche politiche*, ed. by M. Bovero, Milan 1982, p. xxi.

those "higher norms" postulated as endowed with different qualities from those promulgated by political power, that is, were they seen as the dictates of reason, nature or God, or – in a legal formalist conception – an intrinsic guarantee associated with their general and abstract nature, these conceptions would find it hard to escape the accusation of being idealistic. The higher norm that limits political power, in order to be effective, must have behind it some power that desires it and brings it into being. It is then not so much the norm in itself that limits political power as another power that is to some extent counterposed to the first and constitutes a counterweight and a brake on it. It was from such considerations that the theory of separation of powers took shape, which saw as the limit to political power its fragmentation, not the law considered abstractly.

But what is the "higher norm" to be founded on? For some the solution is contractualism: "If it is not possible to make a norm attributing legitimate power derive from another power which is not de facto power", writes Professor Bovero, "I cannot see any other way to keep to the superiority of the norm over legitimate power, than to consider the obligation of obedience contained in the norm as the result of the members' own will [· · ·] This brings us back to the contractualist view".[81] But from where do we derive the norms that dictate us to obey contractual relations?

The relation between "higher" norm and power calls for some further reflection. At the basic level of social structure, power and norm coincide. They coincide because the typically human (social) behaviour is not in itself natural, the necessary product of naturally (by nature) determined instincts and needs. Typically human behaviour is largely "symbolically" (which amounts to saying "normatively") based. In this very general sense, all social behaviour is legal (normative), and law and society coincide. Political power is accordingly norm, as based upon this diffused network of norms that is society itself. In essence and at a very basic level one complies with because the culture of a given society lays down that one ought to comply with or simply because there is no other way to act in certain spheres. In this very general sense power and law coincide, because both are expressions of being in society.

But there is a further normative level, the one of positive law (of law in force in virtue of written or customary norms), which constitutes the "institutional" level of a society. It is only here that the question of a distinction between norm (law) and political power is actually posed and has meaning. But the distinction (or else the non-distinction) between (positive) law and (political) power is not a distinction of fact; it is a normative, or better *symbolic* distinction, which has its origin at the first, normative level of society. This (its members) construct(s) its/their own institutions by *thinking them*, not in an idealistic sense, note, but by positing the cultural-symbolic referents of which these institutions are largely made up. Thus, for instance, a society may conceive of its own political power as untied from any limit (or norm), or else may conceive the opposite: political power limited by a norm that is superior to it. In fact, though at the original normative level, power is always

---

[81] Ibid., p. xxv.

limited, since it cannot be constituted except within the norms that a society gives itself. (Even where political power takes as its objective a *tabula rasa* of the previous society, it is always from the society that it derives, from its customs, from its culture, from its language, however strong and radical its rejection of these). The subsequent limitation of power at the institutional level cannot be a de facto matter. Power will be limited and law will be superior to it if it is symbolically constructed as limited by and *inferior* to law. But it cannot be constructed (symbolically, or by symbols) as *unlimited.* This construction will obviously be the more effective in one sense or another the more consistent it is in relation to its objectives, and the more it is endowed with material means (of social force) to protect itself against possible attacks. The norm-power relation at institutional level is accordingly not a "datum", but a problem that has to be continually faced and solved by the members. This solution may come unconsciously as the undesired result of intentional acts, or else, where the problem is known to society, may come in some conscious fashion.

At the original, basic, level of society, every social structure is autonomous, that is, gives itself its own norms, since the social rules are very probably not reflections of universal laws of nature or reason or of divinely determined will. This primordial "autonomy", this "autonomy" in the most general sense, may not be reflected at an institutional level and correspond with "autonomy" in the strict sense. ("Autonomy in the strict sense" means here as a situation in which the institutional rules are the conscious, voluntary and discussed product of the members of the society). At a "superstructural" level the most rigid "heteronomy" may apply: there could be a strongly oligarchic or hierarchical political power, for instante. But in any case it applies on the basis of the underlying "autonomy", however paradoxical that may seem. Even if men obey a dictator and their life depends on the will of one or of few, it cannot be said that this position is governed by extrahuman rules. The concept of "autonomy" in the most general sense used here is equivalent to that of "positive law" *lato sensu*, that is, to law laid down by man.[82] Even in the case where men obey a tyrant, they continue nonetheless, quite unconsciously and spontaneously, to give themselves their norms of conduct.

In fact, when we speak of a norm distinct from political power, this norm does not exist. What instead exists is a normative conception of the institutional level that prescribes a separate norm and power. In reality these are strictly connected in the sense that political power is erected on a preceding normative basis and is in turn an issuer of norms. The normative conception sets, as far as the "secondary" level of social norms at which the political and legal system are found is concerned, the division between legal system and political system, between law and power. This does not mean that this division is imaginary. It is instead real, has very concrete effects on the life of the members of the society, but is a "construction", a symbolic function in relation to the social reality given by the inextricable relationship of norms and possibilities of action. This division is the content of *some* of the social

[82]In this connection, cf. M. La Torre, *Anarchismo, giusnaturalismo e positivismo giuridico*, in *Archivio giuridico 'F. Serafini'*, 1989, pp. 133ff.

norms laid down at the level we have called "institutional". One can't but share the opinion of two German scholars: "Law and power cannot be opposed in abstract terms. We would otherwise get a distorted view of law's sphere of action as power or else of power's practice as law. We would not thus be able to understand law. Only by considering the internal connection between a power under forms of law and of law under forms of power would we make possible a distinction betwen legitimate and illegitimate powers".[83]

Here, however, a further problem arises, that of the so-called "ideologies". The term "ideology" can be assigned at least three meanings, the first drawn from ordinary language, and the other two from the tradition of Marxist thought: (i) "ideology" as a body of ideas, as a theory or doctrine, (ii) "ideology" as an area distinct from that of material reality, that is, as ideal reality or also, using Marxist terminology, as "superstructure"; (iii) "ideology" as "false consciousness", as a *Weltanschauung* that does not correspond with actual reality or gives a distorted image of it, in general serving the consolidation of particular interests. It is on this last meaning of the term that I wish very shortly to dwell here. I maintained earlier that the institutions of a society are constituted by its members through a largely shared normative conception. The obvious objection to this point is as follows. Many political regimes have (and still do) spread a conception of themselves that does not correspond with the actual reality. For instance, National Socialism asserted that it assured the effective participation of the *Volksgenossen* in running the *Volksgemeinschaft*, but we all know that de facto the decisions were concentrated in a restricted handful of *leaders* of the Nazi party, the NSDAP. How, then, can this disparity (between the conception one has, or is presented with, of one's own institutions and the actual reality of those institutions) be reconciled with the thesis that the institutions are constructed in virtue of the idea one has of them?

A possible reply to this quite legitimate objection could be summarized in the following steps. Not all the representations (conceptions) of institutions are ideological. No ideology (as mere "false consciousness") is a conception that is constitutive of institutions. A normative conception is ideological (in the sense just mentioned of "false consciousness") if and only if it does not fit the actual functioning of the institution concerned. The constitutive normative conception of the given institutions is the one that fits the actual functioning of the institutions.

To distinguish ideology (as "false consciousness") from the fundamental normative conception of a society, it suffices to consider whether certain postulates do or not fit with the actual social reality of the society. For instance, when the 1936 Soviet constitution proclaimed certain rights of citizens like those of association, assembly etc., then in order to establish whether those proclamations were "ideological" or instead elements of the fundamental normative conception of the Soviet Union, it was sufficient to go and look whether Soviet citizens could actually (without incurring penalties) freely meet and associate. Once, however, the "ideological" nature

---

[83] F. Müller and R. Christensen, *Testo giuridico e lavoro sul testo nella Struktuirierende Rechtslehre*, in *Ars Interpretandi*, 1997, p. 90.

of this proclamation had been established, the further conclusion to be drawn is not the one common to so many thinkers with a functionalist, realist approach (from Marx to Pareto to the Scandinavian realist Vilhelm Lundstedt) that the reality of the institutions in question is based solely on purely material forces and hence that any normative conception is always just ideology (or even – as in the case of Marx and Lundstedt – that law itself is ideology). In order validly to reach such conclusions one would have to insert a further premise, namely that human actions are governed exclusively by material needs and instincts. If one does not share that position, and instead holds that man acts in accordance with his ideas of action, according to values of action that always to some extent presuppose types (ideas) of action,[84] then the above-mentioned conclusions are not argumentatively justified. This does not mean excluding needs from the vast spectrum of determinants of human actions, but only holding that these are either accompanied by other determinants hinging on deliberations, or else come to form part of the latter as premises of some practical reasoning. But to do this, to be presented as the premises of an argument, these needs have to take on propositional content, that is, become part of the semantic content of judgements and propositions.[85] Accordingly, the capacity for such needs to determine human action passes through the understanding and interpretation of the semantic content of the statements as which they are expressed, and then through the deliberative operation within which these statements are fitted. All these operations could be implicit and embedded in a practice. One could thus maintain that the internal point of view has priority over the external perspective – that of the observer who considers the conduct of the agent to be the cause of material effects or just a matter of behavioural regularities.[86] The internal aspect is essential to the understanding of the conduct.

If in Stalin's Russia the 1936 constitution was waste paper, mere "ideology", this does not authorize us to deny that there was any other normative conception that was *indeed* constitutive of the functioning of the Stalinist Soviet institutions, which is not actually too hard to find, being Marxism-Leninism as "invented" by none other than Stalin himself. Equally, in a so-called primitive society, in which the prevailing social conception maintains that the office of shaman is open to all and it is instead found this office is always held by members of a given family, one should not confine oneself to asserting that this conception is mere "ideology" and reach the conclusion that the society is accordingly based only on the force of events or the functions of the social group. It should instead be said that the true internal viewpoint of the primitive society in question is not the one that the post of shaman is open to all, but the one for which it is reserved to those belonging to a given family to which particular qualities and a special *status* are attributed. Certainly,

---

[84] Cf. D. Farias, *Per una definizione scientificamente utile di ideologia*, in Id., *Saggi di filosofia politica*, Milan 1977, pp. 313ff.

[85] Cf. C. S. Nino, *La validez del derecho*, Buenos Aires 1985, Chapter 7.

[86] Cf. C. S. Nino, *Derecho, moral y política. Una revisión della teoría general del derecho*, Barcelona 1994, Chapter 3.

it might very well be that a family, against the generally shared social conception that lays down that the post of shaman is accessible to all, succeeds through fraud or force in monopolizing the position of shaman for a certain period of time. But this situation will with all probability have one of two developments: either that family's monopoly will be consolidated, that is, recognized by the collectivity (and then come to form part of the normative social conception); or else it will become attenuated and, failing to impose itself further and become a social norm, become overturned by the reaffirmation of the previous social norm that proclaimed free access to the post of shaman for all members of the society. In any case, access to the post of shaman will not be explicable in terms of "material" relations, of "functions", foreign to the symbolic and cultural (and hence normative) constitutions of that given society.

Part II
Language, Norms, Institutions

Chapter 3
Meaning and Norm

3.1 Preliminary

"There is a far-reaching analogy between law and language"– said Jacob Grimm in his inaugural lecture in 1841.[1] Today, the position that there are manifold relationships between law and language and that law is in certain aspects a form of language is widely accepted and needs no additional justification.[2] As Uberto Scarpelli, a distinguished Italian legal philosopher, has written, "some problems that have been raised and tackled in relation to the regulatory structure of a language and a way of speaking, to its function, acceptance etc., strikingly resemble traditional problems in the theory of law".[3] Or, as it is stressed by Alessandro Passerin d'Entrèves, language and law seem to us somehow similar: such similarity being confirmed by the vicinity between the lawyers' and the grammarians' work, for both aim to lay down general rules for the use of certain signs or symbols that human beings employ to qualify given states of affairs.[4] The assumption of a relationship between law and

---

[1] J. Grimm, *Über die Altertümer des deutschen Rechts. Antrittsvorlesung*, in J. Grimm and W. Grimm, *Schriften und Reden*, ed. by L. Denecke, Stuttgart 1985, p. 103.

[2] For an acknowledgement of the close links between the phenomenon of law and language see e.g., among philosophers, B. Croce, *Filosofia della pratica*, 4th ed., Bari 1950, p. 347, and among jurists S. Pugliatti, *Sistema grammaticale e sistema giuridico*, in Id., *Grammatica e diritto*, Milan 1978, pp. 3ff. Cf. also F. A. Hayek, *The Counter-Revolution of Science*, Chicago, IL 1952, p. 30. It is interesting to note that the relation between law or normative phenomena and language has also been recognized by more than one linguist and philosopher of language. Thus, while theorists of law seek to explain the law by relating it to linguistic phenomena, linguists and philosophers of language (e.g., Karl Bühler and Ludwig Wittgenstein) explain language by basing it on normative phenomena or situations of direction of behaviour (see e.g., K. Bühler, *Die Krise per Psychologie*, Frankfurt am Main 1978, pp. 50–51). One indication of this "juridification", so to speak, of the linguistic phenomenon is the following definition by Jean Piaget: "Un langage est une *institution* collective dont les *règles* s'imposent aux individus, qui se transmet de façon *coercitive* de générations en générations" (J. Piaget, *Le structuralisme*, Paris 1972, p. 63, my emphasis).

[3] U. Scarpelli, *La meta-etica analitica e la sua rilevanza etica*, in Id., *L'etica senza verità*, Bologna 1982, p. 79.

[4] A. Passerin d'Entrèves, *Natural Law. An Introduction to Legal Philosophy*, with a new introduction by C. J. Nederman, New Brunswick, NJ and London 2007, p. 114.

M. La Torre, *Law as Institution*, Law and Philosophy Library 90,
DOI 10.1007/978-1-4020-6607-8_3, © Springer Science+Business Media B.V. 2010

language at a meta-theoretical level also seems plausible. This would imply a link between theories of language and theories norms, in the sense that adoption of a certain theory of language influences or determines adoption of a certain theory of norms, and vice versa (the formulation of a particular theory of norms presupposes a particular theory of language).

In this chapter I propose to analyse briefly some of the possible connections between theories of meaning on the one hand and theories of norms and of legal validity on the other. In particular, I propose to link the institutionalist theory of law with the theory of meaning as "use". To this end I shall consider critically some of the most important and best-known theories of meaning, making use of the objections to these theories raised by Ludwig Wittgenstein. In conclusion, I shall adopt as my own the "use" theory of meaning proposed by the "late" Wittgenstein, seeking to clarify the sense in which this approach could also be called "institutionalist". The Wittgensteinian theory of language, based as it is on a more general analysis of social rules, indeed constitutes an excellent introduction to the study of normative phenomena and hence of society and law.

In the following chapter I shall go on to set out some of the most significant aspects of Santi Romano's theory, in the light also of the more recent presentation of an institutionalist theory of law by Neil MacCormick and Ota Weinberger. I shall then venture to state some propositions intended to clarify the concept of "institution" and to apply the institutionalist viewpoint to the definition of questions intrinsic to the theory and philosophy of law. In Chapter 5, I aim to apply the neo-institutionalist theory to the study of the concept of power, and in particular to the analysis of the relation between it and law. The object of my study is accordingly to reconcile (where necessary) both two distinct fields of study, analysis of language and consideration of legal and political phenomena, and two different theoretical traditions, analytical philosophy and legal institutionalism.

3.2 Theories of Meaning

Among the various theories of meaning, the one I find most convincing is the theory of meaning as "use" (*Gebrauch*) developed by Ludwig Wittgenstein and elaborated by philosophers of language like Friedrich Waismann and William P. Alston. The theory of meaning as "use" is proposed by Wittgenstein and scholars taking inspiration from him through a critique of three chief theories of meaning: (a) the verificationist theory, (b) the representation theory, (c) the behaviourist theory.

The verificationist theory considers, as is well known, that the meaning of a proposition is the method used to verify it. It should be recalled in relation to this that Moritz Schlick – following the early Wittgenstein[5] – grafts the verificationist

---

[5]See *Ludwig Wittgenstein und der Wiener Kreis*, reports and notes by F. Waismann, ed. by B. F. McGuinness, Frankfurt am Main 1984, p. 244: "Der Sinn eines Satzes ist die Art seiner

theory onto that of use.[6] He adheres to Wittgenstein's idea that the meaning of a word or a combination of words is determined by the rules governing its use. He accepts Wittgenstein's conception insofar as it takes the shape of a verificationist theory through interpretation of the notion of "use" as verification of the state of affairs asserted by the statement. Use is understood by Schlick as the *method used to verify* the statement.

The so-called theory of "representation" is that which considers the meaning of a statement to be constituted by the image or representation of a state of affairs. There are two chief variants of this theory: (i) a mentalist variant ("ideational" theory) for which meaning corresponds to the mental representation, the "idea", of which the statement is the sign; (ii) a logicist variant (*Abbildungstheorie*, or "pictorial" theory), according to which the statement's logical form reflects the ontological structure of the state of affairs to which it refers. It is worth stressing that for the theory of "representation", especially in its mentalist version ("ideational" theory), the meaning of a term or a statement is above all what it means for the *utterer*, that is, what the utterer *intends* to represent by means of that particular term or statement. The "ideational" theory can thus verge on an "intentional" theory of meaning for which meaning is given by the *intention* governing the linguistic utterance.

The behaviourist theory holds that the meaning of a term or utterance is the response or causal effect produced by the term or utterance. The words and the utterances – according to this theory – are consequently stimuli that either directly or indirectly (through a conditioning process like the one exemplified in Pavlov's dog experiments) *cause* a response (or "disposition" to respond). This is the meaning of those particular words and those particular utterances. The behaviourist theory ignores the state or intentions of the utterer of the linguistic expression, instead concentrating attention exclusively on the *receiver* of the linguistic expression, or on the latter's reactions. The meaning is here sought and determined on the basis of these reactions.

For the late Wittgenstein, and for Waismann who clarifies and systematizes Wittgenstein's thought (sometimes rather obscure), the theories of meaning just mentioned are all equally unsatisfactory.

3.3 Objections to the Verificationist Theory

Wittgenstein and Waismann do not underestimate the role that the procedure for verifying a statement may play in determining the assertion's meaning. Waismann even readily accepts that assertions that are in principle unverifiable are without meaning. He writes: "We say only that if someone makes a statement, he should

Verifikation. Die Methode der Verification ist nicht ein Mittel, ein Vehikel, sondern der Sinn selbst".

[6] See M. Schlick, *Meaning and Verification*, in *The Philosophical Review*, 1936.

indicate some possible method of verification; otherwise he does not know what he is saying".[7]

What Wittgenstein and Waismann dispute is that the meaning of an utterance is *reducible* to the method of verifying it. They do not by contrast dispute that the verification of an utterance, or the indication of the method of verifying it, may *contribute* to determining its meaning. Thus, in Wittgenstein's *Philosophical Investigations* (I, 353) we find the following thought: "Asking whether and how a proposition can be verified is only a particular way of asking 'How d'you mean?' The answer is a contribution to the grammar of the proposition."[8]

Waismann brings forward at least two objections to the verificationist theory. (i) The event or fact that serves to verify an utterance is not equivalent to the utterance's meaning. The facts that verify the utterance are not what the utterer intends to say by that particular utterance. If for instance I say "it rained yesterday", one way of verifying the statement might be to observe the degree of humidity present on the ground today. The degree of humidity is a method to verify the statement "it rained yesterday". However, it is clear that I did not by that utterance mean to say anything just about the dampness of the ground.[9] (ii) I can proceed to the verification of a statement only once I have understood its meaning.[10]

However, as mentioned above, Waismann does not deny all value to the verificationist theory. There are, he maintains, cases in which the method used to verify a statement is necessary in order to understand its meaning. There are, according to Waismann, two ways of knowing the meaning of a statement. One is that which follows from explication of the meaning of the individual words constituting the statement according to a certain natural language, plus recourse to the grammatical rules of that language. "Der eine ist der, daß wir die Bedeutung der Worte und die Regeln der Satzfügung angeben".[11] This is the ordinary way of understanding the meaning of a statement.

The other way is to establish the conditions on which a particularly statement would prove to be true or false respectively, that is, to supply a method for verifying the statement. This is the way to understand the meaning of a *scientific* statement, where everyday experience and grammar no longer suffice to understand the terms of a theory that introduces new features in comparison with the ordinary vision of the world. "Der Satz 'Das weiße Licht ist aus den Spektralfarben zusammengesetzt' drückt seinen Sinn noch nicht so deutlich aus, dass ihn jeder verstehen müßte, der die deutsche Sprache kennt. Was hier 'zusammengesetzt' heißt, kann ich nur

---

[7]F. Waismann, *Logik, Sprache, Philosophie*, ed. by G. P. Baker and B. McGuinness with the collaboration of J. Schulte, Stuttgart 1976, p. 488.

[8]L. Wittgenstein, *Philosophical Investigations*, English trans. by G. E. M. Anscombe, Oxford 1976.

[9]See F. Waismann, *Logik, Sprache, Philosophie*, pp. 479–480.

[10]See *ibid.*, p. 480. Cf. I. Berlin, *Verification*, in Id., *Concepts and Categories. Philosophical Essays*, ed. by H. Hardy, Oxford 1980, p. 29.

[11]F. Waismann, *Logik, Sprache, Philosophie*, p. 481.

dadurch erklären, dass ich die Erfahrungen beschreibe, die dieses Satz verifizieren; damit definiere ich die Bedeutung, die das Wort in diesem Zusammenhang hat".[12]

3.4 Objections to the Theory of "Representation" and to the Psychological Conception

3.4.1 As has been said, we can distinguish two main versions of the so-called "representation" theory. There is first a logicist version according to which words and statements correspond to the essential features and the structure of the world. We can define this theory as the *Abbildungstheorie* theory or "pictorial" theory, or again the "referential theory".[13] There is then a psychological or mentalistic version, according to which the meaning is the mental representation that the word (or statement) evokes in our minds. For this second version of the theory meanings are sensations, emotions, mental states, concepts or ideas. In the context of this psychological version, the conception that holds that meanings are eminently concepts and ideas has also been called the "ideational theory".[14]

One important version of the *Abbildungstheorie* is that which appears in Wittgenstein's *Tractatus logico-philosophicus*. That work upholds the position that language reproduces or reflects the structure of facts in the world, which are always composed of the same simple elements, which take on changing configurations. Here – we shouldn't forget – Wittgenstein makes his own Bertrand Russell's view of linguistic propositions according to which the world, is made, apart from objects and properties, of relations; and propositions are mainly assertions of relations and thus *functions*.

Language, claims Wittgenstein in his celebrated *Tractatus*, reproduces the core of the world structure through names (which correspond to the simple features of facts) and, combinations thereof. "A name means an object. The object is its meaning".[15] "In a proposition a name is the represenative of the object".[16] "A proposition is a picture of reality. A proposition is a model of reality as we imagine it".[17] However, Wittgenstein subsequently modified his first theory of meaning, subjecting it to rigorous criticism.[18]

---

[12] *Ibid.*, p. 482. On the other hand, Waismann disputes the possibility of *definitive* verification of scientific laws and "existential" statements, since even empirical concepts are never *completely* and *exhaustively* defined: see F. Waismann, *Verifiability*, in *The Theory of Meaning*, ed. by G. H. R. Parkinson, Oxford 1973, pp. 35ff.

[13] See W. P. Alston, *Philosophy of Language*, Englewood Cliffs, NJ 1964, pp. 12ff.

[14] See *ibid.*, pp. 22ff.

[15] L. Wittgenstein, *Tractatus logico-philosophicus*, English trans. by D. F. Pears and B. F. McGuinness, London 1966, p. 23 (§ 3.203).

[16] *Ibid.* (§ 3.22).

[17] *Ibid.*, p. 37 (§ 4.01).

[18] See e.g., the reference to the author of the *Tractatus*, in L. Wittgenstein, *Philosophical Investigations* (I, 23), pp. 12.

Against the logicist theory of representation Waismann – following the "second" Wittgenstein – raises three chief objections. Firstly, the *Abbildungstheorie*, like any referential theory, ends by exchanging the meaning of a name for the bearer of the name, at the point when it asserts that the meaning of a term is its object. The meaning of a term and the object it refers to in ordinary linguistic usage do not coincide. Frege maintains that the meaning of the utterance "morning star" is the planet Venus. This however, objects Waismann, clashes with ordinary linguistic usage. Were a comet to destroy the planet Venus, we would not say that the meaning of the utterance "morning star" had been destroyed by a comet. We say, for instance, "John has left", but we never say "the meaning of John has left": this last statement is, in ordinary language, devoid of meaning.[19]

According to Wittgenstein, the "referential" theory of language clashes with the use ordinarily made of words. In ordinary use, in fact, the meaning of a term is quite distinct from the "thing" designated by that term. I may, for instance, sensibly say "the King of Spain is dead", but I shall never, by contrast, be able sensibly to say "the meaning of the King of Spain is dead". Moreover, should some term accidentally cease to have meaning, it could not be said on that account alone that the bearer, so to speak, of the term, the object it served to designate, is no more, has ceased to be. "It is important to note that the word 'meaning' is being used illicitly if it is being used to signify the thing that 'corresponds' to the word. That is to confound the meaning of a name with the bearer of the name. When Mr. N. N. dies, one says that the bearer of the name dies, not that the meaning dies. And it would be nonsensical to say that, for if the name ceased to have meaning it would make no sense to say 'Mr. N. N. is dead.'".[20] Referential theory, Wittgenstein goes on, ends by treating all linguistic terms as proper nouns. But nouns, as real pictures, cannot express grammatical moods, for instance a negation. And how could indeed a picture "represent" negating a state of affairs? However grammatical moods are a not peripheral part of meaning. "If a proposition is conceived as a picture of the state of affairs it describes and a proposition is said to show the possibility of the asserted state of affairs, still the most that the proposition can do is what a painting or a relief does: and so it can at any rate not set forth what is just not the case".[21]

A further objection is as follows. If language reproduces or represents the structure of the fact, then all statements describing the same fact have to have the same

[19] "Frege sagte z.B., daß der Planet Venus das ist, was das Wort 'Morgenstern' bedeutet. Dies aber steht überhaupt nicht in Einklang mit dem gewöhnlichen Gebrauch von 'Bedeutung'. Würde die Venus etwa durch einen Kometen vernichtet werden, so würden wir nicht sagen: "Die Bedeutung des Worts 'Morgenstern' ist durch einen Kometen vernichtet worden". Die Sprache macht einen deutlichen Unterschied zwischen 'Bedeutung' und 'bezeichneter Gegenstand". Wir sagen "Die 'N' genannte Person ist fortgegangen, gestorben, sitzt auf diesem Stuhl", aber wir können nicht sagen: "Die Bedeutung des Namens 'N' ist fortgegangen, gestorben, sitzt auf diesem Stuhl" (F. Waismann, *Logik, Sprache, Philosophie*, p. 456).

[20] L. Wittgenstein, *Philosophical Investigations* (I, 40), p. 20. Emphasis in original.

[21] L. Wittgenstein, *Philosophical Grammar*, ed. by R. Rhees, English trans. by A. Kenny, Berkeley 1978, p. 127 (§ 82).

logical structure. This is not however the case. The same facts may be described by statements whose logical structure is entirely different. For instance, wishing to describe the geographical position of three towns, we may say: (i) A is north of B and B is north of C. We can equally well say: (ii) A is north of C and B is between A and C. But (i) and (ii), Waismann notes, are entirely equivalent to the extent that one of the propositions can be converted into the other. They represent the same state of affairs. Nonetheless, (i) and (ii) have a different logical form, which may, in Russell's way, be rendered as follows:

(i) ANB. BNC;
(ii) ANC. T (B, A, C).

He then goes on: "In the one case the fact is described by two dyadic relations; in the other case by a dyadic and a triadic relations. And these two expressions have quite different forms. Now, which of the two structures is to be called the 'structure of reality'?".[22] But there is a further objection here to be raised. Bertrand Russell, to exemplify this theory, suggest to consider the sentence "Socrates loves Plato". "xRy" could then represent the "structure" of the reality which that sentences refers to.[23] However, should Socrates instead hate Plato or even kill him, the logical structure of the sentence reproducing such state of affairs in the world would again be given through "xRy" so that one might conclude that the meaning of "Socrate loves Plato" and "Socrates hates Plato" should be the same, since both by having the same logical structure seem to refer to the same "structure of reality".[24]

The third objection runs as follows. *Abbildungstheorie* has to assume that any statement is complex or compound, since every fact in the world is compound (resulting from the combination of simple elements). "Whoever says that the sentence is a picture of the fact imagines the sentence consisting of words the combination of which mirrors the structure of the fact. It is essential to this view that the sentence should be complex; for only what is composed of parts can picture what is complex in the world – the fact".[25] This does not, however, according to Waismann, correspond to reality. Not every statement endowed with meaning is made of different parts, compound or complex. On the other hand, sometimes it is not the state of affairs that is complex, but only the sentence referring to it. A brown armchair is not, unless we are to fall into absurdity, the "complex" of armchair and the colour brown. It is, so to speak, a *simple* fact. Nonetheless the statement describing it consists of a subject, verb and attribute: "the armchair is brown". One may thus fall into the temptation of inferring from the "complexity" of the statement a "complexity" (non-existent in reality) of the state of affairs. On the other side, if we find the word

[22]F. Waismann, *The Principles of Linguistic Philosophy*, ed. by R. Harré, London 1965, p. 315.
[23]See B. Russell, *Propositions: What They Are and How They Mean*, in *Proceedings of the Aristotelian Society*, Supplement 2, 1919.
[24]See F. Waismann, *The Principles of Linguistic Philosophy*, p. 314.
[25]*Ibid.*, p. 317. Emphasis in original.

"restaurant" written above an entrance in a building, it as a matter of fact means "this is a restaurant", so that here a *simple* and *single* word expresses a sentence, thus a more complex linguistic structure – which nevertheless refers to a simple and single fact (one restaurant).[26]

3.4.2 Waismann, again following Wittgenstein, brings to bear three chief objections to the psychological conception of meaning. The first is that this theory is said to lead to the most radical subjectivism, reaching the absurd consequence of asserting the impossibility of human communication. If anyone were to seek to understand the meaning of a word or utterance by considering only his mental representations, then that word or utterance would mean something different to everyone. "If for an expression to convey a meaning means to be accompanied by or to produce certain experiences, our expression may have all sorts of meanings".[27] It would then be impossible to attribute any common intersubjective meaning to a word or utterance.[28]

Further, as Wittgenstein notes, as far as what goes on in my mind is concerned, my word is decisive. My hearer can do no more in this regard than take note of my assertion. At most, he can accuse me of expressing myself incoherently. When, however, I say something on the meaning of an utterance or a word, my understanding of it may – rightly – be criticized.[29] If I tell a psychoanalyst that the word "sea" evokes in me the image of a sail or arouses a certain emotion or sensation in my mind, this assertion cannot be disputed by anyone; I am the absolute arbiter of its truth. If however I say that the word "sea" means a piece of cloth used to make vessels move using the wind (the meaning of "sail") this statement of mine could be disputed by speakers of the language in question (in this case English). I am not the absolute judge of the truth of an utterance asserting the meaning of a term.

The second objection is the following. The psychological conception – in particular the "ideational" theory – presupposes that the word or utterance evoke a series of images corresponding to the meaning of the word or utterance. But there are many terms and utterances to which it is rather difficult to attribute a corresponding "image" that fixes or constitutes its meaning. This is the case for many terms in mathematics and geometry, and, adds Waismann, in law. What "image" do terms like "pledge" or "equity" evoke? And even if these terms do evoke some image, in the first case, let us say, the image of a pawn shop, in the second that of a serious

---

[26] See *ibid.* In this connection see also Waismann's critique of the conception that reality consists in a set of *individual* facts ("Verifiability", pp. 57–58).

[27] L. Wittgenstein, *The Blue Book*, in Id., *The Blue and Brown Books*, Oxford 1989, p. 65.

[28] See F. Waismann, *Logik, Sprache, Philosophie*, p. 233.

[29] Note that for Wittgenstein meaning clarification could solve any difference of views about meaning: "die Erklärung der Bedeutung kann jede *Meinungsverschiedenheit* in Bezug auf eine Bedeutung beseitigen" (L. Wittgenstein, *Philosophische Grammatik* (24), Frankfurt am Main 1973, p. 60, emphasis in original).

gentleman in wig and gown, do these perhaps constitute the meaning of those terms? And what images do conjunctions like "when", "because", or "though" evoke?[30]

A further objection to the "emotivist" version of the psychological theory is that the meaning of an utterance or word is not a sensation, a psychic or mental state, in the sense that, say, depression, excitation or pain are. In this version, the mental state or sensation are not the effects of the linguistic expression, but their cause. We can define this version as the "expressionistic" or "emotivistic" theory of meaning. "The word 'fine', 'oh', 'perhaps'... can each be the expresion of a feeling. But I don't call that feling the meaning of the word".[31] Wittgenstein accordingly rejects any emotivistic theory of language. Emotions may accompany or even motivate certain meanings, but nonetheless remain quite distinct from them.

"The difference between the propositions 'I have pain' and 'he has pain'", writes Wittgenstein, "is not that of 'L. W. has pain' and 'Smith has pain'. Rather, it corresponds to the difference between moaning and saying that someone moans".[32] It is wrong to establish a strong psychological connection between a name and that object referred by the name.[33] The meaning of a linguistic expression, continues Wittgenstein, has indefinite duration in time, whereas a sensation or a mental state (a pain, for instance) has very definite time coordinates. On the other hand, the meaning of a linguistic expression has a duration in time independent of the duration of the sensation or mental state ("idea") that (perhaps) accompanies in the utterer's (or recipient's) mind the utterance of that expression.

Finally, the "ideational" theory, by explaining terms through reference to an element external to them, a concrete "image", ends up committing the same error as the referential theory, namely that of treating all words like proper nouns. "This is again connected with the idea that the meaning of a word is an image, or a thing correlated to the word (this roughly means, that we are looking at words as though they were all proper names, and then we confuse the bearer of a name with the meaning of the name)".[34]

The "referential" and the "ideational" theory again lose plausibility when we move from considering the meaning of individual words to analysing the meaning of utterances. Reducing utterances (even if descriptive) to proper nouns, as those theories tend to do, is clearly doing violence to the ordinary use and logical status of

---

[30]F. Waismann, *Logik, Sprache, Philosophie*, p. 233. Cf. L. Wittgenstein, *The Brown Book*, in Id., *The Blue and Brown Books*, pp. 78–79.

[31]L. Wittgenstein, *Philosophical Grammar*, ed. by R. Rhees, English trans. by A. Kenny, p. 9 (§ 30). "Wir werden sagen, dass das Wort 'herrlich', das Wort 'ach', aber auch das Wort 'vielleicht' der *Ausdruck* einer Empfindung, eines Gefühls, ist. Dieses Gefühl nenne ich aber nicht die Bedeutung des Wortes" (L. Wittgenstein, *Philosophische Grammatik* (para. 30), p. 66, emphasis in original).

[32]L. Wittgenstein, *The Blue Book*, p. 68.

[33]"Es ist der Ausdruck einer unrichtigen Auffassung, wenn man sagt: die Verbindung zwischen Name und Gegenstand sei eine psychologische" (L. Wittgenstein, *Philosophische Grammatik* (56), p. 97).

[34]L. Wittgenstein, *The Blue Book*, p. 18.

utterances. (Descriptive) sentences, for instance, are capable of being true or false. This is however not the case with proper nouns, of which one may not predicate truth or falsity. This is well put by Waismann: "What is the difference between 'fire' when I mean it as a *word*, and 'fire' when I mean it as a *statement*? Simply this, that in the latter case it has a specific use – a use, that is, which makes it meaningful to apply to it the terms 'true' or 'false'. It is made part of a system of operations, of a two-valued calculus. It is this which explains *why a sentence is not a sort of name given to fact, a label tacked on to it: if it were the question of truth would not arise*".[35]

The "ideational" theory, notes Wittgenstein, is in some respects subsidiary to the *Abbildungstheorie*, and comes to the latter's help when it is not possible to ascertain the presence of an object or fact that corresponds to the linguistic sign. In this case, within the conception of the relation of meaning as sign-object relation, an image, fact or object is postulated that is no longer material but "spiritual". "And we do here what we do in a host of similar cases: because we cannot specify any *one* bodily action which we call pointing to the shape (as opposed, for example, to the colour), we say that a *spiritual* [mental, intellectual] activity corresponds to these words. Where our language suggests a body and there is none: there we should like to say is a *spirit*".[36] The *Abbildungstheorie* and the "ideational" theory thus form part of one and the same theoretical paradigm, for which meaning is an object coexistent with the sign.[37]

3.5 Objections to the Behaviourist Theory

The behaviourist theory, also defined by Waismann as the "causalist conception of language", basically asserts that the meaning of a linguistic expression lies in the response this expression, as auditory or visual stimulus, arouses in its recipient (albeit not directly, but only in the presence of further conditions). This theory seeks to resolve what we call "sense" or "meaning" into a chain of physical and at any rate verifiable events, by observing the behaviour of the recipient of the linguistic expression. Wittgenstein's and Waismann's objections to the behaviourist theory number at least five.

(i) The theory in question does not, maintains Wittgenstein, cover the important difference between "signal" or "indication" (*Anzeichen*) and "sign" (*Zeichen*), or between *stimulus* and *sign*, or the correlative one between *effect* and *meaning*. A clue is not a sign endowed with meaning. A sound "hm" can be

---

[35] F. Waismann, *Fiction*, in Id., *Philosophical Papers*, ed. by B. McGuinness, Dordrecht 1977, p. 117, my emphasis.

[36] L. Wittgenstein, *Philosophical Investigations,* p. 18 (I. 36), emphasis in original. Cf. A. G. Gargani, *Introduzione a Wittgenstein*, 2nd ed., Bari 1980, p. 82.

[37] Cf. A. G. Gargani, *Op. cit.*, pp. 78ff.

considered as a clue or symptom or an "indication" of being perplexed, but it does not *mean* "being perplexed".[38]
The effect of a linguistic expression does not correspond to its meaning. One may, for instance, not understand the meaning of a statement but nonetheless be influenced by it, or else a statement may not be understood and nonetheless have some effect on the person it is addressed to. I may, for instance, ask someone who speaks, say, only German "Che ora è?" in Italian. My question, even if not understood, may nonetheless have the effect of causing the person in question to understand that the speaker is Italian. "Der ist ein Italiener" is not, however, obviously, the meaning of "che ora è?". Or a linguistic expression may even be entirely devoid of meaning and nonetheless bring about a certain effect on the recipient.[39]

If I assert that a linguistic symbol is what brings about a certain effect and hence define the meaning of the symbol as this particular effect, then the problem arises, as the Viennese philosopher notes, of how I can manage to recognize the effect as meaning. "'A symbol is something that produces this effect'. – H*ow do I know that it is the one I meant*?".[40] In other words, how do we manage to recognize the meaning of a linguistic expression among its various effects, if we do not already have an idea of what that expression was intended to mean? In addition, if the meaning of a linguistic expression is completely identical to its effect, then when I pronounce the expression – that is before it could have any effect – I am engaged in an act devoid of sense; the expression has no meaning. Why then should I utter it? One could reply that I do so because I want to obtain a certain result or cause a determinate effect. In order to claim this, however, my expression has to be supplied with a prior meaning comparable to the effect obtained with the same expression, so that this effect is connected to my expression and consitutes its meaning.[41]

38"Man darf übrigens hier Zeichen mit Anzeichen nicht verwechseln. Den Laut 'hm' kann man einen Ausdruck der Bedenklichkeit nennen und auch, für den Andern, ein *Anzeichen* der Bedenklichkeit, wie Wolken ein Anzeichen des Regens sind. 'hm' ist aber nicht der *Name* der Bedenklichkeit" (L. Wittgenstein, *Philosophische Grammatik* (31), pp. 67–68, emphasis in original).

39Wittgenstein writes: "Wenn ich sage, der Befehl 'bring mir Zucker' und 'bring mir Milch' hat Sinn, aber nicht die Kombination 'Zucker mir Milch', so heißt das nicht, daß das Aussprechen dieser Wortverbindung keine Wirkung hat. Und wenn sie nun die Wirkung hat, daß der Andre mich anstarrt und den Mund aufsperrt, so nenne ich sie nicht deswegen den Befehl, mich anzustarren etc., auch wenn ich gerade *diese* Wirkung hätte hervorbringen wollen. 'Diese Wortverbindung hat keinen Sinn' heißt nicht, sie hat keine Wirkung" (*Philosophische Grammatik* (136), p. 189, emphasis in original).

40L. Wittgenstein, *Philosophical Grammar*, English trans. by A. Kenny, § 33, p. 10, emphasis in original.

41As Wittgenstein states, "Wenn ich sage, 'Symbol ist das, was diesen Effekt hervorruft' –, so ist eben die Frage: Wie ich von 'diesem Effekt' reden kann. – Und wie ich weiß, daß *der ist, den ich gemeint habe*, wenn er eintritt. –Es ist drum keine Erklärung, die die Wurzel dieser Beunruhigung trifft, zu sagen: sehr einfach, wir vergleichen ihn mit unserem Erinnerungsbild. Denn wie ist uns die Vergleichsmethode gegeben, nach der wir vergleichen sollen, d.h.: Wie wissen wir, was wir zu tun

(ii) A second objection to the behaviourist theory is raised by Waismann: the theory in question renders communication problematic. If the meaning of a linguistic expression depends on its effect on the recipient, it is possible that the meaning the recipient attributes to the linguistic expression (in other words, its effect on the latter) turns out entirely different from the meaning the utterer intended to convey by uttering the linguistic expression in question. In this case there is no communication between utterer and recipient. Since on the behaviourist view we cannot exclude this happening, namely the effect of the linguistic expression on the recipient being different from or even opposite to the desired or "intended" effect, we fall back into a subjectivistic and relativistic conception. Meaning is in the power of the individual reception or response, and of the greater or lesser efficacy of the individual expression. "Suppose we say," writes Waismann, "'All right, the meaning of a sign lies in the effect'. But suppose the sign just once fails to effect the movement, and the machine, instead of moving, stops? Then we shall have to say that stopping is what '*a*' means. So that this sign has a definite maning is a hypothesis, and future experience could teach us that it has a different meaning from what we thought".[42]

(iii) A third objection is related to the one above. The meaning of an action, asserts Wittgenstein, cannot be deduced simply from the behaviour of the agent and his satisfaction, since an inseparable element of action is the agent's *intention*.[43] That is, for instance, if when playing chess I am checkmated and say: "I won, since that was the goal I was aiming at", one would say that in fact I was not playing at chess but some other game. If however a behaviourist view is adopted, it would instead have to be said that *I* have won, since I was moving pieces on the board and am content with the outcome of the game. This is true for language too: If from language we take away any intentional element, language will lose its proper function.[44] In order to understand a linguistic expression, one cannot, then, do without the intention of the one using it (the utterer).

---

haben, wenn uns befohlen wird 'zu vergleichen'?" (L. Wittgenstein, *Philosophische Grammatik* (33), pp. 70–71, emphasis in original).

[42]F. Waismann, *The Principles of Linguistic Philosophy*, p. 115. "Gesetzt, wir sähen die Bedeutung eines Zeichens in seiner Wirkung. Wie nun, wenn das Zeichen einmal nicht die Bewegung bewirkt sondern das Stehenbleiben? Dann wird man sagen müsen, dass *dies* die Bedeutung des Zeichens *a* ist. In diesem Sinn ist es eine Hypothese, welche Bedeutung dieses Zeichen hat, und zukünftige Erfahrungen könnten lehren, daß es eine ganz andere hat, als wir geglaubt haben" (F. Waismann, *Logik, Sprache, Philosophie*, p. 172, emphasis in original).

[43]Wittgenstein gives the following example: "Wie wäre es, wenn einer Schach spielte und wenn er matt gesetzt wäre, sagte 'siehst du, ich habe gewonnen, denn *das* Ziel wollte ich erreichen?' Wir würden sagen, dieser Mensch wollte eben nicht Schach spielen, sondern ein anderes Spiel, während Russell sagen müßte, der hat im Schach gewonnen, der mit den Figuren spielt und mit dem Ausgang zufrieden ist" (L. Wittgenstein, *Philosophische Bemerkungen* (24), Suhrkamp, Frankfurt am Main 1981, p. 65, emphasis in original).

[44]"Wenn man das Element der Intention aus der Sprache entfernt, so bricht damit ihre ganze Funktion zusammen" (*ibid.* (20), p. 63).

(iv) A fourth objection linked to the first is that the behaviourist conception confuses logical consequences with causal effects, and therefore the "reason" or "basis" (*Grund*) for a behaviour with its "cause" (*Ursache*). If we ask a train driver "Why did you stop?" and he answers "Because the light is red", we are in the presence not of the "cause", but of the "reason" for a certain piece of behaviour.[45] A command may be obeyed or not, a norm or a principle complied with or not, a meaning understood or not, while it is meaningless to say that a cause is not obeyed, not complied with, or not understood. The cause, if it is one, is followed inevitably by its effect.

In opposition to behaviourism, Waismann asserts that the meaning of a linguistic expression cannot be understood from a purely causal viewpoint (from the "external" viewpoint, we might say, taking up Peter Winch's terminology[46]) but only from a *normativist* viewpoint (from the "internal" viewpoint, as Herbert Hart might say[47]). "In the conception of the mental mechanism according to which language pulls the lever that moves another's body, the concept of meaning has not yet appeared. This concept can be apprehended only when we consider language from a normative point of view. 'Meaning' (like 'sign', 'expression') is a grammatical term, not a term used in natural sciences. Hence, in scientific reasoning, it is always felt to be something alien and our analysis shows whay that is so".[48] Wittgenstein did in fact emphatically deny that the explanation of the meaning of a linguistic expression might be supplied by the description of a mere empirical experience, the indication of regularity or any sort of causal explanation.[49] The explanation of the meaning of a linguistic expression is, rather, the statement of a *rule*, of a *norm*, that is, of the rules for using that expression.

(v) The behaviourist theory of meaning verges on a verificationist theory. Once meaning is conceived of as the causal effect of a linguistic expression, the determination of this meaning takes on the nature of a hypothesis about the occurrence of the effect held to be bound up with that particular expression.[50] Understanding a statement amounts, on this view, to noting or at least

---

[45]"Die kausale Auffassung der Sprache rührt nun her von einer Verwechslung der logischen Folgen mit den kausalen Folgen. Wenn der Lokomotivführer gefragt wird: 'Warum hast du hier gehalten?', so sagte er etwa: 'Weil hier das Signal *HALT*! steht'. Diese Antwort hält man nun fälschlich für die Angabe einer Ursache, während sie die Angabe eines Grundes ist" (F. Waismann, *Logik, Sprache, Philosophie*, p. 180. See also F. Waismann, *The Relevance of Psychology to Logic*, in Id., *Philosophical Papers*, ed. by B. McGuinness, especially pp. 77–79).

[46]See P. Winch, *The Idea of a Social Science and its Relation to Philosophy*, 11th reprint, Routledge & Kegan Paul, London 1985, p. 110.

[47]See H. L. A. Hart, *The Concept of Law*, Clarendon, Oxford 1961, pp. 86ff.

[48]F. Waismann, *The Principles of Lingustic Philosophy*, pp. 190–191.

[49]"Wir sagten aber: unter 'Bedeutung' verstünden wir das, was die Erklärung der Bedeutung erklärt. Und die Erklärung der Bedeutung ist kein Erfahrungssatz und keine Kausalerklärung, sondern eine Regel, ein Übereinkommen" (L. Wittgenstein, *Philosophische Grammatik*, p. 68, § 32).

[50]See F. Waismann, *Logik, Sprache, Philosophie*, p. 172.

predicting the effect the statement has produced, is producing or will produce on the recipient. "The proposition that your action has such and such a cause, is a hypothesis – the hypothesis is well-founded if one has had a number of experiences, which, roughly speaking, agree in showing that your action is the regular sequel of certain conditions which we then call causes of the action".[51]

For Wittgenstein the proposition that gives us the meaning of a term is profoundly different from the proposition hypothesizing a particular causal relation. To understand the meaning of a linguistic expression, I do not necessarily need to turn to observing regularities of behaviour. "In order to know the reason which you had for making a certain statement, for acting in a particular way, etc., no number of agreeing experiences is necessary, and the statement of your reason is not a hypothesis".[52] The proposition giving the meaning of a linguistic expression is instead more a proposition supplying a "reason" for a particular action. And the "reason" for a particular action (linguistic or otherwise) refers either to the psychology of the individual, or to rules, norms, accepted within a given context. "Giving a reason for something one did or said means showing a *way* which leads to this action. In some cases it means telling the way which one has gone oneself; in others, it means describing a way which leads there and is in accordance with certain accepted rules".[53]

There nonetheless remains one important difference between the behaviourist and the verificationist theories. For the latter, the event that is the object of the (possible) verification is not the *effect* of the utterance, but *the state of affairs around which the utterance turns*. Thus while the behaviourist theory resolves the semantic dimension into the pragmatic one, the verificationist theory maintains the distinction between these two dimensions.

3.6 Theories of Norms and Theories of Validity

3.6.1 One might maintain the existence of a link between theories of meaning and theories norms, in the sense that once a certain conception of meaning has been adopted, if one is to remain with it consistently, one must assume a corresponding conception of the norm. This link may also be implicit, and is sometimes adopted almost unreflectively. So that its is not uncommon for many theories of the norm that they do not concern themselves with, or refer to, the connections between normative and linguistic phenomena.

The links between the theory of meaning and the theory of norms, however, become extremely close if one adopts the philosophical perspective of the later

---

[51] L. Wittgenstein, *The Blue Book*, p. 15.

[52] *Ibid.*, p. 14, emphasis in original.

[53] *Ibid.*, p. 14, emphasis in original.

Wittgenstein according to whom "there exists a correspondence between the concepts 'rule' and 'meaning'".[54] For the Austrian philosopher, in fact, the meaning of a linguistic expression is a particular type of rule or norm: it is a norm relating to the use of the linguistic expression in question. The theory of meaning thus assumes the contours of a special theory of norms.

Thanks to the convergence of hermeneutic philosophy and neopositivist and analytical philosophy, in recent decades the study of law and of language have become increasingly interwoven, so that a view of the analysis of conceptions of norms like the one adopted in this study seems legitimate, at least in relation to contemporary theories of law. I believe, however, that it may plausibly be stated that adopting a particular theory of meaning determines (or is the prerequisite for) a particular theory of norms (and of legal validity).[55] Below I shall seek to indicate some possible links between theories of meaning and theories of norms.

3.6.2 Anyone who adopts a verificationist theory of meaning and accordingly attributes "sense" only to *statements* or *assertions*, that is, to *descriptive* sentences, is faced with this alternative: either to consider that a norm is a statement endowed with meaning or to consider that a norm is devoid of meaning. In the first case the norm will in some way be reduced to an assertion. In the second case the norm will be equivalent to a mere exclamation, an expression of a feeling or of an emotion.[56]

Where the norm is reduced to a proposition of assertive type, we customarily face two principal conceptions: (i) that the norm is nothing but the prediction of a future event (in general the behaviour of judges); (ii) that the norm is nothing but a technical rule, in turn seen as the "description" of the most suitable way or "means" of reaching a particular goal. A conception of type (i) is, for instance, that upheld by Judge Oliver Wendell Holmes, who considered that the law consisted in predicting the behaviour of courts.[57] A conception of type (ii) is, instead, defended by, say B. F. Skinner. "Important social contingencies," he writes, "are implied by 'Thou shalt not steal', which may be translated as 'if you want to avoid punishment, do not steal', or else 'stealing is wrong, and wrong behaviour is punished'. Such a proposition is no more normative than 'if coffee keeps you awake, don't drink it when you want to go to sleep'".[58]

---

[54]L. Wittgenstein, *On Certainty*, p. 10, § 62.

[55]This is, for instance, the position taken by J. Wróblewski, *The Problem of the Meaning of the Legal Norm*, in Id., *Meaning and Truth in Judicial Decision*, 2nd ed., ed. by A. Arno, Helsinki 1983, pp. 1ff.

[56]On this see U. Scarpelli, *Contributo alla semantica del linguaggio normativo*, 2nd ed., ed. by A. Pintore, Milan 1985, p. 86.

[57]See O. W. Holmes, *The Path of the Law*, in *The Holmes Reader*, ed. by J. J. Market, 2nd ed., Doblesferry, NY 1964, p. 42. On this cf. also U. Scarpelli, *Semantica, morale, diritto*, Turin 1969, p. 111.

[58]B. F. Skinner, *Beyond Freedom and Dignity*, Harmondsworth 1979, p. 114. For a more or less analogous conception in the meta-ethical field, see the so-called "technical foundation" of norms attempted by Paul Lorenzen and the "Erlangen school": cf. R. Alexy, *Eine Theorie des praktischen Diskurses*, in *Materialien zur Normendiskussion*, vol. 2, *Normenbegründung. Normendurchsetzung*, ed. by W. Oelmüller, Paderborn 1978, pp. 29–30.

The theories of validity corresponding with the two theories of the norm just stated are as follows. If a norm is a mere emotional utterance and it is assumed that it is "without meaning", the problem of its validity does not even arise. The problem of the "validity" or "justification" or even "truth" of an utterance can be posed only in relation to its *meaning*. A sentence without meaning is neither valid nor invalid, neither justified nor unjustified, neither true nor false.

In the case where the norm is seen as the prediction of a future event, the validity of the norm will coincide with its *verification*, that is, with verification of the event (behaviour) foreseen. The validity of the norm here ends by coinciding with its efficacy: a norm is valid if it is actually complied with, that is, is efficacious. This is also true as far as the validity of the norm conceived of as a technical rule goes (where it is understood as a type of descriptive sentence, as a description of the means necessary towards a certain end): the norm as technical rule will be valid if it is actually *true*, that is, if it is verified by the reaching of that particular end through use of that particular means as it describes.

The "ideational" (psychological or mentalistic) theory of meaning can be made to correspond to the theory of the norm as declaration of will. This theory may in my view be linked both to many natural-law (voluntarist) theories and to various imperativist theories that see the norm as command, imperative, or else as "meaning of an act of will", and at any rate maintain that the norm is the product of a mental act of will. The norm is valid here when it corresponds to the will (to the "idea", to the "representation" or to the "intention") of the subject that issued it.

The second (objectivistic or "logicist") version of the theory of representation can instead be made to fit a "Platonist" conception of norms according to which they would be real (ideal, non-material) entities, represented, reported or "portrayed" by the normative sentence. This sort of conception has recently been called "hyletic", in contradistinction to an "expressive" conception of norms.[59] For the "hyletic" conception, the validity of a norm would depend on criteria of an eminently ontological nature, that is, on the norm's belonging to a particular normative "world". For "normative Platonism", the validity of the norm is entirely independent of the actions of human beings. Human behaviour may be an index of the validity of the rules, but never a condition of that validity.[60]

Finally, the behaviourist theory corresponds with the conception of norm as a particular type of stimulus (linguistic and/or extra-linguistic). Since here the "meaning" of the norm is nothing but the effect produced by it on its recipient, the validity of the norm can only be superimposed on its effects, accordingly on its *efficacy*. Here too, as in a version of the theory of the norm based on the verificationist conception of meaning, validity and efficacy end up coinciding. A conception of this type has been reaffirmed by Georg Henryk von Wright, who maintains that the norm

---

[59] See C. Alchourron and E. Bulygin, *The Expressive Conception of Norms*, in *New Essays in Deontic Logic*, ed. by R. Hilpinen, Dordrecht 1981, pp. 95ff.

[60] Cf. A. Kemmerling, *Regel und Geltung im Lichte der Analyse Wittgensteins*, in *Rechtstheorie*, 1975, pp. 106–107.

is a "external determinant of human action". But what are these external determinants? Here is von Wright's answer: "The external determinants of our actions are like stimuli to which we react. These responses must be learnt, *as in the case of conditioned reflexes*".[61]

Quite apart from the fact that the foregoing theories of the norm (and of validity) are based on largely unsatisfactory theories of meaning, they are, in my view, unsatisfactory themselves, and in their outcomes. The theory of the norm based on verificationist theory has two outcomes, both rather unconvincing. On the one hand it falls into what has been called the "descriptivist fallacy", for which there is only one type of meaning (the descriptive), with the consequence that it can no longer distinguish between statements of what "is" and what "ought", and has to give up so-called "divisionism",[62] which however remains fruitful in the area of social science methodology. On the other hand, verificationism ends up by depriving of "meaning" any normative sentence, evaluative or prescriptive, with the rather questionable result of consigning to the "meaningless" a considerable and relevant part of human experience and theoretical reflection. "Since it is obvious to every lawyer that a rule has a meaning, in any ordinary sense of the word 'meaning'" writes Glanville L. Williams, "it follows that a lawyer must reject the definition of meaning advanced by the Logical Positivists as a complete definition of the word."[63]

I would recall in relation to this that considerations of this type impelled Uberto Scarpelli, a scholar of strong analytical and neo-positivist convictions, to abandon the principle of verification (or verifiability) in favour of what he has called the "principle of significance".[64] For similar reasons, verificationism was rejected also by, say, Jerzy Wróblewski. The emotivist theory, argues Wróblewski, fails to explain on the one hand the fact that norms are often linguistically complex and far from reducible to the simple form of exclamation or interjection, and on the other hand their grip on reality, the fact that the norms really do serve to make social institutions operate in a certain manner.[65]

3.6.3 Another possible outcome of the verificationist theory is the one I would define as its "analogical" application to normative sentences. This is a proposal put forward several years ago now by Luigi Ferrajoli, who sought a principle of significance similar to that of verifiability, but valid for normative sentences. Ferrajoli started

---

[61] G. H. von Wright, *Determinism and the Study of Man*, now in Id., *Philosophical Papers*, vol. 1, *Practical Reason*, Basil Blackwell, Oxford 1983, p. 38.

[62] On this see U. Scarpelli, "La 'grande divisione' e la filosofia della politica", Introduction to: F. E. Oppenheim, *Etica e filosofia politica*, Italian trans. by M. C. Galavotti, Il Mulino, Bologna 1971.

[63] G. L. Williams, *Language and the Law*, in *Law Quarterly Review*, 1946, p. 405. Williams who here makes reference to the verificationist theory, remains however a defender of the emotivist theory of meaning.

[64] See U. Scarpelli, *Contributo alla semantica del linguaggio normativo*, 2nd ed., pp. 85ff. For a critique of verificationism with reference particularly to the meaning of normative sentences, see also P. F. Strawson, *Meaning and Truth*, in *Philosophy As It Is*, ed. by T. Honderich and M. Burnyeat, Harmondsworth 1984, pp. 526–527.

[65] See J. Wróblewski, *The Problem and Meaning of the Legal Norm*, p. 10.

principally from a theory of representation. "In order to determine the 'meaning' of a proposition, be it assertive, preceptive or of some other type, the first operation is certainly that of identifying the representational content it evokes in *its recipient* or interpreter or user".[66] We are here in the presence of a combination of an "ideational" theory (but centred on the "recipient", not the "utterer" of the sentence) and of a "referential" theory. "Both an assertive and a preceptive proposition have meaning to the extent that it is possible empirically to determine the state of affairs they represent".[67]

Ferrajoli speaks of a more general criterion of "acceptability" of sentences, which would take a different shape according to the different (semantic) nature of the sentence. The distinction between descriptive or assertive sentences and normative sentences would then *also* be semantic, and not only pragmatic.[68] "The possibility of being either accepted or not accepted is, then, the characteristic feature that any sentence must possess in order to come into consideration as a proposition, irrespective of whether as an assertion or as a precept. It seems possible, accordingly, to identify a general criterion of meaning, consisting in a general *principle of acceptability*, valid, then, for assertions as well as for precepts, taking the shape for the former of a *principle of verifiability* and for the latter of a *principle of executability*".[69] A norm, here seen eminently as a precept, would accordingly have meaning, would be endowed with meaning, if the conduct it prescribes is "performable". "A preceptive proposition has meaning if it is in principle *performable*, that is, if it prescribes behaviour whose execution is possible, or conceivable (or its coming into being)".[70]

Really the "executability" Ferrajoli speaks of constitutes a rather "liberal" and perhaps even vague criterion, since executability is connected not only with the material (empirical) possibility of execution, but also with its *conceivability*, and this obviously transcends the bounds of empirical executability, and may be projected into imaginary or "possible" worlds, in any case ones that do not empirically exist. Nonetheless, "executability", be it with the broadest outlines attributed to it here, is not a true criterion of meaning, but more of "making sense" or of "rationality", or of "justification" of the utterance, since it is not operational unless it is assumed that the utterance in question has already been understood. In order to execute a prescription, just as to verify an assertion, I must first have understood its meaning. The example of an utterance that is meaningless because it is "inexecutable" given by Ferrajoli, "Paint the Absolute green!", is not however devoid of meaning. We understand it, but we find it "meaningless" or "irrational" or "unjustified", since we

---

[66] L. Ferrajoli, *Linguaggio assertivo e linguaggio preceptivo*, in *Rivista internazionale di filosofia del diritto*, 1966, p. 522.

[67] *Ibid.*, p. 523.

[68] See *ibid.*, p. 525, note 23.

[69] *Ibid.*, p. 526. Emphasis in original.

[70] *Ibid.* Emphasis in original.

cannot imagine what behaviour would bring about the state of affairs that utterance is intended to contribute to bringing about.

Equally, the principle of verifiability constitutes a criterion not of meaning but of "making sense" or of "rationality" or of "justification" of a certain descriptive sentence. That the principle of "executability" is here nothing other than analogous application of the principle of verifiability is clear from the way Ferrajoli resolves the problem of the validity of a normative (prescriptive) sentence. This validity is resolved into the *truth* of the sentence meta-linguistically made as to the validity itself. This is possible, but at the price of conceiving "validity" not so much as a predicate of the prescriptive sentence as the predicate of a sentence about the prescription in question. Better, validity is conceived of here alternatively (i) as reiteration of the bindingness of the sentence, so that the expression "it is valid" would be entirely equivalent to "you must" and would have no independent semantic content in relation to the prescription it deals with. Alternatively, (ii) as a predicate that connotes a property of the sentence. "In this way," writes Ferrajoli, "two different acceptations of the word 'validity' and 'invalidity' or 'must' and 'must not' have been singled out, parallel to those already of 'truth' and 'falsehood'; a first acceptance corresponds with their directly *imperative* use, and the second with their *declarative* use. In the imperative acceptation, that is, when they are used as expressions of the same language in which the precept has been uttered, they refer directly to the behaviours prescribed and express an act of will by the one making the precept. In the declarative acceptance, that is when used as expressions of the meta-language describing the preceptive proposition, they instead refer to properties of the precept and accordingly express a theoretical judgement".[71]

We thus find ourselves, firstly, before an imperativist, voluntarist theory of validity, and secondly before a reduction of validity to verifiability or to truth. To reach this second thesis, however, it must be postulated that (a) the meta-language about the prescriptive sentence must necessarily be descriptive, whereas in order to maintain the first thesis (the judgement of validity of p is nothing but a reiteration of p) it must be maintained that (b) this judgement belongs to the same linguistic level that p is on. But neither (a) nor (b) are correct. "The normative proposition p is valid' – writes Ferrajoli – is certainly a proposition in a meta-language that is about the language in which p is expressed, and yet this meta-language is not necessarily descriptive or declarative, since the correctness of this statement may be ascertained by criteria that have nothing to do with empirical correspondence with a certain state of affairs, but instead with recourse to reasons or principles which in turn are normative statements (not necessarily prescriptive). In other words, in order to ascertain the validity of a normative sentence I have to have recourse to practical reasoning, and cannot trust exclusively to the observation of empirical facts. Nor can this

71 *Ibid.*, pp. 530–531. Emphasis in original.

practical reasoning turn solely around syntactical relations of coherence, even if augmented by pragmatic criteria of success or efficacy".[72]

3.6.4 An example of "normative Platonism" is supplied by the semantics proposed by the Franco-Polish scholar Georges Kalinowski. He starts by accepting the existence of a prescriptive language distinct from descriptive language. A prescriptive language, here, is characterized by the fact that it contains the deontic operators of obligation, prohibition and permission. And legal language, as being made up of sentences that explicitly or implicitly use these deontic operators, is considered as prescriptive.[73]

Kalinowski accepts a "representational" or "ideational" theory of meaning: "The *significatum* is, properly, the idea expressed by an utterance".[74] This is, however, an "ideational" rather than a psychologistic conception: the "idea" in question here is more a logical class than the content of a mental act. There are then, according to this scholar, two chief types of meaning: (i) through one, knowledge is expressed; (ii) through the other, creation. We thus have *pensée-connaissance* and *pensée-creation*. The first corresponds with some sort of reality, the second with no entity that can be termed real. One must accordingly distinguish within the *significatum* between (a) *designatum* and (b) *significatum* proper, so that it is possible to have utterances devoid of *designatum* that nonetheless have *significatum*. Utterances devoid of *designatum* are called "empty expressions".

However, for Kalinowski there may be *designata* that do not consist of real entities. These would then be so-called "intentional" objects, or ideal entities such as, say, the nymph Calypso. The "empty expressions" might then similarly designate something, have some type of referent. "Non-empty" utterances would designate in the strong sense, so that in them *significatum* and *designatum* would be quite distinct. "Empty" utterances would instead designate in a weak sense, referring to entirely ideal entities, so that in these the *designatum* would be absorbed by the *significatum*.

Then comes the decisive passage in which Kalinowski assumes a "normative Platonist" position. If ideal entities – arguments – are accepted as *designata*, that is, if the existence of that which is not immediately perceptible or sensible is accepted, then even that which is not material, that is, not within space and time coordinates, may be real, or better existent. But if this is so, then normative relations too, in particular those expressed by the deontic operators of obligation, prohibition and permission, may be termed real. Consequently, the truth or falsehood of a norm expressing a normative relation may be predicated, according to whether there is

---

[72]Cf. *ibid.*, pp. 537ff. This is one of the reasons perhaps that persuaded Ferrajoli to distinguish later between "validità" and "vigore" ("validity" and "in force"); see L. Ferrajoli, *Diritto e ragione. Teoria del garantismo penale*, Bari 1989, pp. 915ff.

[73]See e.g., G. Kalinowski, *Zur Semantik der Rechtssprache*, in *Argumentation und Hermeneutik in der Jurisprudenz*, ed. by W. Krawietz, K. Opalek, A Peczenik and A. Schramm, Berlin 1979, pp. 239ff.

[74]*Ibid.*, p. 245.

or is not a correspondence relationship between its meaning and the "normative relation" that the norm designates or refers to.

Kalinowski goes as far as affirming that the norm is a "non-empty" sentence, that is, designates in the strong sense, since the "normative relation" to which the norm refers and which it designates is not an "intensional object", or ideal object, but a reality in the strict sense, where the existence of that which is not immediately perceptible to the senses is not excluded a priori.[75]

Kalinowski's "normative Platonism" is fairly radical: norms, for him, do not designate "ideal entities", but real entities in the proper sense. A norm can accordingly be true or false in a similar sense to the way one may predicate the truth or falsehood of an assertion, of a descriptive proposition. In consequence legal norms – the norms themselves, note – and not the propositions stating them (the later Kelsen's *Rechtssätze*,[76] to clarify, or Ronald Dworkin's *propositions of law*,[77] or better still von Wright's *norm-propositions*[78]) may be termed true or false according to whether their meaning does or does not correspond with their referent (the "normative relation").

For Kalinowski the epistemological and semantic distinction between assertions and prescriptions, between descriptive sentences and prescriptive or normative ones, turns into an ontological distinction, a distinction that operates no longer at the level of *significatum*, but on that of *designatum*. There would then be descriptive *designata* or "real entities", and normative *designata* or "real entities". The semantic relation between *significatum* and *designatum*, or "real entity", would in both cases be the same: essentially that of correspondence, of the "*adaequatio rei*", or a truth relation.

A form of normative Platonism seems also to constitute the nucleus of the conception of norm of Jan-Reinard Sieckman. Partly following Robert Alexy, he adopts a semantic concept of norm, that is to say, he maintains that a norm consists in the "meaning of a normative statement".[79] Accordingly, given the normative statement "lying is forbidden" the norm that this expresses would be "one shouldn't lie". The difficulties start however when on poses the problem of the nature of the meaning of the norm or rather of what this is or represents. At this point Seickman, adopting a representational theory of meaning is constrained to construct a strong analogy between meaning of descriptive and normative sentences. The meaning of an assertion is the proposition or rather the state of affairs that the assertion expresses or represents. Equally, normative sentences would express normative propositions or rather would indicate normative states of affairs. Here normative propositions refers

[75] See *ibid.*, p. 247.

[76] See H. Kelsen, *Reine Rechtslehre*, 2nd ed., Deuticke, Vienna 1960, pp. 59, 73ff., 209ff.

[77] See R. Dworkin, *Introduction*, in *The Philosophy of Law*, ed. by R. Dworkin, Oxford University Press, Oxford 1977, p. 5.

[78] See H. von Wright, *Norm and Action. A Logical Enquiry*, London 1977, p. 93, p. 106.

[79] J.-R. Sieckmann, *Regelmodelle und Prinzipienmodelle des Rechtssystems*, Baden-Baden 1990, p. 26.

to largely descriptive content, that is to states of affairs or objects or ideal entities that are as such normative. The norms thus end up as normative sentences that are in turn as assertions the semantic content of which is supplied by normative propositions. One might say that "according to a semantic conception of norms these could be understood as *normative states of affairs* or as normative propositions which should not necessarily be true".[80]

"Normative Platonism" ought not however to be taken *sic et simpliciter* for the theory that asserts a specific existence of norms as non-material entities. What characterizes "normative Platonism" is not so much the assertion of the existence of norms as entities endowed with specific reality, as the thesis that the norms, or better the normative propositions, however existent, reflect or are expressions of specifically normative objects or facts or relations. The norms, accordingly, as in Kalinowski's theory, have the truth or falsehood attributed to them. We are here dealing, as Kalinowski himself claims, with an extreme "normative cognitivism", which is true as much for moral norms as for legal norms.

It should be borne in mind that the typical feature of meta-ethical cognitivism is instead only the assertion that *moral* values, principles and rules are knowable, not also *legal* norms. Inversely, meta-ethical non-cognitivism defends the non-knowability of specifically normative entities such as moral values and principles, but not of social phenomena or of propositional content, and so doesn't also claim the non-knowability of legal norms if understood as social phenomena and propositional content. Obviously, in speaking here of the knowability of legal norms we refer to, as it were, a strong knowability, irrespective of any foregoing normative production. For "normative cognitivism", the knowability of norms concerns not the possibility of knowing the positive norms, but the knowability of the entities or relations to which the positive norms, on this view, may or may not correspond. (Put in other terms, the normative knowledge claimed by the "cognitivist" here has as its object not norms already issued, the "real" norms, but those to be issued, or the "ideal" norms.) For a normative cognitivist, it is accordingly possible to assert that a certain possible norm – let us say Article 1 of the German Civil Code or Article 12 of the preliminary Provisions of the Italian Civil Code – is false. Falsehood and truth are, for a Kalinowski-style normative cognitivist, predicates of statements in a first-order "normative" language, not of statements of a second-order language (of the type: "Article 1 of the German Civil Code states that...").

A more moderate position, asserting the existence of the (social or legal) norms as specific entities, is not necessarily compromised by any form of meta-ethical cognitivism or "strong" normative cognitivism. Ota Weinberger, for instance, conceives of norms as "ideal entities" existing in the world, and yet is a radical non-cognitivist in meta-ethics. Still less does he believe that the language of legal norms may be true or false. Weinberger asserts a less controversial position, namely that norms, like other cultural phenomena, have a specific existence, which cannot be reduced to that of merely empirical facts, "brute facts". Norms would instead be "institutional

[80] *Ibid.*, p. 30. Italics mine.

facts". To justify these theses, Weinberger refers in part to the ontology developed by Nicolai Hartmann and still more to Popper's ideas of *World 3*.

For our purposes it is sufficient to accept the theses of norms as entities endowed with specific existence in virtue of the following criteria; (i) that which acts or has effects on existent beings or states of affairs is itself also endowed with existence; (ii) that which is produced by existent beings is itself also endowed with existence; (iii) that which has existence independently of the existence of other beings is endowed with existence specifically its own.[81] These three criteria are all met by the "things" we commonly call "legal norms". For: (i) the norms constitute reasons or motives for, and hence act on, existent human behaviour; (ii) the norms are products of existent beings, humans; (iii) the norms are, however, independent of the act of their utterance or production, since every norm has as logical consequence a plurality of other norms of which the utterer or producer is not and cannot yet be aware.[82]

3.6.5 The outcomes of the behaviourist theory of norms are equally unsatisfactory, in particular the reduction of their validity to their efficacy (which is also common to the verificationist theory). If a norm is valid only when it is effective, this has as a consequence that it can never be breached. For on the behaviourist view, if the norm is breached that means it is not valid, or else does not exist as a norm. But if it does not exist as a norm, it must be concluded that there is no obligation to comply with it, and if there is no obligation to comply with the norm, it cannot really be breached.

For the behaviourist theory the norm is a sort of "stimulus" to act, a "command". But as Friedrich Waismann writes, "it is typical of the use of the word 'command' that one may speak of breaking it. But if a provision that brings about a certain movement is termed a command, then there is no meaning in speaking of breaking a command, and hence the word 'command' is being used improperly. For the command to do something is the command to do that even where it is broken. If, however, it is so because of its efficacy [*Wirkung*], then the command to do something is no longer that in the case where it no longer brings about that action. According to this conception, we are able to know what one man has ordered another only by observing what the latter does because of the command. *On this conception, no child is disobedient*".[83]

On the other hand, a characteristic feature of a norm is the fact that in relation to it one takes up a "critical reflective attitude".[84] The norm, that is, is taken as

---

[81] I am here taking up ideas of A. Schramm, *Zur logischen Rekonstruktion des Problems der Normrechtfertigung*, in *Argumentation und Hermeneutik in der Jurisprudenz*, ed. by W. Krawietz et al., Berlin, pp. 275ff.

[82] Cf. *ibid.*, p. 274.

[83] F. Waismann, *Logik, Sprache, Philosophie*, p. 173. Italics mine.

[84] In this connection see H. L. A. Hart, *The Concept of Law*, p. 56. Hart warns that "we must cease to regard the law as merely a causal factor in human behaviour" and that "we must cease, therefore, to regard the law simply as a system of stimuli goading the individual by its threats into conformity" (H. L. A. Hart, *Legal Responsibility and Excuses*, in Id., *Punishment and Responsibility. Essays in the Philosophy of Law*, Oxford 1992, p. 44).

a guiding criterion of our *reasoning* in relation to our and *others'* behaviour. One typical element of norm-governed behaviour (social or legal) has been identified as the fact that the behaviour in question is open to criticism by those forming part of the context of action within which this behaviour comes about. One indication that we are in the presence of norm-governed behaviour and not of individual behaviour or mere regularity is supplied by the fact that this conduct is subject to criticism by those taking part or having an interest in it.

This statement has been doubted by those who see in it the danger of an infinite regress. If it is maintained that norm-governed behaviour is distinguished from mere regularity of behaviour by the fact that the former is subject to criticism by those taking part in or concerned by it, one is obliged to state what one means by "criticism". This can in turn not be just any sort of hostile behaviour or reaction towards the piece of behaviour considered, but must be "qualified" conduct. This qualification has, then, to be found in the fact that the "critical" behaviour is in turn subject to rules, and hence to criticisms. But in order then to identify the latter, we must look for further "critical" behaviour, and so on *ad infinitum*.[85]

This objection however is really rather captious. In fact the criticism through which we can identify behaviour based on norms, or engaged in compliance with certain norms and not conforming to them by chance, is some other behaviour that can be interpreted as a negative reaction vis-à-vis conduct based on norms. The criticism alone does not yet tell us that this conduct is based on norms; it constitutes only an indication of that. In order for the hypothesis that conduct is founded on norms induced in us by the indicator represented by the "criticism" to be confirmed, it is necessary to resort to other criteria. It will be necessary to verify whether the criticism in question is an act of purely personal aversion, or instead refers to a body of norms and is justified in relation to these. We must, that is, verify whether this "criticism" is based on *arguments* and not mere emotional reactions, and then ascertain whether the arguments make referencc to norms. Only in the last case can we conclude that as far as the conduct criticized is concerned it is action based on norms. The act of criticism we refer to in the first instance is, however, an empirically observable and comprehensible fact, quite apart from the body of norms which that act in some way shows to be in force. The act of criticism as an empirical fact is only a *prima facie* reason for asserting the

[85]This objection is well summarized by Eike von Savigny: "Regelfolgendes Verhalten unterscheidet sich von bloß regelmäßigem Verhalten wesentlich dadurch, daß es der Kritik augesetzt ist. Als Kritik kann man ein Verhalten aber nur dann bezeichnen, wenn es selbst bestimmten Regeln folgt; nicht jede negative Reaktion auf des Verhalten eines Anderen ist Kritik. Es kann auch eine reflexhafte Ohrfeige sein, ein Wutausbruch, ein Ausdruck der Enttäuschung, eine angewöhnte Handlung des Liebensentzugs oder was auch immer. Kritisieren als Handlung folgt dagegen zumindest der Regel, weiteren Argumenten zugänglich zu sein. Allem Anschein nach läßt sich also regelfolgendes Verhalten nur daran erkennen, daß man zuvor ein anderes Verhalten als regelfolgendes Verhalten erkannt hat, und so weiter ad infinitum" (E. von Savigny, *Die Philosophie der normalen Sprache. Ein kritische Einführung in die "Ordinary language philosophy"*, 2nd ed., Frankfurt am Main 1974, p. 274).

existence of norms. The objection of the "infinite regress" accordingly seems to me unjustified.

In order to constitute a *reason* justifying our behaviour, the norm must be capable of supplying a valid criterion for a potentially infinite number of cases.[86] This has been put very well by John Searle too: "Two of the marks of rule-governed as opposed to merely regular behaviour are that we generally recognize deviations from the pattern as somehow wrong or defective and that the rule unlike the past regularity automatically covers new cases. Confronted with a case he has never seen before, the agent knows what to do".[87] The norm, in so far as it develops a directive function for human conduct, is fundamentally directed to the future, always regulating new situations, similar and yet different from those for which the solution had originated. The norm is then not so much a "stimulus" followed by direct or indirect (conditioned) reflex, and at any rate *non-reflectively*, by certain behaviour (Pavlov's dog's salivation, for instance, when the red light went on) but a *general* model of action which, in order to "bring about" certain behaviour has to come to form part of our chain of reasoning, which ultimately leads us as conclusion to the representation (and intention) of the *specific* action to be performed.

Thus the behaviourist theory can scarcely succeed in giving an account of judicial error. If the law consists in the behaviour of judges, and only in that, there will not by definition be any criterion for assessing the "correctness" or "legality" of this behaviour. The problem of "correctness", indeed, does not even arise. It would not, then, be possible, from the viewpoint of behaviourist theory, to speak of judicial errors. This is also true for the verificationist version, which resolves the norms into "predictions" about courts' behaviour.[88]

3.6.6 The mentalist or psychologistic theory of representation, by which the meaning of a proposition depends on the mental representation of the utterer, leads to considering a norm valid only when it in some way corresponds to the will of the subject producing it.[89] Here too the norm tends to be identified with a prescription or a command. But the "command" too, like the "stimulus", by contrast with the norm, acts only in specific contexts, in concrete situations, so that their being typified by legal norms would seem to be ruled out. Commands, like "stimuli", can be directed only at definite subjects, so that one would have to rule out the possibility of norms being directed to indefinite *generalities* of subject. In short, commands

[86] "In der Natur der Regel liegt es," writes Waismann, "*wiederholt* angewendet zu werden in einer unbegrenzten Zahl von Fällen" (F. Waismann, *Logik, Sprache, Philosophie*, p. 209, my emphasis).

[87] J. R. Searle, *Speech Acts. An Essay in the Philosophy of Language*, Cambridge 1969, p. 42.

[88] On this cf. the critical considerations of D. N. MacCormick, *Institution Morality and the Constitution*, in D. N. MacCormick and O. Weinberger, *An Institutional Theory of Law*, Dordrecht, pp. 171ff. It is interesting to recall that in Wittgenstein's philosophy it is fundamental to the notion of following a rule that it be logically inseparable from the notion of *making a mistake*. If it is meaningful to say that a certain person is following a rule, that means that it may also be asked whether what they are doing is being done correctly or not or else is mistaken.

[89] The concept of the norm as "declaration of will" often leads to reducing the normative statement to a descriptive statement: see R. M. Hare, *The Language of Morals*, Oxford 1986, pp. 5ff.

act *inter-personally*, between identified or identifiable subjects; the same cannot be said of norms. As Waismann notes, "a command necessarily presupposes a subject giving the command; a rule does not".[90] The mentalist theory is, then, particularly unsatisfactory when it comes to interpreting the norm.

If the meaning of the norm depends on the legislator's mental representation and its validity on his will, the interpreter's activity must consist in ascertaining the historical will of the legislator. This however raises a series of problems that are hard to solve. It is very hard to ascertain the "historical" will of the legislator, for at least two reasons. (i) There are no means of knowing with certainty the actual psychological will of a subject. (ii) The legislator is in actuality often not a physical subject, but an *institution* (parliament, the central committee, the administrative board etc.), to which will in the psychological sense cannot properly be ascribed.[91]

Norms have a duration in time that often goes beyond the instance of their promulgation. They serve to guide the behaviour of subjects in very different situations from those in being when they were issued. Interpreting norms by reference to the "historical" or "orginal" will of the legislator would mean restricting the sphere of operationality of the norms to particular situations, preventing them from instead having their efficacy extended to *new* situations and relations. An "historical" or "originalist" interpretation of norms often, therefore, has the grave defect of frequently being entirely inadequate in relation to the problems it is called upon to solve.[92] It is also possible that a norm has been laid down as concretisation of a more basic principle which is part of a general moral or political coneption. In such case the norm is valid only as an instantiation of a principle that has to be traced back to give the norm its sense. In this context the lawgiver's intention refers back to a normative standard (a principle and its conception) which is the bearer of an independent content and hence could not be singled out simply through "history", "originality" or "genealogy".

An interpretation founded on the sense attributed to the statement only by thc utterer or only by the recipient, that is, centred on the *intention* or will of the persons, leads to unacceptable consequences both in the case of the law, and, if not even more so, in that of the contract. In the case of a law, if it is to have ascribed to it the meaning originally attributed to it by the legislator, then any extensive, analogical, evolutionary or "principled" interpretation would not seem very plausible (quite apart from the almost insuperable difficulties involved in ascertaining the actual will of the subjects that might come under the denotation of the term "legislator"). Where it is instead held that the law is to be interpreted according to how it has been understood by the recipient or addressee, or according to the meaning the latter attributes to it, it would be hard to justify the principle "ignorantia legis non excusat", that is, a standard according to which citizens' ignorance of laws' content does not supply an

---

[90] F. Waismann, *Logik, Sprache, Philosophie*, p. 209.

[91] Cf. K. Olivecrona, *Law as Fact*, Copenhagen 1939, pp. 35ff.

[92] Cf. A. Falzea, *Introduzione alle scienze giuridiche*, Part One, *Il concetto di diritto*, 3rd ed., Milan 1988, pp. 241ff.

excuse for any breach of the law – actually a clause which is generally accepted in modern legal orders. Moreover, ascertaining breach of the norm, and hence responsibility for this, would be strongly dependent on the individual subject's wish to comply with it. This consequence would make futile the very function of law, that of guiding the behaviour of those in society over and above, and even contrary to, the permanent consensus of individuals in relation to the norm's content.

In the case of contract, the negative consequences of a subjectivist conception (from the viewpoint of both utterer and recipient) of interpretation have been highlighted by countless generations of jurists. These may be exemplified by what Karl Anton von Martini, an Eighteenth century Austrian natural lawyer, wrote regarding this: "It is here first of all to consider that interpretation cannot be made dependent either on the speaker's or on the addressee' will. In fact, if they were both free to give words whatever meaning they like, then the promissor would soon give less than he promised, and the promissee would claim more rights than those that were given to him".[93]

3.7 An "Institutionalist" Theory of Language

3.7.1 The theory of meaning that seems to me to give the best account of the linguistic phenomenon is the one called that of "use". As we know, this theory was developed by Ludwig Wittgenstein after he had rejected the positions maintained in his *Tractatus logico-philosophicus* that he had defended until the end of the Twenties.[94] "The meaning of a phrase for us," maintains the Viennese philosopher, "is characterized by the use we make of it".[95] The theory of "use", however, perhaps largely because of the aphoristic style adopted by Wittgenstein in expounding his ideas, seems rather obscure, and has, I feel, sometimes been misunderstood.[96] This is especially true of the idea that "use", connected to the intention of the speaker, would be nothing but a contextual and individual employment of the term.[97]

One point is important to stress. The "use" Wittgenstein refers to, in placing this at the foundation of linguistic meanings, is not a pure and simple "habit", the

---

[93]"Vor allem ist hier dieses zu beobachten, daß die Auslegung weder ganz dem Willen des Redenden, noch ganz dem Willen des Hörenden gemacht werden dürfe. Denn wenn es von ihnen abhinge, den Worten eine beliebige Bedeutung zu geben, so würde bald der versprechende Teil weniger leisten wollen als er wirklich versprochen hat, bald der annehmende sich mehr Recht anmaßen, als ihm übertragen worden ist" (K. A. von Martini, *Lehrbegriff des Naturrechts*, Vienna 1799, pp. 235–236).

[94]See e.g., *Wittgenstein und der Wiener Kreis*, ed. by F. Waismann, pp. 47–48.

[95]L. Wittgenstein, *The Blue Book*, p. 65, see also *ibid.*, p. 69: "The use of a word in practice is its meaning" (emphasis in original).

[96]In this regard, cf. the considerations of V. Villa, *Conoscenza giuridica e concetto di diritto positivo*, Torino 1993, pp. 303ff.

[97]Cf. Q. Skinner, *Meaning and Understanding in the History of Ideas*, now in *Meaning and Context. Quentin Skinner and His Critics*, ed. by J. Tully, Oxford 1988, p. 65.

mechanical repetition of particular behaviour, but resembles a "custom" in the legal sense, that is, the repetition of conduct in awareness (where we ask or are asked about the meaning of this conduct) of its "rightfulness" (the *opinio iuris* of legal doctrine). Linguistic "use" in Wittgenstein's sense is founded not upon "regularity" but on "rules".

The use Wittgenstein refers to must possess three fundamental requisites: (i) it must be continuous in time, repeated and consolidated, that is, there must be "ständiger Gebrauch"[98]; (ii) it must be a collective human activity, a "gemeinsame menschliche Handlungsweise"[99]; (iii) it must, finally, be based on norms, not so much in the sense that the behaviour in question can be made to agree with these, but that it presupposes them,[100] that is, that these norms constitute a condition or better a *reason* for the behaviour.

The "normativist" interpretation of Wittgenstein's theory of meaning as "use" is accepted, among others, by one of the most respected German logicians and philosophers of language, Franz von Kutschera. "By use", he writes, "it is not a number of individual uses that is intended, but the *mode of use*. This mode is determined by general rules of use, which tell us in what cases that particular word is used".[101] If, then, the meaning of a term is to be made to coincide with its use, adds von Kutschera, one has to indicate the rules for its *correct* use. Thus von Kutschera distinguishes between the meaning of a linguistic expression and the meaning of its utterance. While the first type of meaning results from the rules determining the "use" of the linguistic expression, the second type of meaning results from those rules plus the actual context in which the utterance occurred. One example of this difference (which, significantly, we again find in Ota Weinberger's work[102]) is the linguistic expression "it is raining", which (i) has a meaning as such (determined by the rules for its "use") and (ii) a meaning as a statement in a given pragmatic context: it may serve as information or warning (say, to suggest not forgetting an umbrella) or as a request for action (to suggest closing the window, for instance).[103]

The concept of "use" (and that of meaning connected with it) are intimately bound up in the thought of the "late" Wittgenstein with two other concepts: "language game" and "form of life". The use of a sign that determines its meaning is not, for Wittgenstein, the merely individual use, but the use that forms part of

[98] L. Wittgenstein, *Philosophische Untersuchungen*, p. 198.

[99] *Ibid.*, § 206, *Philosophical Investigations*, p. 82e.

[100] See L. Wittgenstein, *The Blue Book*, p. 13.

[101] F. von Kutschera, *Sprachphilosophie*, 2nd ed., Munich 1975, p. 141. Emphasis in original. Against, however, G. P. Baker and P. M. S. Hacker, *Wittgenstein: Rules, Grammar and Necessity*, Oxford 1986, who interpret the concept of "rule" in Wittgenstein as "regularity", not bound up with any use by a community. For a critique of Baker and Hacker's theses cf. N. Malcom, *Wittgenstein on Language and Rules*, in *Philosophy*, 1989, pp. 5–28.

[102] See O. Weinberger, *Die Norm als Gedanke und Realität*, in D. N. MacCormick and O. Weinberger, *Grundlagen des Institutionalistischen Rechtspositivismus*, Berlin 1985.

[103] See F. von Kutschera, *Op. cit.*, pp. 143ff. Cf. A. J. Ayer, *Freedom and Morality and Other Essays*, Oxford 1985, p. 24.

a "language game", or of a certain "language".[104] Not every use of a sign, then, attributes to it a "meaning", but only use taking place within a "language game". On the other hand, not every individual use of a sign, term, or utterance constitutes a "language game". This is because, according to Wittgenstein, the "language game" is (i) governed by rules and (ii) the expression of a "form of life", that is, of a certain community practice. I cannot, accordingly, agree with those who maintain that for Wittgenstein a linguistic expression "has meaning only in the use made of it, indeed, only in the use made of it within an utterance, indeed, only in the use made of it *within the specific utterance of a statement, as an atomic move* in the language game".[105]

To determine the meaning of linguistic expressions, Wittgenstein goes back to their typical use, and hence to the "language game" to which that use belongs. The meaning of a sign is defined as the role that sign performs in a certain language game.[106] Thus "nonsense" originates in the fact that a sign is used outside the "language game" proper to it, that is, in breach of the rules governing that game.

The theory of meaning as "use", in short, is a *normativist* theory in the sense that it connects the meaning of linguistic expressions to compliance with certain norms and rules, and understanding of the meaning with knowledge of the rules in question. Without rules, the words and statements have no meaning, and if the rules change, words and statements either lose their meaning, or take on a new one.[107] On the other hand, the theory of "use" is an *institutionalist* theory because the rules which according to the theory guide language use are the expression of an organized or institutionalized social reality, of a "form of life", or of an "institution". Wittgenstein speaks explicitly of "institution": "Ein Spiel, eine Sprache, eine Regel ist eine *Institution*".[108] "It is not possible," he writes in a famous passage, "that there should have been only one occasion on which someone obeyed a rule. It is not possible that there should have been only one occasion on which a report was made, an order given or understood; and so on. To obey a rule, to make a report, to give an order, to play a game of chess, are *customs* (uses, institutions)".[109] As we see, here the term "use" is employed as a synonym for "institution".

According to Wittgenstein, rules by themselves are not enough to determine the meaning of linguistic expressions. Rules must, in order for the meaning of the "uses"

---

[104] It is interesting to note here that Karl Bühler distinguishes between an "occasional aspect" and a "usual aspect" of linguistic meaning, attributing to the latter the quality of being the basis for the dictionary and the grammar of a language: see K. Bühler, *Die Krise der Psychologie*, pp. 124–125.

[105] M. Barberis, *Il diritto come discorso e come comportamento. Trenta lezioni di filosofia del diritto*, Giappichelli, Turin 1990, p. 144. My emphasis.

[106] See L. Wittgenstein, *Philosophical Investigations* (I, 49, 261), pp. 24e, 93e.

[107] See L. Wittgenstein, *Philosophische Grammatik* (133), p. 184.

[108] L. Wittgenstein, *Bemerkungen über die Grundlagen der Mathematik*, Frankfurt am Main 1989, p. 334. Italics mine.

[109] L. Wittgenstein, *Philosophical Investigations* (I, 199) p. 80e, emphasis in original. On the other hand, *believing one is following a rule* is not, for Wittgenstein, equivalent to *following* a rule (on this see also J. Schulte, *Wittgenstein. Eine Einführung*, Stuttgart 1989, p. 161). See 3.7.3 below.

they govern to be understood, be connected with the "form of life" of which they are an expression. It is the "form of life" that is the original source of meaning. Language, for the Austrian philosopher, is not an "instrument" for some end (even the end of communication), but an end in itself as a cultural phenomenon. Regarding this Anthony Kenny notes, "language cannot, taken all round, be seen as a means for some extra-linguistic purpose; it cannot be held that the 'communication of ideas' constitutes an end as such, since there are so many ideas that cannot even be thought of without language".[110]

3.7.2 As has been noted,[111] the theory of meaning as use is charged with a considerable dose of ambiguity and indeterminacy. This is in part due to its eminently critical and polemic nature: it is, as we know, directed chiefly against the language philosophy expressed by the "early" Wittgenstein in the famous *Tractatus*. In the theory of use, in short, the Austrian philosopher was settling accounts with himself. This ambiguity obviously lends itself to the most varied interpretations and the most eccentric misunderstandings. In particular, the theory of use is often seen as an instrumentalist conception, that is, an individualistic, behaviourist, pragmatic conception, of language.

Accepting the instrumentalist interpretation of the theory of use, then "for Wittgenstein", as Eike von Savigny writes, "an expression has meaning if and insofar as a certain purpose is achieved by its use; and the object achieved sets the meaning. For instance 'close the door!' is a command to close the door because it is uttered with the intention of having the door closed, and because this object is in fact achieved by it. In contradistinction with this, our interpretation maintains that the expression has its meaning because closing the door is sanctioned as the appropriate conduct in relation to the expression by all those speaking the language, irrespective of whether its utterer intended that conduct thereby".[112]

Savigny accordingly holds that the meaning of a linguistic expression is not the (individual) object intended to be secured by it, but the conduct that is considered appropriate in relation to the expression by members of the language community. Savigny's proposal has, however, the flaw of falling back into behaviourism. For

---

[110] A. Kenny, *Wittgenstein*, Harmondsworth 1976, p. 168. Cf. L. Wittgenstein, *Philosophische Grammatik* (133ff.), pp. 184ff. "Notice that all these theories which I have sketched – Frege, the *Tractatus*, logical positivism – have certain characteristics in common. They all assume that the only, at any rate the primary, aim of language is to represent and communicate factual information, that the part of language that really counts is the 'cognitive' part. The aim of language, in short, is to communicate what can be true or false [...] In the late thirties and especially after the Second World War these assumptions came to be vigorously challenged, especially by Wittgenstein. Wittgenstein argued that stating facts is only one of the countless jobs we do with language" (J. R. Searle, *Introduction*, in *The Philosophy of Language*, ed. by J. R. Searle, Oxford 1971, p. 6). The "gratuitousness" of language and its link not so much with the phenomenon of "communication" as with that of "ideation" is asserted on the basis of very plausible argument by S. K. Langer, *Philosophy in a New Key*, second printing of 3rd ed., Cambridge, MA 1960, pp. 109ff.

[111] See E. von Savigny, *Die Philosophie der normalen Sprache. Eine kritische Einführung in die "ordinary language philosophy"*, Frankfurt am Main 1969, pp. 76–77.

[112] *Ibid.*, p. 77.

the German scholar, meaning, though not being a "response" causally determined by the "stimulus" constituted by the linguistic expression, is nonetheless what is considered to be the correct *reaction* to the expression. Meaning here is still a *behaviour*, which this time does not derive directly or causally from the linguistic expression (or, if you wish, because of a relation between two subjects, the utterer and recipient of the expression). It is instead the outcome of a twofold process of social conditioning. Above all, meaning has its origin in the *sharing* supported by the community for which that behaviour would be the one correctly "corresponding" to the linguistic expression. Moreover, the community's "sanction" is held to be necessary (social pressure exercised on the individual speakers) in order for that particular behaviour to be regarded as that which *ought* to correspond to the linguistic expression.

Yet quite apart from the many problems common to behaviourist theories that obviously arise here again, the most obvious weakness of Savigny's proposal is that it is silent on the crucial point: that of the "correspondence" between linguistic expression and a behavioural act. How can it be affirmed or denied that a piece of behaviour "corresponds" with a linguistic expression? Is there perhaps not a need, for such an affirmation or denial, to assume some sort of representational quality, some sort of semantic element, that can be drawn from the linguistic expression and may constitute the main criterion for the "correspondence"? The only other way to ascertain the "correspondence" with linguistic expression is that based on a causalist hypothesis whereby conduct "corresponds" with an expression when the latter is either only the sufficient or the necessary and sufficient condition for the conduct. But this path is ruled out by Savigny, and, as we have seen, is still more loaded with problems than Savigny's moderate behaviourist proposals. All that is left, then, is to take the road of a definition of meaning in terms that are *also* semantic (representational).

The problem of the "correspondence" between linguistic expression and certain behaviour (held ultimately to constitute its meaning) brings us back to the more general question of *compliance* with a rule or norm. It might be said that a norm is complied with when the normative act succeeds in "bringing about" or "causing" the addressee's conduct. This opinion presupposes a conception of the norm specifically as (normative) *act*, that is, either as a stimulus to act or as a "speech act". On a more moderate version of the same conception it might be stated that a norm is observed when it succeeds not so much in causally bringing about in the strong sense (according to the stimulus/response scheme) the addressee's conduct, as in *motivating* it. "But surely", noted Kazimierz Opalek, a distinguished Polish legal philosopher, "there are numerous instances in which the conduct 'fulfilling' or 'not-fulfilling' the normative act is by no means motivated by the latter. Whatever the motive of the addressee would be, his conduct can be said either one 'fulfilling' or one 'not-fulfilling' the directive act. By simply confronting the normative act and a given conduct one can say that the latter 'fulfils' the former, or not".[113]

---

[113] K. Opalek, *Norm and Conduct. The Problem of the "Fulfillment" of the Norm*, in *Le raisonnement juridique. Actes du Congrès mondial de Philosophie du Droit et de Philosophie Sociale* (Brussels, 30 August–3 September 1971), ed. by H. Hubien, Brussels 1971, p. 113.

Nonetheless, by simply comparing the normative act and the given behaviour it is not so easy to ascertain whether the norm has been complied with, especially if the idea of the norm as an "act" or a "performative" is maintained, rather than in some sense a *semantic* entity. How could there be a "comparison" between one act and another, in short between one piece of behaviour and another, such as to enable us to define the ensuing act or piece of behaviour as a "realization" or "accomplishment" of the previous act or behaviour? In order for a "comparison" and therefore a possible "correspondence" (or "realization" or "accomplishment") to be possible, as Professor Scarpelli noted in his *Contributo alla semantica del linguaggio normative*,[114] it is necessary as terms of comparison to have on the one hand a class of states of affairs or events in some way evoked or represented by the norm, and on the other a specific piece of behaviour that may be subsumed within the class of events represented and prescribed or described by the norm in question. This observation, which seems to me hard to contradict, has to have its influence on the adoption of the most suitable theory of meaning for giving an account of the normative phenomenon. The lesson that may be drawn from this observation is that in order to explain the semantics and the functioning of norms as reasons or motives for action, a theory of use is not enough. It is necessary for the latter to include, in some way and in some sense, or to also take into consideration, the *representational* element of normative statements in which rules and norms of every type can be expressed.[115]

"Use" in Wittgenstein's theory, in any case, is not a merely arbitrary, entirely subjective, fact (on the part of the utterer and/or recipient of the linguistic utterance), as, for instance, those who see use as only "individual use" or even those who stress the "intentional" element end up maintaining. Nor is, according to Wittgenstein, use a fact founded entirely on conventional rules. "Use" is here an element in a *context*: a programme or a form of life. Is the meaning, asks Wittgenstein, really only the use of the word? "Isnt't it the way this use meshes with our life?".[116] And he replies: "Well, language does connect up with my own life. And what is called 'language' is something made up of heterogeneous elements and the way it meshes with life is infinitely various".[117]

What is not perhaps too clear is *how* Wittgenstein sees language meshing with life. Sometimes he tends to refer the "use" to a "calculus", to some kind of syntactical exercise whereby signs or "things" in a table or scheme are conventionally related to other signs or "things" in another table or scheme. So that Waismann, faithful to his master's original inspiration, can conclude that "it is often impossible to give the meaning of a word without paying attention to the way it is

---

[114]Second edition, ed. by A. Pintore, Milan 1984.

[115]Not prejudging here the question whether, for a norm to be observed, there must also be the *intention* to observe it, as some affirm (see, e.g., G. J. Warnock, *The Object of Morality*, London 1971, pp. 35–36). In this regard, read the sixth paragraph of the following chapter.

[116]L. Wittgenstein, *Philosophical Grammar* (§ 29), p. 65. Cf. J. Habermas, *Vorlesungen zu einer sprachtheoretischen Grundlegung der Soziologie*, in Id., *Vorstudien und Ergänzungen zur Theorie des kommunikativen Handelns*, Frankfurt am Main 1984, p. 73.

[117]L. Wittgenstein, *Philosophical Grammar* (§ 29), p. 66.

connected with other words in speech, that is to say, to the rules of its syntactical employment".[118] Now, this "sintactical"exercise is then related to "training", and is based on this as its "bedrock" or final explanation and justification. "Training" here becomes the source of meaningful action, and seems to be founded on behavioural responses, thus more or less implying a causalist view of the relationship between sign and meaning. On the other hand, "training" here seems also to be able to do without an opening to some objective world external to it.[119]

3.7.3 If the theory of language as "use" in Wittgenstein's sense is accepted (albeit with the reservations just mentioned) one is in some way committed to an institutionalist theory, first of language and then in general of normative phenomena (and hence also of law). The "use" Wittgenstein speaks of can well be defined as an "institution" in the sense of a complex of actions rendered possible by rules. This conception enables us to uphold a fundamental distinction for understanding the dynamics of normative phenomena, specifically legal ones: the distinction between the validity and the efficacy of the norm. The validity of a norm can not be reduced to its efficacy, so that the empirical observation of regularity of behaviour does not yet tell us anything about the norm that (possibly) governs it, or is "implicit" (involved, in Wittgenstein's words[120]) in that series of pieces of behaviour. "Whether a rule is followed or not", writes Waismann, "can only be discovered by actually observing the moves people make in the play. The validity of a rule is independent of such observations".[121]

For Wittgenstein, the existence of a rule does not depend on its "recognition" by the subject or the majority of subjects. For instance, when we employ "equal" as a predicate, we do not mean that equal is what most people believe it is such, but we raise a claim that can be fulfilled in an independent way.[122] Nor can the existence of a rule be reduced to the *conviction* that it exists, just as following a rule does not perfectly coincide with the conviction of following it. We usually say that we believe, for instance, that a contract is put into force so-and-so. But, remarks Wittgenstein, what in this case we really mean is not that we believe in a special contract rule, but that we believe that a rule's content is such-and-such.[123]

118 F. Waismann, *The Principles of Linguistic Philosophy*, p. 187.

119 For a criticism to Wittgenstein's approach, stressing his behaviourist and causalist assumptions, see U. Steinvorth, *Warum überhaupt etwas ist. Kleine demiurgische Metaphysik*, Reinbeck bei Hamburg 1994, Chapter 3.

120 See L. Wittgenstein, *The Blue Book*, p. 13, where a distinction is drawn between being in accordance with a rule and involving a rule.

121 F. Waismann, *The Principles of Linguistic Philosophy*, p. 142.

122 "Und heißt das nun etwa, die Definition von 'Gleich' wäre die: Gleich sei was alle oder die meisten Menschen übereinstimmend so ansehen? – Freilich nicht" (L. Wittgenstein, *Bemerkungen über die Grundlagen der Mathematik*, p. 406).

123 "Vergleiche: Wenn du sagst: 'Ich glaube, daß das Rochieren so und so geschieht', so glaubst du nicht die Schachregel, sondern du glaubst etwa, daß *so* eine Regel des Schachs lautet" (*ibid.*, p. 78, emphasis in original).

For Wittgenstein, the rule does not exist independently of the practice in which it is observed. A rule and its sense are part of a "language game" and this is a practice. To speak of rules is to tell about the rule following conducts; so that it is a practice what gives a rule its real dimension.[124] The very concept of "complying with a rule", accordingly, implies the idea of *practice*.[125]

Further, there is more than one similarity between Wittgenstein's philosophy of language and "classical" institutionalist theory of law, in particular Santi Romano's. Regarding this one should recall the comparison drawn by Romano between "society" and "games" ("Society being like a game that cannot exist without rules"[126]) and the conception of the phenomenon of law and that of language as homologous, as both being (i) normative (ii) human and yet (iii) involuntary. "Usage and spoken language", writes Romano, "insofar as they start from the formation and stabilization of practice, are in and for themselves nothing but facts: both 'normative facts', from which 'oritur ius' and, respectively, the complex of rules that the language obeys".[127]

On the other hand, it is not by chance that one of the neo-institutionalist theoreticians of law, Professor Ota Weinberger, explicitly adopts the theory of meaning as "use". "What statements of ordinary language mean depends", writes this scholar, "on the way they are understood by those who use the language".[128] Weinberger explicitly posits a link between his institutionalist theory and the conception of language developed by the "late" Wittgenstein. This is particularly so where the Czech scholar notes that neither legal norms nor the rules of ordinary language are always explicitly formulated, and stresses that each have a constitutive nature, in

---

[124]"Ja, der Ausdruck der Regel und sein Sinn ist nur ein Teil des Sprachspiels: der Regel folgen. Man kann mit dem *gleichen* Recht allgemein von solchen Regeln sprechen, wie von den Tätigkeiten, ihnen zu folgen" (*ibid.*, p. 409, emphasis in original). "Die Regel ist als Regel losgelöst, steht, sozusagen, selbstherrlich da; obschon was ihr Wichtigkeit gibt, die Tatsachen der täglichen Erfahrung sind" (*ibid.*, p. 357).

[125]"Der Begriff des Regelfolgens ist untrennbar mit dem Gedanken der Einübung in eine praktische Handlungsweise" (J. Schulte, *Wittgenstein. Eine Einführung*, p. 161).

[126]S. Romano, *L'ordinamento giuridico*, 3rd ed., Florence 1977, p. 125. On the genesis of this work cf. S. Cassese, *Ipotesi sulla formazione de "l'ordinamento giuridico" di Santi Romano*, in Id., *La formazione dello Stato amministrativo*, Milano 1974, pp. 21ff.

[127]S. Romano, *Frammenti di un dizionario giuridico*, 2nd ed., Milano 1983, p. 45. The analogy between "institution" and language is met with again in another Italian "institutionalist", W. Cesarini Sforza, *Filosofia del diritto*, 3rd ed., Milano 1958, p. 38; and cf. A. Baratta, *Presentazione*, in M. Hariou, *Teoria dell'istituzione e della fondazione*, ed. by W. Cesarini Sforza, Milan 1967, p. XIX. "There are important formal analogies between language and other social institutions", writes no lesser "Wiitgensteinian" than Peter Winch (P. Winch, *Nature and Convention*, in Id., *Ethics and Action*, London 1972, p. 70).

[128]O. Weinberger, *Ontologie, Hermeneutik und der Begriff des geltenden Rechts*, in Id., *Recht, Institution und Rechtspolitik. Grundprobleme der Rechtstheorie und Sozialphilosophie*, Stuttgart 1987, p. 124. See also C. Weinberger and O. Weinberger, *Logik, Semantik, Hermeneutik*, Munich 1979, pp. 161–162. Here the importance of the theory of meaning as "use" to those who study so-called "practical" languages (moral, legal etc.) is stressed.

a broad sense.[129] It should further be recalled in this connection that the Czech scholar rejects the referential theory of meaning, since this has two outcomes for normative statements that are both unacceptable: (i) on the one hand, it deprives them of all meaning; (ii) or else on the other it presupposes – à la Meinong – a series of "entities" that correspond to those statements.[130] Thus – for Weinberger – the norm is not an object standing by itself, "which can be recognized [*erkannt*], but always an ideal construction that can be grasped [*erfaßt*] only hermeneutically [*verstehend*]".[131] Moreover, Weinberger rejects all approach that says that a statement can have two different meanings, depending on which side of the language relationship (either the addresser's or the addressee's) is taken into account. Meaning – to allow information and communication – should have a common, unitary core which cannot be too much differentiated according to the speaker's or hearer's perspective.

3.8 The Concept of Law. A First Approximation

From the "late" Wittgentein's philosophy, once the institutionalist theory of language is accepted, we could draw a few first, tentative conclusions about the concept of law.

In legal theory we usually find four basic approaches. (i) The first and traditionally more common is the voluntarist theory, that according to which law is a set of commands or wills or decisions. This approach relates either to the "ideational" theory of meaning or to a "causalist" approach to language. It could also correspond to an "intentional" theory of meaning, which says that statements' meanings are basically "intentions" of the speaker, or better refer to these conveying them to an addressee. (ii) A second, quite widespread approach connects law and "rules" or "norms". This is a normativist conception, according to which norms are semantical contents, or "judgments" (*Urteile*), as is the case of Hans Kelsen's "pure" doctrine of law. This approach as well often relates to a lingustic "representational" or "ideational" theory. Or else it may also base on a "referential" theory, once the content of norms is seen as a picture of specific and idiosincratic states of affairs in the world in a descriptive mood, as is the case of "normative platonism". (iii) We the have a third approach which tends to see law in terms of natural laws, or "regularities", the fact of some conduct regularly and consistently repeated in time. Legal validity here is often reinterpreted in terms of effectiveness. An approach of this kind more or less explicitly refers to linguistic theory shaped as a causal effect

[129] See O. Weinberger, *Institutionentheorie und institutionalistischer Rechtspositivismus*, in Id., *Recht, Institution und Rechtspolitik*, p. 176. It is hard, however, to understand the reason for Weinberger's decisive criticism of the theory of constitutive rules as rules distinct from regulative (prescriptive) ones.

[130] See O. Weinberger, *Soziologie und normative Institutionentheorie. Uberlegungen zu Helmut Schelskys Institutionentheorie vom Standpunkt der normativistischen Institutionenontologie*, in Id., *Recht, Institution und Rechtspolitik*, p. 187.

[131] Ibid., p. 188.

or as verification. (iv) A fourth approach is the one upheld by several sociological theories. Here legal facts are a variable of natural states of affairs or are a version of these, or else they can be referred to an ontology which is akin to the empiricist one. Law in any case is a "system" among other "systems" governed more or less through similar functional laws. This conception is very close to the idea of law as "regularity", but is distinct from it in its greater stress on the functional relationships between law and other parts of the social system. It also base mostly on a teleological perspective. This conception, nonetheless, also relates to a causalist, or "naturalist" theory of meaning.

Now, if the "institutionalist" theory of language offered by the "late" Wittgenstein, with the many associated considerations on the notion of "rule", is accepted, then all the four approaches to the concept of law just listed have to be rejected.

Chapter 4
Law as Institution

4.1 Preliminary

Now that some of the major theories of meaning have been analysed, albeit perhaps too rapidly, and a certain theory of meaning (the so-called theory of meaning as "use") and a certain view on the analysis of social and legal phenomena (the "institutionalist" one), have been linked, we need to consider this perspective more closely. The previous chapter sought to show, first, that the institutionalist approach finds justification in its analysis of normative phenomena in the broad sense, that is, of phenomena expressed in, or governed by, rules. There is an inextricable link between language, social behaviour and rules, the institutionalist perspective contributes to identifying it fairly clearly. This nexus is relevant not only to the analysis of language, but also, and chiefly, to the study of law.

Second, the previous chapter sought to show that a "liberal" approach, attentive to the problems of analysis of language and oriented (*cum grano salis*) towards the neo-empiricist, positivist *Weltanschauung*, in the field of legal theory, does not necessarily lead to prescriptivism, or to a reductionist realism. Between "analytical philosophy" and "analytical jurisprudence" (à la Bentham or à la Austin, to be specific) there is not much more than a terminological resemblance. Nor does analytical philosophy, understood in a broad sense and incorporating the "institutionalist" approach to the theory of meaning pioneered by the "late" Wittgenstein, have inevitably to end up in prescriptivist meta-ethics (à la Hare). This was used for the internal reform of imperativist, legal positivist doctrine. From Bentham's and Austin's "commands" to the "prescriptions" or "precepts" of Richard M. Hare, Alf Ross and Uberto Scarpelli, the distance is by no means far. On the other hand, one can remain a noncognitivist without necessarily having to embrace a prescriptivist theory of value judgements and of norms. One can plausibly claim that the class of normative sentences is larger than the class of imperative or prescriptive sentences (if one thinks of norms which instead of creating obligations, attribute powers).

M. La Torre, *Law as Institution*, Law and Philosophy Library 90,
DOI 10.1007/978-1-4020-6607-8_4, © Springer Science+Business Media B.V. 2010

4.2 Santi Romano's Theory of Law

4.2.1 The most significant texts on the institutionalist theory of law are the works of Maurice Hauriou and Santi Romano. Institutionalist legal thinking has in the Twentieth century been very influential particularly in France, Italy and Germany. However, there has been a steady exhaustion of the "driving force" of this theory. We are indeed indebted to the work of Neil MacCormick and Ota Weinberger for reopening discussion of institutionalism in the context of the theory of law. Here I shall concentrate my attention on Santi Romano's work. I begin with some particularly important methodological questions, in relation to which there are four points that need emphasis.

Above all, remember that Romano always claimed that the legal scholar should use the positive-law method. He proposed to proceed keeping "strictly to the ground of a legal positivist conception of law, avoiding any natural law view".[1] But what does Romano mean by "positive conception of law"? I would say a conception of law as it *is* in reality, and not as it ought to be according to certain principles.

Romano draws a clear distinction between the spheres of law and of morals. He uses this separation as a further argument in favour of his thesis of the plurality of legal orders. Consider, for instance, the following section: "It is", he writes, "well known how, under the threat of State laws, there often live, in the shadows, associations whose organization might be said to be almost analogous, in miniature, to the State's: they have legislative and executive authorities, tribunals that resolve controversies and give punishments, agents that inexorably execute the punishments, statutes drafted and clarified like governmental laws. They accordingly create an order of their own just like the State's and the institutions it makes lawful. Denying these orders the quality of being legal can only be the consequence of an ethical evaluation, because such entities are often criminal or immoral; which would be admissible, were that necessary and absolute dependency of positive law on morality shown which, according to us, does not in that sense, which seems to us very ingenuous, actually exist".[2] "So-called immoral or unjust law", Romano adds still more explicitly, "is no less law than the moral kind".[3]

The Sicilian theorist conceives the notion of institution not as a merely systematic concept, but as representation of a segment of reality. "The institution", he writes, "is not a requirement of reason, an abstract principle, some ideal thing; it is instead a real, actual entity".[4]

Romano anticipates the distinction drawn by Hart, following hints from Peter Winch, between "internal viewpoint" and "external viewpoint" in the study of legal

[1] S. Romano, *L'ordinamento giuridico*, p. 96. On the continuing adherence of Romano's institutionalism to legal posititivism cf. G. Fassò, *Il giudice e l'adeguamento del diritto alla realtà storico-sociale*, in Id., *Scritti di filosofia del diritto*, ed. by E. Pattaro, C. Faralli and G. Zucchini, vol. 3, Milan 1982, p. 993.

[2] S. Romano, *L'ordinamento giuridico*, pp. 123–124.

[3] S. Romano, *Frammenti di un dizionario giuridico*, p. 72.

[4] S. Romano, *L'ordinamento giuridico*, p. 96.

phenomena.[5] Romano asserts that the typical viewpoint of the lawyer – which he takes – is not the "external", but the "internal". Consider the following passage. "We", he writes, "have considered this entity [the institution] not from the viewpoint of the material forces that produce it and govern it, not in relation to the environment in which it develops and lives as a phenomenon interdependent with others, not in relation to the causal nexuses and effects bound up with it, and thus not sociologically; but in itself and for itself, as it results from a legal order, indeed, is a system of objective law".[6]

One fundamental distinction in Romano's institutionalist theory is the very basic one between (a) the law as one or more norm considered individually and (b) the law as the entire legal order. Romano concentrates his attention on the latter aspect, on the law as an order, since he considers that it is the fundamental one. In a certain sense, Romano here anticipates Kelsen's distinction between "nomostatic" and "nomodynamic", highlighting well the "dynamic" element in the legal order, in particular, as far as the State order is concerned, conceived of as an order of orders.[7]

Let us now seek to identify the, as it were, "differential" characteristics of the legal order according to Romano's theory. First of all, some negative features. The legal order is not a mere sum of norms. "The nature of a legal order is not fully grasped and cannot be if one considers not its entirety but the various norms making it up: the *quid* that constitutes that entirety is something different from the latter, and at least to a certain extent independent of them".[8] The legal order, according to Romano, is not a sum of legal relations either.[9] This thesis differentiates him from some other Italian theorists of legal institutionalism, in particular from Widar Cesarini Sforza and from Guido Fassò.[10]

Cesarini Sforza – following Hauriou – counterposes "objectivist" to "subjectivist" conceptions of law. The former are, he asserts, founded on the supremacy of the norm, and the sole legal relationship conceivable for them is that between the norm and its addressee. The latter, instead, conceive of legal reality as a complex of relations between rights and obligations. Cesarini Sforza adheres to what he calls the "subjectivist" conception of law.

But what is a "legal relationship" for this author? "A legal relationship is", he writes, "the interdependency of the actions of two subjects (or 'persons' in the legal

---

[5] See H. L. A. Hart, *The Concept of Law*, pp. 55ff., and cf. P. Winch, *The Idea of a Social Science and its Relation to Philosophy*, pp. 57ff.

[6] S. Romano, *L'ordinamento giuridico*, pp. 96–97. My square brackets.

[7] Cf. G. Tarello, *Ordinamento giuridico*, in Id., *Cultura giuridica e politica del diritto*, Bologna 1988, pp. 186, 188. On some parallels between Kelsen's work and Romano's cf. V. Frosini, *Kelsen e Capograssi*, Milan 1988.

[8] S. Romano, *L'ordinamento giuridico*, p. 14. Romano, in order to assert the primacy of the order over the norms, also uses an organicist metaphor: see ibid., p. 12.

[9] See ibid., pp. 70–71.

[10] On the response to Romano's ideas by Italian legal doctrine see A. Agnelli, *L'istituzionalismo giuridico italiano dal 1945 ai giorni nostri*, in *Annuario bibliografico di filosofia del diritto*, Milan 1965, pp. 267ff.

sense) established by a norm, such that one of them is the bearer of a right in relation to the other, and the other has a duty towards the former".[11] Legal relations are those in which "*ego* and *alter* are in a situation of equilibrium and of equivalence".[12] The legal relationship is here "the primary cell and the irreducible nucleus of all social reality", and the legal order amounts to the "relationship or relationships in which it is manifest".[13] This order is conceived by this author essentially as a relation or relationship among individuals.

Guido Fassò, too, closely connects law and legal relationships. The law, according to him, *is relation.* "Where there is co-existence", he writes, "there is relation, and accordingly law".[14] "Relation means law".[15] "Relationship means law".[16] "The law, in fact, presupposes a relationship or complex of relationships".[17] Here too the institution is conceived of essentially as a relation between individuals. For Fassò, accordingly, not only are the Camorra, the game of football, or a queue, "institutions", but even "a couple making love".[18]

For Santi Romano, instead, the law as relation presupposes, rather, the law as order. This is also true for norms. According to Romano, the legal order is made up not just of norms, but above all of organizations. The norms are instrumental in relation to the order, not constitutive of it. "In other words", he writes, "the legal order, understood comprehensively in this way, is an entity that in part moves according to the norms, but above all, moves the norms themselves, as it were like chessmen on a board, so that they represent more the object and also the means of its activity than an element in its structure".[19] It is interesting to note how Cesarini Sforza criticizes the prevalence Romano attributes to "institution" over norm. "What is unacceptable in Romano", writes Cesarini Sforza, "is the logically secondary position of the legal norm, as product of the institution-organization. The norm does not come before the institution-organization, nor even after: it is *coeval*".[20]

Carl Schmitt adheres to the, in some respects, "autopoietic" version of the legal order offered by Romano's institutionalism. "In his book Santi Romano has rightly said that it is not right to speak of an Italian, or French, or whatever law by simply conceiving it as a sum of legal rules, while the truth is that the Italian, or French State, as complex and differentiated organizations of a concrete order, produce such law. The several agencies and structures of State power or authority produce,

---

[11] W. Cesarini Sforza, *Il diritto dei privati*, 2nd ed., Milan 1963, p. 11.

[12] Ibid., p. 12. Emphasis in original.

[13] Ibid., p. 13.

[14] G. Fassò, *La storia come esperienza giuridica*, Milan 1953, p. 100.

[15] Ibid., p. 102.

[16] Ibid., p. 105.

[17] Ibid., pp. 106–107.

[18] See ibid., pp. 82–83. For an opposite opinion cf. G. Gurvitch, *L'idée du droit social*, reprint, Aalen 1972, p. 118, and M. Oakeshott, *On Human Conduct*, Oxford 1975, p. 123.

[19] S. Romano, *L'ordinamento giuridico*, pp. 15–16.

[20] Cited by A. Baratta, *Presentazione*, in M. Hauriou, *Teoria dell'istituzione e della fondazione*, ed. by W. Cesarini Sforza, Milan 1967, p. xxiv. Emphasis in original.

change, apply and guarantee legal rules".[21] In this view it is not a change of rules that modifies the legal order, but it is rather a change of the concrete order that is then reflected through a change of rules. Schmitt's institutionalism, or better *Konkretes Ordnungsdenken*, is, however, quite different from Romano's doctrine. This is for at least two reasons: (a) behind Schmitt's institutionalism one can fairly clearly discern the sinister shadow of decisionism, a conception that clashes with Romano's decisive anti-voluntarism and anti-imperativism; (b) Schmitt is attracted by a vital, moralistic *Weltanschauung* that tends to confuse and combine the spheres of ethics and of law, which, on the contrary, remain quite distinct in Romano's doctrine. The most striking difference between Romano and Schmitt lies, however, in the latter's fierce anti-pluralism.

While Romano, as we know, is a tireless defender of legal pluralism, Schmitt sees it as the chief cause of the ills of State and society. This anti-pluralist position, an expression of a deep-lying anti-democratic prejudice, is a constant in his work, almost constituting an obsession well before his conversion to National Socialism. In his writings after May 1933, the date Schmitt joined the Nazi party, his anti-pluralism even reaches the point of paroxysm in his affirmation of the unity and "totality" of the State. On the other hand, it should be recalled, the expression "total State" was used by him in writings before May 1933.[22] Romano's pluralism is, accordingly, to be counterposed to Schmitt's "totalitarianism". "However manifold the viewpoints on the regulation and organization of the various spheres of life", writes the German scholar, "on the other hand one unitary, consistent fundamental principle must certainly be recognized and upheld. All uncertainty and all dissent turn into points at which forces originally neutral, and subsequently hostile, towards the State can press, and where pluralistic disintegration and laceration can make a breach. A strong State is the prerequisite for a strong life, just in its most varied components. The strength of the National Socialist State lies in the fact that it is dominated and permeated from top to bottom and in every atom of its being by the idea of the authority of the *Führer*".[23]

4.2.2 Let us now consider the essential features of the conception of law according to Romano. The conception of law "must first and foremost be linked to the concept of society".[24] By "society" one must here understand not a mere relationship

[21] C. Schmitt, *Die drei Arten des rechtswissenschaftlichen Denkens*, Hamburg 1934, p. 24. On the divergence between Schmitt and Romano on the point of the one's rejection and the other's acceptance of the positive-law tradition, see A. Catania, *Carl Schmitt e Santi Romano*, in Id., *Il diritto tra forza e consenso. Saggi sulla filosofia giuridica del Novecento*, Napoli 1987, pp. 150ff.

[22] Cf. I Maus, *Bürgerliche Rechtstheorie und Faschismus. Zur sozialen Funktion und aktuellen Wirkung der Theorie Carl Schmitts*, 2nd ed., München 1980, pp. 152ff.

[23] C. Schmitt, *Staat, Bewegung, Volk. Die Dreigliederung der politischen Einheit*, Hamburg 1934, p. 33.

[24] S. Romano, *L'ordinamento giuridico*, p. 25. It is, then, questionable whether Romano is engaged in a "juridification of the social", or perhaps more a "socialization of the legal": in this connection see G. Tarello, *Progetto per la voce 'Ordinamento giuridico' di una enciclopedia*, in *Politica del diritto*, 1975, pp. 72ff.

between individuals, but a concrete unity distinct from the individuals that make it up, an effectively constituted (effectively organized) unity. Thus, for Romano, a caste group or social class, if not organized, does not constitute a true society.

The concept of law, according to this view, must contain the idea of social order. "Any social manifestation", writes Romano, "by the mere fact that it is social, is ordered, at least in relation to the members".[25] The social order whose expression is the law is not however the one given by the existence of norms or rules.[26] Law, before being norm, is organization.

The decisive assertion of the social nature of the phenomenon of law and the conception of sociality as "organization" are the two prerequisites for the definition of law as institution. An institution is, according to Romano, "any entity or social body that has a stable and permanent pattern and forms a body in itself, with a life of its own".[27] Law and institution thus become equivalent concepts. "Any legal order", he writes, "is an institution, vice versa any institution is a legal order: the equation between the two concepts is necessary and absolute".[28]

Romano clarifies his conception by comparing it with Maurice Hauriou's doctrine; Hauriou had preceded him in using the concept "institution" as central notion in the phenomenon of law in *Principes de droit public*, 1910. Romano raises four chief objections.[29]

(i) The limitation of the denotation of the concept of "institution" solely to the organizations Hauriou calls "corporative", that is, organizations that have reached a high degree of development, which is to say modern States, is unjustified. (ii) It is even more incorrect to identify "institution" with bodies organized according to the constitutional/representative model. (iii) It is inaccurate to maintain that the institution is a source of law, or that one is the cause of the other, since there is "perfect identity" between the two concepts and phenomena. (iv) Finally, Hauriou's conception that the "institution" is "une sorte de chose" is obscure: "what is true", writes Romano, "is that Hauriou wished to bring out the objective nature of the institution, but for this nature there is no need for it to be considered as an object, as a *res*: the institution is, instead, an objective legal order".[30]

Having distanced himself from Hauriou, Romano indicates what in his view are the fundamental features of the phenomenon of the institution. He starts by giving a definition: "By institution we mean any social entity or body".[31] A social entity, to be termed an institution, must have the following characteristics: (a) it

---

[25] S. Romano, *L'ordinamento giuridico*, p. 27.

[26] For Romano the two terms are equivalent: see S. Romano, *L'ordinamento giuridico*, p. 4, note 2.

[27] S. Romano, *Frammenti di un dizionario giuridico*, p. 82. "Any social entity, that is, any institution in the sense in which that word is synonymous with social entity [. . .] is a legal order" (S. Romano, *Principii di diritto costituzionale generale*, 2nd ed., Milano 1946, p. 55).

[28] S. Romano, *L'ordinamento giuridico*, p. 27. "Every institution is a legal order and every legal order is an institution" (S. Romano, *Principii di diritto costituzionale generale*, 2nd ed., p. 55).

[29] See S. Romano, *L'ordinamento giuridico*, pp. 33–34.

[30] Ibid., p. 34.

[31] Ibid., p. 35.

must be objectively and concretely existent: "however immaterial, its individuality must be exterior and visible".[32] (b) It must be a "manifestation of the social rather than purely the individual nature of man". (c) It must be "a closed entity that may be considered in and for itself, just because it has an individuality of its own".[33] (However, "the autonomy of any institution need not be absolute"[34]). (d) It must be "a fixed, permanent unit".[35] The social entity termed an institution must, that is, be able to maintain its identity even when its individual elements change (the persons making it up, its possessions, its interests, and even – be it noted – its *norms*[36]). Romano considers it possible that an institution have all of its norms changed yet still remain identical to itself.

(e) The concept of institution implies that of *organization*. The institution is, in particular, *organization of force*. "Every force", writes Romano, "that is effectively social and accordingly is organized, is *ipso facto* transformed into law".[37] As we see, with this idea he preempts the similar theses of Hans Kelsen and Karl Olivecrona. There is, however, a difference that perhaps reduces the apparent resemblance between Romano and Kelsen (Ross and Olivecrona). For Kelsen (and Ross and Olivecrona) "force" signifies "coercive force", physical violence in the last instance; for Romano, instead, the concept of force – in this context – is much broader, more or less coinciding with that of "social force".

It should be noted that Romano does not conceive of organization solely as *hierarchical* organization. "We, however", he writes, "do not feel that the concept of organization necessarily implies a relation [. . .] of superiority and correlative subordination".[38] If hierarchical structure is not an essential requisite, it may then without difficulty be admitted that the international community too is a legal order.[39] This recognition is also justified considering the fact that the existence of an institution does not presuppose its full autonomy. For Romano, accordingly, the international community represents the broadest institution.

---

[32] Ibid.

[33] Ibid., pp. 37, 38.

[34] Ibid., p. 38. Cf. the entry for "Autonomia", in S. Romano, *Frammenti di un dizionario giuridico*, pp. 14ff.

[35] S. Romano, *L'ordinamento giuridico*, p. 39. "Every institution [. . .], as an entity with a structure and organization of its own, is accordingly an order, *a more or less stable and permanent pattern*, and brings to unity the individuals and other elements making it up, taking on in relation to them a life of its own and forming a body in itself, constituting a 'legal order'" (S. Romano, *Principii di diritto costituzionale generale*, p. 55, my emphasis).

[36] See S. Romano, *L'ordinamento giuridico*, p. 39.

[37] Ibid., p. 43.

[38] Ibid., p. 54.

[39] See S. Romano, *Frammenti di un dizionario giuridico*, p. 68.

Indeed, as has frequently been noted,[40] the concept of "institution" supplied by Romano remains rather vague, since, as he himself recognizes, further clarifications of the concept come down to reformulating the definition of institution as "social entity or body".[41] Nonetheless, Romano avoided confusing "institution" and "legal institution".[42] The confusion of these terms is however present in the neo-institutionalist authors, in particular in Neil MacCormick's writings; when implying "institution" he repeatedly refers to the contract.[43] This marks one first important difference between Romano's theory and MacCormick and Weinberger's. In the latter, "institution" means primarily "institutional fact" (in the sense this term is used by John Searle[44]); while for Romano "institution" means chiefly "social entity" or "organization".

Though any organization constitutes an "institutional fact", not every "institutional fact" constitutes an organization. The case of the contract cited so frequently by MacCormick[45] is an example of this. A contract that is existent or in force may certainly appear within the category of "institutional facts". It is not, however, always possible to bring it into the category of "organizations" or "social bodies". Thus, even those accepting a rigidly monistic, statalist conception of law (according to which the only law possible is the State's) could recognize the plurality of "institutions" in the sense in which the term is used by MacCormick. They could not, however, recognize the plurality of "institutions" in Romano's sense without falling into contradiction with the assertion of the exclusivity of State law.

---

[40] Cf. e.g., V. E. Orlando, *Stato e diritto*, in Id., *Diritto pubblico generale. Scritti vari (1881–1940)*, Milano 1954, pp. 291–293, and N. Bobbio, *Teoria e ideologia nella dottrina di Santi Romano*, in Id., *Dalla struttura alla funzione. Nuovi studi di teoria del diritto*, Milano 1977, p. 173. "Romano's theory", notes Uberto Scarpelli, "does not offer any well-defined model or precise criteria for the legal resolution of the antinomies and alternatives that emerge from social issues" (U. Scarpelli, *Istituzione*, in *Gli strumenti del sapere contemporaneo*, vol. 2, *I concetti*, UTET, Turin 1985, p. 437). The "slipperiness" of the concept of "institution" is stressed also by Sabino Cassese, who then arrives at the conclusion that the concept has now become "useless" (S. Cassese, *Istituzione: un concetto ormai inntile*, in *Politica del diritto*, 1979, p. 53)

[41] See S. Romano, *L'ordinamento giuridico*, p. 40.

[42] See ibid., p. 36, note 30.

[43] See e.g., N. MacCormick, *Law as Institutional Fact*, in N. MacCormick and O. Weinberger, *An Institutional Theory of Law*, pp. 49ff., and O. Weinberger, *Bausteine des institutionalistischen Rechtspositivismus*, in O. Weinberger, *Recht, Institution und Rechtspolitik*, pp. 32–34.

[44] See J. R. Searle, *Speech Acts. An Essay in the Philosophy of Language*, Cambridge 1969, pp. 50ff.

[45] See e.g., N. MacCormick, *Institutions, Arrangements and Practical Information*, in *Ratio Juris*, 1988, pp. 73ff. In relation to the "institution", MacCormick distinguishes between "institutive", "terminative" and "consequential" norms: see N. MacCormick, *Law as Institutional Fact*, pp. 52ff. On this distinction cf. H. Rottleuthner, *Rechtstheorie und Rechtssoziologie*, Munich 1981, pp. 58ff. Cf. also A. Pintore, *Da Ross a MacCormick: Recenti sviluppi nella teoria analitica dei concetti giuridici*, in *Studi economico-giuridici in memoria di Antonio Basciu*, Naples 1986, pp. 267ff., and A. Pintore, *La teoria analitica dei concetti giuridici*, Naples 1990.

Romano, however, recognizes two concepts of law. The first (and fundamental) one is that of law as "an order in its fullness and unity, that is, an institution".[46] The other (subordinate to the former) is that of law as a set of precepts or norms that draw their *raison d'être* from the overall order: "a precept or complex of precepts (be they norms or particular provisions), variously grouped or arranged, which in order to distinguish them from non-legal ones we call institutional, thereby bringing out the connection they have with the order as a whole, that is, the institution of which they are elements, a connection which is necessary and sufficient in order to attribute the qualification 'legal' to them".[47]

These two types of law correspond, in Romano's theory, to two different concepts of legal validity. Law as "institution", or as "order", is valid only insofar as it is effective, and forms part of reality.[48] Law as norm, or as "institutional precept", is instead valid insofar as it is in some way (not better defined) connected with law as "order". "The institution is an institution", writes the Sicilian jurist, "insofar as it lays down norms, and *the norm draws its force from the institution*".[49]

This twofold structure of the concept of validity obviously recalls Kelsen.[50] Indeed, it is the idea of "legal order" that is the link between the theories of Kelsen and Romano. One has to add, though, that the idea of "legal order" is very different in the work of each theorist. For Kelsen it is a system of norms, something resulting solely from norms, and reducible to these. For Romano, on the other hand, the idea of "order" (which really amounts to that of "institution") is not reducible to a mere sum, or organization, or system, of norms. Thus, to Kelsen's "presumed fundamental norm" corresponds a sort of "material constitution" or "tacit law", founded on the "normative force of fact". While Kelsen conceives of the legal order as a sum of norms and as "closed" or "founded" on one norm (albeit of higher rank), Romano has a, so to speak, "holistic" vision of order, basing it upon a sort of material necessity.[51] This is the part of his theory that met with the greatest appreciation from the proponent of *Konkretes Ordungsdenken*. "Were one to seek to reduce the contrast between Kelsen and Romano to one between two definitional formulas," wrote Vittorio Frosini, "one could however note the alternative between the 'fundamental legal norm' at the foundation of the pure theory of law, and the 'tacit

[46] S. Romano, *L'ordinamento giuridico*, p. 27.

[47] Ibid., pp. 27–28. See also S. Romano, *Frammenti di un dizionario giuridico*, pp. 68–71. The use of the term "precept" does not, however, commit Romano to an imperativist conception (see S. Romano, *Op. cit.*, pp. 140–141). In this connection it should be noted that for Romano "neither the individual norms nor the order receiving and accommodating them considered as a whole have addressees" (Ibid., p. 142).

[48] See S. Romano, *L'ordinamento giuridico*, pp. 35–36

[49] Ibid., p. 42. My emphasis.

[50] Cf. G. Tarello, *Ordinamento giuridico*, pp. 186–188, and V. Frosini, *Kelsen e Romano*, pp. 55–56.

[51] Cf. A. Tarantino, *La teoria della necessità dell'ordinamento giuridico*, 2nd ed., Milan 1980.

fundamental law' on which the institutionalist doctrine is built".[52] Moreover, as emerges from their differing conceptions of international law (Kelsen's unitary one versus Romano's pluralist one) and the different legal status they attribute to the Catholic Church, Kelsen has a tendency to assert one legal order and one only, whereas Romano is radically pluralist in this area.

4.2.3 I believe we might summarize the main features of Romano's legal theory as follows.[53] It is a theory of law that is (a) positivist (anti-natural-law), (b) realist, (c) moderately anti-normativist, (d) anti-statist but not imperativist (pluralist and pan-juridicist), (e) formalist, and (f) non-sanctionist.

As for legal positivism, Romano's doctrine may be called positivist once one adopts a broad version of legal positivism, that is, the version according to which law is produced solely by the action (though not necessarily the intention) of human beings: "Legal positivism has many different forms, but they have all in common the idea that law exists only in virtue of some human act or decision".[54] Moreover, insisting on the distinction between law "as it is" and law "as it ought to be" and hence on the separation between law and ethics, Romano accepts one of the strongest precepts of legal positivism.

As regards realism, Romano is a realist in the sense that, as we have seen, he seeks to reconcile the (normative) sphere of law with the world of what "is", accordingly conceiving the law as a sphere of reality, as a set of *facts*. In reference to anti-normativism, it should be stressed that, while counterposing the concept of "institution" to that of "norm", he does not think he can do without the latter; instead he subjects it to the concept of "institution", without eliminating it. Thus, while it is the institution that is prior, not the norm, the latter also plays an essential role in legal experience, although it is "deduced" from the institution.

Romano brings out very explicitly the theme of the counterposition between institutionalism and traditional normativist theory. The institutionalist conception, he writes, "is not taken over from the traditional doctrine on the concept of law which, according to it, is instead a complex or system of norms the specific nature of which to distinguish them from other norms is sought – though in vain. To this so-called normative conception we counterpose the *institutionalist conception of law*".[55] According to Romano's view, norms do not represent the central element in the phenomenon of law. Here they are no more than an externalization or manifestation of the *institution*, which is the primary and fundamental reality of law. The

[52] V. Frosini, *Op. cit.*, pp. 53–54. Cf. O. Condorelli, *Il 'diritto fondamentale'*, in Id., *Scritti sul diritto e sullo Stato*, Giuffrè, Milan 1970. Compare also C. Mortati, *La costituzione materiale*, Milano 1940.

[53] Cf. G. Gavazzi, *Santi Romano e la teoria generale del diritto*, in *Le dottrine giuridiche di oggi e l'insegnamento di Santi Romano*, ed. by P. Biscaretti di Ruffia, Milan 1977, pp. 67–86.

[54] R. Dworkin, *A Matter of Principle*, Oxford 1986, p. 131. See also H. L. A. Hart, *Legal Positivism*, in *The Encyclopedia of Philosophy*, ed. by P. Edwards, vol. 4, New York, NY 1967.

[55] S. Romano, *Principii di diritto costituzionale generale*, p. 55.

norm draws its nature as legality from the institution of which it is a manifestation or derivation. Legal norms are accordingly distinguished from other types of norms not by their specific characteristics, but rather by the institution from which they are derived.

Moreover, without the institution, without its existence, one could not speak of efficacy of norms. "The individual norms, or even the set of norms, called legal are only particular externalizations of a given order in the sense mentioned, which may, moreover, even remain latent in simpler or less evolved institutions. Their practical importance is so great that it has been possible to identify with them every legal order considered in its entirety. It is, however, more correct to consider that an order does not in the objective sense break down solely into norms, which in fact presuppose the institution considered comprehensively and unitarily, and are an aspect and manifestation of it and derive from it the nature that differentiates them from non-legal norms, their efficacy and their guarantee, which do not result from the intrinsic features of any norm nor from their being linked with other norms that protect them, but instead rest on all the gears and levers, the whole structure of the institution".[56] Here we find a further difference with respect to Kelsen's "pure theory". For Romano an institution as a legal order is not a logical compound, a unitary system made of rules, but it comprises and consists of more than just norms. Procedures, agencies, sanctions, principles are equally original members of the legal order and as such they are not reducible to a bundle of rules. They have an ontological "thickness" or density and a social efficacity that are well beyond the normativity of a ruling or an ought.

For Romano, however, "institution" and "norm" are not mutually incompatible notions. They do not rule each other out: "on the contrary, they integrate".[57] The institution, which for Romano constitutes as it were the "essence" of the phenomenon of law, is always accompanied by a body of norms (even if not explicitly formulated). "The law is also norm, but as well as being norm it is often, before being norm, organization or social body, and it is this which communicates to the norm, as it were to its product or derivation, the nature of being legal, not vice versa. In other terms, the existence of an institution never fails to be accompanied by a series of norms, which may be, and in part always are, implicit in its structure and in its essential features and are accordingly coeval with it, but are in part also expressly declared and formulated by the institution itself, after it has arisen, or by a higher, greater institution of which the first is an element".[58] The institution is not equivalent to a body of norms, nor, on the other hand, can it exist without these. The norms are only a necessary condition of the institution, never a sufficient condition

56 Ibid., pp. 55–56.

57 S. Romano, *Osservazioni sulla completezza dell'ordinamento statale*, in *Scritti minori*, vol. 1, ed. by G. Zanobini, 2nd ed., Milan 1990, p. 458.

58 S. Romano, *Principii di diritto costituzionale generale*, p. 56.

for it. This does not however prevent the norm from in some cases preceding the social practice in which the institution is embodied.[59]

As far as anti-statism is concerned, it should once again be recalled that Romano's institutionalism supports the plurality of legal orders, of which the State is only one variety. Romano does not believe that legal phenomena are quintessentially commands, prescriptions, precepts, imperatives or acts of *imperium*. As we know, legal statism (which asserts that the only law is the State's) is fed by presciptivism, and vice versa. For a theory that identifies State and law, or better, reduces law to the "State form", it is natural that it (the law) should consist in the commands of State power. Romano is accordingly anti-Statist in two ways. On one side, because he denies that the law is made up only of those acts that have been regarded as typical of State activity: prescriptions, imperatives, sanctions. On the other, because he denies the State's claim to be the *sole* legal order valid and effective in a given territory, by opting, as he does, for the thesis of the plurality of legal orders. "The State is to be considered as, and is as a rule so regarded by itself, not only as the sole legal order existing but as one of the orders that constitute the legal world, living sometimes in relations of social coexistence with each other, sometimes in conflict, sometimes ignoring each other".[60] In Romano's theory the law does not break down into nor is exhausted in either the norms laid down by the State (here anti-statism is combined with anti-normativism), nor in the State as institution, since this is not the sole form of institution (legal pluralism and anti-statism).[61]

Moreover, legal pluralism, used in rather extreme fashion by Romano, ends up in pan-juridicism, that is the position (typified by Romano's) that every social group constitutes a legal order. It is interesting to note that Romano links the position that the State is the sole expression of the "legal", or the sole source of law, with the natural-law conception that tends to conceive the law in monistic terms, as one and universal. "The definition of the State as legal order is not complete unless it is brought out that it is one of the various legal orders that may exist, and in reality do exist. It derives from a transposition to the theory of positive law of the natural law conception of law, that is, the now very frequent opinion, which does not however antedate the principles of the eighteenth century, that the sole legal order is the State's: the others could be legal only by reflection and as being instituted or at least

[59] A contrary view seems to be taken by Gianluigi Palombella. See G. Palombella, *L'istituzione del diritto. Una prospettiva di recerca*, in *Materiali per una storia della cultura giuridica*, 1990, p. 378: "In the institutional theory, the notion of law/order/social body rules out the possibility that the norm may effectively precede social practice".

[60] S. Romano, *Principii di diritto costituzionale generale*, p. 59. For a critique of the legal pluralism defended by Romano see A. Passerin d'Entrèves, *La dottrina dello Stato. Elementi di analisi e di interpretazione*, Turin 1967, pp. 184ff., where the centrality of the notion of sovereignty is affirmed (the capacity to produce and *impose* norms) in the definition of legal order: "In these two combined attributes, reaction and the imposition of law, which are by definition contained in 'sovereignty', the other orders do not partake, or do so only in part" (ibid., p. 187). In Pietro Costa's view, instead, Romano's doctrine remains "Statocentric": see P. Costa, *Lo Stato immaginario. Metafore e paradigmi nella cultura giuridica italiana fra Ottocento e Novecento*, Milano 1986, pp. 127ff.

[61] Cf. G. Gavazzi, *Op. cit.*, p. 76.

recognized by the State itself. However absolute and therefore single natural law may be, the positive orders are plainly as numerous as the social bodies in which they are manifested".[62]

As far as Romano's "formalism" is concerned, it lies in the fact that he is not concerned with identifying contents or functions that are typical of law, or substantive conditions (specific normative contents or particular institutional configurations) that a certain group has to meet in order to be recognized as having attained the quality and prerogatives of a legal order. The law, on his view, has no necessarily predetermined objects, ends, or distribution of competences.[63] Finally, Romano's "anti-sanctionism" is expressed in the denial that sanction is a distinctive or central element of the legal norm, or better, the legal experience as a whole. Spontaneous order is too important and central to him to allow for the view that law and compliance to rules are mainly driven through an explicit threat of some evil.

4.3 Old and New Institutionalism. Santi Romano Compared with Neil MacCormick and Ota Weinberger

It might be useful to consider the points of contact, and some divergences, between Romano's institutionalism and MacCormick and Weinberger's neo-institutionalism. Common features in my view are at least four theses more or less clearly encountered in both Romano's writings and those of MacCormick and Weinberger: (i) the thesis that law and language are related phenomena, in some respects homologous; (ii) the affirmation of the existence of a specific legal reality distinct from the physical or "brute" one[64]; (iii) the support for the so-called "positive" method, by which the law is studied as what it "is", distinguishing the planes of description and of prescription (or evaluation) of norms and institutions, so that the study of law for both the institutionalist theories (both Romano's and MacCormick and Weinberger's) is seen as neutral, *wertfrei*; (iv) the separation of law from morality (justified by Romano with the argument that law is an eminently *involuntary* phenomenon, whereas morality is seen as having its roots in the will of individuals[65]).

Also common is the conviction that a plurality of normative orders (institutions) exist. However, the neo-institutionalists, by contrast with Romano, think they can

[62] S. Romano, *Principii di diritto costituzionale generale*, p. 58.

[63] Cf. G. Gavazzi, *Op. cit.*, p. 76.

[64] See S. Romano, *Frammenti di un dizionario giuridico*, pp. 204ff.; O. Weinberger, *Bausteine des institutionalistischen Rechtspositivismus*, p. 17; O. Weinberger, *Die Bedeutung der Logik für die moderne Rechtstheorie*, in O. Weinberger, *Recht, Institution and Rechtspolitik*, p. 91; O. Weinberger, *Ontologie, Hermeneutik und der Begriff des geltenden Rechts*, p. 117; and N. MacCormick, *On Analytical Jurisprudence*, in N. MacCormick and O. Weinberger, *An Institutional Theory of Law*, pp. 97ff.

[65] See S. Romano, *Frammenti di un dizionario giuridico*, pp. 65ff. This obviously does not commit Romano to the adoption of a neo-cognitivist meta-ethics. Cf. O. Weinberger, *Bausteine des institutionalistischen Rechtspositivismus*, p. 42.

find "legal" and "non-legal" institutions: "There are legal and extra-legal", writes Weinberger.[66] This amounts to saying that not every "institution" is *ipso facto* a *legal* order, despite being a normative order. To Romano's "legal" pluralism there thus corresponds the "normative" pluralism of Weinberger: "It is a feature of modern society that there are within it a *plurality of social normative systems*. They are partly general rule systems, that apply to the whole of society members, partly special rules concerning particular".[67] But Weinberger's "normative" pluralism is immune from the "pan-legalist" temptations to which Romano's thought is instead constantly exposed.

Indeed, the differences between Romano's institutionalism on the one hand and MacCormick and Weinberger's on the other are manifold. First and foremost comes the diversity in their cultural background. The most important difference seems to me, though, to be the one (which I have already mentioned) of the meaning they attribute to the concept of institution. For Romano, "institution" is equivalent to "society", or to "legal order". For MacCormick and Weinberger (but perhaps more for MacCormick than for Weinberger), "institution" is equivalent to "institutional fact".[68] Not every "institutional fact", however, constitutes a "society", and a "legal order", so that the concepts of "institution" used by Romano and by MacCormick and Weinberger respectively, remain distinct.

One other important difference is that Romano repeatedly speaks of the need to trace the "ought" (of the norm) back to the "is" (of the institution). If law is defined as "institution", or as a specific part of reality, then, Romano argues, the phenomenon of law can no longer be conceived of as an aspect of the "ought", but as belonging to the sphere of what "is". "If the law", he writes, "lies chiefly in the institutions, it will be necessary when it comes to defining it not only to go beyond the voluntarist dogma [...], but also *to rise from the sphere of what ought to be to that of what is*".[69] This, according to the Sicilian lawyer, marks a further difference between law and morality: morality belongs to the world of what "ought to be",[70] law to what "is", or better, law belongs to both areas, since the institution expresses

---

[66] O. Weinberger, *Verfassungstheorie vom Standpunkt des neuen Institutionalismus*, p. 103.

[67] Ibid., italics in the text.

[68] See N. MacCormick, *Law as Institutional Fact*, in N. MacCormick, O. Weinberger, *An Institutional Theory of Law*, pp. 49ff. and N. MacCormick, *Institutions, Arrangements and Practical Information*, pp. 76–77 (here MacCormick speaks of "legal institutional facts" (p. 77)). Weinberger does in fact distinguish between "institution" and "institutional fact" in the sense that "institutional facts are facts that depend on institutions" (O. Weinberger, *Ontologie, Hermeneutik und der Begriff des geltenden Rechts*, p. 117). However, there is in Weinberger's work no further explanation of the difference between "institution" and "institutional fact". In fact, this work lacks any precise definition of "institution". Weinberger's defence that it is not always necessary to define the phenomena one deals with (see O. Weinberger, *Bausteine des institutionalistischen Rechtspositivismus*, p. 30), seems to me rather weak.

[69] S. Romano, *Frammenti di un dizionario giuridico*, p. 70, my emphasis. See also ibid., pp. 80, 84.

[70] It would accordingly seem that Romano sometimes treats the phenomenon of law as a mere "brute fact"; which has led more than one person to take a distance from institutionalism because of its apparent insensitivity to the eminently normative aspects of law. See e.g., L. Lombardi Vallauri, *Corso di filosofia del diritto*, Padua 1981, p. 125: "Unlike Santi Romano, we do not necessarily

an "is", while the norms (which derive their validity from the institution) express an "ought".

For the neo-institutionalist theorists (really particularly for Weinberger, since MacCormick displays some ambiguity in this area[71]), "is" and "ought" are instead clearly distinct planes that never come into contact (in the sense of its being possible to derive an "ought" from an "is", as Romano seems to believe[72]), and law is defined in terms of "ought" and not of "is". Nonetheless, if the neo-institutionalist theories are considered more closely, this difference fades considerably.

First of all it should be noted that Romano and Weinberger attribute a different meaning to the distinction between "is" and "ought". For Romano, the terms express the idea of two distinct spheres of reality. His is an ontological thesis. Weinberger, instead, distances himself from this way of understanding the distinction (which he, by the way, attributes to Kelsen[73]). "According to the ontological conception", writes Weinberger, "there is a sphere of what is and a sphere of what ought to be, the world of what is, revealed to us in empirical experience essentially on the basis of observation, and the world of 'ought', which cannot be observed but only understood, since it consists of ideal entities".[74] To the "ontic" or ontological conception of the distinction between "is" and "ought", Weinberger raises two chief objections.

(i) On the one hand, this conception must presume a "world" (that of the "ought") that includes *all* the "conceivable" norms, hence also those that contradict each other. But, objects Weinberger, a "world" is a world, for instance in the theory of possible worlds, only insofar as it does not include states of affairs that are mutually contradictory. If instead the "world" of the "ought" were confined to including only norms effectively in force and efficacious, then we would be in the presence no longer of a "world" of the "ought", but of a plurality of normative systems.[75] It follows, in the Czech scholar's view, that the law cannot be conceived of as *one* "world".

---

identify the law with the social body, since this would mean reducing law to a mere fact, depriving it of its normative nature".

[71] See N. MacCormick, *Ein Postskriptum zu Weinbergers Einleitung*, in N. MacCormick and O. Weinberger, *Grundlagen des Institutionalistischen Rechtspositivismus*, Berlin 1985, pp. 57–59.

[72] See e.g., Weinberger and MacCormick's critique of the claimed derivation of an "is" from an "ought" by John Searle: see N. MacCormick and O. Weinberger, *An Institutional Theory of Law*, pp. 21, 24. For an analogous critique cf. K. O. Apel, *Das Apriori der Kommunikationsgemeinschaft und die Grundlagen der Ethik*, in Id., *Transformation der Philosophie*, vol. 2, Frankfurt am Main 1984, p. 416. Cf. also J. R. Searle, *Speech Acts*, pp. 175ff.

[73] See O. Weinberger, *Ontologie, Hermeneutik und der Begriff des geltenden Rechts*, p. 113. However, see O. Weinberger, *Hans Kelsen als Philosoph*, in Id., *Normentheorie als Grundlage der Jurisprudenz und Ethik. Eine Auseinandersetzung mit Hans Kelsens Theorie der Normen*, Berlin 1981, p. 186, where we read: "Die Unterscheidung von Sein und Sollen ist im Kelsenschen Sinne [...] als begriffliche Differenzierung von Denkinhalten, als *semantische* Unterscheidung verschiedener, gegenseitig ineinander unübersetzbarer Satzarten zu verstehen" (my emphasis).

[74] O. Weinberger, *Ontologie, Hermeneutik und der Begriff des geltenden Rechts*, p. 112.

[75] See ibid.

(ii) On the other hand, the ontological conception is wrapped up in the contradiction that a norm, which by definition is a "non-being", insofar as it is conceived of as belonging to a sphere different from that of what "is", is nonetheless taken as "existent". One might endeavour to find a terminological solution to this contradiction, in the sense, for instance, of distinguishing "being" from "existing". This solution is, however, considered unsatisfactory, "since existences, material existence and the existence of norm-systems, are both being [*Dasein*] in time".[76]

For Weinberger it is not of "is" and "ought" that one should speak, but of sentences that express "is" (or descriptive sentences) and sentences that express "ought" (or normative sentences). The distinction between descriptive propositions and normative propositions can however be maintained on the basis of various arguments. Traditionally, the distinction is affirmed on the basis of the following argument: while the former (descriptive propositions) can, it is said, have a truth value assigned to them, this is not possible in relation to normative propositions. Descriptive propositions may be true or false; normative propositions cannot be either true or false. Yet this is not the path Weinberger follows in order to distinguish descriptive from normative propositions. Weinberger assigns to normative propositions a semantic "value" that is in a certain sense analogous to the "truth" value ascribed by propositional logic to descriptive propositions. It is thanks to this "value" that Weinberger believes in justifying, for instance, the conception that two norms may logically contradict each other.[77]

Weinberger reconstructs the distinction between descriptive and normative propositions starting from his theory of action. (Human) action is, for the Czech scholar, "a process of elaboration of data".[78] This process is based on two distinct types of information: (a) theoretical information (descriptions of states of affairs, nomic-causal information); (b) practical information (determination of purposes, values, rules). But from the point of view of the acting subject, argues Weinberger, it is not possible to derive any "practical information" from "theoretical information". The distinction between "descriptive" and "normative" propositions is accordingly reformulated, and with it also the thesis that the latter cannot be derived from the former. This distinction lies, accordingly, in the sphere of semantics,[79] and does not commit one to the adoption of any particular ontology.[80] One might

---

[76] Ibid.

[77] See O. Weinberger, *Rechtslogik. Versuch einer Anwendung moderner Logik auf das juristische Denken*, Vienna-New York 1970, pp. 212ff.

[78] O. Weinberger, *Bausteine des institutionalistischen Rechtspositivismus*, p. 25.

[79] See O. Weinberger, *Eine Semantik für praktische Philosophie*, in *Beiträge zur Philosophie von Stephan Körner*, ed. by R. Haller, Amsterdam 1983, pp. 219ff.

[80] See O. Weinberger, *Ontologie, Hermeneutik und der Begriff des geltenden Rechts*, p. 114. I would recall in this connection that for the Czech scholar ontology is above all stipulative in nature: see e.g., O. Weinberger, *Bausteine des institutionalistischen Rechtspositivismus*, p. 15.

thus without contradiction adopt simultaneously Romano's "ontological" theory and Weinberger's "semantic" one.

In reality, on this point Weinberger is closer to Romano than might at first sight be supposed. I shall concentrate on Weinberger's thought, because on the point of the distinction between "is" and "ought" MacCormick is, as mentioned above, rather less decided.

Weinberger affirms what he calls the "primacy of practice", that is, the primacy of the practical sphere (of action) over the theoretical one (of knowledge),[81] and in general over the linguistic one (that is, over various types of proposition, over "theoretical" and "practical" information, and hence also over norms, which can always be formulated for him as normative propositions, that is, as "practical information").[82] Thus for Weinberger logical operations are tools not only of knowledge but also of action.[83] This last position is to defend his conception of a specific logic of norms against the claim that deontic logic should be patterned more or less on propositional logic.[84] But practice is an "is", and if to it are to be subordinated the various types of proposition, including normative ones, and hence also the norms (which express an "ought"), that means that the "ought" is here too "reduced" in some way (or in some sense) to "is". This in my view emerges still more clearly from the conception of the validity of legal norms sketched out by Weinberger.

Weinberger on the one hand rejects the conception of validity of norms based on the type of realism that identifies it with the efficacy of the norm itself, and on the other distances himself from Kelsen who makes the validity of norms depend on a non-existent, "assumed" though not posited, *Grundnorm*. Weinberger accuses the realist conception of neglecting the normative element of validity. He brings against Kelsen's "pure theory" the reproach of neglecting the need to link the validity of norms with reality, that is, with real processes empirically observable and confirmable.[85] "The law", he writes, "is not valid [*gilt nicht*] in itself or for itself, but always in connection with observable communicative processes".[86]

Weinberger returns to the very clear distinction in the *Pure Theory of Law*, which is, as we have already seen, present also in Romano's doctrine, between the validity of the legal order as a whole and the validity of individual norms. The validity of an individual norm can, according to Weinberger, be ascertained primarily through recourse to what he defines as "genealogical criteria", which are the formal ones of ascertaining respect for the necessary procedures and responsibilities required in the

---

[81] See O. Weinberger, *Op. cit.*, p. 20.

[82] See O. Weinberger, *Die Bedeutung der Logik für die moderne Rechtstheorie*, p. 91. Cf. also O. Weinberger, *The Role of Rules*, in *Ratio Juris*, 1988, p. 225, where we read: "To follow a rule does not presuppose being explicitly aware of the rule or being able to formulate it in a linguistic form".

[83] See O. Weinberger, *Ontologie, Hermeneutik und der Begriff des geltenden Rechts*, p. 116.

[84] See ibid.

[85] See O. Weinberger, *Bausteine des institutionalistischen Rechtspositivismus*, pp. 37–38.

[86] O. Weinberger, *Ontologie, Hermeneutik und der Begriff des geltenden Rechts*, p. 111.

issuing of the norm.[87] When however one traces back the "genealogical tree" of the norm, or the *Stufenbau* (to use Kelsen's terminology once again), then the formal criteria are no longer enough, and it has to be ascertained whether the "fundamental norms" of the legal system to which the norm in question belongs are elements of institutions that actually exist.[88] Thus, in Weinberger's theory too, the "ought" of the norm is "reduced" to the "is" of the "institution", in so far as the need is recognized, as Romano says, to base the concept of law "not on the form of what ought to be, but on the other one of what is".[89]

A further difference between Romano's theory and Weinberger and MacCormick's – possibly related to their different ways of seeing the distinction between "is" and "ought" – is that the former counterposes the institutionalist conception to the normativist one, while the latter two defend a "normativist institutionalism"[90] in the sense that "the institutions possess a core that has the nature of the practical information",[91] that is, of the norm. "The institutions", writes Weinberger, "are realities located in the context of action; they constitute models of action, spheres of possible action, and organize interaction among men. Accordingly, it is necessary to produce rules that determine what ought to be, the *licere* [*Dürfen*] and the *posse* [*Können*] (the empowerments [*Ermächtigungen*]) of the authors".[92] Institutions and norms are thus strictly connected, and mutually dependent. The nature of this connnection and the true difference between norms and institutions are not clarified however.

The neo-institutionalist theory of Weinberger and MacCormick sometimes falls into a sort of vicious circle. For in it the institutions are the source of validity of the norms, and on the other hand, according to the theory, without norms it is not possible to have institutions, in the sense that the former (the norms) constitute a condition for the possibility of the latter (the institutions). The confusion is, in short, in this theory, between what constitutes a sphere of action and the sphere of action itself. Weinberger does not distinguish between these two aspects, so that the "institution" is sometimes defined as "a sphere of action",[93] and sometimes as what constitutes and produces or renders possible that sphere, or results from it. "The interplay between individual and society", he writes, "understood in the context of

---

[87] See ibid., pp. 122, 124.

[88] *See* ibid., p. 122.

[89] S. Romano, *Frammenti di un dizionario giuridico*, p. 84.

[90] See O. Weinberger, *Bausteine des institutionalistischen Rechtspositivismus*, p. 14, and O. Weinberger, *Reine oder funktionalistische Rechtsbetrachtung*? in *Reine Rechtslehre im Spiegel ihrer Fortsetzer und Kritiker*, ed. by O. Weinberger and W. Krawietz, Vienna-New York 1988, p. 219.

[91] O. Weinberger, *Ontologie, Hermeneutik und der Begriff des geltenden Rechts*, p. 117.

[92] Ibid.

[93] See e.g., O. Weinberger, *Bausteine des institutionalistischen Rechtspositivismus*, p. 33: "Institutionen sind Rahmensystemen des menschlichen Handelns"; and O. Weinberger, *Norm und Institution. Eine Einführung in die Theorie des Rechts*, Vienna 1988, p. 29: "Sie [the institutions] sind Handlungsrahmen".

action, is the locus of the institutions: the institutions render that interrelation possible, and the institutions are the outcome of these individual-social relations and interactions".[94] Elsewhere we meet the statement that not only the institutions but also the norms constitute a sphere of human action: "The norms and legal institutions constitute [*bilden*] a framework for the action of human beings".[95] This certainly does not help to clear up how the concept of "institution" differs from that of "norm".

4.4 The Concept of "Institution". A Proposal

At the end of Chapter 3, I sought to indicate possible connections between theories of meaning, theories of norms and theories of validity. To the verificationist theory of meaning there corresponds, I said, two conceptions of norms: (i) the norm as exclamation without meaning, a meaningless sentence; (ii) the norm as prediction of a future event (a behaviour). These two conceptions of norm in turn correspond, as I have attempted to show, with two different attitudes towards the validity of the norms themselves: (i) that the problem does not even arise, since it is not possible to "justify" (in this case attribute validity to) a statement devoid of meaning; (ii) that validity coincides with verification of the prediction contained in the norm.

The ideational theory of meaning corresponds, as mentioned above, with the conception of the norm as manifestation of will or command. Here the norm will be valid when it actually expresses the will of the subject that issued it. The "pictorial" theory instead corresponds with a so-to-speak "Platonist" theory of the norm according to which it exists (and is valid) irrespective of specific conduct conforming to the norms. Finally, the behaviourist theory of meaning corresponds, we have maintained, with the conception that the norm is a particular type of linguistic stimulus. Validity in this last conception ends up coinciding with the norm's efficacy.

Once the theories of meaning just mentioned have been rejected and the so-called "use" theory adopted instead, in the sense clarified in the seventh section of Chapter 3 of this work, according to which "use" is no longer conceived of as mere "regularity", but is behaviour or a series of behaviours regulated or governed by one or more norms, I believe we may reach the following conclusions regarding the concept of rule or norm.

(A) A rule, or a norm – I am using these two terms as synonyms – has to do with a practice, or better, with the constitution of a practice. Weinberger expresses this idea by saying that "the meaning and the use of rules in the lives of those who use a language are connected essentially with action",[96] that is, that the notion of "rule" or "norm" is an *action-relative* one.

---

[94] O. Weinberger, *Institutionentheorie und institutionalistischer Rechtspositivismus*, in O. Weinberger, *Recht, Institution und Rechtspolitik*, p. 151.

[95] O. Weinberger, *Bausteine des institutionalistischen Rechtspositivismus*, p. 34.

[96] O. Weinberger, *The Role of Rules*, p. 225.

(B) Following a rule means acting in a manner endowed with meaning. The meaning indeed results from behaviours corresponding with a particular rule. A linguistic expression has meaning to the extent that there are rules governing its use. An action, or a piece of behaviour, is endowed with meaning, if there are rules governing it. These rules or norms, both those applying to linguistic expressions and those that "govern" actions, are not however the outcome of a regulation that everyone takes on in an entirely private and personal manner. The constitutive rules of "meanings" and "senses" are in turn the outcome of practices, or of "institutions". As Wittgenstein writes: "And hence also 'obeying a rule' is a practice. And to *think* one is obeying a rule is not to obey a rule. Hence it is not possible to obey a rule 'privately': otherwise thinking one was obeying a rule would be the same as obeying it".[97]

(C) Rules and social practices, or norms and institutions, are intimately connected. It may indeed be maintained that certain rules or norms "constitute" certain social practices and institutions. To illustrate this, recourse can be made to the notion of "constitutive rule" formulated by John Searle. As is well known, he distinguishes between "regulative" and "constitutive rules". The former do not constitute the object they relate to: that is, this object is independent of the formulation of the norm. The latter instead "constitute" the object they relate to, that is, their object is not independent of the formulation of the rule. "Regulative rules regulate a pre-existing activity, an activity whose existence is logically independent of the rules. Constitutive rules constitute (and also regulate) an activity the existence of which is logically dependent on the rules".[98] Significantly, Searle connects the distinction between "regulative rules" and "constitutive rules" with another distinction he introduced: between "brute facts" and "institutional facts". This distinction, in particular the concept of "institutional fact", constitutes, as we have seen, the theoretical soil from which MacCormick and Weinberger's neo-institutionalism has sprung. "Institutional facts", according to Searle, are facts that presuppose certain "institutions". The "institutional fact" of Mr Smith's marriage to Miss Jones is possible thanks to the existence of the "institution" of marriage. Equally, the institutional fact of my possession of a five-dollar bill is made possible by the "institution" of money. And "institutions" are systems of constitutive rules. "These institutions are systems of constitutive rules. Every institutional fact is underlain by a (system of) rule(s) of the form '*X* counts as *Y* in context *C*'".[99]

For some authors, the constitutive norms are not only a necessary condition but even a necessary and sufficient condition for a certain state of affairs. This seems, for instance, to be the position defended by a Spanish jurisprudent, Professor Gregorio

---

[97] L. Wittgenstein, *Philosophical Investigations* (I, 202), p. 81e. Emphasis in original.

[98] J. R. Searle, *Speech Acts. An Essay in the Philosophy of Language*, Cambridge 1969, p. 34. See also J. R. Searle, *The Construction of Social Reality*, London 1996, pp. 79ff.

[99] J. R. Searle, *Speech Acts*, pp. 51–52.

Robles: "The rule saying that a chessboard consists of sixty-four squares is not describing any concrete game field and it does not either say anything about the quality of the chessboard; *it simply produces* that board, that is, the field to play that game".[100] This conception is, however, rather problematic,[101] since it has to attribute to the norm creative powers of its own over and above its being complied with or realized, which obviously imply very strong metaphysical assumptions. For the presence of a rule, if understood as a mere linguistic expression or semantic entity, does not yet tell us that the corresponding sphere of action, or the state of affairs to which it relates, indeed exists. It would instead be necessary to find at least one sample of action that can be traced to that particular sphere in order to be able to assert that the constitutive norm of that sphere of action is in force.

I would accordingly propose adopting the following definition of the constitutive rule or norm of a practice (or "institution"). Such a norm is the condition for the conceivability (*ex ante*) and perceivability (*ex post*), and hence possibility, of a sphere of action.[102] I propose calling this sphere of action "institution", where the possibilities of action contained in it are actually made use of in time (or realized). The concept of "institution" thus defined is close to that of "practice" or "praxis".[103] The institution is here effective and structured praxis. The definition of "norm" formulated above does not indeed apply to all norms of a normative system, but only to the "fundamental" ones (the meaning of which will be clarified below).

This view of the norm corresponds to the following conception of validity. A norm is valid if and only if its statement or formulation is (i) the condition for the possibility of an institution (in the sense just given), or (ii) authorized by a norm under (i), or else logically deducible from its semantic content, or is arguably justifiable with regard to this content.

At this point there is a need to clarify on the one hand the concept of "fundamental norm" (just mentioned) and on the other that of "institution". First of all, in my view, two types of norms should be distinguished: (a) "fundamental" ones, which are the condition for the possibility of the "institution", and (b) "inferior" ones, which may be derived by logical inference or by delegation of powers (what Kelsen calls *Ermächtigung*) from the "fundamental norms". This distinction finds arguments in its favour in a well-known article by John Rawls, *Two Concepts of Rules*.

---

100 G. Robles, *Was ist eine Regel?* in *Vernunft und Erfahrung im Rechtsdenken der Gegenwart*, ed. by T. Eckhoff, L. M. Friedman and J. Uusitalo, Berlin 1986, p. 28.

101 No less problematic is the position of those who recognize that the constitutive norms are not reducible to regulative (prescriptive) norms but end up conceiving of the former as "quasi-commands" (A. Ross, *Directives and Norms*, New York, NY 1968, p. 57) thus going back on all they had previously conceded to a "liberal" vision of norms.

102 I am here adopting ideas contained in the writings of Amedeo Giovanni Conte. See e.g., A. G. Conte, *Materiali per una tipologia delle regole*, in *Materiali per una storia della cultura giuridica*, 1985, pp. 345ff.

103 See e.g. A. G. Conte, *Regola costitutiva in Wittgenstein*, in *Uomini senza qualità. La crisi dei linguaggi nella grande Vienna*, ed. by F. Castellani, Trento 1981, pp. 65ff.

Rawls too, like Wittgenstein, starts by noting that there is a connection between rules or norms and practice. "Rules", writes Rawls, "are not generalizations from the decisions of individuals applying the utilitarian principle directly and independently to recurrent particular cases. On the contrary, rules define a practice".[104] Note however that these rules serve according to Rawls not only to (i) "define" the practice but also (ii) to learn it (and hence engage in it) and (iii) to correct the conduct of those who engage in that particular practice. Establishing a practice involves, according to Rawls, "the specification of a new form of activity".[105] The norms of the practice, further, are not followed on the basis of utilitarian considerations nor prudential calculations: "a practice necessarily involves the abdication of full liberty to act on utilitarian and prudential grounds".[106]

This conception of norm, which Rawls terms the *practice conception*, is contrasted with what is called the *summary view*. According to the latter conception "rules are pictured as summaries of past decisions arrived at by the direct application of the utilitarian principle to particular cases".[107] Rawls adopts the practice conception, distinguishing between (i) "a practice" and (ii) "a particular action", and hence between (i) "rules of practice", and (ii) "particular rules to particular cases".[108] The conclusion reached by Rawls, whose fundamental problem here is the "justification" of these practices, actions and rules, is that a utilitarian argument may "justify" a practice and the rules that define and constitute it, but cannot be applied to the particular actions and rules that are a specification of a particular practice. The "justification" of the particular actions and rules is according to Rawls always given in terms of the practice of which they are a specification, and thus by recourse to the rules of the practice of which the action or rule in question represents an application.

In this perspective, the problem of "justification" properly arises only as far as the practice is concerned. Thus, if a child asks its father why the neighbour has been put in jail, the father may reply that he has been arrested because he has been sentenced by a court, referring to a rule of the "practice" of criminal law. But if the child were to ask "Why is there a jail?", the father's answer could no longer refer to the rules of a "practice", but would have to have recourse to a justification of strictly moral type, perhaps an argument of utilitarian type like: to protect good people from criminals.[109]

Now Rawls's distinction between "rules of a practice" and "particular rules" is similar to the one I propose between "fundamental norms" and "inferior norms". The former are the norms that "define" and "constitute" the practice in question, that is, according to the definition given above, the "institution". The "inferior"

---

[104] J. Rawls, *Two Concepts of Rules*, in *Theories of Ethics*, ed. by P. Foot, Oxford 1970, p. 163.

[105] Ibid., p. 162.

[106] Ibid.

[107] Ibid., p. 158.

[108] See ibid., p. 146.

[109] See ibid.

norms are the rules that apply to the actions occurring within the framework of the "institution" made possible by the "fundamental norms".

A norm, then, is valid, if "fundamental", if and insofar as the "institution" of which it is the possibility condition actually exists in reality, that is, if the particular actions that those norms make conceivable and possible actually occur. If "inferior", a norm is valid if and insofar as it is correctly derived (a) by logical inference, and (b) by normative delegation, from a "fundamental" norm. (b) corresponds, as we have said, to Kelsen's *Ermächtigung*.[110] (a) instead corresponds to what Ota Weinberger calls the principle of "co-validity" or *Mitgeltung*.[111] As I have said, I propose calling "institution" the sphere of action of which one or more norms are the possibility condition, provided that this possibility is actually made use of. In this proposal of mine the concept of "norm" and that of "institution" do not coincide and indeed remain quite distinct.

Consider the definition of "institution" given by John Rawls in *A Theory of Justice*: "Now by an institution I shall understand a public system of rules which defines offices and positions with their rights and duties, power and immunities, and the like".[112] In this definition the concept of norm and that of institution overlap. This confusion can have two outcomes: (a) on the one hand, the position that the statement of normative propositions is sufficient to give rise to an "institution"; (b) on the other, a circular definition of the concept of "institution". Proposition (a) may have paradoxical consequences, such as for instance the position that a constitution formulated only on paper gives rise to the corresponding constitutional regime. This would rightly incur the reproach often brought against theorists of constitutive rules by scholars with a realist orientation, of attributing to linguistic statements a "magic power" such that they are *by themselves* capable of producing extra-linguistic entities.[113]

Consider again what Rawls writes: "An institution exists at a certain time and place where the actions *specified by it* are regularly carried out in accordance with a public understanding that the system of rules defining the institution is to be followed".[114] This assertion is problematic. It in fact asserts the existence of an institution when the actions that are "specified" by it are actually engaged in (with awareness of their mandatoriness, a sort of *opinio iuris ac necessitatis*). But the actions can only be "specified" by an institution if it is already in some sense existent. The institution is here existent – when it is existent.

One way to avoid this tautological outcome is to assert that an "institution" is nothing but a *system of norms*; this seems, for instance, to be the opinion of John

[110]See e.g., H. Kelsen, *Reine Rechtslehre*, 2nd ed., Vienna 1960, pp. 15–16, 57–58, 150ff.

[111]See O. Weinberger, *Norm und Institution. Eine Einführung in die Theorie des Rechts*, pp. 67, 103

[112]J. Rawls, *A Theory of Justice*, Cambridge, MA 1971, p. 55.

[113]Cf. e.g., what R. Guastini writes in *Cognitivismo ludico e regole costitutive*, in *La teoria generale del diritto. Problemi e tendenze attuali. Studi dedicati a Norberto Bobbio*, ed. by U. Scarpelli, Comunità, Milano 1983, p. 170.

[114]J. Rawls, *A Theory of Justice*, p. 55. My emphasis.

Searle.[115] If that is the case, we once again lose the distinction between the two concepts of "norm" and "institution", that is, the latter is transformed into an "order", a more or less logically coordinated complex of normative statements. At this point, however, the following question arises: given that by "institution" one understands an extra-linguistic reality, and that the "institution" is nothing but a "system of norms", in what sense does a system of norms that is only thought of or written on paper constitute an "institution"?

Another way to avoid the tautological outcome or *petitio principi* above can be seen in a distinction that I feel is appropriate between (i) actions made possible by one or more norms and (ii) actions, made possible by one or more norms, *that are actually executed.* Only the latter actions, of which the norm is a necessary but not sufficient condition, give us what should in my view properly be defined as an "institution". The norms, that is, produce *possibilities* of action, not the actions themselves. This is very well put by Riccardo Guastini: "What the constitutive normative systems produce is only the *possibility* of events, situations, objects and activities. (The rules of a game, for instance, are productive not of gaming activities, but of a game system, which is just a system of rules)".[116] If the distinction just mentioned is adopted, one will not come up against the realist criticism, and the confusion that is a source of so many misunderstandings between norms and "institutions" will be avoided. The "institutions" are not systems of rules or norms, but systems of possibilities of action that are actually made use of.

I do not find it possible to share the opinion that constitutive norms by themselves produce the state of affairs with which they are concerned. "The norms we are concerned with," writes Professor Carcaterra in connection with constitutive norms, "produce the effect that is their object and their content by *realizing it themselves*: they constitute it – this is their characteristic – at the very moment when they come into force".[117] "The constitutive norm is an ought [. . .] that is identified with an 'is', that by itself immediately actuates its own content [. . .] Norming and realization coincide [. . .]; the reality envisaged is produced immediately". "In the phenomenon of constitutivity", writes Carcaterra again, "the normative act and the act of its execution coincide".[118] To develop his concept of "constitutive norm", Carcaterra does not refers so much to Searle's concept of constitutive rule (which is the possibility condition for what it relates to, but does not immediately produce its object) but rather to the concept of *performative utterance* proposed by John Langshaw Austin. Carcaterra constructs his "constitutive norms" on the model of Austin's performative utterances, which, as we know, produce the object they relate to by their mere utterance. (Thus, for instance, the utterance "I promise *p*" immediately produces promise *p*.)

---

[115]See J. R. Searle, *Speech Acts*, p. 51.

[116]R. Guastini, *Op. cit.*, p. 171.

[117]G. Carcaterra, *Le norme costitutive*, Milano 1974, pp. 60–61.

[118]Ibid., pp. 100, 106. On this cf. G. Azzoni, *Il concetto di condizione nella tipologia delle regole*, Padova 1988, pp. 55–56, 61ff.

Carcaterra's theses do not convince. The norms do not have the power to change real situations, except on the condition that they are followed or observed or "made use of". They have this power, that is, on the condition that some human conduct conforms to them or comes about taking these norms as models or uses that possibility of action offered by the norms. To corroborate his thesis of the immediate productivity of effects of constitutive norms (irrespective of any other human intervention), Carcaterra gives the examples of Article 45 of the Italian Civil Code, which used to state, before it was replaced by Article 1 of Law no. 151 of 19 May 1975 reforming family law: "A wife not legally separated has the husband's residence..." But what does it mean to "have residence" in a certain place? It means that, for certain purposes, certain documents will indicate that a particular subject resides in that particular place, that communications directed to that particular subject will be addressed to that particular place, etc. I mean, that "having residence" is not a state of affairs unless confirmed by actions and conduct in conformity with it. It is not entirely correct to maintain, accordingly, that a constitutive rule produces *by itself*, by its intrinsic force, a state of affairs, *quite apart from any other human intervention or behaviour*.[119] Without further human action in conformity with or constituted through the norms in question these would be nothing other than *flatus vocis*. The relation between norms and action is more or less similar to that between the text of a play and its performance on stage. Theatre, the phenomenon of theatre, comes about only once the text is performed, so that there is a "theatrical performance". Equally law, the phenomenon of law, comes about only once the norms are "represented", that is, when there is an action effected according to or through norms. This doesn't of course prevent us reading and appreciating a work of theatre aside from its enactment. In the same way one can appreciate a law that is no longer in effect, for the values of which it is an expression and the practical consequences to which it might eventually lead.

Let us suppose that together with some friends I conceive the rules of a new game. These rules are carefully worked out and then put down in writing. This is not, however, sufficient, if the definition of "institution" I propose is adopted, for it to be possible to maintain that these rules constitute an "institution". Only once the game is actually and repeatedly played, and the actions made possible by its rules performed, can it be said that game is an "institution".

For the "institution" in this sense represents a portion of what "is", which cannot however be conceived of in the same way as the "is" of physical beings (the heavenly bodies, for instance) or even living organisms (a cell, let us say). It is a typically human, cultural reality, with a normative foundation: that is, it is made possible by the production (conscious or unconscious) of norms or rules, and makes sense in reference to them. Think of any natural language; it constitutes a piece of reality, a significant space of human action (thinking, communicating, discussing). This

[119] For a critique of Carcaterra's idea that constitutive rules immediately produce the object they relate to, see R. Guastini, *Teoria delle regole costitutive*, in *Rivista internazionale di filosofia del diritto*, 1983, pp. 563–564.

reality, the thinking and communicating, let us say in Italian, is possible *thanks* to the rules of the Italian language.

Thus, following the institutionalist view here adopted, we arrive at a theory of validity that emerges as a sort of fusion of "is" and "ought". The "is" of an "institution" depends here on the "ought" of the norms, and vice versa the "ought" of the norms draws its ultimate justification (validity) from the "is" of the "institution".[120] This is, moreover, what Weinberger defines as the fundamental ontological thesis of his normativist institutionalism: "There exists an essential connection between institutions and institutional facts on the one side and practical informations (rule-, ends-, and value-systems) on the other".[121] Note that this "tracing back" of the "is" to the "ought" and vice versa does not necessarily invalidate the non-cognitivist meta-ethical thesis nor the methodological position of the *Wertfreiheit* of science, where the "great divide" is intended as a *semantic* rather than an ontological distinction. On the other hand, when it is said that the "ought" of the norms is traced back to the "is" of the institution, nothing is affirmed other than that only *existent* norms are norms, that is, norms which "ought to be" are nothing other than the norms that "are", or which, on the view adopted here, constitute possibilities of action actually made use of, and "precipitated"[122] in the "institutions". This however is not true of all types of norm, but only of those that are social or, rather, socially existent. It is not valid above all, for moral norms as the "moral ought" is so strong as to not be reconcilable with "is". According to the "strong" moral point of view the norms that "ought to be" can never be equivalent to the norms that "are", except by virtue of a chance act by an autonomous subject. The legal and social norm insofar as it is democratically produced as the product of an open, discursive process, maintains an element of involvement (as its adoption is not independent of the circumstances of its issue). The moral norm, however, is always rigourously autonomous.

The validity of the law, that is of legal or, more generally, social norms, depends on their relation with the corresponding institution. "The social norms are valid – that is, existent as social facts", writes Weinberger, "only when as regulatory mechanisms they determine the functioning of the corresponding institution. By validity of a social norm we mean the existence of an effective link between the norm and the corresponding institution".[123] The validity of social and legal norms thus depends on the existence of particular states of affairs, and cannot accordingly depend on purely normative criteria like moral principles and rules. "The validity of law",

---

[120]The correlation between "is" and "ought" here affirmed is similar to the correlation between *Sein* and *Sollen* of which Amedeo Conte speaks in connection with the "eidetico-constitutive deontic rules" (the *Sein* of what they regulate is determined by the *Sollen* of the rules themselves, which are *constitutive* for that very reason).

[121]O. Weinberger, *Institutionentheorie und insitutionalistischer Rechtspositivismus*, p. 149.

[122]Cf. G. Di Bernardo, *Il ruolo delle regole costitutive e prescrittive nella costruzione della realtà sociale*, in *Nuova civiltà delle macchine*, 1985, no. 3–4, p. 38.

[123]O. Weinberger, *Verfassungstheorie vom Standpunkt des neuen Institutionalismus*, in *Archiv für Rechts- und Sozialphilosophie*, 1990, p. 100.

writes the Czech author, "cannot be made depending on values".[124] Nor can validity be made to depend on the existence of an act of will (the act of promulgation of a norm). "Valid law originates not only through explicit decisions that lay down the law but also through practices, through customary behaviour that can be institutionalised as normative behaviour. In any case we should reject the extreme view defended by imperativist legal positivists that acknowledge a norm as real only when there has been a previous explicit act of will producing a rule with corresponding contents".[125]

This does not, however, lead to identifying the norm's validity and its efficacy. Institution and norms remain separate or separable entities. What is required for the validity of the norms is certainly the existence of the corresponding institution, or if you will its "efficacy" or "effectiveness". The norm may however be valid even if it is not efficacious. Or rather, as far as the fundamental norms of the institution are concerned, validity and efficacy tend to coincide. But for all other norms, the derived or "secondary" norms, it is neither necessary nor possible for validity and efficacy to coincide.

The critique of the voluntarist theory of validity, the rejection – at least at the level of "secondary" norms – of the confusion between validity and efficacy and the rejection of the overlapping of criteria of validity and of morality, and finally the reference, in order to determine criteria of validity, to "fundamental" norms that are effectively in force as corresponding to the institution considered do not necessarily imply acceptance of principles of positive morality as criteria of legal validity. This is justified by the difficulties of identifying a *single* positive morality, and by the need to leave open the possibility of transcending it (or calling it in question through criticizing it). Neo-institutionalism "does not accept either the subsidiary validity of validity as criterion among others for determining what is 'legal', since there is no such thing as *the* social morality, and all the moral principles commonly accepted may be disputed".[126]

According to the institutionalist view here adopted, we ultimately end by upholding a rather less controversial position than might have seemed likely at first sight: that the norms that constitute an "institution", the ones we earlier called "fundamental", are valid because they are effective. This position echoes that of Kelsen that the validity of the legal order as a whole coincides with its effectiveness. It might seem that by accepting this position we fall back into an anti-normativist view of social reality and of law. That is not so, since according to the institutionalist perspective to which reference is made here, the efficacy of norms, that is, compliance with them, comes about through actions made possible by the norms themselves, in a space of action constituted by them. This point seems to be already sufficiently clear in Weinberger's theory. "The validity of social norms", he writes, "is based on their relation with institutions. The norm, for instance a legal norm, exists in social

---

[124] Ibid., p. 104.

[125] Ibid.

[126] Ibid.

reality when it is in functional relation with institutions. The validity of a legal norm is neither an expectation on the basis of a forecast regarding the future behaviour of courts – as some legal realists maintain – nor is it mere ideal existence on the basis of a presumption (as pure normativism asserts), but is based on the essential fusion of norm and reality that comes about in the institution".[127] The validity of the norm here refers to the existence (efficacy) of the institution, which however is not the outcome of a sum of "brute facts" or of mere behavioural regularities, but is made possible (and knowable) through a particular body of fundamental norms. Nor does the validity of the norm serve to exclude any moral evaluation of the norm or the possible realization of the injustice of this. All that it does is to structure the arguments in favour of the obligatory nature of the norm according to a series of hierarchical steps amongst which the evaluation of the norm involves reference to the validity of the "institution". This has to be checked through reference to the "meaning" of the same institution: the efficacy of the "institution" corresponds to its meaning or *Witz*. This doesn't preclude the transcendence of the level of the institution and entrance into a purely normative debate. In contrast to what is said by Wittgenstein it is possible that the "meaning" of a institution refers back to considerations of justice.

In line with the definition I offer here of "institution", this is not understood as a particularly stable model of behaviour, an "institutionalized" one to use the vocabulary of sociology, to be contrasted with still fluid, unregulated behaviour (broadly the "movement" that Professor Alberoni speaks of), "crystallized" or norm-governed behaviour (Alberoni's "institution"[128]). In my view all the models of social behaviour actually followed are "institutions". On the other hand, there are no models of behaviour or spheres of action apart from a system of norms that prescribes these models and is the possibility condition for the existence of those spheres of action.

This does not, however, imply an underestimation of the element of stability within the framework of the spheres of action. As Wittgenstein writes "a language game is something which consists in the recurrent procedures of the game in time."[129] A sphere of action is practicable, that is, can be "made use of", only as long as it is stable in time. This is for at least two reasons: (a) first, because an action is an event developed in time, and hence requires constant conditions, a fixed reference framework; (b) second, because actions are often mutually interdependent, connected by reciprocal expectations, which would be frustrated – the prospect of the action – if they could not count on a stable space within which it would be possible to project, undertake and bring to a conclusion certain actions.[130] Social actions are also collective actions and collectivity is expressed here as a

---

127 O. Weinberger, *Soziologie und normative Institutionentheorie. Überlegungen zu Helmut Schelskys Institutionentheorie vom Standpunkt der normativistischen Institutionenontologie*, p. 192

128 See F. Alberoni, *Movimento e istituzione. Teoria generale*, Bologna 1981, e.g., pp. 223ff.

129 L. Wittgenstein, *On Certainty*, § 519, p. 68e

130 Cf. N. MacCormick, *Institutions, Arrangements and Practical Information*, pp. 73ff.

history of actions the meaning of which is perceivable as the narration of a more or less coherent series of events.

In relation to the problem of the dynamics between "institution" and "institutionalization", Ota Weinberger's notion is more than plausible. "As far as the phenomenon of institutionalization is concerned, the relative stabilization of forms of behaviour is mostly seen as the essential fact. In my view, however, the stress should be laid particularly on the fact that the institutions have a practical nature, that is, are systems of action, and are constituted around a core of practical information. In this connection, naturally, from a sociological viewpoint, the question of relative stabilization plays an essential part. This follows already from the fact that institutions are systems of action, since practical activity requires a certain quantity of stable frameworks".[131]

Weinberger gives an example in relation to this. Take the case of two children who decide to play at football on a lawn. Their behaviour is governed by the rules of football, and their game constitutes an "institution", even if in the case under consideration the action of the two children is of limited duration. "I favour the conception", concludes Weinberger in this connection, "that the nature of the institutions and of the social process of institutionalization should be treated as two distinct though often mutually connected questions. In the case of individual situations too, a system of rules of interaction comes into being, which may be considered an institution quite apart from the fact of its being constituted as a lasting, stable organism. Ad hoc interactions in communities cannot be ruled out of the sphere of the theory of institutions, since they constitute spaces of action in a similar way to that of stable institutions".[132]

4.5 Binding Force and Mandatoriness of Norms

Weinberger and MacCormick have not particularly concerned themselves with the problem that has tormented generations of philosophers and theorists of law, that of the so-called binding force of norms. I nonetheless believe that the institutionalist view can supply some useful insights into this question. Weinberger, for instance, occasionally denies that the bindingness of norms is a product of the sanctions ensuing on their breach. "From a sociological perspective it is fundamentally false", he writes, "that rule following conduct could only be reached through incentives of various kind: sanctions, punishment, or rewards".[133] The Czech scholar repeatedly criticizes the conception that a norm is observed only from a prudential or utilitarian

[131] O. Weinberger, *Ontologie, Hermeneutik und der Begriff des geltenden Rechts*, p. 118. See also O. Weinberger, *Institutionentheorie und institutionalistischer Rechtspositivismus*, pp. 151–152.

[132] O. Weinberger, *Soziologie und normative Institutionentheorie*, p. 191.

[133] O. Weinberger, *Verfassungstheorie vom Standpunkt des neuen Institutionalismus*, p. 104. And this is one of the points on which the Czech author takes his distance from Kelsen (cf. e.g., H. Kelsen, *Hauptprobleme der Staatsrechtslehre, entwickelt aus der Lehre vom Rechtssatze*, Tübingen 1911, p. 202).

calculation, that is, to avoid a penalty (damage) or to gain a reward or in some way derive a benefit. "It would be wrong to consider the efficacy of heteronomous rules only as a prudential reaction to penalties or rewards".[134]

In particular, the institutionalist view enables us, I believe, to escape a solution frequently put forward in the theory of law (I am thinking, for instance, of Julius Binder's "absolute idealism",[135] and of Olivecrona's legal realism[136]) which ends by conceiving of the "binding force" as a sort of moral obligatoriness. This solution, I feel, has paradoxical outcomes. It should be noted, for instance, that all norms in force, not just legal ones, are binding. This is put very clearly by Hermann Kantorowicz: "The most widely spread, but often unconscious misuse of the term 'law' is to restrict it to *(absolutely) binding rules*. This quality is often called validity (*Geltung*), i.e., obligatory character, but obligatory character of some kind or degree is of course inherent in *any* rule, not only in those of law".[137] On the other hand, if all rules or norms in force are "binding", certainly not all are also binding "morally".

Think, for instance, of a game of chess. There is no doubt that when I play chess I am "bound" by the rules of this game. But am I bound to them "morally"? Is breach of the rules of chess perhaps a moral infraction? I may certainly seek to deceive my opponent, by covertly moving a knight as a bishop. This could perhaps be called immoral conduct. But does its immorality result from the breach of the rules of chess, or rather from breach of mutual trust (trust that the other will act loyally), which is in some sense the condition for any game or, we might say, any social relationship?

The paradoxical outcome of the theory that sees the binding force of norms in terms of moral obligatoriness appears still more clearly if the theory is applied to the rules of natural languages. In what sense can it be said that I am morally obliged when I say something in German always to put the verb second? And is the beginner who repeatedly commits howlers in speaking the language of Goethe perhaps committing immoral acts? It might be objected that the theory in question here is understood solely in reference to *legal* norms. But even in that case there is no lack of paradoxical outcomes. In what sense can it be said, for instance, that the so-called "Nuremberg laws" of 1935 (valid and effective within the National Socialist legal system) were morally obligatory? The theories that assert the binding force in the moral sense of legal norms thus risk overlapping the *normative* and the *moral* viewpoint, which instead remain distinct. If they were indeed not so, we could not ultimately distinguish law and morality, and still more serious, we could not assert the bindingness of a norm without asserting its morality. As Wittgenstein writes:

---

[134]O. Weinberger, *Die formal-finalistische Handlungstheorie und das Strafrecht*, now in Id., *Recht, Institution und Rechtspolitik*, p. 132.

[135]See e.g., J. Binder, *Zur Lehre vom Rechtsbegriff*, in *Logos*, vol. 18, 1929, pp. 1–35

[136]See e.g., K. Olivecrona, *Law as Fact*, Copenhagen 1939, p. 14, according to which the binding force of law is said to be "a certain *feeling* of being bound by the law", emphasis in original. For an opposite view, M. Oakeshott, *On Human Conduct*, pp. 155–156.

[137]H. Kantorowicz, *The Definition of Law*, ed. by A. H. Campbell, Cambridge 1958, p. 16, emphasis in original.

"once I have grasped a rule I am bound in what I subsequently do. But this of course means only that I am bound in the *judgements* I deliver on what conforms with the rule and what does not".[138] The *normative* viewpoint is certainly a "genus", part of which makes up the *species* of the "moral" viewpoint. Not every "normative" viewpoint represents a "moral" viewpoint. The moral one is a strong, or extremely strong, normative viewpoint, characterised by a large dose of counterfactuality.

I would propose distinguishing between an "objective" and a "subjective" binding force of norms. The first is connected with their constitutive nature. Consider the following passage, from Professor Guido Fassò's *La storia come esperienza giuridica*: "If on the basis of my direct or indirect experience I have grounds for believing that the existence of a family, a State, a band etc., right up to the whole human community, is subordinate to performance by their members of certain acts, I, if and when I choose to become a member of them, will abstractly consider those acts and subsequently perform them in those particular circumstances in which I find myself having to perform them, thus applying what, for me, is the law (simultaneously theoretical and practical) of the family, of the State, etc.".[139] Within the space of action created by the norms, these are binding insofar as compliance with them is a condition for that space of reality to continue to exist. For we said that an "institution" exists not when there are norms that constitute possibilities of action, but only when these possibilities are actually and repeatedly "made use of". An institution may accordingly be extinguished by *desuetude*, that is, by the fact that there are no longer behaviours that make use of the possibilities opened by the norms in question.

Anyone who chooses a certain course of action is bound by the rules that make possible the action itself. Anyone acting within a certain reality space, playing at chess, for instance, is objectively bound to respect the rules of chess, on pain of leaving the game itself, and not completing the action he intended to accomplish. Moreover since human life is necessarily social life, and since this is given through the norms that constitute it, the "objectivity" of the norms is equivalent to that social context into which one is "thrown" without the possibility of exit. All this is very well expressed by Hannah Arendt: "For the point of these rules is not that I submit to them voluntarily or recognize theoretically their validity, but that in practice I cannot enter the game unless I conform [. . .]. Every man is born into a community with pre-existing laws which he 'obeys' first of all because there is no other way for him to enter the great game of the world".[140] We might also remember the Duchess of Sanseverina's recommendation to Fabrizio, his beloved nephew: "Figure-toi qu'on t'enseigne les règles du jeu de whist; est-ce que tu ferais des objection au règles du whist?".[141]

---

[138] L. Wittgenstein, *Bemerkungen über die Grundsätze der Mathematik*, ed. by G. E. M. Anscombe, R. Rhees and G. H. Von Wright, Frankfurt am Main 1989, pp. 328–329. English translation mimne, emphasis in original.

[139] G. Fassò, *La storia come esperienza giuridica*, Milan 1953, pp. 60–61.

[140] H. Arendt, *On Violence*, in Id., *Crises of the Republic*, Harmondsworth 1972, p. 157.

[141] Stendhal, *La chartreuse de Parme*, Paris 1964, p. 147.

This "need" to respect "constitutive" rules could also be clarified in the following way. "At every step of the process leading to accomplishment of a particular project", writes Professor Di Bernardo, "the agent, if he wishes to maintain the responsibility incumbent on him, is obliged to respect the rules that define the relevant functions. They are necessary and sufficient conditions for that social agent to carry out the functions of the role he fills. It can also be said that this obligation has more the nature of an alethic modality (the need to do this or that, or the impossibility to do this or that), than of obligation in the deontic sense true and proper".[142] "Subjective" binding force seems to coincide, hence, with the motivation, or motive, to act in a certain way. The chief reason for which norms are observed is, on this view, that of wanting to "enter" the sphere of social reality that those norms constitute. This has to do also with the problem of constructing the subject's social identity, bearing in mind that "individual action is prevalently identity-oriented, that is, centred round the process of constructing individual identity (doing for being)".[143] The identity of the subject is not "given". but "constructed", and often "conquered".

Consider the following case. A famous university teacher, flying back from Argentina, crashes in the Amazon in an accident. He is the sole survivor, and finds himself in the midst of a tribe of Guaraní Indians. His former identity as a learned, esteemed intellectual disappears at a stroke as soon as he finds himself in a social context, a sphere of action, entirely different from the one in which he had constructed his identity as a university teacher. To be sure, this example is too much of a *reductio ad Amazoniam*,[144] as unlikely as you wish, yet not impossible. What I wish to stress, however, is that the individual social identity is connected with a certain sphere of action, that is, with one or more institutions, and further that "if persons act, they always do so in connection with some identity".[145] The identity that an individual gives herself is connected with the type of social reality, of sphere of action, of game, in which she may represent herself as *actor*. If I constitute my subjective identity at a certain point in time as that of a chess player, I shall have very good grounds for regarding the rules of chess as binding and complying with them.

All this does not, however, imply, let it be noted, either that one cannot rebel against the existing norms and institutions or that the individual's subjectivity is something void or a vain illusion, as being dependent on the individual's "role" or "social identity". Above all, it should be made clear that according to the view taken here, if norms constitute possibilities of action, the actions always remain the product of the will or intention of the subject. Rules, in any case do not determine their application, but must be used: the rules that an individual "accepts" do not tell her what to say.

---

[142] G. Di Bernardo, *Il ruolo delle regole costitutive e prescrittive nella costruzione della realtà sociale*, pp. 37–38. See also G. Di Bernardo, *Le regole dell'azione sociale*, Milan 1983, p. 181.

[143] M. Livolsi, *Identità e progetto. L'attore sociale nella società contemporanea*, Firenze 1987, p. 139.

[144] See A. Pizzorno, *Sul confronto intertemporale delle utilità*, in *Stato e mercato*, April 1986, p. 15.

[145] Ibid., p. 14.

4.6 Institution and Intentionality. The Problem of the Social Identity

The intentionality of subjects in relation to "institutions" is deployed at two chief levels. (i) One may or may not want to "enter" a given sphere of action, a given "institution". One may decide to play chess or not. I may decide whether or not to wear the uniform of a conscript. And so forth. This decision is determined by the subject's life project, by his goals, and not by those of the "institution" one may, let us say, wish to "enter". I decide, say, to play chess to freshen a mind dazed by too many hours of reading, to relax, to give a lesson to some upstart, to divert my convalescent sister, and so forth.

(ii) Within the sphere of action constituted by certain rules, within a definite "institution", if the scheme of action is already modelled by the constitutive norms of the "institution", the token action, the "sample" action that I accomplish, is largely, in its specificity, an interpretation, or somehow an *invention* of mine. The "Sicilian defence", for instance, is an invention, a "creation", within the schemes of action made possible by the rules of chess. Indeed the specific application of the norm in practice in some way alters (in general imperceptibly, but sometimes dramatically) the norm itself, that is, its semantic content. To refer once more to Wittgenstein's philosophy, it is quite obvious that – as he says – "the rule does not work itself, for whatever happens according to the rule is an interpretation [*eine Deutung*] of the rule".[146]

Moreover, in order for a piece of behaviour to be termed performed in conformity with a norm, it is not enough for the behaviour to correspond with the norm; there must be the *intention* to conform with the norm (or at least it must be possible to presuppose the existence of that intention, for instance by feeling oneself bound to perform particular behaviour even if one is not capable of explicitly formulating the corresponding behaviour). This is well put by Jürgen Habermas: One observable behaviour can be said to fulfill a valid rule only when this can be understood as the production of an acting subject that has grasped the rule meaning and decided to follow it.[147] Here, perhaps, we have a first element in the solution to Kripke's paradox that (repeating a phrase of Wittgenstein's – but isolated from its more general context) no behaviour can be determined by any rule, since any behaviour can be made to correspond to that particular rule.[148] Where the other element is given by the intersubjective validity of the rule and by its being rooted in an (intersubjectively recognizable) practice: "The application of the concept of 'following a rule' presupposes a habit. Accordingly it would be nonsensical to say that just once, in

---

146 L. Wittgenstein, *Bemerkungen über die Grundlagen der Mathematik*, p. 249. English translation mine.

147 See J. Habermas, *Vorlesungen zu einer sprachtheoretischen Grundlegung der Soziologie*, p. 14.

148 Cf. C. M. Yablon, *Law and Metaphysics*, in *The Yale Law Journal*, 1987, pp. 613–636; J. Bjarup, *Kripke's Case. Some Remarks on Rules, their Interpretation and Application*, in *Rechtstheorie*, 1988, pp. 39–49; F. Schauer, *Rules and the Rule-Following Argument*, in *Canadian Journal of Law and Jurisprudence*, 1990, pp. 187–318.

the history of the world, someone had followed a rule (or a road sign); had played a game, uttered a proposition, understood a proposition, etc., once only".[149]

The intentionality governing human actions cannot be regarded as "internal" to rules, in the sense of being explicable through them. I find unacceptable the following statement by Habermas: "Intentional I call a behaviour that is directed through rules or that is oriented to rules".[150] In particular, it should be noted that there is intentional conduct not directed or oriented by any system of rules: for instance, drinking water, walking towards some destination, smoking a cigarette etc. Moreover, as far as behaviour directed or oriented by norms is concerned too, for instance writing or speaking, or playing football, the individual behaviour or action (writing a particular phrase, pronouncing a particular word, kicking the ball in a particular direction) cannot be explained entirely or solely by reference to the system of rules governing or guiding them. The norms have to be "intended", or put more simply, *applied*. And their application cannot in turn be regulated (fully) by other rules. The rules as such have no power to "apply themselves" or to bring about anything at all unless some factor external to them comes in: the intention (to follow or apply the rule).

This is indeed recognized by Habermas himself in discussing the concept of language rule in Wittgenstein. Understanding a game means that one understands something that one "can do". Understanding is mastering some technique. By such mastering there is a spontaneity expressed, whereby one can independently apply a learned rule. There is also a creative production of new examples and cases that can be considered as a valid application of the.[151] The "spontaneity" and "creativity" that he refers to here are obviously *external* to the rules, that is, to their semantic content, instead belonging to the "world" of "intentional" or psychological facts. This corroborates the Wittgensteinian thesis, shared by Habermas, that a cognitive capacity to understand a rule, to grasp its semantic content, at the same time implies a *practical ability*: to carry out operations in accordance with that rule for a potentially infinite number of cases, that is, for new cases different from the ones the rule has been seen applied to (and hence learned).

Peter Winch, speaking of an "institution", refers to two types of means-ends relation: (a) an "extrinsic" relation and (b) an "intrinsic" relation. In the former the action possible within the institutional context appears as a means, in relation to an end "external" to the institution. Winch's example is of someone playing chess to improve his ability at the game, in order to impress his employer who attaches great importance to that ability. In the second type of relation, the action in question acts as means to an end "internal" to the institution. Winch's example is of a

---

[149] L. Wittgenstein, *Bemerkungen über die Grundlagen der Mathematik*, pp. 322–323. English translation mine.

[150] J. Habermas, *Vorlesungen zu einer sprachtheoretischen Grundlegung der Soziologie*, p. 13.

[151] See ibid., p. 70.

player who, asked why he is playing, replies, "To checkmate my opponent".[152] In the "extrinsic" relation, accordingly, it should be added, the subject of decision has as its object "entry" to the "institution" or otherwise, in that particular context of action. In the case of the "intrinsic" relation, instead, the subject's decision concerns not "entry" into the "institution", but adoption of the most suitable conduct for pursuing an end already implicit, intrinsic in his word, in the framework of that context ("institution") in which he is moving. Subjectivity is, then, doubly relevant in an institutionalist perspective: as regards the decision to "enter" the "institution" and hence accept it as it is (in reference to what Winch calls the "extrinsic" means-end relation), and as far as performance of the individual actions is concerned (in the framework of what Winch calls the "intrinsic" means-end relation); this performance is highly creative and inventive in relation to the schema offered by the constitutive norms of the "institution".

Further, the subject's social identity, if dependent on a certain sphere of action, that is on an "institution", is not, according to this perspective, the *whole* identity of the subject, nor does it coincide with subjectivity itself (as is the case in, say, the theories of Julius Binder, Karl Larenz and to some extent Arnold Gehlen and Hans-Georg Gadamer[153]). The subject's identity does not, that is, coincide with the subject's *social* identity, which comes from taking on a certain role within an institution, nor does the social identity so conceived coincide with either a "pure" type of collective identity (where "the subject sets his own identity through belonging to a group, indeed identifies himself *without residue* with the group"[154]) or a "type of fundamental identity resulting from dependency of the individual element – differentiating it from the collective-assimilating type".[155]

The individual's identity, if constructed in relation to a social context, is also, and perhaps particularly, *reflexive*: it is constructed in relation to oneself. This emerges clearly from the fact that individuals are always capable of rejecting the tradition they have been brought up in and taking their distance, albeit only morally, from the social context in which they are embedded. Voltaire was educated by Jesuits. A rigidly Catholic family may produce a rabid anti-clerical, and vice versa; an aristocrat may turn into an intransigent revolutionary, and so forth.[156]

---

[152]See P. Winch, *Popper and Scientific Method in Social Sciences*, in *The Philosophy of Karl Popper*, ed. by P. A. Schilpp, La Salle, IL 1974, pp. 894ff.

[153]See e.g., J. Binder, *Der Idealismus als Grundlage der Staatsphilosophie*, in *Zeitschrift für Deutsche Kulturphilosophie*, 1935, p. 151; K. Larenz, *Sittlichkeit und Recht. Untersuchungen um Geschichte des deutschen Rechtsdenken und um Sittenlehre*, in *Reich und Recht in der deutschen Philosophie*, ed. by K. Larenz, Stuttgart and Berlin 1943, pp. 379–380; A. Gehlen, *Urmensch und Spätkultur. Philosophische Ergebnisse und Aussagen*, Bonn 1950, pp. 233ff.; H. G. Gadamer, *Wahrheit und Methode. Grundzüge ener philosophischen Hermeneutik*, in Id., *Gesammelte Werke*, vol. 1, Tübingen 1986, pp. 276ff.

[154]M. Bovero, *Identità individuali e collettive*, in *Ricerche politiche due. Identità, interessi e scelte collettive*, ed. by M. Bovero, Milan 1983, p. 49.

[155]Ibid., p. 51.

[156]On this point cf. R. M. Hare, *The Language of Morals*, p. 166. Cf. also B. Williams, *Morality. An Introduction to Ethics*, London 1976, Chapter 6.

Subjectivity is not identified with social identity, with the "role", though it does need these, since it has to be explicated in social actions, which arise eminently within institutional contexts. However, subjectivity transcends the identity acquired, since it "lives" and is hence subject to "novelty". The identity just acquired may at any moment be "lost" or rejected.

4.7 The Particular Character of Legal Norms

Anyone who has read the foregoing pages will perhaps not be able to avoid a sense of dissatisfaction. Much has been said of rules, norms and institutions, but really not much about *legal* rules, norms and institutions. At least, the theme of the specific nature of legal norms and institutions has not been sufficiently tackled. Is it appropriate and correct to deal with norms indiscriminately, putting language rules, rules of games, other social rules and legal norms all into the same basket? Is there perhaps not a specific feature of the "legal" that risks getting lost in a generic, undifferentiated treatment of rules as such? If the law is defined according to the nature of the "institutional" criterion (in the sense clarified above), and the same applies to language (as Wittgenstein seems to suggest), how can one manage to understand the difference, important as we know it to be, between law and language? The same question applies as far as the criteria for distinguishing between law and games goes, or between legal and economic institutions.[157]

Should the reader be assailed by this doubt, he may be comforted to know that the author is too. What follows is intended to be a first attempt at an answer.

Allow me a long quote. It is again from Jürgen Habermas: "But does the grammar of a language presuppose experience in the same way as the rules of a strategic game? The meaning belonging to the moves of a game means nothing outside the game's context. Language refers to something in the world. One talks about something that is not in language, but in the world. In the context of a game, we can do nothing that does not form part of the game. Games, by contrast with statements, cannot represent anything. Accordingly, grammatical rules are 'constitutive' in a different way from the rules of a game; they constitute the possibility of experiences. Accordingly, even if they precede that possible experience, they are nonetheless not free of limitations depending both on invariants in the constitution

[157]Max Weber speaks of the "decisive difference" between legal rules and conventional rules in moving from dealing with the rules of *Skat* to the norms of law, though without clarifying what the difference consists in (see M. Weber, *R. Stammlers Überwindung der materialistischen Geschichtsauffassung*, in Id., *Gesammelte Aufsätze zur Wissenschaftslehre*, ed. by J. Winckelmann, 8th ed., Tübingen 1988, p. 343). The need to distinguish at any rate the specific nature of the institution of the "State" by comparison with such an institution as bridge, tennis, a Church or a club is however stressed by A. Passerin d'Entrèves, *La dottrina dello Stato*, pp. 184–189

of our organisms and on constants in ambient nature".[158] Really, this conception of Habermas' remains ambiguous. Especially because the rules of a game precede experience (of the game), and constitute the possibility of experiencing the game. What interests us here, however, which Habermas more or less confusedly brings out, is that the rules of a natural language make reference to something outside the language itself, and hence outside its rules and compliance with them, and that this "something" means that the rules of a language cannot be entirely arbitrary or conventional. By comparison with the rules of a game, Habermas tells us, language rules are endowed with weaker "constitutive force". Now, I believe that law shares with natural languages this "weak constitutivity".

Legal rules are not entirely based on convention, or at least not to the degree of the rules of games. Legal norms, instead, as is the case for language rules, have to make reference to something beyond and not "constituted" by themselves. This "something" outside is the "world" as far as language is concerned; there has to be a certain referential or representational capacity, though not necessarily thereby committing us to seeing this as the only or even chief criterion of meaning in linguistic expressions. "Use" is not enough to give us the meaning of terms and statements. Otherwise there would be no difference between a "bishop" as an element ("piece") in the game of chess and the term "sun" as an element ("noun") in a certain language (understood eminently as a language *game*). The bishop as piece does not represent or refer to anything other than itself (a piece in the game of chess), something that is possible only within the game itself. The term "chair" represents something different from itself (the word "chair"), and refers to something that is not linguistic (an object in the world). The game turns around itself; language by contrast turns around the "world", an extra-linguistic reality, or better one external to the language considered. If it were, say, a meta-language, it would indeed be concerned with a language (and accordingly not with an extra-linguistic reality), which would however still be different from, outside, the language in question.

The inadequacy of a treatment of rules that ignores their content and their "purpose" or "sense" was seen by Wittgenstein himself, not so much in his dwelling on the problem of meaning as in tackling the topic of social rules, in particular the rules of games. Wittgenstein disputes the theories of the absolute conventionality of such rules, since they might be subordinated to the participants' *enjoyment*. "Are the rules of chess arbitrary? Imagine that it turned out that only chess entertained and satisfied people. Then the rules aren't arbitrary if the purpose of the game is to be achieved. 'The rules of the game are arbitrary' means: The concept 'game' is not defined by the effect the game is supposed to have on us".[159] This means that to

---

[158] J. Habermas, *Vorlesungen zu einer sprachtheoretischen Grundlegung der Soziologie*, in Id., *Vorstudien und Ergänzungen zur Theorie des kommunikativen Handelns*, Frankfurt am Main 1984, pp. 74–75. Translation mine.

[159] L. Wittgenstein, *Philosophical Grammar*, ed. by R. Rhees, English translation by A. Kenny, Berkely, CA and Los Angeles, CA 1978, p. 192, and compare L. Wittgenstein, *Philosophische Grammatik*, ed. by R. Rhees, Frankfurt am Main 1983, para. 140, p. 192. See also ibid., p. 193: "Die Sprache ist für uns ein Kalkül; sie ist durch die *Sprachhandlungen* charakterisiert. Woher

define the rules of games it is not enough to describe the use made of these and the corresponding "institution". One must, Wittgenstein tells us, take into consideration a third factor: the effects the use of the rules has on those taking part in the sphere of action constituted by them. This amounts to saying that the rules of games are not arbitrary, since they are subordinate to that purpose, those effects. Indeed, the very concept of "use" refers to the notion of "end" or "purpose". "Use" is not an end in itself, but is directed towards the result, an *end* in the world held by subject acting intentionally.

Reference to the "world" or "purposes" or "effects" applies analogously to the rules of law, that is to legal norms. Though constituting the possibility of certain conduct, legal norms have to presuppose the existence of certain constants of human experience, and with these, certain interests and values.[160] A legal norm more than any other type requires reference to the end to which it is directed and the specific effects that should be produced.

A legal system is not "constitutive" to the same extent as a game, because it centres on facts and behaviour largely conceivable *even outside* that particular legal system. In part, as we have seen, this may even be said of a game, where it is considered that its normative system is subordinate to the satisfaction of certain needs, or tends to bring about certain effects (the entertainment, recreation or amusement of participants and spectators). This may also be so if it is considered that playing presupposes the "idea" of a game, and hence certain anthropological invariants, and ultimately a "value" of the game, that is, the fact that human beings are "homines ludentes", interested in games and deriving from them pleasure that gives them value in the context of their individual social life.

All this is true, *mutatis mutandis*, for rules of law, which centre on the fundamental interests of human beings: life, dignity, well-being, security. Thus, although the "institutional" nature of law has been confirmed, we have not yet said all there is to say about it. It remains to define the most important part of the phenomenon of law: "interests", "purposes", "values"and the "ideas" which give them "meaning" for human experience. To be operational (for example, to justify a practical syllogism required for a decision to apply a norm) the "institutional" conception of law refers one to an "ideal" concept of law, that is to say to a "strong" normative viewpoint. To the "institutional" concept corresponds, therefore, varied and opposing "ideal" concepts, or principles. The (eminently descriptive) reconstruction of legal phenomenon as "institutions" needs to and can be reconciled with a "strong" normative perspective.

---

die Bedeutung der Sprache? Kann man sagen: 'Ohne Sprache könnten wir uns nicht miteinander verständigen'? Nein. Der Fall ist nicht dem analog: Ohne das Telefon könnten wir nicht von Europa nach Amerika sprechen. Wohl aber kann man sagen: 'Ohne den Mund könnten sich die Menschen nicht verständigen'. Der Begriff der Sprache dagegen *liegt* im Begriff der Verständigung" (emphasis in original).

[160] Cf., among others, H. Coing, *Vom Sinngehalt des Rechts*, in *Die ontologische Begründung des Rechts*, ed. by A. Kaufmann, Bad Homburg 1965, pp. 33ff.

Chapter 5
Law and Power

5.1 Preliminary

The dualism arising in political and legal philosophy between conceptions asserting the priority of power over law (or norm)[1] and conceptions that maintain the primacy of law (or norm) over power turns up again in the context of sociological theory. There are two distinct basic approaches to the relationship between law and power: an empirical and descriptive approach which sees a causal relation between the two phenomena such that one is the cause or the effect of the other; a normative or ethical approach which in some way fixes the axiological priority of one or other of the forms of action, and envisions possible conflict between the two. It is obvious that the sociological perspective is concerned only with the former. Here, however, the vision of the relations between the two phenomena (law and power) becomes more complicated, as a consequence of the entry into the scene of a third factor, fundamental (obviously) to sociological theories, to which both power and law can be reduced: society.

In order to understand how the relation between power and law is structured in these theories, reference must be made to their way of conceiving society and social action. For a conception that sees society as a set of relations of mere force and social action as purely utilitarian action, governed by prudential calculation, will almost inevitably subordinate law, and normative phenomena more generally, to power (which will chiefly be deployment of physical or material force). A conception, by contrast, which assumes that social relations are intrinsically normative, that social action is governed by (or constituted) by rules, will probably maintain that political power presupposes some sort of normative element, and not define such power merely in terms of material force. We can define the former conceptions as "realist" or "naive realist", and the latter as "normativist" or "normative realist".

In this chapter I intend first to bring out the two chief ways of understanding the relation between law and power traditionally upheld in political and legal

[1] "The general theories of law and State may be distinguished into two broad categories according to whether they assert the primacy of power over norm, or conversely, of norm over power" (N. Bobbio, *Kelsen e il potere giuridico*, in *Ricerche politiche*, ed. by M. Bovero, Milano 1982, p. 3).

M. La Torre, *Law as Institution*, Law and Philosophy Library 90,
DOI 10.1007/978-1-4020-6607-8_5, © Springer Science+Business Media B.V. 2010

philosophy, but this time seen against the background of sociological conceptions. To do so, I shall use a few examples taken as "ideal types" or "models" of theories. To represent "realistic" conceptions I shall take the theories of Ludwig Gumplowicz, Michel Foucault and Teodor Geiger, and as "normativist" versions those of Eugen Ehrlich and Georges Gurvitch. The account of these authors' thought in this context has no claims to completeness.

What I am most concerned with, however, is to elaborate on the views of legal institutionalism regarding the relation between law and power, starting with its "classical" representatives and ending with the most modern institutionalist theories, in particular Ota Weinberger's. In conclusion I shall seek to put forward some proposals as to the way in which the relationship between law and power can be seen in a theoretical framework referring to an institutionalist (and "culturalist") interpretation of the phenomenon of law. In moving from language to power, particularly from the philosophy of language to political theory, there is certainly more than one hurdle (above all methodological) to be overcome. Nonetheless, the phenomenon of law, the ramifications of which extend from the rarified world of linguistic meanings to the cruder landscapes of political power, compels us to risk interdisciplinary research, despite doubts we may have regarding the connections there may be between apparently remote fields.

5.2 The Sociological Tradition. Two Models

5.2.1 The relations between the phenomenon of law and that of political power are seen by the Austrian Pole Ludwig Gumplowicz as different according to whether they relate to a *homogeneous* or *heterogeneous* social group. In the former case it is considered that the group needs no law (nor power), since in it there are no inequalities and hence no conflicts. In the primitive horde, he writes, that is, in a homogeneous, unitary and indifferent group, there is no law, which is indeed *not at all necessary* here, since at this level and in this situation the various religious conceptions plus *custom* suffice.

In "heterogeneous" groups, by contrast, where coexistence is made possible by the predominating power of one stratum or class over another, law is nothing other than this predominating power, which by habit has become rule and precept. It is only with the clash between heterogenous groups once some of these have secured the others' submission, and have to think about the coexistence of technically unequal elements and hence of an organization of power – a purpose for which the custom of one of the parties is not enough, since the foreign element is not recognized by custom – only then do the violence and predominating power of the stronger introduce the possibility of coexistence and of the order of life. The forms of coexistence, one beside the other, of *unequal elements*, created in this way, condense through practice and habit into norms and precepts, and constitute the *law*.

According to this conception, law is functional to the establishment and maintenance of political power conceived of as the violent control of one group by another. In a word, all law arises from inequality and aims at maintaining and consolidating this inequality by introducing the *rule* of the stronger over the weaker. From this viewpoint, all law is a faithful mirror-image of the *State* to which it owes its birth, and similarly aims at nothing other than the maintenance and *ordering* of the coexistence of *unequal* elements through the control of some by others. Law is, accordingly, a product of political power, and is functional for underpinning it.

For Gumplowicz, however, the law is not a mere instrument in the hands of the wielder of power, but more a sort of "signpost", the signal that indicates how far a certain power can be exercised: "It is nothing other than the determination [*Festsetzung*] of the limits between the opposite frameworks of power and spheres of action".[2] The law, that is, "shows to us the borderline [*Grenzscheide*] reached by the social components of the State in their fight for power and authority".[3] The law here seems almost to lose its normative function, that of guiding human conduct, in order instead to take on a kind of descriptive function.[4]

5.2.2 Gumplowicz's position is in part echoed by Michel Foucault. The latter, however, puts forward a conflictualist view of law in much more dramatic terms. The picture he offers us has the apocalyptic tones of a Dürer etching and the violent chiaroscuro of a Goya drawing. "Law is born of real conflicts: massacres, conquests, victories that have their dates and their terror-wielding heroes; the law is born of burnt-out cities, of lands laid waste; the law is born of innocents breathing their last in the rising dawn".[5] Thus, to analyse its concepts and legal mechanisms, "what we have to trace, behind the transience of history, is the blood drying on the law books, not the law as absolute".[6]

That "the law is the instrument of domination [...] goes without saying".[7] But to the extent that law and statutes are instruments of domination, they cannot manage to produce peace, to make conflict cease; instead, they reproduce it incessantly, because they obscure it. "The law is not pacification, since behind the law the war

---

[2] L. Gumplowicz, *Was ist Recht*? in Id., *Ausgewählte Werke*, vol. 4, ed. by G. Salomon, Innsbruck 1928, pp. 2–3.

[3] Ibid., p. 3.

[4] This same conception was taken up many years later by Vincenzo Tomeo, a distinguished Italian sociologist, fascinated by a view that seems not to attribute to the law the virtues (or defects) of an agent in settling social conflicts. Thus, Tomeo affirms that "the law represents and delineates the structural schema for conflict between interests and between groups" (V. Tomeo, *Il diritto come struttura del conflitto. Una analisi sociologica*, Milano 1981, p. 85). Outlining this position, Tomeo refers explicitly to Gumplowicz: see V. Tomeo, *Il diritto come segno del potere*, in *Sociologia del diritto*, 1980, pp. 37–39. "The law, in short, is the instrument that records and verifies the reciprocal power position of groups" (ibid., p. 38); this is the central idea Tomeo thinks he can attribute to the sociology of the Austro-Polish author.

[5] M. Foucault, *Difendere la società. Dalla guerra delle razze al razzismo di Stato*, in the version ed. and trans. by M. Bertami and A. Fontana, Florence 1990, pp. 44–45. For the view that it is violence that is at the root of law, see also T. Mann, *Das Gesetz*, in Id., *Die Erzählungen*, Frankfurt am Main 1986, pp. 1010–1011.

[6] M. Foucault, *Op. cit.*, p. 48.

[7] Ibid., p. 32.

continues to rage, and in fact rages within the mechanisms of power, even the most law-governed".[8]

On the other hand, for Foucault power is not concentrated at a given point, in a subject or an institution, nor does it move in accordance with hierarchical dynamics set up between a dominator and a dominee; it is *diffuse*, and circulates among various subjects, in their "bodies" (a term of which the French thinker is very fond). More than sovereignty, it is *discipline*. The discourse of power is thus seen as developing *transversely*. "In short, let us not forget that we are dealing with a discourse that ultimately cuts off the king's head, a discourse that in any case does without the sovereign, and denounces him".[9] "Sovereignty" is rather a legal category which, structured according to the pattern of the opposition between a subject wielding power and a subject coming under power, "obscures" the true political reality, which is that of a diffuse power, namely that of disciplinary coercion. "Legal systems – be they theories or codes – have made possible a democratization of sovereignty through the constitution of a public law structured around collective sovereignty, at the very point at which the democratization of sovereignty was established, at bottom by mechanisms of disciplinary coercion".[10]

Foucault on the one hand returns to a classical "realistic" conception of the law/power relation, according to which law is an instrument of domination, an *arcanum imperii*.[11] On the other, he radicalizes the conflictualist view of law, starting by standing on its head Clausewitz's well-known thesis that war is the continuation of politics by other means. "Power", writes Foucault, "is war – war continued by other means. This hypothesis – upholding that politics is war continued by other means – is the inverse of Clausewitz's assertion".[12] This inversion has three theoretical consequences. (i) Power relationships are conceived of as relations of force, or of open and declared hostility, that is, of war. (ii) Civil or social peace is considered as an ideological, hypocritical cover-up of the war with no locus that is under way. That is how it is to be read and interpreted; thus, "no other history can ever be written than the history of war".[13] That means that *everything* is war: there is no area of human experience that escapes. (iii) The decisive criterion for judging what is right, fair, true or beautiful is that of the most powerful, that is, what is laid down by the victor in the war in question. "The definitive decision as to the criteria of correctness in all the spheres of operation concerned cannot come but from war, that is, from a trial of strength in which, ultimately, only arms can be the arbiters".[14]

---

[8]Ibid., p. 45.

[9]Ibid., p. 50.

[10]Ibid., p. 38.

[11]As the Italian editors note, Foucault's positions "are [...] the harsh, disquieting ones of Thrasymachus" (*Op. cit.*, p. 15). And it is the "Thrasymachus argument" that is at the origin of the "realist" attitude in politics (cf. A. Passerin d'Entrèves, *La dottrina dello Stato*, pp. 23ff).

[12]M. Foucault, *Op. cit.*, p. 27.

[13]Ibid., p. 28.

[14]Ibid.

We thus arrive at a sort of absolute, totalizing decisionism, much more extreme than that set out by Carl Schmitt, since in Foucault's thought the "decision" as to who emerges victorious from the death struggle between "friend" and "enemy" does not determine just the criteria for what is legal, for what is to count as "constitution" or "norm", but also the criteria to judge what is "true", "beautiful" and "just".

So far, Foucault's thought appears as an exasperation, a dramatization, of the most insistent political "realism" or legal decisionism. "As far as the relations between law and power are concerned", he writes, "the following general principle applies: in Western societies, since the Middle Ages, the development of legal thought has taken place essentially around royal power. It is under the pressure of royal power, for its benefit or to serve it as an instrument or justification, that the legal edifice of our societies has been built up. Law in the West is law commissioned by kings".[15] The positions of Hobbes, Marx or even Schmitt pale or take on the vague colouring of moderation by comparison with Foucault's fury.[16] Nonetheless his work can be seen as the continuation of a sequence in which these names appear. He says, "the system of law and the legal sphere are the permanent vehicles of polymorphous relations of domination and techniques of subjection. The law should be seen [. . .] not from the aspect of a legitimacy to be established, but from that of the procedures of subjection it employs".[17]

The novelty in Foucault in comparison with the tradition of political "realism" is marked more by the conception of the relation between law and power than by his interpretation of the political phenomenon. For Foucault power, as already said and widely known, is something slippery that passes through subjects without remaining in any of them, something that conflicts with the "subjectivist" view of politics represented by Hobbes, Marx and Schmitt. For them, power is always *someone's*: a sovereign's, a class's, a victor's; and power is always exercised *against someone*. It is certainly possible in this model for there to be intermediate aspects, someone who has power who is in turn the subject against whom someone else's power is exercised. But ultimately and in principle, both for Hobbes and for Marx and Schmitt, power in the proper sense is only *sovereign* power, power is not in turn subject to any other power. This is not, however, Foucault's opinion. "Power", he writes, "is [. . .] something that circulates and functions – so to speak – chain-wise. It is never localized here or there, never in the hands of anyone, never appropriated as wealth or possession. Power functions if exercised through a network organization [. . .] Power is not applied to individuals, but passes through individuals. The point is not to see the individual as a sort of elementary nucleus or primitive atom, as manifold, inert matter to which power is applied or against which power impinges [. . .] The individual is not the opposite pole to power. The individual is an effect of power, and

---

[15] Ibid., p. 31.

[16] As Habermas notes, Foucault radicalizes Horkheimer and Adorno's critique of instrumental reason into a theory of the "eternal return" of power (see J. Habermas, *Die Krise des Wohlfahrtsstaates und die Erschöpfung utopischer Energien*, in Id., *Die Moderne – ein unvollendetes Projekt. Philosophisch-politische Aufsätze 1977–1992*, 2nd ed., Leipzig 1992, p. 109).

[17] M. Foucault, *Op. cit.*, p. 32.

at the same time, or just to the extent that it is an effect of it, is the linking element of power. Power passes through the individual that has constituted it".[18]

Power is "slippery", but so much so that conceptualizing it becomes so. And Foucault's definition is equally "slippery". Though it does have the merit of drawing our attention to the fact that power is also above all a phenomenon manifested in the remotest, apparently least political spheres of human life, it does not help us greatly in understanding the dynamics it helps to bring to light. Power "circulates", passes through bodies, without stopping or being concentrated in any of them. Power "constitutes" the individuals themselves. All this is certainly interesting, and in a sense, plausible. But in what is this "circulation" manifested? Why has it arisen? Where does it originate? What is its end? How can we oppose it or escape it? How is it possible to attribute truth value to theses that make truth into a dependent variable of power?[19] Especially when it is maintained that they come from the camp of the "conquered". These are questions to which Foucault has not given an answer, and unfortunately will never be able to.

5.2.3 In Gumplowicz's thought, however, despite its apparent crude realism, the liberal faith in the capacities and progressive potential of law survives. His article *Was ist das Recht?* concludes with words that entrust the law with the role of guarantor of civil liberties and bogey of "reaction": "Law is a barrier that must from time to time be shifted according to the cultural evolution of peoples, as a guarantee to freedom and to spite reaction [*der Freiheit zum Schutz, der Reaktion zum Trutz*]".[20]Here there is thus some ambiguity in the subordination of law to power; the subordination occurs with respect to *political struggle.*

A much sharper version of the sociological way of conceiving the law as a phenomenon subordinate to that of power is the theory of Theodor Geiger, a German sociologist who lived for many years in Denmark. In one sense Geiger is one of the most extreme representatives of the "realist" viewpoint. His, however, is a "naïve" realism, that yields nothing to normativism and tends to interpret social events as merely "brute" facts, and human actions as events observable and to be studied exclusively from an external viewpoint, that is, without having to consider the intentions or conceptions of agents. It is not by chance that Geiger is one of the theorists of "ideology", that is, one of those social scientists who consider they can clearly distinguish among social facts a subjective or psychological or normative component from an objective or physiological or material one, the latter constituting the real motor or "true" reality of social action, yet obscured and mystified by the "subjective" component, that is, by "ideology".[21]

Geiger, rightly, stresses that the way of conceiving the relations between law and power is largely a question of definition, depending as it does on the respective

---

[18]Ibid., pp. 34–35.

[19]See e.g., M. Foucault, *L'ordre du discours*, Paris 1971, p. 15.

[20]L. Gumplowicz, *Op. cit.*, p. 11.

[21]See T. Geiger, *Ideologie und Wahrheit. Eine soziologische Kritik des Denkens*, 2nd ed., Neuweid am Rhein 1968.

definitions of "law" and "power". Let us, then, see what Geiger means by law, and what definition of it he gives us. First, he identifies law (or the legal order) with State law (or legal order), and the latter with the State itself. "We speak of legal order", he writes, "only when within a social environment differentiated into contiguous or mutually limiting social groups a super-ordinate central power [*eine übergeordnete Zentralmacht*] has been constituted".[22] He goes on to give us this definition of legal order: "The order of social life of a large social structure centrally organized, insofar as that order rests on an apparatus of penalty monopolistically controlled by special organs".[23] The definition of power (*Macht*) refers to Max Weber's, with some important differences, explicitly stressed by Geiger.

While for Weber power is every possibility (*Chance*), within a social relationship, to impose one's own will on another even against the latter's resistance,[24] whatever the basis for that possibility, Geiger defines power as follows: "The possibility [*Chance*] of being able to control [*steuern*] the course of certain occurrences".[25] As we see, there are two novelties in this definition in comparison to that of Weber's. First, the mention of both the will of whoever is exercising power and the resistance of those undergoing it is dropped. The concept of will, Geiger clarifies, is already contained in that of "control". Then, the elimination of mention of the "resistance" of whoever power is exercised on makes it possible to include among the cases of "power" also those where the subject on whom it is exercised accepts without resisting the behaviour prescribed for him. Further, from Geiger's definition reference to the social relation, which for Max Weber is the sphere in which the power relation is seen to come into play, disappears. Thus, the conception of power becomes applicable both to *extra-social* relations between men and things and to *social* relations among men.

Power is, in this view, the ability to control certain occurrences. Those who have this ability have power over the objects in the context of which these occurrences take place. "Social power" is accordingly the ability to control the behaviour of another person. Those who have this possibility have power over the other. A power relation is, then, one in which one of the subjects can control the behaviour of the other.

"Power factors" (*Machtfaktoren*) are those facts on which the possibility of controlling others' behaviour is based. These factors are of various types. Here, Geiger

[22]T. Geiger, *Vorstudien zu einer Soziologie des Rechts*, 2nd ed., Neuwied am Rhein 1964, p. 161.

[23]Ibid., p. 339

[24]See M. Weber, *Wirtschaft und Gesellschaft. Grundriss der verstehenden Soziologie*, 5th ed., ed. by J. Winckelmann, Tübingen 1985, p. 28.

[25]T. Geiger, *Op. cit.*, p. 340. It is interesting to note that Ralf Dreier, in distinguishing the various positive-law theories into those (a) "oriented to the efficacy" and (b) "oriented to the production" of law, and those "oriented to efficacy" into (i) "according to the external aspect" and (ii) "according to the internal aspect" of norms, locates both Geiger's and Weber's conceptions among the positive-law theories "oriented to efficacy" "according to the external aspect of norms". See R. Dreier, *Der Begriff des Rechts*, in Id., *Recht-Staat-Vernunft. Studien zur Rechtstheorie 2*, Frankfurt am Main 1991, pp. 96–97; and cf. R. Alexy, *Begriff und Geltung des Rechts*, Freiburg 1992, pp. 31ff.

distinguishes among, (a) "*primary* power facts", supplied by nature (for instance physical strength, availability of weapons, sexual charms, cleverness, capacity to suggest and persuade, knowledge etc.) and (b) "*secondary* power factors", resulting from social organization, for instance from the roles held in such an organization.

For Geiger, the power relationship is "accidental" (*akzidentell*) when it is between persons taken individually, and when the main "power factor" results from personal qualities or other circumstances concerning those individuals. A power relationship is by contrast "categorical" if based (even though being between single individuals) on the subject's belonging to a particular group (the example mentioned by Geiger is the power of a soldier in an occupying army over inhabitants of the occupied country). The German sociologist's conclusion on this point is as follows: "The whole network of relations in a social structure can be conceived of as a web of innumerable power relations founded upon distinct power factors".[26] Here the whole of society seems to rest on one single type of action, fairly similar to what Habermas will call "strategic action".[27]

A further distinction drawn by this scholar is between "intercursive power relations" (*interkursive Machtverhältnisse*) and "integral power relations" (*integrale Machtverhältnisse*[28]). The former are the set of "categorical" power relations existing among the members of a certain social structure. The latter are the power relations in which the members of a society exercise social pressure among themselves. When in the "integral" power relation the object and subject of the social pressure are clearly distinct, and the relation accordingly becomes unilateral or unidirectional, and this unilaterality is lasting in time and becomes constant, then we are dealing with a *Herrschaftsverhältnis*, a relation of "supremacy".

"Supremacy" in this view is the "monopolization of integral power".[29] There are in turn two types of supremacy: (a) "arbitrary" (*Willkürherrschaft*), or (b) "legal" (*Rechtsherrschaft*). The first is when "supremacy" is exercised without fixed criteria in relation to the context and intensity of its exercise. The second is when *regularities* (*Regelmäßigigkeiten*) take shape in relation to the sphere, intensity and direction of the "supremacy". Law here does nothing but follow the statistical uniformity of the exercise of the "supremacy" (the monopolized "integral" power), thus representing a sort of measuring instrument or "signpost", devoid of normative function. The law comes to be a sort of signal, an indication, a descriptive criterion of the level reached by the "supremacy", this is similar Ludwig Gumplowicz's view considered above. In Geiger's thought, in conclusion, the law is entirely subordinate to the phenomenon of power.

5.2.4 Things are otherwise according to another sociologist of the German cultural area, Eugen Ehrlich. In his best-known and most important work, *Grundlegung*

---

[26] T. Geiger, *Op. cit.*, p. 342.

[27] See e.g., J. Habermas, *Hannah Arendts Begriff der Macht*, in Id., *Politik, Kunst, Religion. Essays über zeitgenössische Philosophen*, Stuttgart 1982, pp. 103ff.

[28] See T. Geiger, *Op. cit.*, p. 342.

[29] Ibid., p. 345.

der Soziologie des Rechts, Ehrlich at first seems to conceive of power, political domination, as a situation which has little to do with law, and is indeed historically prior to it. The fact, says Ehrlich, that there exists a relationship of power and subjection everywhere preceded the legal propositions that govern this relation as an element in the legal order. All power is only the other aspect of the lack of defence and need of assistance of the person subjected. The latter is subject to power because he does not enjoy legal protection, and on the other hand, does not receive this protection either because he is not part of a group that can protect him or because the group he belongs to is too weak to protect him. Here, then, power is thought of as the result of the weakness of the ruled in relation to the force exercised by the ruler.

Nonetheless, Ehrlich manages to maintain that power cannot be sustained merely by physical force, and thus needs a normative underpinning. Inability for defence, he believes, cannot by itself found a legal relation. It abandons the undefended person, like an object or animal without an owner, to the one who brings it under his control, but does not give him a master nor assign anyone any right over him. Power by contrast is something more than the mere possession of a person and utilization of his work, being a legally regulated relationship between the one exercising the rule and the one subject to it.

Much more decisive in asserting the supremacy of law over power in strictly sociological terms, starting apparently at the level of descriptive theory, is the French-naturalized Russian Georges Gurvitch. First, Gurvitch distinguishes between two types of sociality: "spontaneous" sociality and "organized" sociality. Spontaneous sociality, he says, is manifested both through the immediate states of collective consciousness, and through collective behaviour, whether these be habits inspired by more or less flexible models or collective acts of innovation and creation. Organized sociality by contrast comes back down to collective behaviour, insofar as this is guided by models crystallized into reflex schemes, pre-established and imposed in hierarchalized, centralized behaviour. Organized sociality thus resists the mobile spontaneity of the collective mentality and is separate from it.[30]

"Spontaneous" sociality exercises only *internal* pressures (those originating inside) on the consciousness of individuals, while "organized" sociality organizes *external* sanctions and constrictions (originating outside). Organized sociality is conceived of as "superstructure" in relation to spontaneous sociality, the latter thus taking on the nature of a "structure". This amounts to asserting that organized sociality is founded on spontaneous sociality. This is also a thesis of Pierre-Joseph Proudhon's, an author always present in Gurvitch's work. Also derived from Proudhon is the following thesis. Since spontaneous sociality is more mobile and dynamic than organized sociality, conflicts and tensions unceasingly arise between these two levels of depth of social reality, since the fixed schemes of organized superstructures always lag behind and must continuously be disrupted by the explosions and eruptions of spontaneous sociality, even in the case where, as in democratic regimes, the organizational frameworks remain largely open to

---

30 See G. Gurvitch, *Sociology of Law*, London 1953, pp. 160ff.

the influence of spontaneous sociality. For Gurvitch, in short, there is between "spontaneous" and "organized" sociality, between structure and superstructure, an unbridgeable gap: the former is mobile, the latter rigid, such that the changing requirements of the one can hardly be accepted by the other without harm.

Spontaneous sociality, according to Gurvitch, consists in (i) sociality by "interpenetration" or "partial fusion", and in sociality by "interdependence" or by "simple convergence". The former's foundation "is actual collective intuitions".[31] It can do without symbolic mediations (of language), since it is at their very basis. Just by making possible mediation through signs, patterns and symbols, it dominates them thanks to the topicality of the collective intuitions that act as their effective basis. The second type of sociality just mentioned (sociality by "interdependence") is instead essentially communicative. "The intermediary signs, patterns, symbols, serve as the primordial foundation of this form of sociality. For example, in exchange, contracts, relations of property, only gestures, declarations oral or written, outward marks on an object and so on, can serve as an effective basis for the bonds established".[32]

According to Gurvitch, any social relation has as its basis some sort of sociality by "interpenetration", thus presupposing some sort of commonality of representations (of "collective intuitions", as the Russian sociologist puts it). Symbolic communication, he says, is impossible without that direct, intuitive union that serves as its foundation. Union, sociality through fusion, accordingly prevails over sociality by inter-dependence. In a certain sense, Gurvitch is here reinterpreting the opposition (made famous by Ferdinand Tönnies's work) between *Gemeinschaft* (corresponding in the Russian's sociology to "sociality by interpenetration") and *Gesellschaft* (corresponding to "sociality by interdependence"). The two types of society or of "sociality" are reinterpreted, no longer as two distinct, opposing models of society that succeeded one another in the course of history, but as two states and stages, or aspects, that are present within the same type of historically-given macro-society. Thus, it is possible to assert a position which, though it might well have been dear to Tönnies, would be something he would never have had the courage to formulate: that *Gemeinschaft* takes precedence over *Gesellschaft*, indeed constituting a sort of structural core of it.

According to Gurvitch, every form of sociality is by itself a creator of law, of "normative fact". In his sociology the distinction between "organized sociality" and "spontaneous sociality" corresponds to that between *organized law* and *spontaneous law*. The distinction between "sociality by interpenetration" (intuitive union) and "sociality by interdependence" (symbolic communication) corresponds to that between *social law* and *individual law*. Social law "is the law of peace, mutual aid, common works". Individual law by contrast is "the law of war, conflict, separation. For even when the individual law partly drags together subjects, as in the case of

[31] Ibid.

[32] Ibid., p. 162.

contracts, it simultaneously separates them and delimits their interests".[33] Social law is upheld by distributive justice, individual law by commutative justice. It is worth noting here that Gurvitch overturns the relationship established by Proudhon between the two concepts of justice. While Proudhon considers that commutative justice is the principle that governs the social order and the one on which distributive justice too depends, Gurvitch instead maintains that it is distributive justice that is the foundation proper of social reality, and that commutative justice is erected on the basis furnished by distributive justice.

In Gurvitch's work, "social law" is always autonomous law, an original product of the group it is destined to govern, and can never be imposed from outside. It governs its object immanently. On the other hand, "every legal power is a function of social law, because it is, at first, only an external manifestation of the irreducibility of 'We', of sociality by simple fusion and interpenetration, in regard to sociality by interdependence and delimitation".[34] This power is always impersonal, objective, and immanent. It "never constitutes domination, and is not projected beyond the multiplicity of the members who constitute a 'We'".[35]

When individual law prevails over social law, we have according to the Russian sociologist a *power of domination*. Social power in general is for Gurvitch the manifestation of the irreducibility of the whole vis-à-vis its constitutive elements, while "the social power of a relatively or absolutely sovereign group is only a function of the jural framework of the group, more precisely of the order of its social law".[36] Political power on this conception is always based, even where it takes on the extreme forms of "domination", on some type of sociality, in general that "by interpenetration", sometimes (generally in the cases of "domination") on sociality "by interdependence". Here, however, sociality is always interpreted as a "normative fact", as a fact that is legal per se (as an expression of a certain idea of justice), and political power is solidly bound by the phenomenon of law.

5.3 The Institutionalist Approach: From Hauriou to Weinberger

5.3.1 The two "classical" doctrines of legal institutionalism, those of Maurice Hauriou and Santi Romano, resolve the controversy between law and power in favour of the former, perhaps more clearly done in Hauriou and rather more ambiguously in Romano. Hauriou considers that the constitutive element of the institution is the *idée directrice*, a sort of *Weltanschauung*, which by impregnating human minds and conduct with itself, ends up being reflected in the specific social institutions and organized power that is their core. The law, here understood as "idea of law"

[33] Ibid., p. 167.

[34] Ibid.

[35] Ibid., p. 168.

[36] Ibid., p. 198.

(in a sense recalling the *Rechtsidee* of the German neo-Hegelian philosophers), is superior to, and indeed is at the origin of, organized power.

Hauriou's favourite targets for criticism are what he calls "subjectivist " and "objectivist systems". The former are those that place at the foundation of the law exclusively or chiefly the will either of individuals or of legal persons; the latter are systems that take as the basis of the law exclusively or chiefly the legal norm. As representatives of "subjectivist" systems Hauriou mentions the three founding fathers of German public law, Gerber, Laband and Jellinek.[37] The principal upholders of "objectivist" systems are said to be Hans Kelsen and Léon Duguit.[38]

Hauriou rejects the "subjectivist" systems because in his view they do not take account of the fact that the subjective will is sustained by largely objective subconscious ideas. The "objectivist" systems are rejected as exaggerating the role played by legal norms and reducing to zero the sphere – which for the French scholar is fundamental – of intentional action within legal phenomena. In short, the former ("subjectivist" systems) are seen as taking account only of the aspect of "creation" of the legal order (where what is most relevant is the role of wills), while the others ("objectivist" systems) are seen as considering only the aspect of "conservation" or "continuity" of the legal order, due largely to the efficacy of the norms, that is, to their conformity with human behaviour. Both the systems are accordingly, in the French scholar's view, unilateral, since they take into consideration not the whole range of properties of legal phenomena, but only one specific aspect of them. The solution Hauriou offers is, then, his theory of the institution.

If we use the distinction between "regulative" and "constitutive" rules as a hermeneutic grid to interpret Hauriou's thought, we should immediately say that Hauriou conceives of only one type of rule (or norm): the "regulative" rule. For the French scholar the norm does not create anything but has the functions purely of regulating the existent. They are but limits and constraints: norms "ne sont en réalité que des bornes et des limites".[39] "Quant aux règles de droit", continues the French jurist, "elles ne représentent que des idées de limite au lieu d'incarner des idées d'entreprise et de création".[40] Norms cannot accordingly "constitute" or "create" the institutions in any sense. Indeed, it is the opposite that happens: "Ce sont les institutions qui font les règles de droit, ce ne sont pas les règles de droit qui font les institutions".[41] Thus, the legislator's role too cannot be "creative", "constitutive", but only "regulative": "Le rôle du législateur est celui d'un *agrimentor* qui pose des bornes entre des champs d'activités".[42]

---

[37] See M. Hauriou, *La théorie de l'institution et de la fondation. Essai de vitalisme social*, in Id., *Aux sources du droit. Le pouvoir, l'ordre et la liberté*, Paris 1933, p. 91.

[38] See M. Hauriou, *L'ordre social, la justice et le droit*, in Id., *Aux sources du droit. Le pouvoir, l'ordre et la liberté*, pp. 84ff.

[39] M. Hauriou, *La théorie de l'institution et de la fondation*, p. 94.

[40] Ibid., p. 127.

[41] Ibid., p. 128.

[42] Ibid., p. 94.

But what is an "institution" for Hauriou? The answer is as follows: "Une institution est une idée d'oeuvre ou d'entreprise qui se réalise et dure juridiquement dans un milieu social".[43] To realize this "idea", the following are necessary: organized power, conceived of almost as an "organ" of the "idea", and manifestations of solidarity or communion controlled by the organized power and regulated by formal procedures.

Hauriou distinguishes between two types of "institutions": "person institutions", such as trade unions and various associations, and "thing institutions" (it is interesting to note that the example Hauriou gives of the latter is the legal norm, which in fact only succeeds in making his theory yet more obscure). The difference between "person institutions" and "thing institutions" consists in the fact that in the former we see a process of subjectivization of the "guiding idea" (manifested in the organized power and in the solidarity of subjects), while in the latter this process does not occur. Hauriou does not however dwell overmuch on the "thing institutions", turning his attention chiefly to "person institutions".

The elements making up the "person institution" number three: the "idea of the work to be accomplished" in a certain social group, or "guiding idea"; the organized power put to the service of accomplishing this "idea"; the manifestations of communion (*communion*, says Hauriou) produced in the group in relation to accomplishment of the "idea". Of these three elements the most important – he is explicit about this – is the "idée de l'oeuvre à réaliser".[44] Every social body is thus constituted by the accomplishment of an idea, or task, or enterprise. This "idea", however, he clarifies, should not be confused with the purpose of the social body or institution in question. Nor should the "idée directrice" of an institution be confused with its function. For the "idée directrice", Hauriou continues, includes not only the purpose of an institution but also the means to be employed to accomplish those purposes. In other words, while the "function" of a social body is highly determinate, its "guiding idea" has broad margins of indeterminacy.

However, the most surprising feature of the "idée directrice" is the fact that Hauriou attributes to it an existence entirely independent of the will or any other mental or spiritual activity of the subjects. The "guiding ideas" thus closely resemble the "ideas" of the Platonic philosophical tradition.[45] They are not created or produced, but only found or discovered. The lay in the world around us, embedded in its objects and things. "En réalité", writes the French jurist, "il n'y a pas des créateurs d'idées, il y a seulement des trouveurs. Un trouvère, un poète inspiré rencontre une idée à la façon dont un mineur rencontre un diamant: les idées objectives existent d'avance dans le vaste monde, incorporées aux choses qui nous entourent; dans des moments d'inspiration, nous les trouvons et les débarrassons de leur gangue".[46]

---

[43] Ibid., p. 96.

[44] See ibid., p. 98. Cf. also ibid., p. 116.

[45] On "Platonism" in connection with Hauriou's theory see A. Baratta, *Presentazione*, in M. Hauriou, *Teoria dell'istituzione e della fondazione*, ed. by W. Cesarini Sforza, Milano 1967, p. xii.

[46] M. Hauriou, *La théorie de l'institution et de la fondation*, p. 101.

The second feature of the "person institution" – as we have seen – is a structure power of government, "un pouvoir de gouvernement organisé".[47] This plays an essential role in the constitution of the "institution", enough to make us doubt that for Hauriou power is subordinate to law. If by "law" we understand the "legal rule", we would have to conclude that for him it is power that takes precedence over law, not the converse. "C'est le pouvoir organisé seul", he writes, "qui peut créer des situations juridiques et lui seul peut les maintenir".[48]

The organized power of an institution is, however, conceived of as strictly dependent on the "guiding idea" of the institution itself, in the sense that this power must be able to act in the name of the institution, and that its directives must be able to count as those of the whole of the social group. In the broad sense, then, according to Hauriou, every "person institution" constitutes a *representative regime*. Indeed, the fact that the subjects holding that power can be elected is not a necessary condition for the existence of an institution. Hauriou does not deny that the power in question may become arbitrary and weaken the bonds laid down by the "guiding idea". Nonetheless, in the long run this is always realized.[49] Thus, if we identify the "law" with the "guiding idea", which seems entirely consistent with the French jurist's doctrine, we may calmly conclude that according to this doctrine, power indeed is subject to law.

5.3.2 For Santi Romano political power presupposes organization, which is then "institution", and hence law. Where there are manifestations of political or social power, accordingly, there is also a legal order. The two phenomena – power and law – here overlap and refer to each other, so that it would be more correct to speak of an identification of the two phenomena (from the "normative" or the "legal" side) than of the supremacy of law over power. "In any institution", writes the Sicilian jurist, "the State too does not *have*, but *is* a legal order".[50] Law is not instrumental to power; it is rather consubstantial to it, although the epiphany of power and law according to Romano seems to be the "state of necessity", in a way that does recall much of Carl Schmitt's later decisionism.[51]

Government, the State, however, is not conceived of as the source of law. Indeed, one may even take the contrary view, since political power, the power to issue norms, has its foundation in a logically prior normative order, the constitution, which need not necessarily be contained in a formal document. "The very widespread opinion that the State is prior in relation to the law, an entity not in itself nor by itself legal but which creates the law, a mere source of the latter, proves inadmissible, [. . .] when we consider that if its first affirmation is given by the constitution itself without

---

[47] Ibid., p. 102.

[48] Ibid., p. 114.

[49] See ibid., p. 104.

[50] S. Romano, *Principii di diritto costituzionale generale*, 2nd ed., Milano 1946, p. 56, emphasis in original. Cf. ibid., p. 59.

[51] Cf. Massimo La Torre, *The End of the 19th Century: The Messina Earthquake and the State of Exception*, in *Ratio Juris*, 2011 (forthcoming).

which it would not even exist, and it is this constitution that determines the power to dictate norms".[52] And this constitution, far from being something different from law, is instead an integral feature of it. The fact that according to Romano, following an ancient doctrine, the constitution should be distinguished from the laws does not mean that the constitution is an extra-legal fact.[53]

Think, for instance, of Romano's pages on "revolution" in his *Frammenti di un dizionario giuridico*. The Sicilian jurist here takes a position similar to the one upheld by the Swedish legal realist Axel Hägerström debating with the British jurisprudent Salmond. Hägerström, asserting the supremacy of the normative *Weltanschauung*, the idea of norm or of normative ideology, over de facto power, criticizes the imperativist conception that has found as it were a "classical" expression in John Austin's theory. Salmond offers a continuation of Austin's line. Thus, he explains the birth of *new* legal orders on the basis of the de facto power exercised by revolutionaries. To this Hägerström replies by asserting that a revolution takes place only when norms come into force that govern certain human behaviour differently from the norms of the legal order that has been overthrown.[54] Salmond then counterposes constitutional practice[55] to constitutional law. Sometimes, he says, constitutional practice comes into conflict with constitutional law. Hägerström's reply to this argument is indicative. "But", he writes, "if a constitutional custom comes into being, that of course merely means that certain rules for the exercise of power have gradually come to be applied without being embodied in laws. In that way, they have certainly become positive law".[56]

Romano tackles the problem of the legal force of revolution with outcomes that are, as we have said, similar to those Hägerström reaches. Revolution is according to Romano a legal phenomena in itself, inasmuch as it presupposes what in his opinion is the element that denotes the presence of law: organization. "A revolution that really is one", writes Romano, "is not mere disorder, a revolt or occasional sedition; it is always an organized movement, to an extent and in a way that of course vary from case to case. In general it may be said that there is an organization which, seeking to replace the State, consists of authorities, powers, functions that more or less correspond with and are similar to the latter's: it is a State organization in embryo, which step by step, if the movement is victorious, develops increasingly in that direction. However, it is reflected in a genuine order, imperfect, fluctuating and provisional though it may be".[57] Thus, for Romano, even the political phenomenon (of political power) that seems most opposed to law, the phenomenon of revolution,

---

[52] *S. Romano, Principii di diritto costituzionale generale*, p. 57.

[53] See ibid.

[54] On this, see E. Pattaro, *Il realismo giuridico scandinavo*. I. *Axel Hägerström*, Bologna 1975, pp. 93ff.

[55] See *Salmond on Jurisprudence*, 12th ed., ed. by P. J. Fitzgerald, London 1966, pp. 84ff.

[56] A. Hägerström, *Inquiries into the Nature of Law and Morals*, ed. by K. Olivecrona, English trans. by C. D. Broad, Stockholm 1953, p. 33.

[57] S. Romano, *Frammenti di un dizionario giuridico*, 2nd ed., Milan 1983, p. 224.

is instead in itself neither an expression nor manifestation of mere violence or force, but is possible thanks to, and expresses, a genuine legal order, a law of its own.

As we saw earlier, the relation between law and power may be understood from a sociological (descriptive) viewpoint, as a relation between two real phenomena of which one is the cause or condition of the other, or from an ethical (normative) viewpoint, as a relation between the practical action of power (political power) and a body of moral rules: the law is understood in this sense as "just law" or simply as "justice". This is the perspective taken by Thrasymachus, in Plato's Republic when he maintains that "law" or what is just is the power of the strongest.[58] If as far as the external, sociological viewpoint is concerned Hauriou's and Romano's doctrines have affinities, they diverge by contrast in connection with the normative perspective, namely on the relationship between positive and moral law. Romano never takes up this viewpoint, or so he claims. He wants only to describe phenomena, has no explicit ethical theory to put forward, and in any case declares to keep the spheres of law and of ethics distinct.

Similar to Hagerstrom's is the theoretical approach of his pupil Karl Olivecrona; being close to Hagerstrom's work implies certain similarities with Romano, for which it is worth mentioning him. It is clear in his work how the controversy concerning the supremacy of law or power risks becoming an empty debate – if lacking normative weight or when not linked to an appropriate theory of social action. Olivecrona supports the position that law is superior to power. When tackling the question as to whether a sociological explanation of law is possible he reaches the conclusion that, "it must be recognized as a fact that the power of the State is not prior to law or independent of it".[59]

This recognition of the supremacy of law is in part illusory, since norms that would be superior to political power are not seen as sanction-based rules rather as directives concerning the use of force by the state power. Law thus is superior to political power, yet it also forms – as in the theory of Kelsen – the nucleus of this same power. Law is conceived of as the subjective representative of a certain standard of conduct: "legal rules exist only as subjective representations of a certain standard of conduct".[60] This idea, while important in establishing the existence of law at a level other than the purely material, it doesn't exclude a purely force-based conception. In the inevitable clash between subjective representations, the strongest will always win – in this case the one capable of realizing through exerting persuasion and social control a certain representation of the dominant law of society. In the end this approach does not differ greatly from that which proposes mere physical force as the basis for law. The outcome is much the same, although in this case the accent is put on the psychological rather than purely empirical.

Rather more difficult, and more delicate, is the debate about the third "classical" form of legal institutionalism: Carl Schmitt's *konkretes Ordnungsdenken*, developed in the mid-1930s. This type of institutionalism remains strictly bound

[58] Cf. above Chapter 1, p.

[59] K. Olivecrona, *Is a Sociological Explanation of Law Possible*? in *Theoria*, 1948, p. 206.

[60] Ibid., p. 207.

up with a decisionist conception of law, such that law ends up ultimately being the product of a decision capable of imposing itself, irrespective of the presence of any normative or institutional framework to legitimate it. One of the criticisms Schmitt brings to bear against normativism is that it reduces the figure of the organs that produce law to mere *Normen-Funktionen*.[61] These organs are instead, for the German jurist, instances of "orders". And "the norm or rule does not produce the order".[62] The norms have a regulatory function only within an already given order. On the other hand, according to Schmitt, any order requires a *Führung*, a leadership endowed with supreme decisional powers, so that in his view it is entirely wrong to counterpose norm to command, *lex* to *rex*.[63]

Schmitt's *konkretes Ordnungsdenken* thus is set up on both the sociological (descriptive) plane and on the ethico-political (prescriptive, normative) plane. On the latter plane, *konkretes Ordnungsdenken* is undoubtedly aimed at reuniting ethics and law, in line with the whole National Socialist legal doctrine.[64] The abyss that opened with modernity between "internal forum" and "external forum" – according to Schmitt and his fellow travellers (Karl Larenz and Arnold Gehlen, both of them "institutionalist" thinkers) – must be filled, not just to subordinate all practical activity to the "internal forum", but in order to get rid of the latter's awkward presence. The subordination of law to power (wrapped in the ideological coverings of the theory of the so-called "concrete order") is in these thinkers accompanied by the subordination of ethics to politics.

5.3.3 Let us now look at how the topic of the relation between law and power is dealt with by neo-institutionalism. The clearest work on this is by Ota Weinberger.

According to Weinberger, the typically social behaviour of people is manifested in institutional contexts, that is, is determined by what he calls practical information (values, objectives, norms, principles), and is made possible by the norms that are constitutive of institutions. Law, and more generally social norms, and with them "practical information", are not just a result of the "institution", a particular manifestation of it, but constitute its fundamental core. According to this view there cannot be any institutions without norms and practical information. And it is this point that Weinberger emphasizes to take his distance from Hauriou, in a way that once again recalls a similar move by Santi Romano. Neo-institutionalism is thus said to differ from Hauriou's theory because, by contrast with the latter, it "ne considère pas le droit comme un épiphénomène de l'institution, mais au contraire tient le système d'informations 'pratiques' pour le noyau de l'institution, qui sans ce centre de cristallisation ne pourrait exister".[65]

---

[61] C. Schmitt, *Über die drei Arten des rechtswissenschaftlichen Denkens*, Hamburg 1934, p. 15

[62] Ibid., p. 13.

[63] See ibid., p. 51.

[64] On this, cf. B. Rüthers, *Entartetes Recht. Rechtslehren und Kronjuristen im Dritten Reich*, Munich 1988.

[65] O. Weinberger, *Droit et connaissance du droit au regard du positivisme juridique institutionnaliste*, in *Droits*, vol. 10, 1989, p. 111.

The power (in a social sense) of a subject thus depends on a normative context, and comes about, for good or ill, within it. "The power [*Macht*] of the individual," writes the Czech scholar, "is not only or primarily a function of his physical or psychological force, but a definite status that has an origin through institutional rules and relations. Rule [*Herrschaft*] as exercise of power in society is thus above all an institutionalized situation [*eine institutionalisierte Konstellation*], determined by a network of normative, functional-factual and ideal factors (and perhaps also ideological ones)".[66]

Weinberger's solution, however, does not establish the primacy of one element (law or power) over the other. Thus, he objects to Schmitt's contrast (derived from Aristotle) between the government of men and the government of laws, as follows. It is not, he maintains, possible to have a "government of laws" that is not expressed in powers of specific persons, and on the other hand it is not possible to conceive of a power administered by people outside action contexts always regulated by "practical information", by norms in particular. "There is no rule of law independent from human beings, but only a legally structured and more or less legally constrained rule of human beings [. . .], and in the political domain there is no rule of human beings but based on social practices and norms that *constitute* individuals' power and social authority".[67]

Neil MacCormick, the other "protagonist" of "neo-institutionalism", more or less follows Weinberger's approach. The stress is, however, placed more on the "normative" nature of law than its "institutional" nature. "As for law", he writes, "the essence is not power but normative order. Wherever there is law, there is normative order, wherever there is normative order institutionalized there is law. Law is about institutional normative relations between normatively recognized persons of all sorts".[68] MacCormick, however, maintains a clear distinction between political power and normative power, which, indeed, he further justifies as the foundation for a reconstruction of the notion of the State based on rule of law. This term has in his view a specific meaning, and is not a mere tautology, only if the State (political power) and law present themselves as two quite distinct phenomena, such that it makes sense for the one (law) to be a limit to the other (the State). Otherwise, one would fall back into Kelsen's empty formulation, according to which "every State is a State based on rule of law".[69]

Despite his aversion to the theory of "constitutive rules" proposed by Searle, Weinberger tells us that the social and legal norms *constitute* the structures

---

[66] O. Weinberger, *Institutionentheorie und Institutionalistischer Rechtspositivismus*, in Id., *Recht, Institution und Rechtspolitik. Grundprobleme der Rechtstheorie und Sozialphilosophie*, Stuttgart 1987, pp. 176–177.

[67] Ibid., p. 177. My emphasis.

[68] N. MacCormick, *Beyond the Sovereign State*, in *The Modern Law Review*, 1993, p. 11.

[69] See ibid., pp. 13–14. See also N. MacCormick, *Der Rechtsstaat und die 'Rule of Law'*, in *Juristenzeitung*, 1984, pp. 65–70; and H. Kelsen, *Der soziologische und der juristische Staatsbegriff. Kritische Untersuchungen des Verhältnisses von Staat und Recht*, 2nd ed., Tübingen 1928, p. 191. And cf. G. Zagrebelsky, *Il diritto mite. Legge, diritti, giustizia*, Torino 1992, p. 22.

of political power, and even the power of individuals. Moreover, unknowingly, Weinberger is here echoing a theme present in Romano's doctrine. Legal norms are for Romano "constitutive" in relation to the legal order, and hence vis-à-vis the State. "The law, whether voluntary or not", he says, "is constitutive of the legal order, in the sense that the fact or facts that it provides for take on a given characteristic in virtue of it".[70] Weinberger, like Hägerström, holds that behind every State there is a constitution, even when the State in question does not have a written constitution. The "constitution" is seen here not as a formal document, but as the series of norms that constitute the State's legal and political practice. "Every State", he writes, "necessarily has a constitution, that is, a normative regulation through which the overall institution of the State is constituted as an ordered unit".[71] Weinberger rejects Schmitt's conception of the "political" as a friend/enemy relation, that is, a mere relation of force and violence, since he reconstructs the "political" as "normative", that is, as constituted by social norms. This does not mean that Weinberger denies or ignores the possibility of political oppression or of the most unbridled authoritarianism. In this connection he gives the example of the National Socialist *Führerstaat*. But, he adds, even that State, however much it grossly amplified the power of a single man or a few men, was in the final analysis based on normative constructions. Weinberger's conclusion closely recalls Santi Romano's position. The words are almost the same: "As an institution the State necessarily has a normative core: a legal order".[72] Even in the concentration camps, Weinberger tells us, and tragically he knew them first hand, a normative order held sway. This assertion does not however imply that the concentration camps are to be acknowledged to have had any moral force.

In Weinberger we find a fairly functionalist (à la Malinowski, to clarify) view of political power. This is conceived of as a "function" of the overall social organization. "The power of the individual", writes Weinberger, "is not the purpose of the political organization, but a necessary element for carrying out the tasks falling to it in society".[73] Weinberger criticizes the well-known definition of "power" (*Macht*) given by Max Weber, that power means any chance to impose one's own will even against resistance within a social relationship, whatever is the basis for such chance ("Macht bedeutet jede Chance, innerhalb einer sozialen Beziehung den eigenen Willen auch gegen Widerstreben durchzusetzen, gleichviel worauf die Chance beruht"[74]).

Weinberger justifies his criticism with two chief arguments. First, he believes that Weber's definition could be accepted only within a theoretical framework that conceives of society as a web of *individual* relations among social actors, neglecting

---

[70] S. Romano, *Principii di diritto costituzionale generale*, p. 83. Emphasis in original.

[71] O. Weinberger, *Verfassungstheorie vom Standpunkt des neuen Institutionalismus*, p. 105.

[72] Ibid.

[73] Ibid.

[74] M. Weber, *Wirtschaft und Gesellschaft*, 5th ed., ed. by, J. Winckelmann, Mohr, Tübingen 1985, p. 28.

the *impersonal* element of social phenomena. In Weber's definition, then, there is an excessively positivist or empiricist view, using for the study of society concepts typical of the natural sciences. Weber in fact uses the term *chance*, which seems to designate a possibility in terms of *probability*. But, argues Weinberger, "power is not the *chance* to impose one's own will, but that particular position of a subject – be it an individual person or a collective – in a social structure that provides the basis for that chance".[75]

Weber, finally, seems to neglect the normative element that lies behind any power phenomenon. Unlike Jellinek who saw in the usurper or the dictator an example of "de facto normative force",[76] Weinberger maintains that even in this case the origins of "normative force" lie in normative relations and facts and not in "brute facts". "Actually", writes Weinberger, "every power – even the one held by a fully unconstrained dictator – bases on a plurality of relationships and institutional moments, that is, is upheld through norms and institutions".[77]

Weinberger thus resolves the traditional dispute between the proponents of the "government of laws" and those of the "government of men" in favour of the former, but with one important addition. The "laws" here are the norms that make up the institution within which the power is exercised. Political power presupposes a certain sphere of action actually utilized by social actors: "A precondition of power is a scope of action [*Vorbedingung der Macht ist ein Handlungsspielraum*]".[78] Power, accordingly, is always normatively founded. But the norms considered here have little or nothing to do with the "laws" in the sense of legal norms properly speaking, issued in accordance with certain public procedures. The formula of the "government of laws" in the sense of "rule of law" is regarded as more of an ideal construction, with no descriptive value.[79]

The formula of the "rule of law" tells us not who governs, but rather the values that those who govern attempt to realize. Thus the "rule of law" does not allow for a non-value-laden understanding, such as that presented by legal positivism. The "government of laws" on the other hand, if it is not to be Utopian, has to be conceived of as a sphere of human action, adopted by subjects according to their wills. Laws detached from actions in which they are realized, have a purely hypothetical value. Consequently the "government of laws" as a real phenomenon, cannot but be "government of men". This however, does not dictate the ideals on which this government will be based: they can be either those of the "rule of law" or those of "rule of men".

---

[75] O. Weinberger, *Verfassungstheorie vom Standpunkt des neuen Institutionalismus*, p. 111.

[76] See G. Jellinek, *Allgemeine Staatslehre*, 3rd ed., Darmstadt 1960, p. 340.

[77] O. Weinberger, *Verfassungstheorie vom Standpunkt des neuen Institutionalismus*, p. 111

[78] Ibid., p. 12

[79] "'Herrschaft des Rechts' ist keine Beschreibung der Machtverhältnisse in der Gesellschaft, sondern eine ideelle Konstruktion" (ibid., p. 110).

Even the most brutal despot exercises his power thanks to a certain body of social norms.[80] But these social norms can hardly be conceived of or utilized as effective limits on the exercise of the despot's power. To say, that is, that the political power is *normatively* founded does not in any way amount to defending, as a descriptive position, the actual effect of "government of laws" in contrast to "government of men", nor to defending the superiority of the first with respect to the second. It allows an approach according to which the correctness of conduct, and its correspondence with a norm, pass to the level of justification of the norm itself; law can thus become a strong normative discourse. This possibility is nevertheless rejected by Weinberger, who remains loyal to the most intransigent legal positivism, at least as the internal basis for applying social norms.

5.4 Law as "Culture"

5.4.1 The institutionalist theory manifestly implies a "culturalist" conception of society, a conception, that is, which maintains that social phenomena are not comprehensible if one does not bear in mind that social reality is such for man through a symbolic screen that makes it significant, and through the concepts and norms that make that reality "possible". But there is another, weightier, sense in which it may be said that institutionalist legal theory refers to a vision of law as "culture". The "institutions" derive their meaning not only from the laws that constitute the possibility-condition of that sphere of action whose actual operation gives rise to, and so to speak instances, the institution.

The constitutive rules of an institution are not enough to define the institution itself. We have to have further recourse to an "idea" of the institution, a "concept" of it, which is just a particular cultural form. This seems to be grasped by Wittgenstein when he contrasts the "rules" of a game to the "image" of it, according to which certain rules are dictated. They however cannot succeed in exhausting the "image" in question. It may thus be that certain moves made in accordance with these particular rules clash, as it were, with the "image" that we had of the game, sometimes impelling us to change the rules. "I give the rules of a game. The other party makes a move, perfectly in accord with the rules, whose possibility I had not foreseen, and which spoils the game, that is, as I had wanted it to be. I now have to say: "I gave bad rules; I must change or perhaps add to my rules." So in this way have I a picture of the game in advance? In a sense: Yes."[81] The "image", the *Bild* Wittgenstein speaks of, represents just this "idea" or "concept" of the institution (the game). It is this "idea" and this "concept" that give us the "sense" of the institution in question and

---

[80] "Auch der absolute Alleinherrscher ist ermächtigtes Organ des Staates, er hat eine gesellschaftliche Rolle in der Institution. Falls 'princeps legibus solutus' gilt, gilt dieser Grundsatz als Element des Rechtssystems" (ibid.).

[81] L. Wittgenstein, *Zettel*, English trans. by G. E. Anscombe, Oxford 1967, § 293, p. 53. See also L. Wittgenstein, *Bemerkungen über die Philosophie der Psychologie*, Frankfurt am Main 1984, p. 87.

that may also be used to check the adequacy or appropriateness or the "legitimacy" of certain rules within that particular institutional context.

Indeed, the practice constituted or governed by certain rules is specified or explained by those very rules. Take, for instance, a game of chess, and suppose that an activity governed by rules identical to those of the game of chess instead constitutes a way two priests seek to draw auguries about certain events. If white wins, one particular augury is to be drawn, if black, the augury will be entirely different. But this practice is not that of the game of chess: the two priests are not "playing at chess", but are engaged in a rather different activity, namely a religious rite. But if an activity governed by rules exactly identical to the game of chess is nonetheless a different activity from that of playing at chess, we have to conclude that the perception and description (and implementation) of the game of chess cannot be exclusively secured by indicating (and complying with) a certain series of norms. This argument "shows that the game of chess is not adequately characterized as a 'system of rules'. Playing chess does not *consist* in acting in accordance with the rules. The rules do not explicate the concept of playing chess; they do not establish what it is to play chess".[82]

The norms do not explain to us the concept of the game of chess; nor do they the more general one of game, nor the *concept* of any other institution. For this we must have recourse to the form of life understood as "culture", as a series of conceptions, ideas, world views, present in a *particular social space*. Thus, to define a particular institution, but also and above all to make use of the rules constituting it, we must in some way understand the *Witz*,[83] the "concept", the "idea", that is, the cultural principle that assigns it its meaning, we need to understand the "guiding idea".[84] It is, accordingly, here that the difference between institutions and other practices, like law or sport or religion, or etiquette or the gang of thieves, lies. In fact, "rules (constitutive rules) do not themselves specify how the behaviour in accordance with the rules is to be regarded; that is something that the setting up of the rules must presuppose".[85] Institutions and "guiding ideas", as Weinberger notes, are inextricably linked to each other.[86] Constitutional theory thus finishes as a theory of society and of cultural phenomena.

5.4.2 The institutionalist approach, indeed, both in its traditional versions (Romano and Hauriou) and in its analytical, transformed version (Weinberger and MacCormick), is, before being a theory of law, a theory of society. The "institution" that Romano, Hauriou, MacCormick and Weinberger are talking about is, for all the

[82] H. Schwyzer, *Rules and Practices*, in *Philosophical Review*, 1969, p. 464. Emphasis in original.

[83] See for example L. Wittgenstein, *Philosophische Untersuchungen*, pp. 237–238.

[84] Cf. O. Weinberger, *Verfassungstheorie vom Standpunkt des neuen Institutionalismus*, p. 103 For Weinberger, it is the "guiding idea" that supplies the "conceptual determination of the institution's tasks" and hence the criterion for distinguishing among the various institutions.

[85] H. Schwyzer, *Rules and Practices*, p. 467.

[86] "Leitideen etablieren sich zusammen mit den entsprechenden Institutionen" (O. Weinberger, *Verfassungstheorie vom Standpunkt des neuen Institutionalismus*, p. 108).

differences among these authors, the prototype of social reality, that is, social reality as such. For institutionalism, man does not "submit to" a social reality facing him with the same force and otherness as natural events; instead he in a certain way "constitutes" it, since social reality is seen as a set of "institutions", spheres of action, which exist in virtue of rules that are all human, and of the intentional application of those rules.

It is from the intuition of this phenomenon, the "constitutivity" of human rules in relation to the social world, that modern idealistic thought takes off. Starting from a theory that I feel is plausible (the centrality of man for man, the "constitutivity" of human thinking and acting as far as his social being is concerned), it develops this in radical terms, destroying the link between idea and symbol on the one hand, and material reality (which exists, and is in a proper sense, a non-human sense, the only possible dimension) on the other. Everything thus becomes "idea": material reality is not, from the viewpoint of Hegelian philosophy, anything but the "alienation" of the "idea", of "being in itself" that becomes "other than itself".

On the opposite side, we find the realist radicalism of those who maintain that social reality is a pure fiction, an imaginary element, "ideology", where these terms, "fiction", "imaginary", "ideology", all have a negative or pejorative connotation. For these "naive" realists, the typically social reality is a sort of self-gratification that people obtain by elevating themselves above what is their true being: their animal nature. The properly social dimension is thus coloured by "ideology"; it is, to use Pareto's terminology, a set of "derivations", dependent variables of constant "residues" (reducible to the basic instincts, to the physiological facts that govern the life of man).[87] As is well known, in the Marxist tradition the "structure" of production relations, seen as more or less causal, more or less "natural", objective relations, is counterposed to the superstructure of normative constructions, including politics and law. And recently there have even been those who have sought to explain social facts by referring to the human being's *genes*.

According to this "naive" realist view, institutions, world views, religions, philosophies, politics, law, are all seen as different forms of a single phenomenon: "ideology", which is seen as "false consciousness", self-deception in the best of cases, downright fraud in the worst. For these realists, man's social life is dominated by his instincts, controlled by conditioned reflexes, by automatic (non-reflexive) physiological mechanisms, however refined they may be, or else by objective laws over which he has no control, power or influence. All the rest, ideas, cultural traditions, customs, myths etc., is either stamped as "ideology" or else reduced to "environment", that is, to conditioning situations (in terms more or less of the red light that makes Pavlov's dog salivate).

5.4.3 These two opposing conceptions, idealism and realism, these two opposed extremisms, are not just philosophies, or better, like all philosophies they are also

[87] See V. Pareto, *Compendio di sociologia generale*, Torino 1978, Chapter 6. On this cf. D. Farias, *La demistificazione delle ideologie e Vilfredo Pareto*, in Id., *Saggi di filosofia politica*, Milano 1977, pp. 361ff.

Weltanschauungen, and have great practical repercussions on the basis of their conception of power. The "idealists" in general endow power with moral or religious attributes. Since their view of reality is entirely imaginary and ideal, their view of the relationship of power will also be imaginary and ideal, and ultimately ideological. As Andrea Caffi writes: "Through the monstrous identification of the Idea with being and all the empirical manifestations of reality, one came to attribute priestly and despotic power to the manipulators and interpreters of ideas, or better, of that formless complex called The Idea, in which all the ideological operations come to be confused. Thus at a stroke every human action, but especially every elemental action, was 'sanctifyed' as an expression of The Idea".[88]

In yet another sense, the "idealists" develop their own political theory. They are led to absolutize, to hypostatize, concepts like "virtue", "duty", "morals", inasmuch as they absolutize, by making it the whole of reality, that imaginary element that is instead only a part of the typically human reality. For them, accordingly, the normative element of reality arises unarguably: norm becomes Law, normativity becomes sacrality.

The "realists", conceiving reality as a material and mechanical fact, are led often to identify law with power, and power with force. For them, the power relation is a relation in which someone with physical means compels another to do or undergo something. Power, for "realist" radicalism, is a relation of cause and effect. It is thus asserted that A has power over B if and only if A's behaviour produces B's conduct. For the "realist", the power relation is essentially a command-obedience relationship. A good example of this way of thinking might be the definition of "rule" (*Herrschaft*) given by Max Weber almost at the start of his monumental posthumous work *Wirtschaft und Gesellschaft*: "By rule must be understood the possibility of finding obedience among some people to a command having a certain content".[89]

For the "realists", power is as much that exercised by a king or by an assembly of people's representatives as that exercised by a bandit telling his victim "Your money or your life!": in both cases we are held to be in the presence of the same phenomenon. It is true that "realists" in general distinguish specifically political power, using the criteria of the *habit* of obedience. Note what Bentham writes: "When it is supposed that a certain number of persons (whom we may call subjects) are accustomed to render obedience to a person or a set of persons (whom we may call ruler and ruled) with well-known, definite characteristics, it is said that these persons taken together (subjects and rulers) are in state of political society".[90] From

---

[88] A. Caffi, *Critica della violenza*, Milano 1966, p. 323.

[89] M. Weber, *Wirtschaft und Gesellschaft*, 5th ed., p. 28. However, it is hard to regard Weber as a "realist" (in the sense indicated above), on the one hand because of his conception of social action in general (which turns around the concept of *Sinn* or "meaning"), and then because he, in speaking of power, of *Herrschaft* (which might also be translated as *rule*) hastens to add that in every authentic power relationship there inheres a minimum of *will* to obey, that is, an interest (internal or external) in obedience (see ibid., p. 122), and introduces the concept of "legitimacy" of power.

[90] J. Bentham, *A Fragment on Government*, in Id., *A Fragment on Government and an Introduction to the Principles of Morals and Legislation*, ed. by W. Harrison, Oxford 1960, p. 38.

the viewpoint of the "realist" Bentham here impersonates, that habit of obedience is however seen as an automatic, mechanical fact, induced by the use of penalties or nourished by the fear of incurring these. The "realist" model of learning is that of stimulus and response and conditioned reflex theorized by behaviourist psychologists. When the child grows, they claim, she establishes a verbal conditioning response for every object and every situation present in his external environment.

5.5 Power and Rule

5.5.1 From an institutionalist viewpoint it may be maintained that society is always the outcome (though not always intended or foreseen) of the self-determination of human beings, insofar as these are not governed by mere instincts or unreflective responses, but by norms, and these are the product of the action of men (though not always of their design).[91] Moreover, in relation to norms it is in every case possible to take a reflective position. In relation to norms, that is, it is always possible to ask the question "why should I respect them?". And the problem in any case arises of *how* to respect them, given their generality and abstractness.

According to the institutionalist theory, norms, contrary to the idealist hypothesis, do not exist by themselves, thanks to supra-natural or supra-human entities, but exist insofar as men consciously or unconsciously conform to them. It should however be noted that in the face of a norm adopted unconsciously, for instance a norm of etiquette, it is still possible to take a reflective position in the sense that is it possible to be in a situation where we are accused of non-conformity with the norm, and accordingly asked for a "justification" (always reflective) of our conduct. None of us, before learning to read and write our own mother tongue, knew its grammatical rules, yet we spoke it according to those rules pretty well. Not all peoples have written grammars of their language, nor schools it is taught in; yet they are always capable of expressing themselves linguistically correctly, following language rules that nonetheless remain unknown to them.

The conception of political power as a normative fact, that is, as an "institution", makes the element of voluntariness existing in power relationships explicit. One obeys, in the last analysis, because one wants to. And one wants to obey, often, because this falls under a certain norm that has been produced or that one shares, or else because one wishes, so to speak, to "enter" a certain institution, which makes certain actions possible only on condition of complying with particular rules. On the other hand, "obeying" is not the right verb to define the power relation founded on norms. A more appropriate verb is "keep to". The command/obedience relationship does not arise for the regulatory function in itself, note. One does not "obey", in the proper sense, a norm; one *keeps to* a norm.

---

[91] For this thesis, the necessary reference is to the thought of Hayek. See e.g., F. A. Hayek, *Die Irrtümer des Konstruktivismus und die Grundlagen legitimer Kritik gesellschaftlicher Gebilde*, Tübingen 1975, pp. 5ff.

There are, to be sure, situations in which we are physically compelled, by arms, by torture, or by prison, to accept a situation of domination. Indeed, as Primo Levi writes, drawing lessons from his experience as an Auschwitz inmate, "the harder is the oppression, the more widespread among the oppressed is the readiness to collaborate with the power".[92] However, over and above the fact that in face of the most brutal oppression – as Primo Levi himself says – one may always opt for death, what is intended to be affirmed here is that in the case of mere violence, of pure and simple manifestation of force, we are no longer in the presence of political power, but, if you will, of a fight to the death, of war. It is not plausible, accordingly, to share Walter Benjamin's position when he writes that all force or violence is either production or protection of law.[93]

The case of the robber compelling us to hand over our wallet, or of the Nazi shutting us in a sealed train, are not commensurable with those of a king or a parliament ordering us to pay taxes. The two cases, putting it that way, of the bandit and the king represent very different social phenomena. Confusing them, as Carl Schmitt, say, ends up doing with his extreme decisionism, further means failing to understand that war and peace are very different social situations, and that it is peace rather than war that is the condition *sine qua non* of any sort of society. Clausewitz wrote that war was the continuation of politics by other means' and Lenin inverted the terms of the proposition. Nothing could be more wrong. Political realism here reveals its lack of foundation.[94] No two situations are as distinct, from the viewpoint of common sense, as war and peace. This so-called "realism" is not describing social reality, but imagining one for its own ends and purposes.[95]

5.5.2 Political power is in fact founded on consensus and not on violence, and politics is not war but collective action concerning the fundamental of a society, thus also a search for agreement, for mediation, for common action. Attributing to politics the bloody features of war, as Foucault, say, does, means depriving it of its core. The imperativist conception of law, that reduces it to a body of bare commands, likewise confuses law and politics. This confusion (made on the political side) ends by corrupting the very concept of "politics". Reducing legal norms to mere commands of the political law-giver amounts to maintaining that in modernity the law can be resolved entirely into politics. However, in that way even our concept of

---

[92]P. Levi, *I sommersi e i salvati*, Torino 1986, p. 30.

[93]"Alle Gewalt ist als Mittel entweder rechtsetzend oder rechtserhaltend" (W. Benjamin, *Zur Kritik der Gewalt*, now in Id., *Zur Kritik der Gewalt und andere Aufsätze*, with a postword by H. Marcuse, Frankfurt am Main 1990, p. 45). Cf. E Resta, *L'ambiguo diritto*, Milan 1984, p. 14: "What Benjamin says [. . .] raises a central problem in analysing legal systems: the weight of force, or if you will the structural ambiguity of *Gewalt* in the 'rationality' of modern politics. The alternative Benjamin sets out between theology and mysticism identifies the central node of the *ambiguity* of the political, that is, the irrepressibly theological nature of power and of the law on which it is based. This means that all *auctoritas* on which political systems are based is founded exclusively on force, both when legal power is *created*, and when it is *conserved*" (emphasis in original).

[94]Cf. S. Cotta, *Dalla guerra alla pace. Un itinerario filosofico*, Milano 1989.

[95]On the non-realism of "political realism" see the fine work by N. Chiaromonte, "Il realista e l'utopista", in Id., *Scritti politici e civili*, Milano 1976, pp. 277ff.

politics would have to break down. In any case, on these premises, political power can no longer be understood as legally legitimate authority; law entirely absorbed by politics would end by losing all legitimating force. In thinking that legitimation can become the *exclusive* work of politics, we are also showing that we renounce the concepts of law and politics as we have to date conceived them.

Political power is above all the capacity to issue decisions that are *binding* for at least some of the subjects concerned. This is very well put by Talcott Parsons: "I shall call this capacity to act, or more broadly, that to make and promulgate binding decisions, *power* in a strict analytical sense".[96] The "binding force" of the acts of power cannot be based on mere violence, but requires some sort of consent, or better of intersubjective validity. Political power thus finds its "foundation" in the impersonality typical of social relations. Thus Parsons, following an insight partly shared by Karl Olivecrona,[97] compares political power with money. "Although backed by coercive sanctions, up to and including the use of physical force, at the same time power rests on the consensual solidarity of a system that includes both the users of power and the 'objects' of its use [. . .] Power in this sense is the capacity of a unit in the social system, collective or individual, to establish or activate commitments to performance that contributes to, or is in the interest of, attainment of the goals of a collectivity. It is not itself a 'factor' in effectiveness, nor a 'real' output of the process, but a medium of mobilization and acquisition of factors and outputs. In this respect, it is like money".[98]

Obviously this does not mean that there can be no oppressive political power, the situation I propose to call "dominion". It must even be said that in the story of the human race the very great majority of forms of political power are at the same time a form a "dominion". What is actually disputed here is that "dominion" has its roots in phenomena of mere force or violence, not of consent or of "normative conceptions" of the world. "Dominion", which in my view is *one* form of political power, is like the latter founded on a body of norms shared by associates, and in any case operates within a sphere of action rendered possible by certain rules. Political power (and "dominion", which is one of its manifestations) arises within an *institution*, in large part depending on the content of rules that constitute the sphere of action within which the power is exercised. It is above all a normative *status*, attributed to the rules constitutive of the social institution in question.

The opinion that the fundamental nature of dominion is monopoly of political power wielded by part of the social group over the rest of the members does not succeed in being convincing. According to that opinion, the phenomenon of political oppression is linked with that of class distinction (though the latter does not

---

[96]T. Parsons, *Evolutionary Universals in Society*, in Id., *On Institutions and Social Evolution. Selected Writings*, ed. by L. H. Mayhew, Chicago 1985, p. 309. Emphasis in original.

[97]See e.g., K. Olivecrona, *Ideologie und Realität des Geldes*, Lund 1948.

[98]T. Parsons, *Op. cit.*, pp. 309–310. We are very far here from the approach that power is eminently restrictive, the power to stop something being done. On Parson's reconstruction, political power is exactly the opposite: the power to get done, the power to mobilize a group's social forces.

necessarily need to be structured according to economic criteria). It hardly to dispute the fact that in societies of "dominion", or at least almost all of them, there is a group of dominators and a group of dominees. This, however, constitutes rather an *effect* of something lying behind the classical dichotomy, and strictly linked with the normative quality of the phenomena of political power. It seems that there is "dominion" wherever the normative system of a society has been hypostatized, absolutized, "alienated", so to speak, by its "producers", and thereby rendered inaccessible to and uncontestable for them. How, for instante, could we manage to explain what the totalitarian State is, that entirely modern expression of "domination", by defining "domination" (political oppression) in the terms of the separation of a social group of dominators from the rest of society? Can the totalitarian State be identified with a group of persons?

"Dominion" is in itself anonymous and faceless. If in the past it wore the mask of the prince, in modern times it maintains and exalts its own anonymity. The modern State's "dominion" is no longer concentrated in a physical being that becomes its wielder, but remains abstract, sanctifies this abstractness, or better, elevates it into a person, a subject (think of the theory of the State as "legal person").[99] "The State is not us. Worse, it is not 'them' (a class), nor even 'him' (a king); its transcendence has thus infiltrated social life so insidiously that it has become immanent within it".[100]

Until the eighteenth century the State was identified with the prince and was his personal property. Until the unity of Italy, for instance, the official denomination of the Piedmontese State was "the States of his Majesty the King of Sardinia". "L'Etat, c'est moi", as Louis XIV put it.[101] But could anyone claim the same today, even the most powerful and wealthy politician? Think once again of primitive societies, all too often idealized and uncritically taken as examples of anti-authoritarian societies. In those societies, in general, the individual is annulled, is made one with the social body; his life is rigidly structured by tradition and myth. Many of them lack what might be called a dominant group, yet they still cannot be termed societies without "dominion", that is, societies in which the members consciously produce, discuss, and hence challenge and modify where needed the norms that govern social life.

H. L. A. Hart, after having distinguished between "primary norms" (which impose obligations) and "secondary norms" (that attribute powers) and including

---

[99] On the modern State as abstract entity cf. R. De Stefano, *Il problema del potere*, Milano 1962, pp. 135–137.

[100] J. Gil, *Un'antropologia delle forze. Dalle società senza Stato alle società statuali*, Torin 1983, p. vii.

[101] But see S. Romano, *Principii di diritto costituzionale generale*, p. 54: "Despite any expression that might lead one to believe the contrary, the State has never been fully identified with its government. Even when Louis XIV was able to say 'L'Etat c'est moi', or in such official documents as international treaties the State was designated by the name of its monarch, or where in laws the words State and Crown were used indifferently as synonyms, all that was meant to be indicated was the State, through the person or entity that was its head, and could accordingly represent it more concretely, that is, the whole was being indicated by the part".

among the latter norms of "recognition", "judgement" and "modification", maintained that the legal orders of primitive societies are characterized by the fact that they contain only "primary" norms.[102] This assertion, though questionable from the viewpoint of a general theory of legal orders, nonetheless hits the mark when it stresses the *static* nature of primitive societies. They are said not to have amending norms, "rules of change", that is, are projected as being "eternal" and "immutable", or represent themselves as being without "history". They are said not to confer legal powers on any member, so that compliance with the norms follows not so much from the action of individual members, that is, the activation of individual powers, as from a general and cohesive sense of duty towards the community. In a primitive society, thus, there would be only duties, and no subjective right or power.

At this point it might be relevant to cite Hobbes (*De cive*, V, 9): "A Union so made is called a *commonwealth* [*civitas*] or *civil society* [*societas civilis*], and also a *civil person* [*persona civilis*]; for since there is *one will* of all of them, it is to be taken as a *one person*, and is to be distinguished and differentiated by *a unique* name from all particular men, having its own rights and its property [*res sibi proprias*]. Consequently, no single citizen nor all together (except him whose will stands for the will of all) are to be *regarded as the commonwealth*. A COMMONWEALTH, then (to define it) is a *one person*, whose *will*, by the agreement of several men, is to be taken as the will of them all, to make use of their strength and resources for the common peace and defence".[103] As we see, Hobbes, a theoretician of the absolute, not of the liberal State (he says, indeed, that there cannot be a State that is not per se absolute), bases this on a notion close to that of the general will. There must be a contract, an agreement, whereby individuals give up all their original, "natural" rights. The modern State, the abstract power *par excellence*, finds its foundation, according to its most consistent theoretician, in an idea (the social contract) that a century later was to be regarded as the source of the democratic revolution. The reference to a general agreement or will expresses the idea that political power comes from the whole of the community, considered collectively, and is only justified through it. The idea of a collective power (however initial or ideal) thus need not necessarily clash with the assertion of an absolute and abstract power (the more abstract, the more it is absolute).

5.5.3 It is not that where there is regulation there must also be "dominion". But where there is political power, there must also be a normative system, and hence an *institution*, that is, a sphere of action made possible by norms. It is not mere force, nor violence, that constitutes political power, but a normative system that makes the exercise of that power possible. Nor is "dominion", political alienation and unfreedom, based on the deployment of material force alone. "Dominion" is a way of structuring social rules that arises where these rules lose contact with the social fabric of which they are the expression. To be sure, between rules and social behaviour

---

[102] See H. L. A. Hart, *The Concept of Law*, Oxford 1961, pp. 89–90.

[103] T. Hobbes, *On the Citizen*, ed. by R. Tuck and M. Silverthorne, Cambridge 1997, p. 73. Emphasis in original.

there is an insuperable gap,[104] due to the fact that the norm, by its formal nature (its generality and abstractness, its indeterminacy), on the one hand is not able to precisely determine its own to practical application. On the other, it cannot cover all the new situations that are in some way contiguous with the area it regulates or the specific case with which it deals. The norm, moreover, even if it, where it is constitutive, introduces new possibilities of action, at any rate by constituting a particular sphere of conduct and accordingly delimiting that rules out certain other possibilities. This exclusion of possibilities of action then becomes explicit in regulative or merely prescriptive rules, which order, prohibit or permit types of behaviour.

For a somehow traditional view, in relation to the plurality and wealth of possibilities of social behaviour norms act as a sort of "cage", as a limitation and "normalization". According to this view, norms would bring about a reduction in the complexity of social life.[105] Norms, however, actually "open" as well as "close" possibilities of action.[106] This does not in any case justify the position that the "meaning" of action that conforms with a rule lies exclusively in compliance with or conformity to the rule. The action of playing chess cannot be explained entirely by compliance with the rules of chess. Even an action governed by rules is not governed only by those rules, but also by manifold reasons and motivations, by other rules of a prudential nature (for instance those of good playing strategy in the case of chess), and moreover by particular intentions and deliberations, that is, those deliberations through which a rule (which is a general formulation) is applied to the specific case. There is a general "sense" that presides over the sphere of action which is rendered possible by norms and expressed in norms. This is prior to the rules and moral principles which provide strong justifications for observing social rules.[107]

It is not so much the presence of the gap between norms and behaviour that produces the situation of "dominion", as the lack of links that means that between rules and social life there is always a relationship such that the latter may always burst into the sphere of the rules to suspend them and more or less explicitly and reflectively amend them. It is not the presence of the "gap" but more its dimensions that indicate whether we are facing mere political power, or else "dominion". That means that, in order for there not to be "dominion", it is not enough for the practical application of the norm implicitly to amend the content of the norm itself. This amendment must at the very least be singled out for consideration. Moreover, it must be possible for there to be other procedures (public, explicit and reflexive) for amending the norm, over and above the minimum amendment brought about in general by its application.

---

[104]Cf. R. De Stefano, *Il rifiuto della legge*, Reggio Calabria 1977, pp. 21–22.

[105]For a polished example of this position cf. F. Crespi, *Azione sociale e potere*, Bologna 1989, pp. 78ff.

[106]Cf. N. Garver, *Rules*, in *The Encyclopedia of Philosophy*, ed. by P. Edwards, vol. 7, New York, NY 1967, p. 232

[107]I will tackle this issue in Chapter 8.

Dominion here does not imply interference with the freedom of movement of subjects, or constriction, coercion or the use of force but rather *arbitrary* interference, constriction, force or coercion,[108] where "arbitrary" means *not decided on* by the one subject to interference.[109] The decision referred to here is not mere consensus, but presupposes participation in the production of norms or decisions that serve to justify interference. Dominion has to last for the same amount of time as the contrary condition – access to decision-making. It cannot thus sustain forms of interference such as to put at risk reproduction of the procedures of deliberation on the part of those subject to interference.

Where the norms that govern human conduct within a certain community, even if laid down in various procedures by the community itself and having a libertarian content, cannot be discussed and reformed by those concerned in accordance with certain public modalities, we would nonetheless be in a situation of "dominion". It is not only their content, but also their relationship with social life and public debate that defines the norms in question, and may cause them slip from the sphere of political power in which they are naturally located to that of "dominion". However, behind the procedural justification of legal norms that broadly corresponds to the model of the relationship between law and power outlined here, one may discern the pressing need for material justice and an inescapable taking of sides.

---

[108] Cf. P. Pettit, *Republicanism. A Theory of Freedom and Government*, Oxford, 1997, Chapter 7.

[109] Following this I distance myself from Philip Petit's views presented in his book cited above.

Part III
Meaning and Values

Chapter 6
Meaning and Value Judgements

6.1 Preliminary

In this last part of the book I propose to focus on what are the foundations, or "justifications", that can be offered for a reflexive morality. By "reflexive morality" I mean an ethics ultimately based on the subject's "reflection", or, in Kantian terms, on the autonomy of his will. My purpose here is not precisely to develop a new approach to metaethics or a normative theory of morality. I have another end in mind, more modest but of equal significance for a theory of law: to show how an institutional conception of law can be connected with a non-cognitivist and reflexive view of ethical judgements. One of the risks attached to institutionalism in law is that, concerning metaethics, it becomes radically objectivist, reinterpreting values (the moral ought) as expressions of institutions (part of reality). Another risk is that in terms of ethics it becomes the vehicle for a strong communitarian morality, reinterpreting values as elements of existing ethics as a product of an unreflective, comprehensive ethos of the institution conceived as the only possible normative point of reference. It is reflexive morality, "the view from nowhere" – as Thomas Nagel would say – that is sacrificed due to the granting of ontological (and thus moral) primacy to "institutions".

I shall proceed in the following manner. In this chapter I once more shall devote my attention to language and thus review (and criticize) some of the most influential theories of meaning and seek to bring out some of their implications for views on human conduct and morality. In the following chapter I shall discuss the most important conceptions. There, I shall propose the metaethical solution that seems to me the most plausible, as much in terms of the theories of meaning studied above as in relation to the conception of rules adopted in the central part of this book. After that, I shall deal with the difficult, controversial relationship between law and morality, systematically setting out in the epilogue some of the considerations that remain to be developed.

As can be seen, I shall not concern myself much with ethics as such. I believe, however, that assuming a certain metaethics may have important consequences of an ethical nature. It is possible moreover that my treatment may, because of its brevity, prove inadequate to the vastness and difficulty of the problems tackled, and perhaps even be irritating for its overweening ambition. The object of this part is

M. La Torre, *Law as Institution*, Law and Philosophy Library 90,
DOI 10.1007/978-1-4020-6607-8_6,

not, however, to propose a metaethical theory nor elaborate a normative morality in detail, so much as to explore the possibility of combining an institutional concept of law with a metaethics that is *moderately non-cognitivist*, or – if you like – *prudently cognivist*. This will take place in the epilogue of the book.

Following a well-established usage, I define "ethics" as the set of value judgements an individual makes in relation to his existential reality. On the contrary, I define "metaethics" as the set of judgements relating to the logical, epistemological or ontological status, or the semantics, of the value judgements making up an "ethics". Metaethics consists of statements about moral judgements. I do not distinguish between "ethics" and "morality" as some do,[1] using the two words interchangeably whilst ascribing the same meaning.

Indeed, value judgements can always be expressed as linguistic sentences.[2] The linguistic sentences through which value judgements can be expressed relate to extra-linguistic realities, that is, to certain states of affairs or to our attitude towards certain states of affairs. Metaethical judgements, also always expressible as linguistic sentences, relate instead to linguistic reality, that is, to the sentences through which value judgements are expressed. We may say, then, that ethics is a "language", or also a "first degree language", that is, a language relating to extra-linguistic entities, while metaethics is "meta-language" or "second degree language", that is, a language relating to linguistic entities. The relationship between ethics and metaethics is similar to that between "knowledge" and "meta-knowledge" (philosophy of knowledge or epistemology), that is, to the relation between the set of factual judgements or descriptive statements (assertions) that make up "knowledge", and the set of sentences (descriptive, prescriptive, argumentative) that relate to the assertions making up knowledge.

It should be added, to avoid confusion, that when I use the term "ethics" I am referring to the system of behavioural norms developed autonomously by the individual as part of his relationship with the world (including that with himself and with others), and not the morality actually in force in a particular community at a particular historical moment. The former is also called "critical morality", and the second "positive morality".[3] In the course of this study "ethics" (or "morality") will be taken exclusively to mean "critical morality". In support of such a choice it has to be said that positive morality however is actually dependent – conceptually and practically – on critical morality. It develops in so far as social actors maintain that its rules of conduct are justified and justifiable and such a justification has an irreducible critical character and strong normative content. This is because it can

---

[1] See e.g., P. Ricoeur, *L'éthique et les conflits de devoirs: le tragique de l'action*, in *Etica e vita quotidiana*, Bologna 1989, p. 5, and J. Habermas, *Faktizität und Geltung. Beiträge zur Diskurstheorie des Rechts und des demokratischen Rechtsstaats*, Frankfurt am Main 1991, p. 127.

[2] This is not so, as we know, for Wittgenstein, or at least for the "early" Wittgenstein: "Ethics, if it is anything, is supernatural and our words will only express facts" (L. Wittgenstein, *A Lecture on Ethics*, in *The Philosophical Review*, vol. 74, 1965, p. 7).

[3] Cf. H. L. A. Hart, *Law, Liberty and Morality*, Oxford 1963, p. 20.

only be effected through reasons and procedures that demonstrate an elevated level of idealization.

It is true of morality, even when taken to mean solely or primarily positive morality, that which Quentin Skinner says of politics: "What it is possible to do in politics is generally limited by what it is possible to legitimize. What you can hope to legitimize, however, depends on what courses of action you can plausibly range under existing normative principles. But this implies that, even if your professed principles never operate as your motives, but only as rationalizations of your behaviour, they will nevertheless help to shape and limit what lines of action you can successfully purgue".[4]

For this reason "strong" normative principles (counterfactuals) that govern the process of legitimization of that particular praxis can be used not only to produce the latter but are also necessary to render the practice itself comprehensible and describable. Thus, the descriptive point of view is dependent on the normative one, or parasitical to it, and positive morality (morality – it could be said – from the descriptive point of view) has to refer to critical morality (morality from the normative point of view). From this is derived the centrality of critical morality.

6.2 Theories of Meaning Once More

From a semantic viewpoint – from the viewpoint of one who deals with the meaning of linguistic statements – it may be maintained that the two chief categories or functions of language are (i) to describe states of affairs and (ii) to prescribe behaviour. A multiplicity of categorizations of the uses of language have in fact been proposed, mostly dependent on the theory of meaning accompanying them. These categorizations are particularly important in the metaethical sphere, as part of the study of the logical, semantic and epistemological status of moral judgements.

I am restating below an analysis of the theories of meaning already given in the second part of the book.[5] Here, however, I am less interested in concentrating on the Wittgensteinian positions as in presenting in more general terms the approach that will then enable me to develop my metaethical considerations. By comparison with what was said before, this treatment is marked, though with some perhaps inevitable repetition, by less recourse to Wittgensteinian texts, and by the attempt to articulate objections and arguments in general terms.

In the recent literature we may distinguish, I believe, the following main theories of meaning: the referential theory; the so-called "pictorial" theory; the ideational theory; the behaviourist; and the verificationist theory; finally the so-called theory of "use". I reviewed all of them in Chapter 3. Now I shall quickly recapitulate the main thesis of each of these theories.

---

[4]Q. Skinner, *Liberty Before Liberalism*, Cambridge 1998, p. 105.

[5]See *supra*, Chapter 3.

According to the referential theory, the meaning of a term or sentence always requires, as well as a "significans" (e.g., particular ink lines on a sheet of paper), a real object or state of affairs in the world. Words and statements without such a referent would consequently have no meaning. In the legal theory this is often the theory presupposed by all those, for instance, that have denied meaningfulness to the concept or term of a "right", since – they say – there is no concrete empirical object or state of affairs that could be imputed to such term or concept.

Related to the "referential" theory is the so-called "pictorial" theory – in German *Abbildungstheorie* – according to which the meaning of a statement represents the structure of the outside world by reproducing it in its logical form. "A proposition", writes Wittgenstein, "is a picture of reality".[6] Picture *(Bild)* is, however, not meant here in the psychological sense as a mental image, but as "logical" representation or as kind of model. "The sense of a proposition", writes Wittgenstein again, "is its agreement and disagreement with possibilities of existence and non-existence of states of affairs".[7]

This is explained by Bertrand Russell as follows: "[Wittgenstein] compares linguistic expression to projection in geometry. A geometrical figure may be projected in many ways: each of these ways corresponds to a different language, but the projective properties of the original figure remain unchanged whichever of these ways may be adopted. These projective properties correspond to that which in his theory the proposition and the fact must have in common, if the proposition is to assert the fact".[8]

In relation to this proposition one should not forget Wittgenstein's anti-subjectivist stance in the *Tractatus logico-philosophicus*: "There is no such thing as the subject that thinks or entertains ideas".[9] Consequently, there cannot be merely psychological representations either, nor can the meaning of terms and sentences be made up of such representations. As far as words and terms are concerned, Wittgenstein holds that they acquire new meaning only when used in a sentence: their meaning is however identified with the object that they denote: "A name means an object. The object is its meaning".[10] For this "early" Wittgenstein, words are thus always "proper nouns".

(c) According to the so-called "ideational" theory, the meaning of a term or sentence is the idea represented to the subject through the use of that term or sentence. A "classical" defender of this theory is, as is known, John Locke, who wrote: "Words in their primary or intermediate signification, stand for nothing but the ideas in the mind of him that uses them".[11] Or remember what Kant said in his *Anthropology*,

---

[6] L. Wittgenstein, *Tractatus logico-philosophicus*, Frankfurt am Main 1983, p. 35 (para. 4.021).

[7] Ibid., p. 49 (para. 4.2).

[8] B. Russell, *Introduction*, in L. Wittgenstein, *Tractatus logico-philosophicus*, London 1961, p. xi.

[9] L. Wittgenstein, *Tractatus logico-philosophicus*, p. 90 (para. 5.631).

[10] Ibid., p. 22 (para. 3.203).

[11] J. Locke, *An Essay Concerning Human Understanding*, ed. by R. Woolhouse, London 2004, p. 364 (III.3.ii).

nearly quoting Locke: all language is a mark of ideas ("Alle Sprache ist Bezeichnung der Gedanken").[12] An example of a more sophisticated version is that set out by the Polish logician Adjukiewicz: "The linguistic meaning of an expression of W form in J language is a kind (a species) of T thought, such as, given two persons speaking in J language, in order for them to use an expression of W form without misunderstanding, it is necessary and sufficient that they associate to such expressions a psychological meaning and thoughts of T type".[13]

For the behaviourist theory the meaning of a sign or set of signs consists in the response (or "disposition to respond") evoked by the sign, which is thus conceived of as a sort of "stimulus". This theory is linked to the work of Charles Morris, whose definition of "sign" is as follows: "If anything, A, is a preparatory-stimulus which in the absence of stimulus-objects initiating response-sequences of a certain behavior-family causes a disposition in some organism to respond under certain conditions by response-sequences of this behavior-family, then A is a sign".[14] A variant of this behaviourist theory is the so-called expressive theory according to which it is maintained that "the utterance, as an integral part of a psychological whole, refers back to the experience which causes me to make the utterance".[15] The utterance, here substituting the sentence, is, "the expression or symptom of something".[16]

For the verificationist theory, typical of neo-empiricist philosophical approaches, the meaning of a sentence consists in the verification or verifiability of the state of affairs about which the sentence is concerned. A particularly liberalized version of this theory is well expressed in the following words of Rudolf Carnap: "I regard as meaningful whatever I can, in principle, confirm subjectively".[17] It should be noted that the verificationist theory faces a dilemma: either it becomes a subjectivist theory in which that which is true, verified, or verifiable for me (and my senses) is meaningful (as seems to be suggested by the Carnap's notion, just cited), or it has to presuppose intersubjective truth criteria of criteria of verifiability. Such criteria however are deduced from the average criterion of verifiability, transcending somehow my sensory system, but as such they don't make sense, they're incomprehensible, being incomprehensible they are not communicable, transmissible or otherwise objects of learning and thus they cannot justify the general adoption of criterion of verifiability as criterion of meaning. The verificationalist theory is also closely linked to the referential theory: it is in fact possible to verify the meaning of a sentence in so far as it has a "referent" in the perceptible world that can be reached through observational procedure.

---

[12] I. Kant, *Anthropologie in pragmatischer Hinsicht*, ed. by R. Brandt, Hamburg 2000, p. 93.

[13] K. Adjukjewicz, *O znaczeniu wyrazen*, Lwow 1931, quoted by K. Opalek, *Il problema del significato directivo*, in *Diritto e analisi del linguaggio*, ed. by U. Scarpelli, Milano 1976, p. 156.

[14] Ch. Morris, *Signs, Language and Behavior*, New York, NY 1946, p. 10. See also Ch. Morris, *Signs About Signs About Signs*, in *Philosophy and Phenomenological Research*, vol. 9, 1948, p. 115.

[15] A. Ross, *Directives and Norms*, London 1968, p. 76.

[16] Ibid.

[17] R. Carnap, *Replies and Systematic Expositions*, in *The Philosophy of Rudolf Carnap*, ed. by P. Schilpp, La Salle, IL 1963, p. 882.

Finally, for the so-called "use" theory, the meaning of a term or sentence lies in the use made of it by speakers of the given language. We have seen above that this is the position of the "late" Wittgenstein.

These theories of meaning do not, with the exception of the last, convince me. I shall now rapidly reiterate the reasons for this position.

To the "referential" theory the objection may be raised that in ordinary language there are terms that for us are entirely devoid of meaning in the sense that in the specific situations in which these terms are put forward we understand what they mean, yet they lack a concrete reference; they do not denote any material object in the world. Consider, for instance, such terms as "griffin", "devil", "value", "norm", "State", "God". Moreover, even terms that seem to refer to a concrete object existing in the world, such as "table", "cat", "man", denote not a specific object but a class of those objects, which as such is not the set of all those particular objects existing in the perceptible world at a given moment, but the set of all possible objects capable of assuming certain properties. The "class" in question is, as such, an abstraction, non-existent in the perceptible world.

It should further be noted that the denotation of a term (the class of objects to which it refers) is dependent on its connotation, that is, the class of properties by which the referred objects can be identified (though without the converse being true, namely that the connotation of term depends on its extension): the extension of the class denoted is inversely proportional to the extension of the class connoted. The more properties that make up the connotation of a term, the narrower will be the class of objects denoted by that term. Further, the fact that the particular object falls within the "denotation" or extension of a term depends on the "connotation" or "intension" of that term. The "connotation" is, however, an entirely ideal factor. What is to be emphasized, in short, is that the "denotation" has no autonomy as far as the determination of its own boundaries goes, depending in this respect on the "connotation", which can be reduced even less than the "denotation" to individual subjects existing in the perceptible world. But, if it is held that the elements in the meaning of a term are supplied by its "connotation", it must be concluded that it is not so much the "referent" or "denotation" that constitutes the condition for the perceptibility (or conceivability) of the "meaning" or "connotation" as just the opposite: it is the "meaning" of a term that is the condition for the perceptibility (or conceivability) of the "referent".

In short, "extension" or "denotation" (in the abstract and general terms) and meaning are two quite different things. This is expressed very well by Quine: "The class of all entities of which a general term is true is called the *extension* of the term. Now paralleling the contrast between the meaning of a singular term and the entity named, we must distinguish equally between the meaning of a general term and its extension. The general terms 'creature with a heart' and 'creature with kidneys', for example, are perhaps alike in extension but unlike in meaning".[18]

---

[18]W. V. Quine, *Two Dogmas of Empiricism*, in Id., *From a Logical Point of View*, 2nd ed., New York, NY 1961, p. 21.

To the "pictorial" theory, it may be objected that there are no elements capable of plausibly upholding the notion that the structure of statements reproduces a presumed "logical structure" of the world. The very concept of "logical structure" of the world seems to me rather far-reaching, and at any rate underived from observational procedures of verification or falsification. The "pictorial" theory thus seems to be invalidated by its over heavy ontological and metaphysical consequences. At the same time, the "pictorial" theory – as formulated by the "early" Wittgenstein – underestimates the jump or gap there is between an object and the term denoting it. One may indeed with some claim to reasonableness follow Joseph Conrad in saying "words [...] are the great foes of reality".[19] A term is obviously not the object denoted by it, nor is the term the proper name of the object. Suffice to say at this point that a term or statement continues to have meaning even when the object or situation it denotes is no longer in the world. I may sensibly say "the cat has disappeared," but not "the meaning of 'cat' has disappeared", and "cat" would have meaning as a term even if cats as an animal species should happen to become extinct. The *Abbildungstheorie* presupposes that language has the essentially "reproductive" function when it comes to that which is real; language, according to this view, is a sort of mirror in which the reality of things is reflected. To this the objection could be made that language performs a primarily *creative* role, producing the categories through which we confront reality. More than an "*Abbildungs*"- *theorie* we need a "*Bildungs*"- *theorie.* The creative or constructive character of language is already implied by the fact that the relationship between a certain term and its referent is not necessary and changes in every natural language: "Classification," writes Ernst Cassirer, "is one of the fundamental features of human speech. The very act of denomination depends on a process of classification. To give a name to an object or action is to subsume it under a certain class concept. If this subsumption were once and for all prescribed by the nature of things, it would be unique and uniform. But the names which occur in human speech cannot be interpreted in any such invariable manner [...] They are determined rather by human interests and human purposes. But these interests are not fixed and invariable".[20]

Against the "ideational" theory the point could be made that in making meaning a subjective psychological fact it so subjectivizes communication as to make it impossible, or highly problematic. For in order for there to be communication it is necessary for there to be some kind of substantial identity between the meaning intended by the utterer of the sentence (message) and that understood by the addressee or recipient. But if meaning is nothing but the psychological "idea" evoked by the sign, what guarantee do we have that there will be substantial identity between the "idea" evoked by the sign in the utterer's mind and the other idea evoked in the recipients mind? And if there is no such identity, communication between utterer and addressee of the statement is not established. It should be further noted that the "idea" spoken of in the "ideational" theory is generally the representation of

[19] J. Conrad, *Under Western Eyes*, ed. by J. Hawthorn, Oxford 1983, p. 3.

[20] E. Cassirer, *An Essay on Man*, New Haven, CT 1944, p. 134.

a state of affairs, an image, a "figure". But there are signs or terms to which no corresponding "image" can be attributed. What "image" is, for instance, evoked by an adverb like "perhaps", or a phrase like "legal transaction"? It may also be said that a certain word evokes a particular "image", yet this is not the meaning of the term. It is, for instance, possible for the word "caramel" to evoke for me the image of a Swiss governess through some psychological mechanism of associations. It does not however follow that the meaning of "caramel" is the image of a Swiss governess.

The behaviourist conception can be repudiated for its – we might say – hermeneutic deafness. It is incapable of understanding that the meaning of a term or sentence or discourse is something not perceivable from an "external viewpoint". That is, we are not capable from mere observation of a subject's behaviour to establish whether that subject has understood the meaning of a given term, statement or discourse. Let me give an example. Say I am in room with two other people playing cards and I do not know German. The first person gets up, looks out of the window and says, "It is raining". I go on looking at my cards. Then my other companion gets up, looks out of the window and says in German, "Es regnet nicht". I go on looking at my cards. How can an observer establish on the basis of my behaviour whether I have understood the two statements, "It is raining" and "Es regnet nicht" or not? Both statements have had the same external effect on me: I kept on looking at my cards. Yet in the first case, since I know English, I understood the meaning of the statement, while in the second, not knowing German, I was not able to understand the speaker.

The reproach based on the idea of "hermeneutic deafness" also counts against the other variant of behaviourist theory, the "expressive" conception of language, according to which linguistic expressions are symptoms of the psycho-physical state of the one making the statement or expression. As Alf Ross recognizes, and has previously sustained, this conception is deeply mistaken."For it confuses the semantic analisis of discourse with psychological inductive inferences".[21]

Underlying behaviourism is a "causalist" theory of meaning, that is, between a sign and the meaning evoked by it there is a causal relation of the stimulus/response type, making that particular sign a sufficient condition for that particular meaning. The objection may be raised to this conception that in contrast to the stimulus/response relation, where the stimulus is a sufficient condition for the response, the sign-meaning relation is mediated by a code, that is, by rules attributing that particular meaning to that particular sign. In order, then, for there to be a particular meaning, at least two conditions are necessary, though neither is sufficient: the sign and the code. This amounts to saying that since the code is located within the human being's disposition and is subject to change, the sign/meaning relation is conventional, arbitrary somehow, and not necessitated by nature. The behaviourist theory further, in some sense, presupposes a "referentialist" conception, since the

[21] A. Ross, *Directives and Norms*, p. 77.

meaning (the response) has to have a corresponding object or fact in the world (the stimulus).[22]

Note that if we accepted the causalist theory of meaning, we could similarly uphold a causalist theory of normative descriptions. We might, that is, assert that the relation between a natural event and a "legal effect" (between murder and a prison sentence) is "causal" – "causal" in the strict sense, in the sense of the murder being a sufficient condition for the imprisonment. We might thus arrive without contradicting ourselves at the position that legal laws and natural laws are "causal" in the same sense. But were we to assert that, we would be falling into a version of what is today usually called the "naturalistic fallacy", that natural facts are in themselves a sufficient expression of criteria for guiding human social behaviour.[23]

In addition one may criticize the model of communication implicit in the behaviourist theory, according to which communication is above all an interpersonal message, that occurs between an utterer and an addressee.[24] This sort of "simple" communication model is assumed by all theories that make the meaning of terms or statements depend exclusively upon the behaviour or mental operations of their utterer or recipient. This model is therefore common also to "ideational" or mentalistic theories of meaning. But as has been written by Mario Jori, "very often signs, especially linguistic signs, are used in communication situations very different from those where the speaker is in direct, contemporaneous communication with the hearer. Consider communication situations characterized by the impersonality of the relationship, where the text of the message takes on an impersonal, often permanent nature".[25] "This," continues Jori, "is one of the reasons that counsels us not to link the definition of the sign process too closely with psychological facts and events (like the utterer's intention of the interpreter's mental relations). Many communication situations are, in fact, complex social institutions governed by interpersonal norms of communication".[26]

To the verificationist theory at least two objections may be raised. The first is that already mentioned attached to the dilemma of epistemological subjectivism or

---

[22]This has been stressed by William P. Alston: "The attempt to give behavioural analyses of meaning is still in an early stage, and it would be premature to deliver a final verdict. Nevertheless, one must recognize that at present they exhibit some glaring deficiencies. First of all, they are saddled with the assumption that every meaningful linguistic unit is a 'sign' of some discernable extra-linguistic thing, aspect or state of affairs" (W. P. Alston, *Meaning*, in *The Encyclopedia of Philosophy*, ed. by P. Edwards, vol. 5, London 1967, p. 236).

[23]In this connection, see K. R. Popper, *The Open Society and Its Enemies*, vol. 1, *The Spell of Plato*, 5th ed., London 1973, p. 57. The incompatibility of a non-cognitivist metaethics and a "realistic" philosophy of language has been stressed by D. Zolo, *La democrazia difficile*, Roma 1989, p. 23.

[24]This is also the model adopted by one of the astutest Italian philosophers of law, Giovanni Tarello: "We call the 'meaning' of an expression of language the communication that expression makes in relation to each of the three functions of language" (G. Tarello, *Diritto, enuciati, usi. Studi di teoria e metateoria del diritto*, Bologna 1974, p. 140).

[25]M. Jori, *Comunicazione (semiotica)*, in *Gli strumenti del sapere contemporaneo*, vol. 2, *I concetti*, Torino 1985, p. 145.

[26]Ibid.

lack of meaning (and relevance). A last objection can also be raised against the "referential" theory of meaning. As we have seen, the verificationist theory implies a referentialist view. It is possible to verify a statement only in relation to what there is in the perceptible world; a statement is verifiable only in so far as it has a concrete referent in the world of empirical facts. However, as we have seen, there are terms and statements that, though endowed with meaning, do not refer to an object or event in the outside world. The sentences making up theological disputes, for instance, rarely refer to objects or events in the empirical world. The dispute over the Holy Trinity, however it may seem to or actually be *scientifically* devoid of meaning, is not so from a semantic viewpoint. So much so that the dispute was possible, that the parties understood each other, argued, wrote treatises on it and – sometimes – massacred each other. The principle of meaningfulness as a semantic principle (serving to discriminate what has meaning from what does not) should thus be kept distinct from the principle of verifiability as a principle of meta-knowledge (serving to discriminate what can be true from what cannot).[27]

But there is another, more decisive, objection that can be brought to bear against the verificationist theory: the verifiability of a statement depends on its having meaning, on what it means. For how could we verify a statement whose meaning we do not know? Karl Popper puts it well: "Bevor man überhaupt fragen kann, ob ein Satz wahr oder falsch ist, mus man wissen, ob er einen Sinn hat oder ob er Unsinn ist".[28] This idea is confirmed by, amongst others, Bunge: "Meaningfulness, though insufficient for testability, is necessary for it".[29] This is proof that the meaning of a statement is independent of its verification or verifiability, or rather the meaning of a statement is a necessary condition for its verification or verifiability and not viceversa.[30]

It is worth mentioning a further objection raised against the verificationist theory. If the theory is accepted, one must also, as Karl Popper notes, conclude that all "natural laws" are without meaning, since they cannot be reduced to mere observational statements.[31] The "laws" are in fact, according to the inductivist theory, reached by a process of induction from *n* observational statements. From the observational statements to the "law", however, there is always a link, the logical justification for which continues, as we note, to be an object of dispute in the philosophy of science. It is, in any case, certain that even for the most radical neopositivist or neoempiricist theory, the "law" cannot be logically reduced to a series of observational statements.

---

[27] In this connection see U. Scarpelli, *Contributo alla semantica del linguaggio normativo*, 2nd ed., ed. by A. Pintore, Milano 1984, pp. 85ff.

[28] K. R. Popper, *Die beiden Grundprobleme der Erkenntnistheorie*, Tübingen 1979, p. 276.

[29] M. Bunge, *Treatise on Basic Philosophy*, vol. 2, *Semantics II: Interpretation and Truth*, Dordrecht 1974, pp. 73–74.

[30] See also, J. Habermas, *Wahrheitstheorien*, in Id., *Vorstudien und Ergänzungen zur Theorie des Kommunikativen Handelns*, Frankfurt am Main 1984, p. 158, where he affirms that "die Verständlichkeit einer Äusserung mit deren Wahrheit nichts zu tun hat".

[31] See K. R. Popper, *The Demarcation between Science and Metaphysics*, in *The Philosophy of Rudolph Carnap*, ed. by P. A. Schlipp, La Salle, IL, 1963, p. 192.

But if that is so, how can one, if the verificationist theory is accepted, uphold the meaningfulness of natural "laws"?

An additional standard objection is the one reported in the following terms: "If all meaningful statements are, on the principle of verifiability, either tautologies or empirically verifiable, what of the formulation of the verification principle itself? It would be awkward to be put in the position of having to argue that the statement in terms of which we could distinguish between sense and nonsense, namely the statement articulating the criterion of verifiability, is itself nonsensical".[32] We have thus before us a blind alley. There might however be a way out, that of arguing that the verification principle is a *rule* rather than a statement. But to accept this as a way out we should assume that not only statements, utterances dealing with what "is", or with states of affairs, that can be in principle either true or false, are meaningful, but also rules, that is, normative propositions (dealing with what "ought to be") that cannot be in principle true or false, hence that cannot be verified or verifiable. Verifiability as a *rule* (as a normative proposition distinct from a statement) would accordingly be meaningful on the basis of some other standard of meaningfulness opposed or different to that of verification or verifiability. Verifiability could not then be the only possible source of meaningfulness. Nor could it be a pivotal, or foundational criterion, since verifiability to be given sense as a standard or rule should be backed through a different and more basic principle or standard of sense.

At the end of the day the least weak theory of meaning is in my view the one maintaining that the meaning of a term or statement depends on the *use* made of it by those speaking a given language.[33] It is, as we know, the theory developed by Ludwig Wittgenstein, after he repudiated the *Abbildungstheorie* he had defended in his famous early work. However, we should be clear about what is meant by "use". Of this Wittgensteinian notion three main interpretations may be identified. (i) "Use" is understood as regularity, mere repetition of the attribution of meaning, so that this "use" can be conceived of as merely individual, beyond the community.[34] (ii) "Use" is understood in pragmatic terms as a "speech act", as the use of a given statement in a given context for given ends, so that there is no longer any sense in asking about the meaning *in general* of a statement or term. On this interpretation there is no "meaning of meaning", one cannot sensibly speak of what the meaning of a term (or sentence) is, apart from a *given* term (or sentence) and a given concrete

---

[32]R. Plant, *Modern Political Thought*, Oxford 1991, p. 18. This is however what paradoxically Wittgenstein in a sense demands of us in his *Tractatus*: see para. 6.54 (cf. H. Tetens, *Wittgensteins "Tractatus". Ein Kommentar*, Stuttgart 2009, p. 9).

[33]The theory of use is anticipated by Baruch Spinoza: "Verba ex solo usu certam habent significationem (*Tractatus theologico-politicus*, in Spinoza, *Opera*, ed. by C. Gebhardt, 2nd ed., vol. 3, Heidelberg 1972, p. 160).

[34]This is the position defended by, for instance, Baker and Hacker. See G. P. Baker and P. M. S. Hacker, *Wittgenstein, Rules, Grammar and Necessity*, Oxford 1986. Cf. also G. P. Baker and P. M. S. Hacker, *Scepticism, Rules, Language*, Oxford 1984, p. 20.

situation in which that term (or sentence) has been used for given ends.[35] (iii) On a third interpretation, more widespread, more authoritative and, I believe, more faithful to Wittgenstein's text, "use" is understood broadly analogously to the concept of "custom" in the theory of law. The "use" does result from constant repetition of certain attributions of meaning, and therefore of certain uses, but this is combined with a normative element, a type of *opinio iuris seu necessitatis*.

"Use", according to this third interpretation, does not stand for "individual use" or "merely subjective use". Say I decide to call the table "pen" and the pen "table"; the meaning of "table" will remain the one sanctioned by common usage, not the one determined by my private use of the term. "Use", on this interpretation, is *use according to certain rules*. It is accordingly legitimate to speak of the "correctness" of linguistic uses. Not all subjective uses of a term (or sentence) are correct, and it is possible to note "linguistic errors" (of those speaking or writing incorrectly). In this way one could claim, along with Habermas, that a linguistic expression is comprehensible, thus has sense whenever it is formed in such a way that whoever masters the corresponding normative systems could produce the same expression.[36]

The theory of "use", in this last version, has important theoretical consequences. The theory, though accepting a conception of language as a conventional fact, a product of man, recognizes that it (language) is the outcome of largely unconscious or unaware activity of human beings, just like many other usages and rules of social life.[37] Humpty Dumpty is accordingly wrong in saying in *Through the Looking Glass* that a term means just what one wants it to mean. For we find language already there, we do not invent it[38]; it thus contributes powerfully towards determining our very categories of thought.

The decisionistic conception (à *la* Humpty Dumpty, so to say) and the emotivistic one (for which meaning is connected to the unpremeditated, and irrational, reactions of the recipient of a statement) in addition to creating severe problems for inter-subjective communication, render problematic the intellectual activities of the subject in question. If the meaning of a term or of a sentence depends on the single decision or reaction of the subject (be this the utterer or the recipient of the linguistic expression), what guarantees that the same term or sentence used at a different moment in time will not give rise to a different decision or reaction? If there is no such guarantee it becomes impossible, for example, to make logical inferences of

[35] Cf. J. L. Austin, *The Meaning of a Word*, in Id., *Philosophical Papers*, Oxford 1961, pp. 23ff.

[36] See J. Habermas, *Wahrheitstheorien*, p. 158

[37] Cf. A. Flew, *Thinking about Social Thinking. The Philosophy of the Social Sciences*, Oxford 1985, pp. 63ff.

[38] As Searle says, "meaning is more than a matter of intention, it is also a matter of convention" (J. R. Searle, *What is a Speech Act*?, in *The Philosophy of Language*, ed. by J. R. Searle, Oxford, 1971, p. 46) Here Anthony Flew's remarks are also relevant when he notes "how fallacious it is to argue that, if something is the product or result of conscious human agency, then it must always be in practice possible radically to redesign and reshape that product or that result in such a way that it shall better accommodate the wishes of the person concerned" (A. Flew, *Thinking about Social Thinking*, p. 67).

the type: "All men are mortal. Socrates is a man. Therefore Socrates is mortal". In fact this simple operation takes place at three distinct moments in time, and is possible only if the terms in these three moments are imbued with the same meaning. If in the first premise "man" means a certain type of mammal with certain characteristics, such as that of walking upright, and alternatively in the second premise "man" denotes – let's assume – a type of grass, the logical conclusion of the two premises (that "Socrates is mortal") will be rendered impossible. Up the same blind alley we are led into by the decisionistic theory of Humpty Dumpty, we come to an individualistic theory of "use", according to which the use relevant to the production of meaning would be the individual one. This however doesn't seem to be the opinion of Wittgenstein who stresses – as we have seen in Chapter 3 – the communitarian and institutional character of "language games". Moreover, an individualistic theory of "use" is not easy to distinguish from a decisionistic theory. The heuristic autonomy of the theory of "use" resides thus to a large degree in the normative and institutional versions.

The theory of "use" has one further implication very relevant to the topic (justification of moral and normative sentences) that interests us here. The theory of "use" maintains a plurality of "uses" of language founded on "language games" and the normative systems underlying it. There is not, then, one use privileged over others or one main or unique function of language; it is instead employed in, and made up of, a multiplicity of "games" all equally important in the context of the given linguistic community. Thus while traditional theories of meaning, in particular the "referential", behaviourist and verificationist ones, tend to see normative discourse as a set of sentences with a logical status in some sense "inferior" to that of the descriptive or observational sentences typical of science, or "shaky" in relation to them, the theory of use acknowledges that moral sentences and normative sentences in general, have a worth (and meaning) similar or analogous to, or even equal to that possessed by descriptive sentences.[39]

6.3 Two Contrasting Views: Bertrand Russell and John L. Austin

6.3.1 In his well-known work *An Inquiry into Meaning and Truth*, Bertrand Russell distinguishes clearly between the meaning of single words and the meaning of sentences. The theory of meaning of the English philosopher is actually anything but linear, rather it is quite eclectic. We could say that it is a mixture of a referential theory, of a causalist theory and of an expressionistic theory.

Russell seems to favour above all a causalist theory of language. The meaning of words and sentences is the effect that they should provoke in the recipient of a linguistic expression. "When in adult life – he writes – you use a word, you do so, as a rule, not only because what the word 'denotes' is present to sense or imagination

[39]Cf. R. Alexy *Theorie des juristischen Argumentation. Die Theorie des rationalen Diskurses als Theorie der juristischen Begründung*, 2nd ed., Frankfurt am Main 1983, pp. 71ff.

but because you wish your hearer to do something about it".[40] Russell adds that discourse in general are meant to provoke behaviour on the part of others. "We may say, generally, that speech consists, with some exceptions, of noises made by persons with a view to causing desired actions by other persons".[41]

The descriptive or representative role, that of representing the state of things, seems thus subordinate to the primary function of language, that of causing conduct by the recipient of the linguistic message. "It is interesting that language can state facts; it is also interesting that it can state falsehoods. When it states either, it does so with a view to causing some action in the hearer".[42] Russell thus comes to affirm, making explicit one of the results of causalist theory, that "most sentences are primarily imperative".[43] This conclusion is added to also through his conception of that which is a "belief". If, as he sustains, "a belief is an impulse towards some action",[44] the distinction between descriptive and prescriptive sentences dissolves. From this perspective the meaning of both types of sentence is defined in terms of the beliefs they sustain. Such beliefs in each case however turn out to be orientation to act, practical criteria or stimuli for conduct.

The descriptive or prescriptive function becomes the principal function of language. This assists in the overturning of the neo-positivist position according to which the primary function of sentences is "indicative" or "representative" or in fact, "descriptive". Russell however seems to weaken the affirmation according to which the primary function of language is the imperative one when he adds that the principal function of statements is imperative but that such a function is possible only thanks to the "representative" capacity of such sentences. The sentences thus "cannot fulfill their action of causing action in the hearer except in virtue of the indicative character of object-words".[45]

We thus arrive at the difference between words (and in particular "object-words") and sentences. The first have meaning in so far as they refer to (or represent) objects and states of affairs in the real world. The "object-words", according to the English philosopher, are characterized by three properties: (a) they don't presuppose knowledge of any other word; (b) they are meaningful as such, even though they aren't parts of sentences; (c) they are learnt through ostension, that is, with the assistance of somebody who indicates the empirical object to which they refer.

As far as the meaning of sentences is concerned, Russell combines different simple theoretical models. In the first place he claims that the meaning of a sentence lies in the state of being of the speaker. "The 'significance' of a sentence is what it 'expresses'. Thus true and false sentences are equally significant, but a string of

---

[40]B. Russell, *An Inquiry into Meaning and Truth*, London 1985, p. 27.

[41]Ibid.

[42]Ibid., p. 28.

[43]Ibid.

[44]B. Russell, *Human Knowledge. Its Scope and Limits*, London 1948, pp. 519–520.

[45]B. Russell, *An Inquiry into Meaning and Truth*, p. 28.

words which cannot express any state of the speaker is nonsensical".[46] Elsewhere Russell seems inclined towards a theory of representation that conceives the meaning as a psychological (or indeed physiological) fact: "The only thing essential to our inquiry is that sentences signify something other than themselves, which can be the same when the sentences differ. That this something must be psychological (or physiological) is made evident by the fact that propositions can be false".[47] The English philosopher adheres then to the behaviourist theory for which linguistic meaning is discernible in the context of the emanation or in reception of the message: "The meaning of a single word is defined by the situations that cause it to be used and the effects that result from hearing it. The significance of a sentence can be similarly defined; in fact, an object-word *is* a sentence when used in an exclamatory manner".[48]

There is a moment in the pages of an *Inquiry into Meaning and Truth* in which a verificationist theory is even outlined: a sentence would have meaning if one is able to imagine the state of affairs that would render true the sentence in question. "A sufficient but not necessary criterion of significance is that perceptual experiences can be imagined, or actually occur, which make us use the phrase (or its contradictory) as an assertion".[49] The verifiability of a sentence is seen as a sufficient but not necessary condition for the significance of the same sentence, and it counts only for assertions. It should be noted that Russell doesn't deny the importance of other types of sentences, such as commands.

Nevertheless, Russell is critical with respect to the verificationist theory defended by Schlick and in a more moderate form by Rudolf Carnap.[50] He has at least three objections to this theory. First, Russell reproaches Schlick for not taking into consideration the difference, as far as meaning is concerned, between words and sentences. Whilst the "necessary" words of a language are defined in a ostensive manner, and are thus dependent – when assuming meaning – on concrete experience, this is not true of sentences. The meaning of the latter, composed of "necessary words" or "object-words", doesn't refer back to a direct observational experience. "Given the experience necessary for the understanding of the name '*a*' and the predicate 'P', we can understand the sentence '*a* has the predicate P' without the need of any experience corresponding to this sentence; and when I say that we can understand the sentence, I do not mean that we know how to find out whether it is true".[51]

The second objection to Schlick's thesis is that the argument is characterized by infinite regression. If the meaning of a sentence is the means used to verify it and such a means is itself intelligible, it will itself take the form of a sentence. The

[46]Ibid., p. 171.

[47]Ibid., p. 189.

[48]Ibid.

[49]Ibid., p. 175.

[50]See for example M. Schlick, *Meaning and Verification*, in *Philosophical Review*, vol. 45, 1936, and R. Carnap, *Testability and Meaning*, in *Philosophy of Science*, vols. 3 and 4, 1936 and 1937.

[51]B. Russell, *An Inquiry into Meaning and Truth*, p. 308.

meaning of the latter will also dependent on a further sentence (which will provide the means to its verification) and so on *ad infinitum*.

Thirdly, we reach perhaps the most serious criticism directed against the verificationalist theory by Russell, whereby he somehow moves away from logical positivism of the Vienna School. There are sentences – says Russell – which, even though amongst the sentences of which human beings are capable they are the most "certain", don't assume their meaning through any means of verification since they form the basis for every possible verification. Such sentences are the sentences of perceptions, those that express directly the data provides by the physiological system through the different perceptive capacities. "When it is said that 'the meaning of a proposition is the method of its verification', this omits the propositions that are most nearly certain, namely judgements of perception. For these there is no 'method of verification', since it is they that constitute the verification of all other empirical propositions that can be in any degree known".[52]

The fundamental difference between the position of Schlick and Carnap on the one hand and that of Russell on the other is that, according to the first two, knowledge is exclusively in the form of science and knowledge statements are thus universal statements, while for Russell, alternatively, knowledge is above all perception or even evidence, the sum of singular statements that don't require any verification and are not verifiable (exactly because they are singular). "Can anything be learnt, and if so what, from single experience? Carnap and the whole school to which he belongs think of knowledge as scientific knowledge, and as beginning with such propositions as 'metals conduct electricity'. Such propositions clearly require a number of observations. But unless each single observation yields *some* knowledge, how can a succession of observations yield knowledge?".[53] If however it is true that the singular observation and the sentence that expresses it constitute knowledge, and are therefore endowed with meaning, and if it is true furthermore that the singular sentence (that expresses the perception in question) is unverifiable, one cannot sustain that a sentence has meaning only where it is possible to provide the means for its verification.

Russell's theory does however conserve many of the characteristics of neopositivism, and in particular the approach to the linguistic phenomenon, seen as detached from the history, culture and society in which it has developed. Language of which Russell, Carnap and Schlick think is in the end the ideal language of the scientist, purged of any contingent historical or cultural implications and faithful (but abstract) mirror of material reality. Here language is not a set of social rules, and much less a cultural filter that determines the very perception of empirical reality. It is a surrogate, a faithful representation, a reproduction in miniature of the ontological structure of material reality, a "model". Thus, Russell recommends that in the study of language this should not be considered a social phenomenon and the speech of the subject has to be conceived fundamentally as a sort of soliloquy or

---

[52] Ibid., p. 308.

[53] Ibid., pp. 314–315.

rather as a dialogue with a subject exactly identical to the speaker. This means, adds the English philosopher, eliminating the concept of correctness from the study of language and also, I would say, abandoning the normative point of view (the point of view internal to the rules of a language) so precious to the late Wittgenstein and to the Waissman of *Logik, Sprache, Philosophie.*

It is unfortunate, but there is no space for society in Russell's conception of language. The theory derived is a sort of linguistic Hobbesianism in which one has to assume that even time has no relevance to the linguistic preferences of the actor who necessarily prevents himself from modifying his preference criteria. "I think – he writes – that, in fundamental discussions of language, its social aspect should be ignored, and a man should always be supposed to be speaking to himself; or, what comes to the same thing, to a man whose language is precisely identical with its own. What remains – if a man is to be able to interpret notes written by himself on previous occasions – is constancy in his own use of words: we must suppose that he uses the same language to-day as he used yesterday".[54] In this vision there is place neither for society nor for history. Rules are substituted by deterministic regularity (the only resource for guaranteeing that the subject is always the same), society by the individual, or, better still, by an automaton that doesn't change linguistic preference and can speak only to himself, and history by a temporal evolution conceived like the addition of similar quantities, numerical progression. No room is allowed to community, altenity and change.

6.3.2 The theory of language developed by John Langshaw Austin is quite different. One could maintain in fact that it is the diametrical opposite of the model represented by Russell's philosophy. However, the theory of the so-called "speech acts" developed by Austin could be seen as a realistic (and individualistic) interpretation of the theory of use originating in Wittgenstein.

For Austin, the function or uses of language are multiple and go far beyond the traditional dichotomy or tripartition (according to the case) of the function of language offered by scholars neopositivist in orientation. For Austin it is necessary above all to overcome the distinction between the semantic and pragmatic nature of a sentence. In his opinion language is essentially pragmatic, it produces conduct and effects on the conduct of others and more generally on the empirical world. On the other hand according to a realist philosophical perspective which seems also to be part of Austin's thought there are no other states in the world, beyond empirical facts, and meanings as ideal entities are rendered ontologically inadmissible.

Rather than propositions or sentences one should therefore speak of speech *acts*. Of these there are various types that might be classified according to the effect that they provoke on the recipient of the message and the context in which the message belongs. There is not one use, but multiple uses of the same word and the same sentence, and such uses give rise to as many acts and different typologies. The meaning of a sentence seems thus to be absorbed by the effect of the speech act of which it

[54] Ibid., pp. 186–187.

is a part. The semantic element is in a sense dissolved into the pragmatic element, that is, the *effect* of the act.

There are thus, according to Austin, two basic classes of sentences: those that represent and describe the world ("constatives"), that can thus be true or false, and those that have as their function the constitution of certain facts in the world that is in a certain way an intrinsic part of the act itself ("performatives"). Of these latter one cannot claim truth or falsehood. Here, "the uttering of the sentences is, or is a part of, the doing of an action, which again would not normally be described as, or as 'just', saying something".[55] There are no "promises" without the acts of promising nor proper nouns (such as ships) without the formal acts of naming and baptism. In addition, for the performatives alone it would seem that one can say that their meaning is given by the individual use one makes of these statements.

Austin however, with two successive theoretical moves, revives a theory of language *based on procedure or rules*, and therefore not reducible to an unordered set or only statistically regular individual uses, with no internal criteria of correctness and no internal checks.[56] This operation is realized above all through distinguishing three fundamental types of speech act: the "locutionary", the "illocutionary" and the "perlocutionary" act. The latter is directed towards provoking concrete effects and is defined through that which it involves in the empirical world, the effect for example that one brings into being in terms of the conduct of the recipient of the act. The locutionary act is internal to that traditionally known as the syntax, that which one does *in* the language, the bringing into being of the correlation of linguistic signs and grammatical structure which is like the carrying and abstract structure of the statement. There is finally the "illocutionary" act, which is that which one does *with* the language: the *type of act* that one wants to bring into being for example a prayer or an order or the affirmation of a scientific law.[57] This last one is the central case of speech act for Austin.

From this distinction between types of *acts* one reaches the distinction between basic types of element present in every type of speech act that correspond to the three types of act just mentioned. That is because above all "to perform a locutionary act in general is, we may say, also and *eo ipso* to perform an illocutionary *act*".[58] There is thus, in every speech act a locutionary, an illocutionary, and a perlocutionary element.[59]

Of any speech act one can say that it was effected as a prayer or an order or an affirmation, making reference to the procedures or rules that govern its illocutionary moment. The "meaning" of an act is thus correct according to rules, and its comprehension is subordinate to the recognition of these rules and checking that

---

[55] J. L. Austin, *How to Do Things with Words*, 2nd ed., ed. by J. O. Urmson and M. Sbisà, Oxford 1982, p. 5.

[56] See ibid., p. 14.

[57] See ibid., pp. 98–101, and p. 109.

[58] Ibid., p. 98.

[59] Ibid., p. 147.

they have been observed in the case under examination. Speech acts are not singular uses of language for so called private beings, not reducible to a common rule of recognition, nor repetitions of the same acts linked only by statistical regularity or fortuitous coincidence. Rather, one is dealing with the realization or use of procedures or rules that are the conditions for the existence of such acts. Speech acts for Austin can only exist if there are procedures to follow such that they are rendered "felicitous", or "happy", that is rules about their validity and "happiness" (that here coincides with their existence or "efficacy" or force – as described by the British philosopher[60]) that is also their meaning, as species of a certain genre of act.

Austin doesn't speak of "constitutive rules" nor of "institutional facts" – both concepts introduced later by John Searle. His idea of the *speech act* however lays the groundwork for Searle's notion of "institutional fact". The speech act (as class of acts) is actually constituted by the procedures for its use, and the single speech act doesn't work, it is not valid or "happy", if these procedures are not observed. One could also say that Austin, after having dissolved semantics into pragmatics, proposes again a semantics (focused on the illocutionary moment) distinct from pragmatic use (reposing fundamentally in the perlocution). Nevertheless, the illocutionary element is differentiated from the semantics of a statement in that it contains not representations but a purely normative or institutional sense, without any reference to the state of affairs in the world independent of the same rules. Speech acts, be they performative or constative, do not rest on the idea of *truth*, but rather on that of "happiness" or rather *correctness*: "It is essential to realize that 'true' and 'false', like 'free' and 'unfree', do not stand for anything simple at all; but only for a general dimension of being a right or proper thing to say as opposed to a wrong thing, in these circumstances, to this audience, for these purposes and with those intentions".[61]

This involves radically overturning Russell's thesis and much of neo-positivist philosophy. For Austin, speech acts, even the constative ones, do not reflect or represent the world but rather contribute – along with the procedures that govern them – to produce it: "Surely, to state is every bit as much to perform an illocutionary act as, say, to warn or to pronounce".[62] To describe, then, is a specific act in the world, it is a *type* of action; it is in addition an illocutionary act. On the other hand any linguistic act, even a constative one, can be seen as perlocutionary in that it produces as any emission of sounds can – effects in the sensible world.[63]

In short, from this perspective, all speech acts end up as *performative*, broadly-speaking "legal", because they are founded on procedures and conventions, on social norms and mechanisms of mutual recognition between individuals. The speaking subject is no longer, as he was for Russell, a Robinson-like individual or a sort of automaton engaged in a continuous, uniform soliloquy, without reflective or critical

---

[60] See ibid., p. 100.

[61] Ibid., p. 145.

[62] Ibid., p. 134.

[63] See ibid., p. 101.

attitude. The speaker has to presuppose intersubjective procedures in force in the context in which he operates and the presence of other individuals that can confirm the "happiness" of his acts. The speech situation is a whole and it is important to take it as such.[64] And it takes place in time and in a community; it has a history.

The speaker, furthermore – according to this point of view – can, despite remaining loyal to the principle of avoiding logical contradictions, fall into incoherence due to the violation of the principles of "happiness" (of "validity") of this type of discourse, which are equally fatal for the meaning of the discourse. Within, for example, a descriptive discourse, if I say "the cat is on the mat, but I don't believe it", I don't fall into any logical contradiction (the two propositions that make up the statement are not in themselves logically incompatible). Nevertheless that sentence – this is John L. Austin's claim – involves a *performative contradiction* (being the negation of the criteria implicitly assumed in the sentence in question, in this case the claim to sincerity that generally accompanies every affirmation of a state of affairs). This contradiction is very damaging to the understanding of the statement and thus as unacceptable as a logical contradiction. Stating something "commits" one to other sentences; it has in a sense pragmatical consequences. A performative contradiction is breaching the commitment one has implicitely taken by uttering a sentence or, said differently, it is opposing, hindering, the pragmatical consequences that are assumed to follow from that sentence

6.4 Meta-ethical Implications

Adopting a particular theory of meaning has considerable implications at the meta-ethical level, that is, for the manner in which value judgements or the sentences that express the individual's ethical choices are conceived and "justified".[65] For those who defend a "referential", verificationist theory of meaning (for which in general the only sentences with meaning are those that describe states of affairs) there are at the metaethical level two diametrically opposed possibilities. The first possibility is to regard sentences containing judgements as radically distinct and different from (and not reducible to) descriptive sentences, and thus to maintain that there are no real ethical sentences ("And so it is impossible for there to be propositions of ethics" writes the "early" Wittgenstein[66]), or that moral judgements are imperatives or commands (as Hans Reichenbach[67] holds), or else meaningless manifestations of feelings or emotions (as Alfred J. Ayer believes[68]), and thus similar to an

[64]See ibid., p. 138.

[65]On the relevance on the theory of meaning in relation to metaethical questions see e.g., E. Tugendhat, *Probleme der Ethik*, Stuttgart 1984, p. 17.

[66]L. Wittgenstein, *Tractatus logico-philosophicus*, p. 112 (§ 6.42)

[67]"In der Ethik werden keine Aussagen gemacht, sondern Anweisungen gegeben", writes Reichenbach (H. Reichenbach, *Der Aufstieg der wissenschaftlichen Philosophie*, Braunschweig 1968, p. 314).

[68]See A. J. Ayer, *Language, Truth and Logic*, Harmondsworth 1982, p. 137.

exclamation or interjection, or to beating one's fists on the table (as Alf Ross says[69]). For all these authors, value judgements cannot be given a rational foundation (that is, on their view, one based on procedures of empirical observation and falsification or logical deduction from postulates that have the status of axioms). Thus in his discussions with the members of the Vienna Circle, Wittgenstein repeated a phrase of Schopenauer's: to preach morality is difficult, to justify it impossible ("Moral predigen ist schwer, Moral begründen unmöglich").[70]

The second possibility open in the metaethical context to the "referential" conception of linguistic statements is to hold that moral sentences, too, are descriptive statements, and thus to propose a naturalistic metaethics (the case of, for instance, Moritz Schlick[71]). According to naturalistic metaethics, moral values have enough objectivity in fact to be *described*.

The two conclusions just mentioned are both unsatisfactory: the first removes the possibility of discussing and arguing and ultimately of thinking (in the sense of reflecting and deliberating) on one's own ethical choices; the second ends up denying the normative (and subjective) character of one's own choices. Other grounds for dissatisfaction will be indicated in Chapter 7. The first conclusion has a consequence that is particularly interesting (and fatal) for the theory of law that claims the supremacy of material forces over values and duties, of power over law. This approach will sometimes explain the "moral ought" through the fear of the sanction that the power from where the rule emanated will use against those who don't respect it. Answering to Waismann, Wittgenstein claims that an "ought" is meaningful only if it is backed by a power able to impose sanctions; indeed an "ought" by itself and as such, he says, without a power behind it, is pointless.[72]

In the context of a behaviourist theory of meaning, it is not so much the question of meaning that counts, as that of the effectiveness and the function de facto performed by moral judgements, or better the question of meaning is subsumed by that of effectiveness and the de facto function of those judgements. Morality, like law, will here be seen as a specific technique for conditioning (others') behaviour. In relation to morality conceived of as a technique of this nature, the only acceptable

[69]"To invoke justice," writes Ross, "is the same thing as banging on the table: an emotional expression" (A. Ross, *On Law and Justice*, Berkeley, CA and Los Angeles, CA 1958, p. 274).

[70]*Wittgenstein und der Wiener Kreis*, ed. by F. Waismann, Frankfurt am Main 1984, p. 118.

[71]See M. Schlick, *Fragen der Ethik*, ed. by R. Heselmann, Frankfurt am Main 1984, p. 67: "Was als die lezten Namen oder die höchsten Werte gilt, muß der menschlichen Natur und dem Leben im Widerspruch stehen, kann nicht die im Leben zugrunde liegenden Werte für schlecht oder falsch erklären. Seine Normen können nicht zu den vom Leben letztlich anerkannten fordernd oder befehlend in einen wirklichen Gegensatz treten".

[72]"Ein Soll hat also nur Sinn, wenn hinter dem Soll etwas steht, das ihm nachdruck gibt –eine Macht, die straft und belohnt. Ein Soll an sich ist unsinnig"(*Wittgenstein und der Wiener Kreis*, p. 118). For a similar, centered around sanction notion of morality, cf. E. Tugendhat, *Fragen der Ethik*, pp. 72ff. *Contra* K. Baier, *The Moral Point of View*, Abridged ed., New York 1965, pp. viii–ix.

rational justification would be one based on the adequacy of that particular morality for determining the behaviour (of others), taken (irrationally) as being endowed with value.

The behaviourist approach is best exemplified by the theory of Charles Morris. In this there is an identification *tout court* of morality with positive morality, that is to say with the dominant morality amongst a certain group, "The appraisals of moral discourse are very commonly the appraisals of actions customarily made by members of the group in question".[73] Morality is thus, above all, habit, dress, social praxis, tradition. The existence of divergent moral opinions is recognized but is related back to cognitive differences rather than to contrasting normative points of view. It consists of differences in recognition of the needs of the groups and in the assessment of the instruments required to satisfy these needs. "Diversity in moral appraisals is made intelligible by the fact that the members of a group may be mistaken both with respect to the needs of the group and to the actions which serve, or best serve, its needs. So it is possible for there to be moral appraisals (appraisals made from the standpoint of group behavior) which differ from the customary moral appraisals of members of the Group".[74]

It should also be remembered that in the behaviourist theory put forward by Morris legal discourse is classified as "designative-incitive", that is to say, as a discourse whose mode of ascribing meaning is "designative" or descriptive and whose use is "incitative" or prescriptive. Morris distinguishes thus between "mode of signifying" and "use of signifying". The difference resides in that the first (the "mode") expresses in the manner in which signs signify and are interpreted; it refers to their semantic content. The "use" on the other hand expresses the instrumental relationship that exists between the production of a sign and a certain end: "A sign *s* will be said to be *used* with respect to purpose *y* of an organism *z* if *y* is some goal of *z* and if *z* produces a sign which serves as men's to the attainment of *y*".[75] This allows one to avoid the dangers of a radically expressionistic or emotivist formulation of normative language, since this requires recognition of a certain semantic value, thus meaning and capacity to represent states of affairs. One can then subject normative language to a check of the correspondence between the event evoked, or rather designated, and the context in which the language is used in a incitative or prescriptive manner. It will not be possible however to lapse into a explicit discourse of justification, a discourse with strong normative content, with respect to norms of conduct, since they derive their ultimate justification exclusively from social praxis and dress.

The defect of this view is that it has to assume a notion of morality that is not the one central to moral deliberation. The morality we are interested in here, indeed what for *us* "is" morality, is not a body of rules or a technique for determining *others'* behaviour, but consists of a set of principles or norms with the object of

[73] Ch. Morris, *Signs, Language and Behavior*, p. 139.
[74] Ibid., pp. 139–140.
[75] Ibid., p. 92.

determining, above all else, *our* behaviour, that is, the behaviour not of the recipient or interpreter of the moral judgment, but of its emitter. Morality in this sense is "critical". This is a highly reflective attitude, and therefore not adapted to explanations based on non-reflective models of behaviour like the stimulus/response mechanism or "conditioned reflexes". As Bertrand Russell remarks, "the moralist is not concerned with actions that are merely reflex or habitual, but with deliberate choices".[76] The behaviourist approach may perhaps explain aspects of what we have called "positive morality", morality in the sociological sense. It does not by contrast help us with defining or elucidating "critical morality".

A different path is taken by views that base on an "ideational" theory. Defenders of an "ideational" theory of meaning which, as we have seen, does not take enough account of the fact that meaning has an inter-subjective, interpersonal component which is uneliminable, risk falling into so-called "moral solipsism". It is certainly true that moral judgements are eminently subjective, yet not every expression of the subject's will or desire can boast the title "moral". In the moral judgment that goes beyond the mere subjective viewpoint, there is some pretence to "universalizibility" which is hard to reach if a merely subjectivist theory of meaning is adopted.

Defenders of a theory of meaning as "use" escape the dilemma facing the verificationist theory and do not necessarily have to conceive of morality in reference to others' social behaviour. Nor do they risk "moral solipsism", if the "use" is conceived of, as proposed above, as normatively determined use, as use determined by rules, in relation to which the question of the correctness of individual or "private" use will always be raised. One may then seek some rational foundation for moral discourse as a discourse distinct from that of science, yet endowed with meaning, as our everyday experience woven of doubts, thoughts, deliberation and discussion on moral questions teaches us.

The theory of meaning as use, however, presents one problem of no slight weight for ethical theory. If it is held that the meaning of words is as it were "deposited" in uses and these are conceived of as determined by the rules of a particular "language game" tied to a particular "form of life", it might be held that the dominant values of that particular "form of life" are also conveyed by the meanings of sentences and words, so that no moral judgment which is not an expression of the morality of the "form of life" or community in question would be possible. This rather extreme conclusion is certainly not present in Wittgenstein, nor in Waismann, nor in Austin, but is clearly formulated by "communitarian" thinkers who take their cue from Wittgensteinian thought. This is the case for, with some variation in tone, say, Michael Walzer or Alistair MacIntyre or Richard Rorty. This position coincides significantly with that of philosophers who are part of the so-called "hermeneutic" tradition such as Hans-Georg Gadamer or Rudiger Bubner. Here a synthesis seems to be coming about between late Wittgensteinian philosophy and Hegelian thought, not without some contribution from the anti-moralist critiques of those such as Nietzsche.

---

[76] B. Russell, *Human Society in Ethics and Politics*, London 1954, pp. 125–126.

Some objections may be raised to this approach that greatly reduce the "use" theory's plausibility and fruitfulness. First and foremost, it should be noted that such an approach ends up eliminating the ethically and methodologically very relevant distinction between dominant or *positive* morality and *critical* morality. Moral judgements as expressed by meanings already charged with moral values would always be inside *one* morality, that of the "form of life" in question. To hold out reflexively against the "form of life" would ultimately be an illusion, merely intellectual vanity.

But if linguistic sentences are already pre-determined in their meaning by the underlying form of life, that does not mean that these meanings are always loaded with moral values. It may reasonably be maintained that the great mass of linguistic meanings of a particular language, or within a particular "form of life", are morally neutral so that they can be used to express differing value judgements or moral judgements that may even sharply contrast with each other. Goebbels and Joseph Roth use the same language, so that it must be maintained, if a strong communitarian approach is adopted, that on the one hand they are the outcome of one and the same "form of life", and on the other that they express good or bad moral judgements that are homogeneous. But this conflicts with reality: Goebbels has Joseph Roth's books burned because dishonourable for German *Volk* and Joseph Roth makes an appeal for his books to be burnt by the Nazis, since he regards it as dishonourable not to be included on the list of authors banned in national-socialist Germany. Where here is the homogeneity of moral values conveyed by the use of a particular language?

A Wittgensteinian approach however does not allow a strong "communitarian" application of the theory of meaning as use. This is not just because Wittgenstein does not endow the "form of life" with that intense moral significance with which it is charged by several "communitarians", but also and especially because Wittgenstein is very clear as to the tension there is between the *rule* as the first necessary condition of meaning and its *application*, which is the second indispensable condition of the meaning of a sentence. Wittgenstein repeats more than once that a rule does not govern its application, and even if there were a rule governing that, there would not be a meta-meta-rule governing that meta-rule. The application of rules is in certain spheres that are defined to varying degrees, but anything but clearly, left up to the subject's creativity and "inclination". Subjectivity, which seemed to have to be chased out of the door of that which Habermas terms *Sprachphilosophie*, language oriented philosophy (as the opposite of *Bewusstseinsphilosophie*, consciousness or mind oriented philosophy) comes back decisively, in through the window.

From the discussion of meaning theories embarked upon in the central part of the book and then taken up again in this chapter one can draw a few initial conclusions as to the character of moral judgements. I will formulate these in negative terms in order to emphasize their provisional nature. Moral judgements are not reducible to emotions or to prescriptions or to purely subjective psychological states. Nevertheless, they cannot be formulated as mere descriptions of factual circumstances. Neither are they reducible to regularity of social conduct. They are not, however, fully subordinate to the "inclinations" of the subject.

Chapter 7
Value Judgements and Justification

7.1 Preliminary

As far as meta-ethical conceptions are concerned, that is, conceptions regarding the "nature" of moral judgements, in the history of philosophy the following views can be picked out: religious voluntarism, naturalism, historicism, utilitarianism, intuitionism, emotivism, prescriptivism, universalism. These are, obviously, only *some* of the solutions that have been presented throughout the history of human thought. Nonetheless, they are most recurrent and significant among the meta-ethical theories. This is the reason why I wish to set them out here – albeit very briefly – and to discuss them. This will allow for a deepening of the discussion of the phenomenology of normative language and for evaluation of the character of moral judgements. This in turn will enable us to draw at the end of this chapter initial conclusions about the controversial relationship between law and morality.

According to religious voluntarism, to be found in the so-called "revealed" religions, it is "revelation" that is the ultimate source of right and wrong. This source can be known by man through faith, which may, depending on the versions of this conception, take on, more or less, rationalist features. At one end, for instance, we have the voluntarist versions, for which the divinity, inscrutable to man, can desire everything and its opposite, good and evil, so that if God wishes evil it becomes good and if God abhors good it will be evil. This amounts to denying that there is any constant criterion of right and wrong, good and evil, beyond that of God's will, which is incomprehensible to man. This voluntarist and irrationalist version of the modern theory based on divine revelation is upheld by, for instance, Ockham and Luther. In relation to this, recall the words of Luther: "Human nature and reason cannot understand God in his majesty; hence we should not look and search for God's will, essence and nature more than He has commanded us".[1]

---

[1] "Menschliche Vernunft und Natur kann Gott in seiner Majestät nicht begreifen, darum sollen wir nicht weiter suchen noch forschen, was Gottes Wille, Wesen und Natur sei, als soweit er's uns befohlen hat" (M. Luther, *Tischreden*, ed. by K. Aland, Stuttgart 1981, p. 43). It is worth recalling that in the *Tischreden* Luther defines reason as "the devil's whore" (ibid., p. 57).

M. La Torre, *Law as Institution*, Law and Philosophy Library 90,
DOI 10.1007/978-1-4020-6607-8_7, © Springer Science+Business Media B.V. 2010

At the other end of the range of versions of religious voluntarism we find a rationalist position according to which God cannot but will good, that is, what appears to men endowed with reason as good. The foundation of right can be attained by use of man's typical rational faculties through which he shares, however modestly, in the God's all-encompassing reason.

Simplifying more than a little, religious voluntarism may be summarised in four propositions: (i) God exists; (ii) God wishes x; (iii) since God exists and wants x, x is good (or right); (iv) Since God exists and wants x, and x is therefore good (or right), x is obligatory. The problems here are numerous; I shall list a few of them. Who tells us that God really exists? What actual proof do we have of his existence? And who tells us there is only God, and not instead several Gods with mutually conflicting moralities? Why then, having ascertained or assuming that God exists, ought we to consider that what he wants is good?

Less problematic, perhaps, is the following question: Why ought what is good for me be obligatory to me? For it might be maintained that calling some behaviour "good", defining it as good, semantically implies the acceptance, or better the assertion of the obligatoriness of that conduct or behaviour. Two considerations, I believe, are enough to invalidate the "revelationist" meta-ethics. The existence of God is controversial, unverified and in all probability unverifiable through empirical experience. It remains a great mystery, around which the human heart can only continue to declare its "anxiety". This anxiety, even for the believer, cannot help reflecting on his moral judgements, rendering them less absolute, in some sense relative, in need of further justification, beyond mere appeal to the divine world. God's will is not a sufficient reason to render an act or behaviour or a state of affairs good or right *for me* too. For it is ultimately I who am the real judge of my ethical choices. "There was a mad woman," writes Sartre, "who had hallucinations: she imagined somebody was talking to her on the telephone and giving her orders. The doctor asked her: 'But who is speaking?' She replied 'He says he's God'. But what proved to her that it was really God? If an angel comes to me, what proves to me that it is an angel? And if I hear voices, what proves to me that they come from heaven and not from hell, or from a subconscious, or from some pathological state? Who proves that they are really directed at me [. . .] *If a voice is directed at me, it will always be I who decides that voice is the angel's voice*".[2] "Ultimately," as has been said, "every man is alone with himself and his own conscience, and has to give a judgement on the good or evil that may result from his own actions".[3] Were it not so, the concept of morality underlying the ideas presented here would collapse: that of a set of autonomous rules the individual adopts for himself and for which he is accordingly

---

[2] J. P. Sartre, *L'existentialisme est un humanisme*, Paris 1970, pp. 30–31, italics mine. Cf. S. De Beauvoir, *Pour une morale de l'ambiguïte*, Paris 1947, pp. 273–274: "'Ecoutons la voix de Dieu', dit le croyant. 'Il nous dira lui-même ce qu'il attend de nous'. Mais un tel espoir est naïf. C'est seulement à travers une voix terrestre que Dieu pourra se manifester car nos oreilles n'en entendent aucune autre; mais comment alors reconnaître son caractère divin?"

[3] R. De Stefano, *Assiologia. Schema di una teoria generale del valore e dei valori*, Reggio Calabria 1982, p. 68.

responsible. One could argue that moral responsibility is, above all, responsibility for the rules, not towards the rules.[4] Denying autonomy would thus imply denying moral responsibility. "The fact that God," writes Popper, "or any other authority, commands me to do a certain thing is no guarantee that the command is right. It is I who must decide whether to accept the standards of any authority as (morally) good or bad. God is only good if His commandments are good; it would be a grave mistake – in fact an immoral adoption of authoritarianism – to say that His commandments are good simply because they are His, unless we have first decided (at our own risk) that He can only demand good or right things of us".[5]

One response to the questions mentioned above is to maintain that the idea of an omnipotent God is necessary for there to be motives to act in a moral way, and thus to put into practice the very idea of morality. In order to eschew His sanctions or to receive His rewards, we need to obey His commands. The idea of recompense however is not always in accordance with moral sense. The argument, as has been remarked, "makes morality something that does not differ from prudence",[6] that is, from the prudential, utilitarian calculation. This, as well as considerably reducing the status of ethics, takes no account of the fact that morality is different from utilitarian calculations. The consideration whether it is, say, more useful to build a bridge between Scilla and Faro, or else between Villa San Giovanni and Grotte (various points on the strait of Messina) bases on a prudential calculation, but cannot be said to be an evident case of moral discourse. Prudential calculation and morality indeed do not coincide, so that any move directed at reducing the latter to the former is bound to prove fallacious.

"Revelationist" voluntarism proves particularly dangerous in the event of conflict among various ethical positions maintained by different subjects. The appeal to the divine rule is absolute and not open to compromise. It may, since in the contemporary world there are *several* revealed religions with different or even opposing ethical content, mean that the dispute becomes one between subjects calling on mutually irreconcilable faiths, thus ending in a situation of incommensurability.

"Revelationist" meta-ethics has in addition an authoritarian tone that can hardly be eliminated. This is a clear example of the ethical relevance of acceptance of a particular meta-ethics and of the possible links between the two levels. Whoever accepts a religious voluntarist meta-ethics can no longer, except at the cost of clamorous self-contradiction, adopt a libertarian morality. The authoritarianism inherent in "revelationism" is well illustrated by one of the Christian thinkers closest, and most sensitive, to libertarian principles: Leo Tolstoy. Tolstoy does not really distinguish between religion (so conceived of as "revelationism") and morality: morality

[4]See E. Pattaro, *Reflexiones sobre pluralismo ético*, in *Anuario de derechos humanos*, 1988, p. 403.
[5]K. R. Popper, *Facts, Standards and Truth: A Further Criticism of Relativism*, in Id., *The Open Society and its Enemies*, vol. 2, *The High Tide of Prophecy: Hegel, Marx, and the Aftermath*, 5th ed., London 1974, p. 385.
[6]B. Russell, *Human Society in Ethics and Politics*, London 1954, p. 98.

is for him the religion that speaks to the individual conscience and is therefore manifest in it. Religion is seen from the subject's viewpoint. The basis of morality is thus, for the Russian novelist, the divine will "revealed" to the individual conscience. Tolstoy's political and social ideals are close to anarchist conceptions[7]; nonetheless in ethical areas Tolstoy proves singularly authoritarian, in open contradiction to his political faith. Recall some of the concluding phrases of *Resurrection*: "Are we not doing the same," Nekhlyudov thought, "when we imagine ourselves to be masters of our lives, and think that life is given us for enjoyment? For evidently, that is absurd. We were sent here by someone's will and for some purpose. And we have made up our minds that we live only for our own enjoyment, and of course things go ill with us, *as they do with labourers when they do not fulfil their master's orders*. The master's will is expressed in these laws. As soon as men fulfil these laws the kingdom of heaven will be established on earth, and men will reach the greatest good they can attain".[8] Right and good are thus contained in the commandments of God, absolute "master" of men's life and death. It is folly and impiety for men to believe themselves masters of themselves and to seek their own happiness.

On the other hand, if divine commands reach us through a particularly authoritative testimony, or through a sacred book passed from generation to generation it would be necessary to evaluate the reliability of the source. However authoritative a testimony is, if it cannot be objectively verified then it is a controversial source of knowledge. This is especially true in a case where at stake is something as fundamental to our lives as the notion of "eternal salvation" or as irredeemable as "eternal damnation". More than often in the chronicles and their history, men express their own opinions rather than the facts that happened. If one has recourse to a sacred text or the charisma of an earthly figure, how does one attribute to that text that particular meaning, or to that authoritative source, moral infallibility? Isn't an act of endorsement necessary in order to do this? We thus find ourselves, faced yet again with the foundational role of individual reflexivity.[9]

God's will can prescribe human conduct through positive law (those that are revealed) or through moral law. The latter are manifested not through the action of human conscience, but are derived from the use of reason. In this case it is reason and not revelation that leads to the discovery of divine laws, which thus coincide with morality. A divine will available to all is – Kant says –"determined solely by purely moral laws".[10] Thus one must have recourse to morality in order to understand divine law, and there can be a universal religion only in so far as the access to the divine will is carried on through morality which is universal.

---

[7] In this connection, cf. G. Woodcock, *Anarchism. A History of Libertarian Ideas and Movements*, Harmondsworth 1983, pp. 207ff.

[8] L. Tolstoy, *Resurrection*, English trans. by L. Maude, Oxford 1962, p. 498, emphasis mine.

[9] Cf. L. Nelson, *Was ist liberal*, in Id., *Gesammelte Werke in neun Bänden*, vol. 9, *Rech und Staat*, ed. by P. Bernays et al., Hamburg 1972, pp. 21–22.

[10] I. Kant, *Die Religion innerhalb der Grenzen der blossen Vernunft*, ed. by K. Vorländer, 9th ed., Hamburg 1990, p. 112.

In the case of revelation however, when the divine will is manifested through positive law, since these laws are connected to a particular time and place and are valid only within a particular historical context, their binding force is only contingent, particular and limited to a certain social group – thus not universalizable. In order for universal binding force to be applicable historical faith (founded on revelation) has to become pure faith (founded on morality).

One can thus confirm, in conclusion, that divine will is either manifested through revelation, in which case it doesn't have universal binding force, or through moral conscience, in which case it can't be distinguished from moral principles as it is from or through them that it derives its universal binding force. Revealed religion, thus, far from supplying a absolute justification for morality, cannot be *strongly* (universally) valid without recourse to morality. Revelationist metaethics is thus an enterprise which in the end seems to be self-defeating.

7.2 Naturalism, Utilitarianism, Intuitionism

7.2.1 Naturalist meta-ethics says that moral values are derivable or deducible by ascertaining, or through description, of certain states of affairs existing in nature. A particular version of "naturalism" is the conception that may be called "subjectivism".[11] According to such view value judgements would be nothing but descriptions or assertions, regarding a mental or psychic state of the subject making the judgements in question. "Thou shalt not steal", or "it is wrong to steal", or "it is good to help one's neighbour", could be reformulated into statements such as "I want you not to steal", "I feel it is wrong to steal", "I hope you will help your neighbour". Here, "I want", "I feel", "I hope", are to be understood in the descriptive sense. This theory is the equivalent in the meta-ethical sphere of the doctrine that legal norms (like contracts) are declarations of will, assertions about the mental state of the one laying down the norm (or stipulating the contract). Historicism, too, can be considered a form of "naturalism". The difference is that for historicism moral values are deducible from the description not of "natural states" but of "historical situation s" or from a (social) nature conceived as a dynamic and evolving concept.

Natural law theory, especially in its secular, liberal version, is a typical representative of meta-ethical "naturalism". For natural law theory, for instance, the descriptive statement that men *are* (by nature) free and equal is the justificatory basis for the normative statement that men *must* (in law) be free and equal. Hence the indignation that rings in Rousseau's famous words: Man was born free, but everywhere he's put in chains ("L'homme est né libre, et partout il est dans les fers"[12]).

Equally, in a historicist conception, in Marxism for instance, the descriptive statement (more properly apparently or allegedly descriptive) that history is tending

---

[11] See R. Alexy, *Theorie der juristischen Argumentation*, Frankfurt am Main 1983, p. 61.

[12] J.-J. Rousseau, *Du contrat social*, Paris 1973, p. 60.

towards a certain end is the justificatory basis for the normative statement that it "is right" to ("one must") pursue that definite end. Once it is ascertained that the end of history is the abolition of class, then that end becomes the (normative) criterion for "right" and "wrong". Moreover, since historicism is often presented as a theory of "phases" according to which history necessarily goes through certain periods which are all directed towards the ultimate goal of the course of history, the "phase" itself turns into a normative criterion. Once it has been found that today we are living in a "bourgeois" phase and since (because of the " iron" laws of history) it is impossible to leap over any "phase", what is "right" is what serves the maturation of the "phase" itself. This is the explanation for, say, the following phrase from Karl Kautsky: "It is capital that creates the material basis for a universally human morality".[13]

Naturalism and historicism may be reproached with falling into what is usually called the "naturalist fallacy", that is, the unfounded deduction of normative conclusions from exclusively descriptive premises. It cannot, in fact, be seen how from a description of a state of affairs one may derive or deduce any value judgment relating to that same state of affairs, still less – as is more or less explicitly done in historicism – a value judgment that is always *positive*: (history, says Benedetto Croce, plays always a justifying, never a condemning role[14]).

Our value judgements, when their object is natural fact, some times evaluate it negatively. A dog breaking a cat's back with one snap may make us exclaim: "What cruelty!". Our moral judgements often relate to really existing states of affairs but do not necessarily describe them positively. However much human beings are a product of the natural order, they are also alienated from it.[15] In fact they couldn't fully participate in this order without renouncing their ability to judge and their desire for autonomy. They thus decide upon their actions, rather than leaving them to chance. One only becomes ruler of ones own life, and thus responsible for it, when criteria for conduct are no longer based on circumstance or inclination or contingent stimuli.

From the descriptive statement or statement of fact that "there is a concentration camp in Guantanamo" it does not logically follow that "in Guantanamo there ought to be a concentration camp". Indeed if it were so, if that logical implication were possible, we would have no need to state moral judgements or morals of any kind, and indeed the moral problem itself would have no reason to be raised. For a moral problem consists in asking about the value of a fact, a question that assumes the possibility of attributing different values to that fact. This attribution always involves some element of evaluation and an endorsement, hence the responsibility of the individual. If we instead assumed that the fact bears a value by itself, the point would no longer be to ask about and deliberate upon the value to attribute to the

---

[13] K. Kautsky, *Ethik und materialistische Geschichtsauffassung*, Stuttgart 1922, p. 109.

[14] See B. Croce, *Teoria e storia della storiografia*, ed. by G. Galasso, Milano 2001, p. 98.

[15] Cf. L. Nelson, *Sittliche und religiöse Weltansicht*, in Id., *Gesammelte Werke in neun Bänden*, ed. by P. Bernays et al., *Sittlichkeit und Bildung*, vol. 8, Hamburg 1971, p. 324: "Als Glied der Natur und ihren Gesetzen unterworfen bleibt er ein Fremdling in ihr, der sich selber nicht genügt".

fact (the moral problem) but to ascertain and prove the existence of the fact (more or less an empirical question). The "truth" and "justice" of a fact cannot have the same meaning in ordinary language or experience. Saying that a fact is "true" in no way implies that it is, also, "right" or "good". On the other hand, saying that a moral judgment is "true" may have as much sense as saying that a logical operation is "healthy". A logical operation can be called correct or incorrect, valid or invalid, but certainly not "sick" or "healthy". Equally a moral judgment or a norm can be "right" or "wrong" but certainly not "true" or "false" in the proper sense.

Naturalist meta-ethics in fact conceals a naturalist *ethics*, namely the conviction that the dictates of nature are good and right or that one must "obey" the principles that govern nature. But this is not obvious. This is shown by the view in the history of human thought that, instead, "nature" as such represents evil and not good: *gnostic* thought. Nor should one forget, in relation to this, the so-called "nihilist meta-ethics": Ivan Karamazov accuses not just the creator, but the creation itself.[16]

Moreover, what counts in a given epoch as "natural" is largely the outcome of cultural and ideological conceptions dominating in that age. The change in sexual morality in various epochs is indicative in relation to this. It should further be recalled that "nature" is today increasingly the work of man; it is no longer "found" but in some respects "invented" by human intervention. Concepts formerly "natural" *par excellence*, such as "mother", become today, with the evolution of genetic techniques, increasingly problematic. "Nature" is no longer able, in such areas as artificial fertilization, to supply us with answers, but instead, must, so to speak, await the answer from us. Accordingly, the reformulation, taking up the same example, of the ethical and legal concept of "mother" cannot derive from an entirely problematic "naturalness" (which even has to be regulated) but has to come from intrinsically moral principle.

Truly, nature is "silent" to those who ask what course to give their own actions, their own social behaviour. As has been said, "there is no validation of justice, thus no human value, that is guaranteed before its realization in the world, because [...] the world as such is indifferent to the values of man".[17] Nature is by its nature – if I

---

[16]Cf. A. Camus, *L'homme revolté*, Paris 1951, p. 81. A good example of a "nihilist metaethics" is offered by the central figure, Doctor de Vriendt, in a novel by Arnold Zweig: see A. Zweig, *De Vriendt kehrt heim*, Berlin and Weimar 1988, pp. 60–61. Not everything that is "natural" is also "positive" for man. An earthquake, cholera, drought, are natural events, yet very harmful for man, who fears them and fights them. Even the death of each of us is a natural fact, and even more inevitable than any earthquake or cholera outbreak; yet our very inner rebel at the idea of it. So we cannot make the "natural" or "nature" the basis for our values. Cf. also M. Frisch, *Homo faber. Ein Bericht*, Frankfurt am Main 1977, p. 107. Whoever acts upon nature, changes it, ipso facto expresses his discontent with the "natural" pattern of things and sets himself up critically towards it. This is an argument used by Ludwig Feuerbach but not so much to assert an anti-naturalist position as to attack faith in a rational divine entity held to be manifest in nature (see L. Feuerbach, *Vorlesungen über das Wesen der Religion*, in Id., *Gesammelte Werke*, ed. by W. Schuffenhauer, vol. 6, Berlin 1984, pp. 191–192).

[17]R. De Stefano, *Il problema del diritto non naturale*, Milano 1955, p. 46.

may be forgiven that horrible word game – entirely deaf to moral questions. This is forcibly expressed in a verse of Goethe's:

> Denn unfühlend
> ist die Natur:
> Es leuchtet die Sonne
> über Bös' und Gute.
> Und dem Verbrecher
> Glänzen, wie dem Besten
> Der Mond und die Sterne.[18]

It may, finally, be objected to historicism that history is not always "rational" or "moral". "Think of the destruction of Carthago – as Leonard Nelson asks –, did it deserve to disappear?"[19] Indeed, it is a privilege of the human being to be able to revolt against the "existent" in the name of principles foreign to and higher than it.[20] If there is an end or purpose in history, it is inscrutable; and why ought that end to offer "salvation", that is, be "right" and "good"? Historicist meta-ethics ultimately proves, perhaps even more than naturalist meta-ethics, to be an "ideology", in a twofold sense: It disguises normative sentences as descriptive statements[21]; it sets up a convenient "false consciousness", allowing to oneself a "morality" that is in any case conform with what happens and hence never fallible, never "wrong". Historicism thus ends up as an extraordinary mixture of opportunism and moral absolutism. This second "ideological" aspect of historicism has been well grasped by Nicola Chiaromonte. "It is not in fact true," he writes, "that those who appeal to history, to science, to the inevitable trend of the world are taking an impersonal course of things to be right. It is primarily themselves they take to be right; and they basically indulge themselves".[22] Historicism ends up as "an ideology that pretends that even truth is determined by circumstances and refuses to consider itself constrained by what it asserted yesterday, which was given as true, when today's conditions require another".[23]

A different version of naturalism is *hedonism*, that is to say, the theory that claims that what is right is that which is pleasurable for the individual (that is what is most "natural" to her). Conversely the criterion for judging what is wrong is that which is unpleasant or painful to the individual (that which goes against the natural

---

[18] J. W. Goethe, *Das Göttliche*, in Id., *Gedichte*, chosen and introduced by S. Zweig, Stuttgart 1983, p. 86.

[19] L. Nelson, *Ethischer Realismus*, in Id., *Gesammelte Werke in neun Bänden*, ed. by P. Bernays et al., vol. 8, p. 282.

[20] Cf. J. Améry, *Jenseits von Schuld und Sühne. Bewältigungsversuche eines Überwältigten*, München 1988, p. 91.

[21] In this connection cf. Th. Geiger, *Ideologie und Wahrheit. Eine soziologische Kritik des Denkens*, 2nd ed., Neuwied and Berlin 1968, pp. 56–57.

[22] N. Chiaromonte, *Credere e non credere*, Milano 1971, p. 197.

[23] J. Benda, *La trahison des clercs*, 2nd ed., Paris 1975, p. 78.

dispositions and tastes or preferences of this individual).[24] However, the realization of pleasure through certain conduct is not enough to qualify that conduct as moral. To eat an ice-cream, despite the pleasure it may give me cannot be described as a moral action. The morality of an action is not equivalent to the realization of pleasure. This doesn't mean that a moral action cannot bring pleasure – the pleasure contingently attached to its execution as much as the pleasure that is structurally connected to it: that of behaving morally. As Leonard Nelson says, "when acting morally satisfies us, it satisfies us insofar as it is moral, but it is not that we consider it moral insofar as it satisfies us".[25]

Hedonism is a particular form of naturalism that falls into ethical relativism, since it is rigidly connected to the feelings of each subject. While relativism of historicism may be considered a sort of moral objectivism, at least as far as a given historical period is concerned, this is not possible for hedonism. Hedonism is an individualistic and antiuniver salistic variant of relativism. Universalism typical of naturalism is no longer possible hcrc as the "nature" to which hedonism refers is that of a particular subject and its contingent states and tastes. "Nature" here does not serve as the general basis of different personal moralities, such as to link and unify them; rather it has an opposite effect: it breaks every bridge between subjects and exalts individual choices and preferences. A source of meta-ethical emotivism is probably also to be found in hedonism.

7.2.2 Arguments similar to those brought against "naturalism" can also be brought against utilitarian meta-ethical conceptions. It is true that in utilitarianism there is not always a clear demarcation line between ethics and meta-ethics. The ethics of utilitarianism is directed towards satisfying the needs (the "happiness") of the greatest number of people with the least possible sacrifice. Utilitarian meta-ethics equally affirms that value judgements, or, better, moral judgements, can be translated into sentences relating to the happiness of the greatest number. Utilitarian meta-ethics thus represents a case of what some define as "rational-universalistic" meta-ethics.[26] Utilitarianism in meta-ethics (and in ethics) is anything but individualistic and idealistic as is sometimes wrongly claimed. It aspires to the happiness of the greatest possible number of people, not that of the single individual. It must howcvcr maintain an individualistic anthropology.

Utilitarian meta-ethics too, may fall into a sort of "naturalistic fallacy", when, as it often does, it holds that utility or happiness can be ascertained objectively or better empirically. If the happiness of the greatest number is ascertainable, calculable, and can be expressed in descriptive sentences, it will be possible to check whether a certain value judgment tends to promote that happiness. Moral evaluations would

---

[24]Such relationship between hedonism and naturalism comes up in a revealing way in one of Georg Büchner's most celebrated plays: "Ich handle meiner Natur gemäß – says Thomas Paine in *Dantons Tod* (III, 1) –; was ihr angemessen, ist für mich gut und ich tue es, und was ihr zuwider, ist für mich bös und ich tue es nicht und verteidige mich dagegen, wenn es mir in den Weg kommt"(G. Büchner, *Dantons Tod*, Stuttart 1989, p. 48).

[25]L. Nelson, *Kritik der praktischen Vernunft*, Hamburg 1972, p. 78.

[26]Cf. P. Koller, *Rationalität und Moral*, in *Grazer Philosophische Studien*, vol. 20, 1983, pp. 276ff.

then be reducible to statements on the most appropriate means to secure the happiness of the greatest number. And in so far as the means/end relationship, that is, the appropriateness of the means to the end, can be verified through observational instruments, moral judgements too can be reformulated as descriptive statements.

But is it really true that the happiness of the greatest number is objectively ascertainable? And is the happiness of the greatest number perhaps not the sum of the happiness of the greatest number of individuals, that is, the sum of so many individual happinesses?

If that is so, however, the problem of ascertaining happiness remains unresolved. What my happiness consists in, and whether I ought to pursue it assuming I know what it is, are the two questions one seeks to answer by adopting a morality. Happiness, indeed, is not the supposition for individual morality, something higher than it, but more often than not the outcome of the thoughts and questions that make up what we assume to be our morality.

In reality, although it sometimes likes to flaunt mathematical formulae and calculations taken from economics, utilitarianism supplies us with rather problematic, counter-intuitive criteria in moral respects. Racism, for instance, directed against a small minority may calmly be justified by utilitarian considerations. Not to speak of torture that more often than not is justified through some sort of utilitarian argument. The fact is that for this meta-ethics/ethics all the desires, needs and preferences of various human beings are placed on the same level: what counts is not their "quality", but their "quantity".[27]

Moreover, utilitarianism tends to reduce considerations of a moral nature to a sort of prudential calculation. But by so doing, as was indicated earlier, it loses the specific feature of morality, which can no longer be distinguished from spheres that are instead ordinarily separate from it. If as an engineer I design a bridge, my aim will be for it to satisfy the needs of the maximum number of users at the lowest possible cost to the firm building it. I shall certainly not set about distinguishing between the needs of white and black users, of Nazis and Jews: the user my design is aimed at will ideally be the whole human race. However, it certainly cannot be maintained that my civil engineering calculations and designs fall within the sphere of what is usually called "moral reflection".

Another point worthy of note, I feel, is the following. If we adopt a utilitarian approach, we may legitimately ask why one ought to adopt a utilitarian meta-ethics, should it prove more useful (to the greater number) to adopt, let us say, a deontological, that is a non-utilitarian meta-ethics. It might be that utilitarianism as a distinct conception of morality could have negative normative consequences on the *fact* of morality, by perhaps loosening the binding force that individuals usually reconnect to moral duties seen as independent from prudential considerations. It might also be that the porose distinction utilitarianism makes between ethics and meta-ethics may mean repudiating utilitarian meta-ethics in the name of utilitarian ethics. But if that

---

[27] Cf. B. Williams, *Ethics and the Limits of Philosophy*, London 1985, p. 86. See also G. E. Moore, *The Nature of Moral Philosophy*, in Id., *Philosophical Studies*, London 1970, p. 339: "Whether the one state," writes Moore, "was better than the other would depend not merely upon the number of desires that were simultaneously satisfied in it, but upon what the desires were desires for".

were so, the strength and the attraction of utilitarianism (which lies in its apparent capacity to supply quantifiable criteria for morality because of its descriptive grasp of moral weights) might in the end be drastically reduced.

There is one further characteristic of utilitarianism which renders it problematic for describing and assessing moral experience. Being a form of consequentialism, utilitarianism is concerned with consequences, that is with outcomes. It is relatively indifferent to conduct as such – not to mention the intentions with which actions are carried out. What counts is results as general facts open to empirical descriptions. Once the greatest happiness for the greatest number of people has been established it is not relevant that the agent (I myself) was responsible for this state of affairs. Now, even if we ignore the impossibility of knowing all the consequences of an action, if the consequences are important and these are already arrived at or would be arrived at if I don't act or if I act in a way that assumes they won't come about, then I find myself obliged to not act or to act in a contrary manner to what is dictated by the greatest happiness of the greatest number (which is however morally illicit from an utilitarian point of view). The paradox of the obligation to act in a morally illicit manner might be resolved only if one assumes that consequentialist morality relates not to the agent, but to the states of affairs. Consequentialism and utilitarianism are thus "eventistic" moralities; they consider a situation not from the point of view of the agent or the interested party, but from that of an observer who can trace all the causal links that hold human action together. Such an observer could however only be a god: human beings are not given such herculean cognitive capacity.

The objective point of view of utilitarianism is not that of an agent who seeks to behave impartially and consider whether the effects of his actions on others would be acceptable to him if she found herself in their position, or whether they would approve of her actions following rational discussion. In both these cases the agent would move from *her* position and seeks in various ways to universalize it.

The objective point of view of "eventistic" morality, however, leaves out of consideration the subjective situation of the agent. Morality is required to answer the question "what should *I* do here and now?". Utilitarianism, and with it any extreme form of consequentialism, restricting me to put myself in the position of the observer, seems to be unable to satisfy the moral need for prescriptive criteria to guide *my action* in the world. In order to be meaningful and effective a moral obligation must be indeed linked to something that the agent herself does, to a situation in which the agent acts.[28] However, there is a point that makes utilitarianism *prima facie* appealing: its focusing on pain as an evil which deserves to be as much as possible lowered and minimized. Indeed, in our world and in human life there is much pain, and morality cannot avoid to be confronted with it.

7.2.3 The meta-ethical positions of intuitionism can be summarised in four chief propositions. "Morality", or "goodness", or "justice", is a quality or property intrinsic to reality. This "quality" cannot be defined and thus cannot be empirically ascertained. Nonetheless, this "quality" is self-evident: analogous to mathematical

---

[28] Cf. N. Hartmann, *Vom Wesen sittlicher Forderungen*, in Id., *Kleinere Schriften*, vol. 1, Berlin 1955, pp. 279ff.

truths. Each of us, even if unable to define them, knows those "qualities" through the intuitive capacities typical of the human being. A formulation (rather fresher and more deeply felt) of the theory can be found in Robert M. Pirsig's fine novel, *Zen and the Art of Motorcycle Maintenance*: "'But how do we know what's good?' but almost before the question was out of his mouth he would realise the answer had already been supplied. Some other student would usually tell him 'you just *see* it'".[29]

One implication of intuitionism should be stressed: at the end of the day it excludes the possibility and need for "proof" (justification and argumentation) of ethical choices. For intuitionism there is no point in asking for a justification or "proof" of the "truth" (better validity) of moral intuitions, because according to it when one is convinced one knows the "good" or the "right" (that is, has a moral intuition), one cannot err. It is worth adding that for this theory knowledge, too, has no need of proof, since if one knows, that is, is *convinced* of knowing, one cannot err. Intuitionism thus ends by also implying the thesis of the unjustifiability of empirical knowledge itself (of facts, not of "qualities").

Intuitionism is a widespread meta-ethics. It is founded on the one hand on hypothetical intuitive capacities of human beings (a kind of "moral sense") and, on the other, on a concept of self-evidence sometimes based on an analogy to mathematical truths (thus a self-evidence alleged to apply also to moral truths). But while some criticism directed at "naturalism" can be raised against intuitionism, in particular that regarding the logical impossibility of deriving an "ought" from an "is", though moral intuitions are sometimes shaped as originally normative, it must be noted that the very concept of self-evidence is anything but unanimously recognised in the mathematical sphere, too.[30] It has, for instance, been shown in the sphere of logic and mathematics that some of what seemed at first "obvious truths" prove on closer analysis to be clamorous errors.[31] Analysis thus has to test intuitive presuppositions and "verify" them.

For intuitionism (as for "naturalism" and for meta-ethical cognitivism in general) there are values (*Werte*) irrespective of evaluations (*Wertungen*). One clear example of this intuitionist position is represented by the Polish philosopher Bochenski. "An evaluation, our insight of values and our reaction to them, is", he says, "something else as values themelves. Evaluations are open to change, are relative, they are ever transient; those values themselves however are eternal and immutable".[32] This distinction between "values" (eternal and immutable) and "evaluations" (transient and changeable) cannot be, however, so sharp from the viewpoint of critical morality. From this perspective a state of affairs, or a piece of conduct, has "value" in so far

[29] R. M. Pirsig, *Zen and the Art of Motorcycle Maintenance*, London 1987, p. 203. Emphasis in the original.

[30] Cf. M. Kline, *Mathematics: The Loss of Certainty*, Oxford 1980, Chapter 10.

[31] See, for example, F. Waismann, *Ethik und Wissenschaft*, in Id., *Wille und Motiv. Zwei Abhandlungen über Ethik und Handlungstheorie*, ed. by J. Schulte, Stuttgart 1983, pp. 164ff.

[32] J. M. Bochenski, *Wege zum philosiphischen Denken. Einleitung in die Grundbegriffe*, 9th ed., Freiburg i. Br. 1985, pp. 76–77.

as the subject attributes values to it, or better endorses it. Value judgements, on this view, are not the ascertaining or recognition or "intuitions" of values already existing in some sphere of reality, but *evaluations*, the production or attribution of values through deliberation.

Intuitionism in the meta-ethical sphere might also lead to a sort of romantic irrationalism. What is "right" is said what I "feel" to be right. In this way, intuitionist meta-ethics exalts monologue, not dialogue. From the moment I "feel", "see", "intuit" what is right, I have no need to face others and explain my reasons to them. This is stated explicitly by, for instance, Bochenski: "The proposition 'you must not cut your mother's throat to get money to drink' cannot be given a foundation. It is obvious; it can only be said that it is so, and that in this connection *there is no room for discussion"*.[33] In this meta-ethical position, by the assertion of the indefinablity of what is right, there might be some anti-intellectual implication. "If you can't define Quality," writes Pirsig, "there's no way you can subordinate it to any intellectual rule".[34] But even if moral qualities cannot be defined, we should be able to put them to some kind of test and allow them to be part of a rational discourse. So that the appeal to the moral intuition cannot be a last word. It should be possible to confront *my* intuitions with *yours*.

Meta-ethical intuitionism also has to face some of the criticisms brought against epistemological intuitionism, namely the theory asserting that the privileged source of knowledge is intuition, especially as regards some allegedly "primordial" concepts like space and time. It can be objected to epistemological intuitionism that: our "intuitions" (for instance that of time) are to some degree determined by the culture we are part of and the theories we hold[35]; intuition, a sort of "flash of genius" that every one of us in fact experiences in understanding or solving a problem has to do with what is usually called the "context of discovery" (as distinct from the "context of justification"). But in speaking of epistemological or gnoseological criteria, reference is made to "proof", "arguments", "procedures", that are intersubjectively verifiable. "Proof", "arguments", "procedures", are hard to apply to the "context of discovery" which represents a strictly individual, unrepeatable position, at any rate one that cannot be shared by others who have not lived that particular experience.

All that can be intersubjective is the "context of justification", which is accordingly the relevant context when one wishes to confirm one's own convictions or "intuitions". This is true also of the experience of morality. I may intuitively hold that some conduct is right. But this is not always enough to justify the "rightness" of the conduct. I may need to communicate my intuition, check it intersubjectively, and this is the task of moral argument. Intuition as such may be a starting point for

---

[33] Ibid., p. 71.

[34] R. M. Pirsig, *Op. cit.*, p. 207.

[35] Cf. K. R. Popper, *Epistemology Without a Knowing Subject*, in Id., *Objective Knowledge. An Evolutionary Approach*, revised ed., Oxford 1986, p. 135.

a process of argumentation and deliberation, but needs in turn to be brought into discussion and given a justification.

Indeed, we come to the moment where we deliberate on our course of action with all our moral presuppositions (intuitions); we need them to start our deliberation. But this cannot just be a procedure of mere registration of what is our moral *Vorverständnis*, or precomprehension of the situation we are confronted with. Thus, we could perhaps accept the following conclusion: "Let's maintain that there is something which is self-evident. Nonetheless, we also maintain: In the process whereby we grasp self-evidence through concepts we get to statements that cannot be in any case uncontroversial and free from error".[36]

7.3 Emotivism and Prescriptivism

7.3.1 Emotivism and prescriptivism are meta-ethical conceptions that derive from (or are implied by) adoption of a certain theory of meaning. This link between meta-ethics and philosophy of language is by contrast not there (at least not so obviously) in intuitionism or "naturalism" nor in utilitarianism.

Emotivism is the meta-ethical theory that maintains that value judgements and in general prescriptive, directive or normative statements are mere manifestations of feelings or emotions. A fine formulation of the emotivist position can be found in Guy de Maupassant: "Nous ne sommes pas de gens logiques ni raisonnables, mais des gens à sentiments subtils; et les plus justes arguments ne valent, dans notre esprit, quelque prejugé poétique. En politique, en morale, même en art, nous ne sommes jamais determiné par des raisonements, mais toujours par des impulsions raffinées et souvent fausses".[37]

Moreover, from adopting a verificationist or referentialist or behaviourist conception of meaning (with the consequence that the only sentences endowed with meaning will be those verifiable or with a "referent" or "effects" in the empirical world) and from conceiving the chief function of language to be the representative or descriptive one, with beside that only one other function, the expressive one (that of expressing emotions or feelings), one will come to the conclusion that value judgements (through which only emotions are expressed) are devoid of meaning. Thus, if value judgements are not regarded as composed of descriptive statements, they will, according to this view, be conceived of as expressions of emotions and equated with mere exclamations. "The exhortations to moral virtue," writes A. J. Ayer, "are not propositions at all, but ejaculations or commands which are designed to provoke the reader to action of a certain sort".[38]

---

[36] P. Strasser, *Gut in allen möglichen Welten. Der ethische Horizont*, Paderborn 2004, p. 64.

[37] G. de Maupassant, *A propos du divorce*, in Id., *Chroniques*, vol. 2, Paris 1980, p. 86.

[38] A. J. Ayer, *Language, Truth and Logic*, Harmondsworth 1982, p. 137. Emotivist meta-ethical positions are also defended by Charles Stevenson, Rudolph Carnap, and by Ogden and Richards

It may first be objected to the emotivist theory, on the level of philosophy of language, that it assumes an over-restricted concept of meaning. It is hard to see why this ought to be confined to the sphere of the empirically observable. Suffice, for instance, to think of symbolic phenomena – like music, which can be "read" as well as " heard", and thus understood quite apart from its material execution – that are not aimed at representing an existing reality, to realise that the explanation of symbolic or linguistic phenomena given by the verificationist, or referentialist, or behaviourist theory is entirely inadequate.

The emotivist theory leads to the unjustifiability of moral judgements. Considering that for it language either describes or expresses or seeks to evoke an emotion, it will not on this theory be possible to find reasons in favour of or against a moral judgement. Such a justification, the presentation of reasons for or against a moral judgement, could not in fact declare its character as being purely emotional without losing its justificatory function. On the other hand, it cannot be purely descriptive either, since one cannot infer from a description (assuming a noncognitivist position denying the deduction of normative statements from descriptive statements), sentences that are normative in the broad sense. And an argument "for or against" is in the broad sense normative: it is a reason for or against a speech-act or an action. From an emotivist point of view it thus proves impossible to argue for (or against) particular ethical choices, and in general to discuss in moral terms. "We cannot bring forward," writes Ayer, "any arguments to show that our system is superior. For our judgement that it is so is itself a judgement of value, and accordingly out side the scope of the argument".[39]

This is an absurd consequence, since it contradicts ordinary experience which, particularly in hard cases, raises the question of justifying moral choices. Emotivism, by denying the possibility of moral argument and discussion, ends up as a conception according to which in moral areas one cannot ask questions (as to the meaning of and reason for our ethical choices), since we do not have the linguistic means for asking such questions. Think also that deliberation is a sort of discussion with oneself, presenting, reviewing and pondering different reasons for action. So that by denying arguments and reasons as meaningful one ends up assuming a phenomenology of decision that is something like the whim of the moment, a *fiat*, without reflection – which is contrary to what we experience and do before controversial courses of action. The conclusion is then irrationalist, as already anticipated in Maupassant's formula cited earlier: all that is possible is to abandon oneself to one's own feelings and one's own emotions. But what about if we don't have any feeling? Shouldn't we act? I have a beggar in front of me, he's really hungry, he needs some help, but I don't have any special feeling towards him: Is that all there is to say?

(see, for example, C. K. Ogden and I. A. Richards, *The Meaning of Meaning. A Study of the Influence of Language upon Thought and the Science of Symbolism*, 10th ed., London 1972, p. 125).

[39] A. J. Ayer, *Language, Truth and Logic*, p. 147.

The criterion of what is "right", moreover, from some emotivist philosophers – consider, for instance, the "early" Wittgenstein, and in his wake Waismann[40] – is the fact that a choice be sincerely felt, be the outcome of a sincere commitment by the subject, accompanied by a strong emotion. (Here emotivism takes on nuances that bring it close to Sartre's existentialism). But how can it be denied that Hitler sincerely believed in and was strongly committed to his value judgements? Well, then, was Hitler "right"?

Two further objections can be brought against emotivism. The first is that the theory is, so to speak, "empty", since it says nothing meaningful. Every human action is in some sense a manifestation of feelings, or at any rate, from any human behaviour one may draw a hypothesis about the emotions of the subject in question. Saying then that moral judgements are expressions of feeling or emotions tells us nothing about them, since ethical judgements too, as well as gastronomical ones, or artistic activity itself, or sitting at table, going for walks, smoking, etc. are expressions of feeling or emotions. As Popper writes, "everything a man as an animal can do is (among other things) an expression of an internal state, of emotions, and of a personality. This is trivially true for all kinds of human and animal languages. It holds for the way a man or a lion walks, the way a man coughs or blows his nose, the way a man or a lion may look at you, or ignore you. It holds for the ways a bird builds its nest, a spider constructs its web, and a man builds his house [. . .] For the same reason espressionist or emotive theories or language are trivial, uninformative, and useless".[41] "The same holds true", he adds, "for expressionist or emotive theories of morals, and of moral judgements".[42]

The second additional objection is as follows. It may be stated that typically human feelings like love, hate, reverence, etc. are present in the human soul only when they can be expressed linguistically. This means that the feeling depends on its being expressible in one or more propositions *endowed with meaning* (that is, not in turn reducible to mere expressions of feeling).[43] Here it is not denied that there cannot be feelings that cannot be expressed in words. But in this case we have to deal with: rather "primitive" feelings not typically human, such as physical pain, hunger, fear, sexual desire, etc., or else confused feelings about which we are unclear.[44]

The emotivist theory, once the unjustifiability of moral judgements is asserted, maintains that in moral areas there can be no room for discussion. This is put very clearly by A. J. Ayer: "It is plain that the conclusion that it is impossible to dispute

[40] See F. Waismann, *Ethik und Wissenschaft*, in Id., *Wille und Motiv*, p. 184.

[41] K. R. Popper, *Unended Quest*, p. 62.

[42] Ibid., p. 209.

[43] Cf. G. Patzig, *Satz und Tatsache*, in Id., *Tatsachen, Normen, Sätze*, Stuttgart 1980, p. 12.

[44] "Violent outcries – of fear, of rage, of pain or joy – are not a specific property of man. We find them", writes Cassirer, "everywhere in the animal world" (E. Cassirer, *Essay On Man*, New Haven, CT and London 1944, p. 115).

about questions of value follows from our theory also".[45] This position leads to absolutism in ethics. But refusing to discuss values means refusing to bring them into discussion even in relation to oneself, such as in internal monologue in dialogue form, in which each of us from time to time evaluates the reason for a moral choice or life decision. Emotivist meta-ethics thus ends up denying the reflectivity of human action.

There is, however, an idea of emotivism that is more than plausible: the pre-eminence at bottom, in moral respects, of feeling over "cold" or abstract rationality. Without feelings one cannot be in a position either to postulate the basic criteria of morality nor, especially, to "live" them, to make them a reality. One may, for instance, with more or less plausibly and rationally justified arguments, hold that the human being's freedom and dignity are the supreme principles of morality, yet nonetheless, apart from declarations of principle, constantly violate those principles in daily relations with others, and indeed adopt opposite ones. This often happens not from hypocrisy or "weakness of will", but because these values have been acquired only as the result of a pure intellectual exercise, but are not *felt*.

There is one respect at least in which emotivism tells us an important truth: we could hardly imagine morality without emotions, in so far as our will implies an emotive status that qualifies the end or the object of our willing. Were we living in a world where we had only conscience or autonomy but no sensation or feelings or emotions, we would not have or sense any pain. But without pain, or some equivalent sensation, or without some *feeling*, nor just idea of loss, whatever damage would count to us only as an abstract formulation: something that does not "touch" or involve "us". There wouldn't be to us any real "damage", but formal subtraction; and there wouldn't be compassion, because there is no "passion". We wouldn't be able to be sympathetic with others, to put ourselves in their shoes. Therefore, we could conclude that without emotions and feelings there wouldn't be a moral point of view.

7.3.2 Prescriptivism is the meta-ethical theory that holds that value judgements are reducible to, or expressible in, or consist of, prescriptive statements, that is, statements that prescribe or command particular behaviour. A first version of prescriptivism can be found in emotivist theories like Carnap's or Ayer's, for which moral judgements are nothing but commands aimed at bringing about certain behaviour in a given subject, yet these commands are in themselves without meaning, and are more expressions of emotions. A value statement – says Rudolf Carnap – is nothing else than a command in a misleading grammatical form.[46]

In speaking of "prescriptivism", however, one generally alludes to a less narrow conception for which, instead, commands are distinguished from mere emotional

[45] A. J. Ayer, *Language, Truth and Logic*, p. 146. In addition, cf. G. E. Moore, *The Nature of Moral Philosophy*, pp. 333ff.

[46] See R. Carnap, *Philosophy and Logical Syntax*, London 1935, Chapter 1.

manifestations, and are endowed with meaning. Below, in speaking of "prescriptivism", we shall be referring to the latter conception.

One "classical" example of prescriptivism is supplied by the first book published by Richard Mervin Hare, *The Language of Morals*.[47] Prescriptivism assumes a theory of meaning broader than that defended by the representatives of emotivism. For prescriptivism adopts a theory of Wittgensteinian extraction: the meaning of a term or statement is here given by its "use". Moreover, this meta-ethical theory holds that alongside a descriptive meaning there may be a normative meaning, or better a prescriptive one. Hare draws a distinction, very well known today, between the propositional (semantic and representative) part of a sentence and the part that indicates the sentence's function. The former designates a certain state of affairs (the closure of a window) and has been called "phrastic"; the latter, indicating the statement's function (either affirming "it is so" – or prescribing – "it ought to be so" added to the representation of state of affairs: "closure of the window"), is called "neustic".[48] In moral judgements we thus find ourselves faced with prescriptive sentences in which a certain "phrastic" part (identical also in the corresponding sentence) is accompanied by a prescriptive or imperative "neustic" part. Thus the sentence "it is wrong to kill a human being" would, according to Hare, break down into a "phrastic" ("killing a human being") and a "neustic" ("it is wrong", or better "there is no need to", "one ought not to").

A prescriptivist conception was also adopted by Norberto Bobbio in the early Fifties. The Italian scholar singled out three main functions of language: descriptive, expressive, and prescriptive. "The descriptive function, typical of scientific language, consists in giving information, communicating particular information to others, transmitting knowledge, in short, *making known*; the expressive function, typical of poetic language, consists in making certain feelings clear and seeking to evoke them in others, so as to *make others share* in the particular emotional situation; the prescriptive function, typical of normative language, consists in giving commands, advice, recommendations, warnings, so as to influence and alter the behaviour of others, in short, in *getting done*".[49]

The link between evaluative and prescriptive language, indeed their equivalence as asserted by prescriptivism, is not very plausible if considered in relation to aesthetic language. The statement "this landscape is ugly" or "this painting is kitsch" can hardly be reduced to the statement "this landscape should be changed" (or "this landscape should not be looked at"), or "this painting should not be bought" (or even "this painting should be destroyed"). It is indeed possible to say without contradiction "this painting is ugly, but I advise you to buy it", or "this is a splendid canvas, but don't go and see it", which proves the fact that in ordinary language

---

[47] Oxford 1952.

[48] R. M. Hare, *The Language of Morals*, Oxford 1986, pp. 17ff.

[49] N. Bobbio, *Teoria della norma*, Torino 1958, p. 83, emphasis in the text. Cf. also, for example, R. Guastini, *Il linguaggio precettivo*, in S. Castignone, R. Guastini, G. Tarello, *Introduzione teorica allo studio del diritto*, Genova 1979, pp. 18–19.

value judgements and commands (and advice) have quite distinct meanings and functions.[50]

Prescriptivism further makes justifying prescriptive statements, in particular moral ones, very problematic. For the justification for a prescriptive statement – on the prescriptivist view – can consist either of prescriptive or descriptive statements (or of expressive statements). But the statements whereby one argues for or against an ethical choice cannot be reduced to any of these types of statement (prescriptive, descriptive, expressive). The justification for a moral statement cannot be constituted entirely of descriptive statements, on pain of falling into the "naturalistic fallacy". Nor can that justification be made up of prescriptive statements, since in that case we would again find ourselves facing an imperative, a prescription, but not an argument.[51]

Nor could this justification be supplied by an expressive statement. The latter could at most express the motive for my making a particular ethical choice, but cannot justify it; that is, give it a rational foundation. The statement "I hate him", for instance, cannot justify my statement "It is right to seek to take Hitler's life", though hatred of the German dictator might be one of the motives, or indeed the only one, for my making the statement in question. In the meta-ethical sphere too, as we have already mentioned, a distinction can be drawn similar to the one employed in meta-knowledge between the "context of discovery" and the "context of justification". In the meta-ethical context one should distinguish between a "context of choice" and a "context of justification", with the consequence that criteria valid for one are not necessarily also valid for the other.

Prescriptivism accordingly has an irrationalist outcome: it does not allow argumentation about ethical choices. This has been astutely grasped by Stephen Toulmin. "Sometimes," he writes, "when we make ethical judgements, we are not just ejaculating. When we say that so and so is good, or that I ought to do such-and-such, we do so sometimes for good reasons, and sometimes for bad ones. The imperative approach does not help us in the slightest to distinguish the one from the other; in fact by saying that to talk of reasons in this context is nonsense, it dismisses our question altogether. However, the doctrine is not only false but innocuous, for it draws on its own fangs. If as we must, as we still refuse to, treat ethical judgements as ejaculations, its advocate can produce no further reasons for his view. By his own account, all he can do is to evince his disapproval of our procedure, and urge us to give it up: it would be inconsistent of him to advance 'reasons' at his stage".[52] Toulmin's remarks are primarily directed against emotivism, but they hold against prescriptivism too, at least in so far as the latter very often cannot but collapse into the former. In fact, even if commands are considered "meaningful", that is endowed with proper meaning and not just "ejaculations", prescriptivism does not allow them

---

[50] Cf. B. Williams, *Ethics and the Limits of Philosophy*, pp. 124ff.

[51] Cf. G. J. Warnock, *Contemporary Moral Philosophy*, London 1967, pp. 27–29, 46–47.

[52] S. Toulmin, *An Examination of the Place of Reason in Ethics*, Cambridge 1970, p. 70.

to be *justified*, since reasons and arguments are still seen in the light of a descriptivist or verificationist theory of knowledge.

The incompatibility between justification of moral judgements and arguing them on the one hand and prescriptive meta-ethics on the other assumes that arguing is taken as an activity done not so much at pragmatic level as eminently on the semantic level. "Justifying", or arguing for, a normative statement is not, in this view, a "discourse [. . .] aimed at convincing the addressees".[53] "Justifying" a moral statement is not equivalent to persuading a subject of its "rightness" or "validity" just as demonstrating a mathematical theorem or verifying an existential statement is not equivalent to convincing a particular subject of their "truth".[54]

Furthermore, prescriptivism obscures one feature of what I would call "moral experience" or "critical morality", as individual morality distinct from and sometimes opposed to "positive morality", to the socially dominant morality. The typical feature of "critical morality" is to be autonomous: it is the individual herself who gives herself her rules and principles. But if the imperativist view is adopted, moral judgements consist of statements directed at *getting done*; that is, at influencing others' behaviour.[55] Moral judgements are however directed above all at doing, that is, at directing the behaviour of the subject stating them. Conceding (though not admitting) that moral judgements consist in direct commands for *others'* conduct it remains for the addressee of the demand to assess and decide, through a moral judgement, whether to comply with that command. But even accepting that this difficulty is overcome, and that prescriptive statements apply also to one's "own" conduct, in what sense can it be said that the individual commands herself by formulating a moral judgement?

If moral judgements were a reason for action that excludes all other moral evaluation, it would be an "exclusionary reason". Obviously a moral judgement that excludes any other form of moral evaluation is not plausible. A moral judgement can also be composite, that is the result of a combination of a number of moral judgements and of the balancing of principles and values. This difficulty could perhaps be overcome through recourse to an authority specifically charged with the task of issuing moral judgements. But this would lead us back to the question of how to justify the exclusionary reasons for action and the infallibility of that authority, a question which in turn could only be answered through reference to moral judgements. Accordingly, maintaining that moral judgements consist in, or imply prescriptions (imperative commands) is, in reference to "critical morality", to say the least, deceptive.

---

[53] U. Scarpelli, *Semantica, morale, diritto*, Torino 1969, p. 92. But cf. U. Scarpelli, *Gli orizzonti della giustificazione*, in *Etica e diritto*, ed. by L. Gianformaggio and E. Lecaldano, Bari 1986, where it is stated that "one should avoid making the connection between argumentation and persuasion an analytical connection, that is, avoid making a doctrine of argumentation into, by definition, a theory of persuasion" (ibid., p. 22).

[54] On this point fundamental considerations are to be found in K. R. Popper, *Objective Knowledge. An Evolutionary Approach*, pp. 106ff.

[55] See N. Bobbio, *Teoria della norma giuridica*, p. 83.

7.4 Universalizabilty of Moral Judgements. Linguistic Community and Discourse Theory

7.4.1 To recap, from the criticisms of meta-ethics considered, some conclusions about the character of moral judgements, and more generally about the nature of moral experience, emerge. From the criticisms of revelationism we deduce that moral judgement must be an act of reason and reflection and not mere adhesion to dogma. From the criticism of imperativism moral judgement is reinforced in so far as it is based on autonomous evaluation, rather than argument from authority. The objections to naturalism and to historicism convince us that a value judgement cannot be fundamentally determined by a factual situation: value judgements act upon facts, react against them, and in this sense they are sort of *counterfactuals*. Criticisms of utilitarianism and of consequentialism illustrate the limited, or not central or exclusive, role played by the empirical consequences of a moral action. Finally objections to emotivism and prescriptivism push us to refrain from excluding rational justifiability of moral judgements.

From a close examination of the criticisms listed above we can deduce six fundamental characteristics of moral judgements. (i) Factual states of affairs or natural qualities cannot be considered sufficient conditions for their being in force and content. (ii) They do not depend for their justification on their being issued by a particular subject considered to be possessed of special (natural or supernatural) powers or charged with a particular social or religious role. (iii) They are reflexive in the sense that they necessarily involve reference to their own propositional content and in that they are the product of reflexive activity on the part of the subject. (iv) They are not merely irrational or emotional responses; they base on and require justification. (v) They cannot be purely subjective; they require intersubjective validation. (vi) They cannot result completely from the consequences of the arising in cases where the action recommended by the moral judgement is taken. (vii) They are not the "exclusionary reasons" of practical reason in that they are imbued with strong normative sense (it is the latter that means that a moral argument cannot consist in a simple "dogmatic" declaration); they cannot thus exclude further normative argument. They are however overriding on any other different kind of argument (for instance, prudential considerations).

7.4.2 Richard Hare's theory – as was mentioned above – is not just prescriptivist; it maintains that moral judgements consist of, or imply, *universal* imperatives. It is worthwhile at this point to dwell on another meta-ethical theory (which, here, combines with "prescriptivism"), asserting that moral judgements are *universalizable* sentences. But what does this mean?

The universalizability of moral statements is spoken of in at least two ways. In the first a value judgement is universalizable in the sense that, if I assert that "x is good (or right)", I am *ipso facto* committed to defining as good or right any act or state of affairs that is similar to x in relevant features. In the second way a value judgement is universalizable in the sense that, when I affirm, in a particular situation, that "x is good (or right)", this must also hold for any other individual in an analogous position to the one which is relevant to me for the occasion of stating my value judgements. In this second case the following question immediately arises: what does "hold" mean here? Various answers can be given to this question. The first is an exercise in empathy. Moreover, for some, a value judgement "holds", that is, is "valid" as universalizable, if it is able to secure the assent of all those interested. For others, instead, a value judgement "holds", or is "valid" as universalizable if, given certain normatively determined and variously (sometimes in detail) specified ideal conditions, that judgement is such as to have to be accepted by any rational subject.

To the universalistic conception maintaining that moral judgements are (or ought to be) universalizable statements in the first sense defined above further objections may be made. Ascertaining what is similar to x in relevant aspects, that is, determining the limits of the class of acts or states of affairs to which (if universalized) that particular moral judgement belongs, refers to a deliberation. That is, it is not ascertaining pure and simple but there is an element of choice. Unless universalizability is conceived in purely formal terms; in which case, however, it will no longer be of any assistance (in determining the class or applicability of moral judgements), since it permits the unlimited entry of acts and states of affairs into the class in question. "If I understand universality in a purely formal way," writes Ota Weinberger, "and admit whatever difference within subsumption conditions, then this postulate indeed will not set any limit to the admission of normative rules; therefore, it will not serve as an evaluative standard for justice".[56]

One could maintain that if universality is conceived of in purely semantic terms, then the difficulty of including x1 in the class of x's is minimized. A rococo table, or a certain piece of furniture, can be recognized as a table without a great deal of effort. Once a class of certain behaviour, or of certain states of affairs is identified in a relatively rigorous manner (through a clear determination and delimitation of defining characteristics), any behaviour or states of affairs in possession of these characteristics can be ascribed to the class in question.

The fact is, however, that as far as value judgments are concerned the class is not merely descriptive (such as that of the tables); rather, it is normative (using the example of table again, it would be that of "beautiful tables"). As a result there are at least two problems: in order to establish the defining characteristics one has to refer criteria external to the same class (that of "beauty" in the case of the "beautiful tables"), thus to criteria that are not strictly semantic. These external criteria are not based on empirical, sensory, observable elements, but on a different type of quality (for example, "happiness", "utility ", "dignity", or "beauty"). They are inevitably vague and make it difficult to identify x1 as part of the class of x's.

The choice of acts or states of affairs to include in the class to which x belongs (or is made to belong) depends on certain normative postulates. Universalizability, or its

---

[56] O. Weinberger, *Die Conditio humana und das Ideal der Gerechtigkeit*, in *Grundlagen des Institutionalistischen Rechtspositivismus*, ed. by N. MacCormick and O. Weinberger, Berlin 1985, p. 252. Cf. also H. L. A. Hart, *The Concept of Law*, Oxford 1961, pp. 155–156.

degree or breadth, of the judgement "x is right (or good)" depends on moral principles endorsed by the subject stating that judgement. "Universalizability" cannot thus constitute the criterion for the "morality" (the moral quality) of a value judgement, since it refers to, and is based on, another value judgement (the normative postulates that lead us to include x in a given class). The conception in the first sense above is accordingly not a meta-ethics (which elaborates on what moral judgements are), but an ethics as such (that tells us what, in its view, moral judgements ought to be).

To the conception that instead upholds (prescribes) the universalizability of a moral sentence in the sense that it ought to be valid for every rational subject finding herself in the same situation as the utterer, the following may be objected. This conception (the second sense above) presupposes the normative principle that all human beings are subjects of equal dignity, "persons". Consider a Nazi saying "every man is entitled to a wage that enables him to live decently". In Nazi literature we frequently find such normative sentences. Jews were nonetheless deprived of their property and, before being physically annihilated, reduced to hunger. How is this to be reconciled with what "our" Nazi asserted earlier? Is it perhaps an internal contradiction in "Nazi morality"? In fact there might be no contradiction here, since when a Nazi says "every man" he could mean "every Aryan"; he does not include Jews in the class of men. Nor is this an absolute novelty in history. Until Christianism it is rare to find in the West a community or a people that does not reserve the status of "man", "person", "subject" for its own members alone. Consider too in this connection the phrase "people of men" by which some North American Indian tribes designated themselves. Without, then, the (moral) postulate of a "humanity" that embraces all human beings, that is, of the equal dignity of all people, the universalist conception of the second type seems to be impossible.

Type two universalism also depends on the adoption of certain normative principles, and is not a meta-ethics but rather an ethics. It does not express a factual truth but only a moral principle. It is however necessary to be aware of this (of the ethical rather than meta-ethical status of this conception) in order not to fall back into the "naturalistic fallacy" (deducing an "ought" from an "is") and into a too strong objectivist position (for which morality is equivalent with "*the* morality"). This is not just manifestly unfounded from the logical viewpoint, but also quite controversial from the ethical viewpoint itself. A morality that is true implies that it is the only possible morality, and hence ends up denying the quality of being "moral" to all other moralities (different from itself), thereby denying that morality is the product of the individual's autonomy and deliberation. This is why intention is so important within the moral sphere: a behaviour by an agent is not just moral because it has certain consequences; to be moral it must be the outcome of a sincere concern for the morality of the act on the part of the agent. It is, then, appropriate to draw a distinction between what is "moral", in the sense of belonging to the context of morality, and what we regard as immoral, cruel, wrong, bad. A position may at the same time be "moral", belong to a class of moral sentences, and yet be for us immoral (in the sense of wrong). It is not contradictory to speak of "wrong morality", or even of "immoral morality", just as it is, by contrast, to speak of "unjust justice". This would also partly explain why it is often easier to ascertain what is "bad" than what is "good", what is "unjust" than what is "just".

7.4.3 Discourse Theory as developed by Karl Otto Apel and Jürgen Habermas is a powerful application of the "transcendental argument" in the ethical domain. For Apel the moral fact *par excellence* is communication: this is valuable in itself with respect to those who follow a series of moral prescriptions. The same activity leaves behind the single individual and presupposes a community of thinking individuals capable of understanding and reaching a consensus among themselves. The transcendental presupposition of a "community of communication" has, for Apel, immediate moral implications. These are contained with the "basic rule" of communication, which is given by the postulates of sincerity and verifiability (in a non-empirical sense) or, better, justifiability of every statement and act of communication. He believes that there are two principles that can be immediately deduced from the "community of communication": the prohibition of lying, as lies render communication impossible, and mutual recognition of the equal dignity of all those who participate in communication, such that a speaker recognizes that listeners have the same communicative capacity and are therefore equal in status.

Mutual recognition is then extended to all human beings and is set out in the normative elaboration of the universal concept of person. This extension stems from the recognition of the equal dignity of all potential participants in the discourse, since every person is a potential participant. This happens because the discourse being based on the idea of the best argument, can't establish limits on the arguments advanced or "advanceable" and thus limitations with respect to new carriers of arguments. However this additional recognition is practicable only at a reflexive level: "In my view", says Apel, "one could even demonstrate that the only possibility of an ultimate rational foundation of morality is in general offered through the reflective belief in a basic norm presupposed by the community of those who argue".[57]

The reflexivity to which Apel refers here relates back to a voluntaristic or deliberative element. The following paragraph demonstrates this: "The basic ethical rule [*die ethische Grundnorm*] as normative condition of the possibility of discourse does not automatically determine the conduct of those who take part in discourse. The basic ethical rule – which according to the ideal of discourse must be previously freely acknowledged [*in Freiheit anerkannt*] – needs once more to be *willingly validated* both by discourse participants as by those that take part in the communication act on the basis of a reflective consideration of that presupposition".[58] The transcendental presupposition of the moral discourse, in order to be operative, has thus to be validated again in discourse. This implies that it must be reflexive; this can only

[57] K. O. Apel, *Der transzendentalhermeneutische Begriff der Sprache*, in Id., *Transformation der Philosophie*, vol. 2, *Das Apriori der Kommunikationsgemeinschaft*, Frankfurt am Main 1984, p. 357, italics mine.

[58] K. O. Apel, *Der Ansatz von Apel*, in *Transzendentalphilosophische Normenbegründungen*, ed. by W. Oelmüller, vol. 1, Paderborn 1978, pp. 165–166, italics in the text.

take place through the process of deliberation of the subjects that take part in the discourse and through an act of will on their part.

Somewhat different is Habermas' way of proceeding: the principle of universalizability is founded by him in two moves. Above all it is based on our common intuitions, according to which an essential requirement of moral judgements is impartiality. This intuition is recognized and rendered explicit through recourse to the internal logic of normative discourse, which is set out in universal terms. The second move consists in the demonstration that the principle of universality is a transcendental presupposition of every argument. Habermas doesn't however attribute a strongly objective status to this "transcendental" argument. It is not an "ultimate foundation" – as it is for Apel – but rather a hypothesis which could be proven to be unfounded. It is more "pragmatical" than "logical".

Habermas defines his meta-ethical approach as cognitivist, universalistic, and formalistic. He declares himself a cognitivist in that he maintains that moral judgements have cognitive content; they are not simply contingent emotional expressions, derived from the preference or subjective decisions of the actor. Discourse theory is cognitivist because it recognizes that moral questions can be decided *through arguments*, "*mit Gründen*". In fact, the proclaimed cognitivism of Habermas is relatively moderate since it doesn't involve superimposing questions relative to the truth of a statement on those relative to the "justice" or correctness of moral values. It can be distinguished from equally moderate forms of non-cognitivism through the accent that it places on the cognitive value of moral judgements, which is however seen as only analogous and not identical to the truth value of cognitive judgements in the strict sense. The transcendental assumptions in the domain of morals are for Habermas very few and quite "thin".

The Habermasian meta-ethical approach is universalistic in its rejection of the relativistic objection according to which moral judgements can only be established through reference to the particular culture or language to which the subject making the statement belongs. In this sense, his reference to language as a pragmatic and transcendental bedrock for the validity of arguments has no communitarian tinge. This is made possible through his conceptualization of language in explicit normative terms which thereby "transcend" the contextual and parochial use of it.

Finally his approach is formalistic, since it is limited to suggesting a *procedure* for examining concrete principles. It is not concerned with the production of substantive or concrete judgements or moral norms, rather it is addressed to test the validity of norms that are hypothetically legitimate. The formalistic element serves also as a criterion for distinguishing between that which Habermas terms "moral" questions and those called "ethical" issues. The first are questions of *justice*, that have as their object inter-subjective relations, the second deal with existential choices ("the good life") of the subject. Only the *moral* issues can be dealt with through the universalistic procedures of practical discourse and reference to the principle of universalizability. The *ethical* questions on the contrary, linked as they are to a concrete form of life, cannot be tackled in an exclusively or strongly normative manner. This could be said, to utilize Thomas Nagel's expression, "the view from nowhere". For ethical questions, however, the place indeed is given, and it is not possible to abstract or distance oneself from it.

The main difference between Apel and Habermas consists in the fact that the former through the transcendental argument arrives at specific moral rulings. Habermas limits himself to obtaining one general principle, a kind of *bridge-rule*, that of universalizability. The transcendental argument in Habermas' philosophy takes the following form: the principle of universalizability derives content through reference to the acceptability of the participants in the discourse (however ideal). Justification of specific moral norms is seen thus as a result and not presupposition of the process of argumentation and discourse.

To render more explicit this point – the deduction of universalizabilty from the pragmatic rules of discourse – Habermas introduces another principle: the "principle of discourse" (D), *Diskursprinzip*.[59] This is prior to the principle of universalizability and morally neutral. It has the following content: the only valid norms are those to which all interested and involved subjects have lent their support as participants in an ideal discourse. While the principle of universalizability (U) has this other content: the effects on the interests of everybody of general observance of a valid norm have to be accepted by all without the use of force. D covers a broader semantic space than U and deals with conduct that is morally neutral. This distinction, according to Habermas, allows one to avoid prejudging the relationship between law and morality, and for the introduction of further principle, which is "ethical" (deals with the "good life" and with a community not an individual) rather than "moral" (concerned with questions of inter-subjective justice). That which is particularly interesting to us is the fact that U is seen as a principle derivable from the structure of the discourse through the use of further arguments. U is not seen as a criterion that is ontologically rooted in the same discourse (which seems to be Apel's view).

7.5 Non-cognitivism and Critical Morality

Let us summarise some conclusions which I believe follow from what has been said in this chapter so far. I hold that the theory of meaning to accept, albeit with supplements and qualifications, is the one of "use", understood as *rule governed use*, and hence as collective use. "Use" here doesn't necessarily exclude reference to strictly semantic elements. Linguistic acts are "intensional" in the sense that they have content, or rather are endowed with propositional content.

The theory of "use" allows us to reformulate in liberal terms the typology of functions of language, since this theory recognises the plurality of linguistic "uses". Following Karl Popper, I believe it is appropriate to introduce alongside the descriptive, expressive and prescriptive functions, at least the argumentative one.[60]

[59] See J. Habermas, *Faktizität und Geltung*, Frankfurt am Main 1992, pp. 138ff.

[60] See, for instance, K. R. Popper, *Materialism Transcends Itself*, in *The Self and its Brain*, ed. by K. R. Popper and J. C. Eccles, Berlin-New York, NY 1985, pp. 57ff.

The theory of use in its Austinian version as speech-acts theory allows us, furthermore, to identify "performative" contradictions, beyond the logical contradictions which are such as to render the same discourse meaningless. Performative contradictions hold implications for the presuppositions of the discourse, or better, for its "felicity" or "validity" which ought to be explicated and respected in order to retain the full significance of the same discourse.

Non-cognitivist metaethics seems hard to refute, if one bases it on the acknowledgment of the "naturalistic fallacy". One cannot deduce from a piece of "theoretical information" – using Ota Weinberger's terminology[61] – a piece of "practical information" (an end, a value, a purpose). Note that adopting a non-cognitivist metaethics does not commit us to accepting that special version of non-cognitivism that is *emotivism*. Emotivism is only *one* variant of non-cognitivism, though some are tempted to make them coincide completely.[62] However, things are less clear and the distinction between "is" and "ought" becomes less evident, once one moves not from what Bernard Williams calls the "fine" normative terms (such as just "ought" for instance), but from what have been said "thick moral concepts" (for instance, "cruel", "compassionate", "tolerant"), where the normative and the factual are so much intertwined that it is indeed difficult to disentangle them.

Moreover, it is important – I believe – to distinguish between three levels (or types) of obligation. There is the socially dominant obligation (which corresponds to the contents of so-called "positive morality"). There is, then, the personal sense of obligation, feeling oneself obliged (perhaps corresponding to the individual's so-called "moral sense"), somehow also dependent on the "positive morality" of which it is the, let us say, "internal" aspect, where the behaviour required (termed "obligatory") and usually followed as such by members of the community in question represents the "external" aspect of "positive morality". Finally, there is moral obligation in the strict sense, corresponding to so-called "critical morality", the outcome of more or less rational reflection by the subject in question, the belief that one has an obligation to *x*.

To these three types a fourth can be added: legal obligation. It has particular characteristics and is derived from the conjunction of the particular "binding force" of the institutions of law and the justifiability of the sense or the *Witz* that precedes the formation of these institutions. This last form of obligation is only *prima facie* autonomous (independent of the moral obligations). Finally, there a fifth kind which is more or less equivalent to be *coerced*. It is however highly controversial whether to be coerced can indeed be defined or conceptualised in terms of being "obligated". An obligation to hold – one could object – should not base on violence or duress.

Consider the following statement by an imaginary "Wehrwolf", a young Nazi educated from childhood in the values of National Socialism: "I feel obliged to fight

---

[61] See, for example, O. Weinberger, *Norm und Institution. Eine Einführung in die Theorie des Rechts*, Wein 1988, pp. 20ff.

[62] This is the case, for example, with M. Riedel, *Normative oder kommunikative Ethik? Zur Begründbarkeit moralischer Werturteile und Überzeugungen*, in *Norm und Werturteil. Grundprobleme der Ethik*, ed. by M. Riedel, Stuttgart 1979, p. 69.

for the Führer, but I do not know if I ought to (or if its right)". In this example the conflict is clear between the psychological or emotive feeling of obligation and "critical morality" based on reflective grounds. Consider this other statement by the imaginary young Nazi: "We have to fight for the Führer, but I don't know whether it is right". Here, the first part of the statement ("We have to fight for the Führer") is apparently descriptive: it describes a socially dominant obligation, as such actually (habitually) complied with. The second part of the statement instead raises a question typical of "critical morality", dealing in a sense with the "truth" of the moral obligation implied in the first part of the statement. In this latter case we might say that there is a conflict between "positive morality" and "critical morality ", in so far as the apparent descriptive part of the statement indeed implies a moral commitment. Otherwise, if "positive morality" is only considered consisting of descriptive sentences and it is "critical morality" that consists of normative ones, there is no real contradiction, since an "is" does not contradict an "ought".

Finally, the possibility should be recognised of rationally justifying moral judgements. This justification here is not a "strong" justification, as happens for empirical statements verified through observational procedures and inductive and deductive logical processes, or with analytic judgements that draw their justification from postulates (conventional according to some, intuitive according to others) from which the analytic statement is deduced by purely logical means (that is, through transformation rules already laid down). The justification of moral judgements can only be "weak". That is, it can come from two procedures: (a) deduction by argumentation (not strictly logical) of descriptive statements using what Hans Albert calls *Brücken-Prinzipien*[63]; (b) logical deduction (not merely argumentative) from other normative statements, which can be accompanied – and indeed usually are – as minor premises by descriptive statements. In the first case the bridging principles (*Brucken-Prinzipien*) and in the second case the same first normative principles can be granted inter-subjective validity only within a discourse that is "constructively" oriented towards both types of principle. They are only *discursively* constraining, when one engages in discussion with others as to the morality of particular conduct.

In order to illustrate the second case, one could recall the so-called transcendental argument. This identifies the presuppositions implicit in a universal practice and demonstrates that denying these presuppositions would be contradictory. To demonstrate the first case, one might recall the model of argument proposed by Stephen Toulmin and taken up by Jürgen Habermas.[64] Suppose we have C that is the normative conclusion of a moral argument (for instance, "I must give John fifty pounds"), and D that is the "reason" for C (here, "John lent me fifty pounds"). W is the rule that makes D a "reason" for C ("One must return sums borrowed"). Finally B is the

---

[63] See H. Albert, *Traktat über kritische Vernunft*, 3rd ed., Tübingen 1975, Chapter 3.

[64] See St. Toulmin, *The Uses of Argument*, Cambridge 1958, pp. 95ff., and cf. J. Habermas, *Wahrheitstheorien*, in Id., *Vorstudien und Ergänzungen zur Theorie des Kommunikativen Handelns*, Frankfurt am Main 1984, pp. 162ff. Cf. also R. Alexy, *Theorie der juristischen Argumentation*, pp. 114ff.

justification, or justificatory principle for W (here the weighting of the respective consequences of complying or not complying with W). In this chain of "justificatory principle", "rule", "reason" and "normative conclusion", while the passage from D to C by considering W can be portrayed as deductive, the passage from B to W is not deductive. The move from B to W can in turn be represented as deductive if one assumes as major premise a further rule W′, which in the above example might run: "one ought not to gain from doing unjust harm to others". Obviously, the question of the justification for W′ remains open.

For Toulmin, however, not all rules of moral argument need justification: it is affirmed that without agreement on some general rules asserted beforehand by those who take part in moral discourse, this discourse cannot even begin.[65] Habermas by and large accepts this position of Toulmin's, though he seeks to provide additional bases for the agreement intrinsic to moral discourse. As we know, the path taken by the German philosopher is that of "pragmatic-transcendental" justification, or as he prefers to say "pragmatic-universal". This consists in identifying rules allegedly implicit in the "happy" conduct (in the sense of speech act theory) of the discourse.[66] Discourse, and we all are within it even unwillingly, bases on assumptions which have a normative purport. Once rendered explicit and elaborated, these assumptions are able to offer general standards for moral deliberation.

7.5.1 The justificatory "weakness" of moral statements may lead us to use as "ultimate" postulates (from which individual moral statements may then be derived) principles that can be widely shared. On this view, the justificatory strategies that avail themselves of the principle of universalizability remain important, though on condition that they retain an awareness that this is an ethical or normative principle, not a meta-ethical one, i.e. one descriptive *in the broad sense*. It is this principle that is closest to what is meant by "the moral point of view", a point of view according to which the interests of all the involved subjects are considered and evaluated in an impartial manner. It is close to the precept that claims that if one doesn't wish to be subject to damaging acts, one should not inflict damaging acts on others.

What in any case seems important, or indeed fundamental, is recognition of the dimension of "critical morality", which is the typical dimension of moral discourse, and the specific schema according to which the justification of ethical choices develops. This recognition in turn derives from a previous discovery, namely that, as Locke writes, "there cannot any one moral rule be proposed, whereof a man may not justly demand a reason".[67] "Critical morality" is just this asking for and giving a reason for the ethical rules followed and to be followed. This "critical" dimension is, more or less, equivalent to "autonomous" morality, a morality of subjects that

---

[65] See S. Toulmin, *The Uses of Argument*, pp. 100ff.

[66] See, e.g., J. Habermas, *Diskursethik–Notizen zu einem Begründungsprogramm*, in *Moralbewusstsein und kommunikatives Handeln*, ed. by J. Habermas, Frankfurt am Main, pp. 53ff.

[67] J. Locke, *An Essay Concerning Human Understanding*, ed. by R. Woolhouse, London 2004, p. 76 (I. iii. 4)

themselves endorse their own principles. This morality is thus eminently "reflexive", and – irrespective of its content – "anti-authoritarian", specifically as morality without truth, unstable, uncertain, entrusted to the freedom, the choice and hence also the responsibility of the subject.

It is worth recalling that widespread recognition of this "critical" moral dimension is a very recent fact, typical of what is today usually called "modernity". Until the eruption of "modernity" it is hard to find a general awareness that "positive morality" is not morality in the normative sense. The separation of individual morality from (socially dominant) "positive morality" and the assertion that only the former is "moral" in the proper sense (that is the normative sense) – but only when it takes the "reflective" form (hence also distinct from the "moral sentiment", the psychology, of the individual) – has anti-authoritarian value as implicitly (but often also explicitly) asserting that the only moral subject is the rational individual. He is the supreme judge of the morality of his actions, and the individual is autonomous in respect of the normative moral qualification of his conduct.

To be sure, this assertion, of the separation of normative morality from dominant morality, is not enough to tell us what should be considered "moral", or "immoral". This necessarily refers to the contents of norms and principles used by the individual's autonomy. However without this autonomy the discourse on content could not even begin. In relation to this, it seems appropriate to spend a few words on the position (of Nietzschian origin) that every morality is repressive and authoritarian, that is, is "le dernier visage de Dieu qu'il faut détruir, avant de reconstruir".[68] This position may be replied to by noting that in reality there are no "amoral" actions, but only immoral conduct. I mean that even the conduct that seems most wrong (by our criteria) is either in turn practised according to certain criteria (immoral for us, but with a normative, or "moral" character that has to be recognised), or else accomplished in breach of criteria accepted as such by the actor in question.

---

[68] A. Camus, *L'homme révolté*, Paris 1951, p. 84. The position of the intrinsically authoritarian nature of morality is upheld by Axel Hägerström, who links the moral sentiment with fear of a higher power: see A. Hägerström, *On the Truth of Moral Propositions*, in Id., *Philosophy and Religion*, English trans. by R. T. Sandin, London 1964, p. 84. "As the product of the need to reduce the complexity of lived experience by excluding some parts in favour of others determination intrinsically has a *violent* nature," writes Francesco Crespi, a distinguished Italian sociologist (F. Crespi, *Azione sociale e potere*, Bologna 1989, p. 154, emphasis in original). Thus moral decision, as a form of determination of human conduct, would have an inescapable "violent" or "repressive" aspect. This view, which echoes Nietzsche's thought, is however, I believe, the outcome of an error. Ethical choice, like the moral norms, does not reduce the possibility of action, but produces it, in the sense that without such a choice (or such a norm) that particular action would not be possible. Think of Buridan's ass who between two sacks of oats could not decide which to choose, and so died of hunger. Had the ass chosen the sack on the right it would have accomplished a necessary condition for the "action" of eating the oats in the sack. This choice does not imply violence or the repression of any action, but accomplishes the necessary condition for carrying out an action. The choice is not then repressive, but productive of actions. The (ethical) choice is an opening, not a closing, of possibilities of action. As Simone de Beauvoir writes, "l'homme n'est qu'en se choisissant; s'il refuse de choisir, il s'anéantit" (S. De Beauvoir, *Pour une morale de l'ambiguïte*, p. 295).

Even those who claim not to have moral criteria are already, in virtue of this very proposition, in possession of a criterion of conduct, like the sceptic who in order to remain one has to repudiate his scepticism. Carefully considered, the alternative is not between accepting criteria and rejecting them absolutely, but between adopting autonomous criteria given by ourselves and obeying heteronomous criteria imposed by others. The alternative is, in short, not between the absence or presence of norms but between autonomous and heteronomous norms.

In connection with the rejection of morality, regarded as "repressive" as such and with a moralism of Nietzcheian stamp, the idea has grown up that any morality accompanied by the feeling of "guilt" ought to be rejected. But it is hard to see how it is possible on the one hand to commit oneself seriously to following a rule and on the other not to feel oneself responsible ("guilty") when that commitment is voluntarily broken. The sense of "guilt" is the inward sanction for breach of the rule autonomously adopted. "The remorse of self-reproach or guilt," writes Bernard Williams, "[...] is the characteristic first-personal reaction within the system, and if an agent never felt such sentiments, he would not belong to the morality system or be a full moral agent in its terms".[69] Absence of the sense of guilt, where a moral rule has been deliberately broken (an autonomous rule, note), would mean that adopting the rule had not been meant seriously and had not come from an actual commitment of the subject, meaning that the rule in question did not "exist". In the extreme and thoroughly improbable case where this happened for every autonomously adopted rule, that is, in the case where someone broke each of his moral rules without feeling guilt for it, one might then speak of an "amoral" subject.

Our final meta-ethical conclusions should thus be the following. From the preceding considerations one can infer that moral judgements have seven characteristics (set out in Section 7.4.1) with the addition of the characteristic of universalizability. Moral judgements thus correspond to normative judgements plus universalizability. The autonomy of these judgements, or rather their "purity" (expressed through their independence of circumstances and consequences of facts) and their being determined solely by normative considerations (intended by the subject) render explicit their *critical* character. Universalizability, which finds expression in the need for them to be accepted by the interested parties, constitutes their rational character.

7.6 The Legal and the Moral Domains: Initial Conclusions

According to the view accepted here, the concept of "institution" and its correlate "norm" are understood in a broad sense that covers not just legal institutions and norms but institutions and norms overall. An "institution" can be defined as any context of action rendered possible by norms, where that context is actually "exploited", where, that is, the norms in question are actually observed, or better "employed" or

---

[69] B. Williams, *Ethics and the Limits of Philosophy*, p. 177.

"used". Norms are the propositional content of normative sentences, understood not just as "prescriptive" sentences but as all those sentences that directly guide or shape human action. The constitutive rules of an institution like chess, according to which a bishop "moves" (is moved) diagonally, are typically not prescriptive; instead of restricting the possibilities of the conduct by human subjects they serve to widen them. Given x possibilities of action the "constitutive" rule does not reduce them to x – n (as the prescriptive norm does), but creates x + n possibilities.

This meaning of "institution" is certainly very broad. In this sense "institution" is both the game of chess and a legal trial and a market of economic exchanges. The problem then arises of delimiting the "intrinsic" sphere of law, or its "nature", vis-à-vis other "institutional" phenomena. In particular, the question arises of distinguishing between the normative system of law and that of morality. If a definition of law is given in terms of "institution", is there not a risk of confusing, or overlapping, the moral sphere and the legal sphere?

The difference between legal and moral norms is that the latter base their validity on recognition or endorsement of the norms themselves by individuals, while legal norms' or social norms' validity is based not so much on recognition by the individual, but rather on their being either "fundamental" rules, conditions for the possibility of "institutions", that is of specific contexts of action, or else rules derivable (by logical argument or by delegation of power) from the "fundamental" rules. It may be objected to the distinction drawn here that legal norms are not the only social norms. It may further be objected that there are social rules of a moral nature that are not legally determined, which are not, that is, legal norms (let us say, the rule that says one should not profit from others' difficulties or weaknesses to gain an advantage at their expense). However, these social rules of a moral nature either are part of the moral rules proper, but thought of as "social" because of an intersubjective construction and practice, or else they are norms enforced in the collectivity through authority, and as such *legal* norms. This view becomes less problematic if the idea of the plurality of legal orders is accepted.

Nevertheless, the demarcation among social norms or legal norms on the one side and purely social or interpersonal norms on the other remains a problem. Ota Weinberger seems on this point favourable to accepting as legal norms only those functional in achieving ends particularly important for society, like the protection of the life and health of its members and the allocation of resources inevitably insufficient to fully satisfy all the demands of each member.[70] Weinberger would not,

---

[70]See O. Weinberger, *Jenseits von Positivismus und Naturrecht*, in N. MacCormick and O. Weinberger, *Grundlagen des Institutionalistischen Rechtspositivismus*, Berlin 1985, p. 148, and O. Weinberger, *Norm und Institution. Eine Einführung in die Theorie des Rechts*, pp. 37–38; and cf. P. Koller, *Meilensteine des Rechtspositivismus im 20. Jahrhundert: Hans Kelsens Reine Rechtslehre und H. L. A. Hart's "Concept of Law"*, in *Reine Rechtslehre im Spiegel ihrer Fortsetzer und Kritiker*, ed. by O. Weinberger and W. Krawietz, Wien 1988, p. 170. Norberto Bobbio speaks of the "minimum content" of law in connection with the definition of law as supplied by modern legal and political theories. This "minimum content" is seen as consisting in preventing actions that threaten the social order, and result in conflicts that threaten the group's subsistence, in short,

then, share this statement by Benedetto Croce: "The legal sphere [. . .] includes not just actions men do in conformity with the laws of the State, but those they do in conformity with any other rule: not just the civil and criminal code, but also the gentlemanly code and etiquette; not just a statute of the fundamental law of the State, but also the rules of games; not just the organisations of the Church and freemasonry but also those of the Mafia and the Camorra".[71]

In a society like the modern one where the State has allocated to itself the monopoly over the "legal", and in which "legal" is by and large equivalent to the product of the State's competent organs, it is hard to accept as legal, over and above the laws and decrees of State organs, the customs, usages and principles that also govern social behaviour. If, however, statist legal positivism, which asserts that the sole source of law is the State, were right, we should have to deny the description "legal" to a large part of the political and social orders that have come and gone successively in human history. This is quite clearly an unacceptable conclusion.[72] It may be held, bearing in mind an intuition of Santi Romano's, that within the context of a given collectivity several legal systems may coexist (sometimes compatible, in the sense that one is the source of integration for the other; sometimes incompatible and opposed), and that the one that we "moderns" usually call "law" is only one of these system.

One might perhaps agree with H. L. A. Hart, according to whom the difference between moral and legal norms lies in the fact that the latter, but not the former, are structured in a system of primary norms (which impose obligations) and secondary norms (which confer powers), though on condition of ceasing to follow that philosopher where he presents moral norms as *social* norms.[73] Hart's position seems convincing as regards individual morality (understood in the character of "critical morality"), but not in relation to "positive morality" (the dominant morality in a given social context, and also the morality de facto followed *unreflectively* by a subject). For all social norms, including so-called moral ones (though not legal ones, according to a statist legal positivism) as well as imposing obligations, also confer *powers*. At least, they authorise fellow members to criticise (give them the power/right to criticise) behaviour that deviates from the norms in question. But there are

in securing and maintaining social peace (see N. Bobbio, "Diritto", in *Dizionario di politica*, ed. by N. Bobbio and N. Matteucci, Torino 1976, p. 320).

[71] B. Croce, *Riduzione della filosofia del diritto alla filosofia dell'economia*, Napoli 1926, p. 50. It should be recalled that Croce is, here, still, maintaining a voluntarist conception of law according to which legal norms are imperatives, or "demands or acts of will" (ibid., p. 49), and accordingly accompanied by sanctions (ibid., p. 47).

[72] In this connection see H. Kantorowicz, *The Definition of Law*, ed. By A. H. Campbell, London 1958, p. 15, where we read: "The State theory of law is unfit to guide us through the mazes of the history of legal thought and science. It rules out any application of juristic analysis to societies before the formation of State".

[73] This position of Hart's seems also to be shared by Neil MacCormick: see his *Law, Morality and Positivism*, in N. MacCormick and O. Weinberger, *An Institutional Theory of Law*, Dortrecht 1986, pp. 127ff.

also moral social norms (those also called "positive morality") which attribute genuine powers to issue further norms: consider, for instance, the powers attributed to the "good father" in Victorian morality, or, to stay closer to home, attributed by traditional Catholic morality in Italy.

On the other hand, once morality is rooted in the individual conscience and it is recognised that morality is the proper sphere of the "obligatory", there is no more point in attributing to law (and to so-called "positive morality") an "ethical" value, some sort of moral character, which is just what legal philosophers call the "bindingness" of law (meaning this in that very sense of "moral" bindingness). Being or feeling oneself bound by a legal norm does not necessarily involve the feeling of moral bindingness, at least no more than does feeling oneself bound by a rule of chess or of the German (or English) language. Certainly, a legal norm may meet with the approval of my moral conscience, and coincide with a rule of my "critical morality". But then I will feel myself bound by the legal norm not because it is one (a legal one), but because it is recognised as legitimate in a moral reflective exercise.

Indeed, the "binding force" of legal norms is not equivalent to moral bindingness. This in no way means that the "binding" nature of legal norms is not somehow related to individual recognition by the individual member of society. Nor does it mean that law "does not oblige anything", thus concluding that the law is observed in so far as it is imposed by force and the threat of punishment. If the "binding force" of norms were to be based on their "moral bindingness", this could amount to maintaining that, for instance, the rules of chess were no longer binding whenever an individual player sets himself up to dispute them. Moreover, if the "binding force" were to be reduced to individual recognition, the law as such would lose all reason for being. The function of law is to guide people's conduct, and in various ways to punish deviant behaviour.

But if everyone were to be able to assert that a particular norm has no "binding force" for him, and were to act in a way contrary to that prescribed by the norm (and hence to break it) adducing in justification his decision not to recognise the norm in question, the law would constitute a set of norms that are not norms, since they are *justifiably* breachable ad libitum. We have seen above a similar problem arising with respect to what we understand as "meaning". This cannot entirely rely on the acknowledgment or choice of the individual speaker, lest what he "means" would not find correspondence and recognition in the addressee's act of understanding.

Law's "binding force" derives first from the, so to speak, "ontic" nature as constituting a context of action, of the "fundamental" rules (in the sense mentioned earlier) of a legal order. Second from the subject's intention to join this context of action, that is, her will to become part of a certain situation and the corresponding practice rendered possible by "fundamental" rules. If I want to play chess, I must play in accordance with the rules of chess. If I want to buy a house, I must conclude a contract on certain terms and with certain effects (by which, accordingly, I am bound). My decision to join a certain context of action rendered possible by particular norms, that is the decision to "make mine" a certain norm of a certain system of norms, binds me not just to observe the norms that I "make mine", but also to respect the norms that follow directly (logically) or indirectly (by normative delegation, by *Ermächtigung*, or by *Empowerment*) from the "fundamental" norms

I have taken as a model or reference framework for my conduct or that shape such conduct.

It has sometimes been said that the arising of distinct normative systems (like those of law and morality respectively) has to do with the "evolution" of the social system, which by growing steadily more complex becomes structured into new, tighter and more specialised "sub-systems". Morality has thus been presented as one of these "sub-systems".[74] However, the "evolution" (admitting that there is a process of this type in relation to social realities) of the social system has very little to do with ("critical") morality, if we take into account that history (like "nature") has hardly a normative content. Nonetheless, morality somehow is an historically and culturally determined entity. There is "morality", as we know it (that is, as eminently "critical morality") from the point when the individual begins asking about the rules of action given her by society, thereby asserting her existential diversity (and distance) from the collectivity. "Critical" morality is, in short, an outcome of "modernity",[75] anticipated in many respects by the secular stage of Greek antiquity. The reflexivity in which ultimately "critical morality" takes shape, deliberation about what one's own actions ought to be, has certainly always been a characteristic of the human condition. Nonetheless, this reflectivity, in order to become "moral" needs what we might, along with Hariou, call an *idée directrice*: the idea that there may be two distinct (indeed opposed) systems of rules, the collectivity's and the individuals', and that the latter is the "higher" system, that is, the ultimate source of normativity.[76]

---

[74]It has also been maintained, on the wave of this "evolutionist" approach, that love in its modern meaning constitutes the outcome of progressive social "differentiation" and of the evolution towards ever more complex systems, and at the same time a mechanism for accelerating this "differentiation" and evolution (see N. Luhmann, *Liebe als Passion. Zur Codierung von Intimität*, Frankfurt am Main 1984). It is hardly to deny that the modern concept of love has come into being historically, constitutes an "idea" that is not at all rooted in man's genetic and physiological structure, and is connected with the arising of a humanist, individualist view of the universe. (In this connection see also the now classic D. de Rougemont, *L'amour et l'occident*, Paris 1984). However, the arising of this new "idea" or conception of love does not need to be connected with any "evolution", if by this is meant a strictly causal process intrinsic to human society and obeying finalistic laws.

[75]"Moral philosophy arises when, like Socrates, we pass beyond the stage in which we are directed by traditional rules and even beyond the stage in which these rules are so internalized that we can be said to be inner-directed, to the stage in which we think for ourselves in critical and general terms (as the Greeks were beginning to do in Socrates' day) and achieve a kind of autonomy as moral agents" (W. K. Frankena, *Ethics*, 2nd ed., Prentice-Hall, NJ 1973, p. 4). Cf. also B. Williams, *Ethics and the Limits of Philosophy*, Chapter 1.

[76]For some time now, indeed, we have been seeing repeated attempts to repudiate ethics as a strongly normative dimension (indicative in this connection is, say, G. E. M. Anscombe, *Modern Moral Philosophy*, in *The Is-Ought Question*, ed. by W. D. Hudson, London, 1969, pp. 175ff.), or to reduce ethics to communitarian morality, that is, reduce critical to positive morality (this is the direction that, say, Richard Rorty has been tempted to move in: see R. Rorty, *Solidarity or Objectivity*? in *Post-Analytic Philosophy*, ed. by J. Rajchmann and C. West, New York, NY 1986, pp. 3–19. In relation to communitarian views, see the critical analysis by C. S. Nino, *The Communitarian Challenge to Liberal Rights*, in *Law and Philosophy*, 1989, pp. 37ff.

Part IV
Epilogue

Chapter 8
Law and Morality

8.1 What is at Stake?

There is no question to which philosophy of law has devoted more attention than that of the relationship between law and morality or, in other (controversial) terms, of the relationship between "right" and "good". One could maintain that all that there is to say has been said. Nonetheless, philosophy – and philosophy of law is no exception – is exactly this: the rethinking of new problems which are in fact always old ones, to which, I would add, there are no definitive solutions. They thus require continual attempts at redefinition. In philosophy one is continually beginning again.[1] When engaged in this endless task, however, there is no need for either disillusionment or despair; it is neither futile nor useless. There are indeed solutions; but they cannot be stored or stockpiled or frozen or "codified". A solution in philosophy to be such should be revived through discussion, and in any new discussion further arguments are possible, and everything or nearly everything here then starts again from the beginning.

The apparently inconclusive nature of philosophy is determined not only by the subjects that it is called to deal with, but also and primarily by its own particular standpoint. This is – to use Thomas Nagel's expression[2] – the "view from nowhere". Philosophy is by nature counterfactual and distinctly normative: it is not always really feasible for a "brute fact" to falsify a fundamental philosophical assumption. This is not meant as an idealistic claim or a glorification of old-style metaphysics. What I want is simply to underline the special character of the intellectual endeavour that is usually labelled philosophy.

Above all, even though lawyers frequently look at philosophy in an ironic condescending manner, it is good to underline the practical relevance of controversy about the relationship between law and morality; it is not a simply an academic question. At least three questions spring to mind in relation to the problem that occupies us now: Why do we have to obey the law? What is the legitimate content of the law?

---

[1] Cf. Helmut Plessner's introduction to *Das Fischer Lexikon – Philosophie*, ed. by A. Diemer and I. Frenzel, Frankfurt am Main 1965, p. 10.

[2] See Th. Nagel, *The View From Nowhere*, Oxford 1987.

M. La Torre, *Law as Institution*, Law and Philosophy Library 90,
DOI 10.1007/978-1-4020-6607-8_8, © Springer Science+Business Media B.V. 2010

Or rather, is the law whatever the effective political authority wants to be law? What type of issues are legitimate or valid in legal reasoning? Or rather, in a legal process can we as lawyers, judges or citizens, use extra-legal – moral – arguments as valid reasons for making a legal decision? Or, said differently, are there moral arguments that serve as legal reasons? They are all, as is clear, questions essential to everyday legal work. The nature of law and legal reasoning are not distant and unrelated issues; on the contrary they overlap and perhaps are even one and the same problem.

The conception of the relationship between law and morality is revealed as of central importance in one specific, significant area of law, that in which law is often identified *tout court* and that which gives it a truculent fame: criminal law. Theories of crime, of that which should be prohibited and legally punished, obviously require detailed awareness of that which is morally acceptable and that which is illicit. It thus requires a articulated theory of morality. As that which is morally speaking illicit doesn't necessarily (logically) have also to be legally illicit, it requires a distinct awareness of the nature of the appropriate relationship between law and morality. Should the punishment be retribution and expiation? Or should it be directed at the re-education of the criminal? In order to answer these questions one needs to start with a conception of the relationship between law and morality, and ultimately with a conception of morality.

In this final chapter it is not my intention nor my task to answer all of these questions. Here they are a point of arrival, not a point of departure. I use them in order to justify and defend myself from the accusation of futility that in a Law School is continually endangering legal philosophy. That which I intend to do is to pull together some of threads of that said in the preceding pages (by now perhaps already too much for the reader) and to unveil the "meaning" of my effort, its *Witz*. It is not, in accordance with its aims, a merely academic effort.

8.2 Definitions and Distinctions

In the first place I need to trace some distinctions and propose some definitions. Some of these are already established. Above all the distinction between "ethics" (the study of morality as a philosophical discipline), "morality" (as "critical morality", the moral attitude endorsed by individual conscience) and "positive morality" (the socially dominant morality or the morality concretely adopted in a certain historical moment by a determinate human group). One could also here distinguish – against what I have done in a preceding chapter[3] – between "ethics" and "morality". Although it is not unusual to merge "morality" and "positive morality" – as various members of the Vienna Circle such as Moritz Schlick[4] attempted to do –, morality, as we have seen in the preceding chapter, is reflexive and strongly normative and it can't be derived from or confused with unreflective conduct, for example simple

[3] Cf. above Chapter 6.1, pp. 169–171.

[4] See M. Schlick, *Fragen der Ethik*, Frankfurt am Main 1984.

regularity of behaviour or mere habit. Morality transcends every concrete state of affairs, every situation of fact; it cannot therefore be deduced from these. Morality has a clearly *individual* character (even though not necessarily individualistic): its ultimate point of reference is the individual, who asks – whatever the others think or do – "What is the right thing to do?", or rather, "What should I do? ". Even if by morality is meant *positive* morality, as dominant practice, it is still possible always to distinguish two aspects: the "internal" and the "external". If from the external point of view positive morality is still an observable sequence of conduct and it can be conceived as a *collective* activity, the internal point of view actually refers to the "intensional" activity of the individual and primarily individual activity (it refers to the propositional meaning of the judgments with which one expresses the content of positive morality).

Here, as has been said, "morality that is positive consists of a combination of judgments and principles assumed as valid, that don't refer back to the positive morality, but rather are considered part of an ideal and critical morality".[5] The individual is invested with concern for the "right thing" to do, not insofar as she carries out a particular social role – as a student for example, or a judge, but rather simply as a human being. This doesn't mean that the individual doesn't enter into moral debate as the real individual that she actually is, with all her social roles and her specific institutional obligations. Also, it doesn't imply that there are not specific moral obligations deriving from the enacting of certain function or the playing of a social role. It means only that the individual can refer to an "ideal" type of function and role, and then compare this to her specific concrete obligations with more general obligations and decide which criteria should prevail. Such a comparison is always possible, not just as the result of a certain abstraction and idealization of our personal conception of "myself", of our normative vision of ourselves, but also because our "myself" is never, in any society, identical to our social identity. The disjuncture and gap between "my" topics and those of society result from the fact that we are subject to a deeper degree to the action of time than society and other collective entities. Subjectivity is identity in *time*, and the time of the individual and that of society don't coincide perfectly. There is a "time-discrepancy between men's private lives and the altogether different life-expectancy of the public world".[6] To bluntly express this idea, "man alone tends towards destruction, to death; and the world, humanity, to life".[7]

The individualistic nature of morality does not mean that human beings have to decide moral questions without taking into consideration the interests of others, or without discussing things with them. This (moral) *discourse*, however, is not a reality in itself, a Luhmanian system that is self-sufficient and self-contained. This is the case, since, even if morality is based on the intrinsic logic of the linguistic practice (something in the vein of Habermas' discourse theory), the moral point of

---

[5] C. S. Nino, *Derecho, moral y política*, Barcelona 1995, pp. 46–47.

[6] H. Arendt, *On Violence*, in Id., *Crises of the Republic*, Harmondsworth 1972, p. 139.

[7] M. Aub, *Campo francés*, Madrid 1998, p. 14.

view is something that cannot be assumed without the conscious, intelligent and *intentional* contribution of the individuals concerned. Speaking about morality in holistic terms is excluded. From the cavern of prejudices and rules followed due to imitation or tradition people exit gradually and one by one.

Here it could be also important to confirm a distinction that is much used in philosophical debate – that between ethics and meta-ethics. This was presented above, but it needs to be confirmed. Metaethics is a meta-language that deals with the language of ethics. It is worth saying that it is a second-order language whose contents deal only with non-empirical entities – sentences, propositions, judgments and meanings. If for any reason the reference to non-empirical entities is worrying we can reformulate that distinction saying that a language deals with *non-linguistic* entities, whereas a meta-language deals with *linguistic* entities. Metaethics thus becomes logical analysis, epistemology and ontology of ethical judgments, that is of the sentences of which an ethics is composed. With reference to the "meta-ethics", ethics – according to the definition above – no longer means the philosophical study of morality, or even of a particular sector of morality, rather it coincides with sphere of morality. *Ethics* and *morality* in this context overlap and become synonyms.

There are those who propose distinguishing between moral questions and questions of justice, although in the majority of natural languages "just" and "moral" are in the same linguistic field and can be used as equivalent in certain contexts. The concept of "justice" would be reserved to those questions that in a way don't concern the entire personality or existential condition of a human subject but are linked only to rules and actions, and in another way are concerned with the allocation and distribution of costs and benefits. One can adopt the following definition, perhaps with the condition that one drops the reference maintained to personal qualities: "Justice is that character of actions, actors, rules or systems of rules, whereby a good scheme of allocation and compensation of costs and benefits is implemented or guaranteed".[8] Indeed, justice and morality are not fully distinct notions; questions of justice are more plausibly but special cases of moral questions.

It remains to be explained why to exclude the personal qualities of individuals from the area covered by "justice". There may be moral, epistemological and logical reasons for so doing. I will leave aside moral reasons and refer only to the two other types. First, the qualities of a person, at least those that are relevant for a moral evaluation of her conduct are revealed only through the action of this person. In this sense anything said about the moral qualities of a person is derived from an evaluation of her behaviour. Furthermore, an argument based on the idea that one is given moral qualities such as these could perhaps lead to a "Naturalistic Fallacy", to the inference of normative consequences from descriptive sentences. If moral qualities are not qualities of actions they can be interpreted as a sort of internal, natural or psychological property of individuals, or even as a species of object with an imprecise (and indeterminable, I fear) ontological status. In the first case psychology and morality would be strongly linked, in such a way that it would be possible to derive

[8] R. Dreier, *Recht-Staat-Vernunft. Studien zur Rechtstheorie 2*, Frankfurt am Main 1992, pp. 12–13.

a moral judgment from the a certain trait or from the psychological character of the person. This would however constitute the deduction of a normative sentence from a descriptive one, and thus it would be a case of Naturalistic Fallacy. We could nonetheless reinterpret the "moral character" of a person as her "virtue", and consider the latter a general disposition or a habit gained by training to act following the appropriate and valid moral principles.

Finally, it is important to distinguish between a *weak* and a *strong* normative standpoint. The first expresses the ideal of, or the claim to, *correctness:* conduct has to be effected in a way so as to conform to certain criteria of "rightness". Given a certain praxis governed by rules, for whoever is involved in, or committed to, a form of that praxis there is the obligation of correctness, that is an obligation to observe the rules on which that particular praxis is built. Nonetheless, this obligation is not, unlike some, equivalent to a moral obligation. (For example, I don't have a moral obligation to put the verb in the second place in a phrase when I speak German; and yet in some other sense I am "obliged" to do so). It is the *strong* normative position alone that expresses the ideal and the claims of *morality.* A statement is *strongly* normative if it doesn't depend entirely on the factual circumstances of its issue, or on the empirical consequences of its execution, and is justifiable through means of a universal or universalizable judgment.

There exists a normative standpoint that is *sui generis* or also – as has been said – detached.[9] This is, in fact, expressed through descriptive sentences but it is "normative" insofar as it assumes the existence of norms or rules as a states of affairs in the world. Thus we could speak of the *sui generis* normative position of an observer who, with the aim of describing a particular society, should take into consideration the system of rules of this society and avoid any evaluation of those rules in terms of moral validity. It is that which has also been called "*cognitive* internal point of view".[10] I set myself up as one who uses, and accepts, certain norms but only in order to describe the conduct that derives from them, without committing myself in any way to adopting these norms as criteria for my own conduct.

In a similar way one could speak, for example, of a "normative" or "normativistic" institutionalism or realism, referring to the fact that the perspective these theories use in order to explain legal phenomena is the "internal" aspect of a rule. This is opposed to the view centered around a "regularity" of behaviour accessible only to a merely observational perspective. "Normative" realism assumes the existence of rules and their efficacy in social behaviour. A *sui generis* normative position doesn't entail either the "strong" or the "weak" position: I can describe the rules of German syntax and grammar and not feel myself obliged to observe them (for example if I have pledged never to speak German again) nor to recommend their observance (if I am not interested in the speaking of that language, the very sound of which evokes unpleasant images). Something analogous holds for the relationship

---

[9]It refers to the "detached normative statements" of Joseph Raz. Cf. J. Raz, *The Concept of Legal System. An Introduction to the Theory of Legal System*, 2nd ed., Oxford 1980, pp. 236ff.

[10]Cf. N. MacCormick, *Legal Theory and Legal Reasoning*, revised ed., Oxford 2003, pp. 275ff.

between strong and weak normative statements. The weak normative point of view (that which deals with "correctness" or "rightness", that is to say, with moral oughts relative to an effectively observed moral system, that is, an "institution") doesn't necessarily imply a *strong* moral position (that deals with "morality" or "justice", that is, with *universalizable,* moral oughts). The "weak" obligation, when speaking German, to use declensions doesn't lead to categorize as *immoral* the actions of those who violate the same obligation.

8.3 The Concept of Law

In order to proceed, we require one fundamental concept: that of *law.* Here, as we have already seen, the field in a manner of speaking, is occupied by three powerful doctrines: *imperativism,* according to which law is reducible to a series of commands directed at subordinates on behalf of the "superior politician"; *realism,* that sees law as the result of social regularity, or rather as a collection of repeated and constant execution of certain external behaviour; *normativism,* which conceives of it as a collection or system of rules and norms meant as an entity expressible in sentences imbued with propositional content.

For imperativism the meaning of a norm is reducible to the state of affairs pertaining at the time of its being issued. For realism the meaning of a norm is reducible to the state of affairs pertaining to its being observed. For genuine normativism, finally, the meaning of a norm is reducible to its propositional content, or its intensional object. We might reclassify these doctrines in the following form, in the way that each one, respectively, conceives of law as "will", as "history", as "form".[11]

An alternative interpretation – we know – is constituted by *institutionalism,* which has sometimes been considered a sort of "spurious" form, the result it is said of a combination of realism and normativism. According to institutionalism – as was seen above in the central part of the book – law is defined as an "institution", that is to say, as a portion of reality (a scope of actions) rendered possible by rules, as soon as they are followed or used, through instances of concrete and continual action.[12] For institutionalism the meaning of a norm is not reducible to either the state of affairs when it is issued (wherefrom it originates) and the when it is observed (or followed) or else to its propositional content.

The adoption of a particular concept of law obviously has an impact on the conception of the relationship between law and morality. For example, a "realistic" concept of law as the sum of regularity of behaviour does, in general, allow for a sharp separation between law and morality. Here, law will be whatever results from the regularity in question. Unless one assumes that social regularity – whatever the

---

[11] For this somewhat antiquated terminology see, R. De Stefano, *Il problema del diritto non naturale*, Milano 1955.

[12] See above, Chapter 4.4, p. 117.

form in which it is conceived – has an intrinsic moral value (as historicism and evolutionism would claim) it will be difficult to find a necessary conceptual connection between morality (a reflective practice) and law, when it is not meant as the product of human design but rather as the result of a combination of chance and necessity. Nevertheless, realism tends to sacrifice the "moral ought" in return for "being"; "in terms of the distinction between *Sein* and *Sollen* realist critique aims to deny such distinction, that is to reducing *Sollen* into *Sein*".[13]

As a consequence, in many realistic theories morality is not considered as a critical or reflective attitude, but, rather, as a social fact amongst others. Law is conceived more or less in the same terms, and thus at this point it is hard to see where law finishes and morality begins and viceversa. One would probably have to refer back yet again to institutional sanctions, or to physical force, or violence, to isolate law from morality (as "positive" morality) which rests primarily on informal sanctions and generalized social pressure.

Another concept of law that can predetermine conclusions as to the relationship between law and morality is institutionalism, at least in its communitarian version (see for example the so-called *konkretes Ordnungsdenken* theorized by lawyers such as Carl Schmitt and Karl Larenz during the Nazi regime[14]). They start by affirming that institutions are the site of action for social actors, and then add that all socially significant conduct has its place only within the sphere of an institution. They are then tempted to conceive of the actor as completely "immersed" in the same institution and incapable of abstracting himself from it, or to leave it out of consideration when engaged in intellectual activities. The actor is thus incapable of reflecting critically on it. They say that behind all conduct or behaviour of the subject or the person and thus behind her critical attitude with respect to the institution is the institution itself rendering it possible and directing (and predetermining) the critical attitude. In other words, adopting, for example the "hermeneutic" perspective of Hans-Georg Gadamer (quite close moreover to the German institutional theories and their particular organicism) we could say that the "judgment", *das Urteil* (the moral evaluation), is rendered possible by the "pre-judgment", *das Vorurteil* (the value-based orientation rooted in a certain community or social institution). The actually-existing (historical) being of the subject is due much more to her "prejudices" than her "judgments". The reflection of the subject is nothing other than a type of "contact" in the electric circuit shut in history. As Gadamer writes, "subjectivity focal point is a magic mirror. Individuals' self-conscience is just a jump spark in the closed electric circuit of historical life. This is why individuals' prejudices, much more than their judgments, constitute the historical reality of their

---

[13]N. Bobbio, *Essere e dover essere nella scienza giuridica*, in *Rivista internazionale di filosofia del diritto*, vol. 58, 1967, p. 250.

[14]Cf. In this connection my own book *La "lotta contro il diritto soggettivo". Karl Larenz e la dottrina nazionalsocialista*, Milano 1988.

being".[15] We could even believe – following the somewhat paradoxical opinion of Arnold Gehen – that every individual is ... an institution.

Were we to accept such organicist or anti-individualistic version of institutionalism, we had probably to conclude that law and morality are intrinsically linked; values held by institutions and by individuals coincide more or less perfectly. Law here incorporates moral values because positive morality, from which the law gains its meaning and importance, is not possible without an underlying institution. Alternatively, the institution of law with the underlying institution of positive morality (according to this perspective they are often fused into one single institution) penetrate so deeply the being of the people who act inside them, since the institutions in question represent the only sphere of meaningful action, that the actors are not able to transcend the institutions or derive their value orientation from a position external to these. Finally, according to this theory, it is not morality that justifies law but, on the contrary, law (as social institution) that justifies morality (as individual value orientation). The Neohegelian political philosopher Joachim Ritter states this clearly: "Morality presupposes a law and an institution where freedom could find its reality; these are its own reality [...] Thus institutional morality means that freedom, the being and the moral conduct of individuals presuppose as their conditions ethical institutions, and a law and a political order that guarantee them. Without an appropriate institution protecting morality [...], this has no reality whatsoever".[16]

According to the communitarian institutionalistic perspective critical (individual) morality, the "view from nowhere", presupposes and depends on positive (collective) morality, that which we can term the "view from here and now". There is a radical and a moderate version of this communitarian institutionalism. For the moderate version, critical morality results from a type of *interpretation* of positive morality. Here, in some way a reflective attitude is recognized, and even praised and encouraged, at least in so far as interpretation is a reflective enterprise, notwithstanding the obligation it has to be faithful to its object and the duties that develops from this.

For the radical version, critical morality is only a type of mirage, hallucination or illusion, the opinion of somebody who takes himself too seriously and ignores the fact that this, individuality, is the product of community and its history. Other subjects, or the entire collectivity, would assess such a person, in the best cases as a deviation from "us", in the worst as the result of natural or historical processes. Whatever the individual thinks or does, it is the institution that thinks and acts through her.

Nevertheless, a different concept of institution is possible – that which has emerged in the course of the preceding chapters. According to this view, the conduct of the individual has an impact on the norms of the institutions and can thus

---

[15] H. G. Gadamer, *Wahrheit und Methode. Grundzüge einer philosophischen Hermeneutik*, in *Gesammelte Werke*, ed. by H. G. Gadamer, vol. 1, Tübingen 1986, p. 281.

[16] J. Ritter, *Institution "ethisch". Bemerkungen zur philosophischen Theorie des Handelns*, in *Zur Theorie der Institution*, ed. by H. Schelsky, 2nd ed., Düsseldorf 1970, p. 64.

provoke a change in them. For this normativist institutionalism norms don't fully govern their application, leaving, thus, a way in for reflexivity. By means of reflexivity the actor, although moving inside the "walls" of the given institution can see the latter, at least partially from outside. She sees it from a perspective that remains irreducible to institutional regulation, that is external to the semantic field covered by the norms to be applied.

In order for the norms to be applied they have to be reinterpreted in light of the concrete situation. Such an interpretation (that develops into an individual norm with particular propositional content, thus with a particular meaning) is added to the propositional content of the general norm (even not reformulated as such). It thus always alters, often minimally and sometimes imperceptibly, the meaning of the general norm. "In every application – Habermas writes – there is potentially a creative moment. A student, after he learnt a rule, through the generative capacity of finding not only novel but imaginary examples has now become a potential teacher".[17] This is true of all types of rules and above all of those whose semantic field cannot be defined and circumscribed by algorithms as is the case with norms of social behaviour.

The "examples" of the student and the "individual norms" (rulings) of the judge are all reinterpretations of general rules and norms (a grammatical rule and a parliamentary law are in this sense more or less the same). They are thus reformulations and (although minimal) modifications of the propositional content of ("general") norms and rules. The change in the meaning of the norms, however, leads to a change in the corresponding "institution" or rather social reality, since this – as has been stated repeatedly in these pages – is the result of the following (application or use) of norms.

The observance (application) of norms, it shouldn't be forgotten, is oriented towards its propositional content. If the assessment of the norm application were fully entrusted to the addressee there could never be certain observance of the norm, which is the same as saying the norm could never be certainly followed. At that point it would be hard to understand what purpose norms served, and why one would make an effort to issue, apply or justify them, even if the sense of the norm generally is that of being used by those that are addressed by the norm itself. In such case, there might be some who would claim that the effort made to realize norms is more like "ideology" – the masking of a more embarrassing and ugly reality. In reply, one could object that, without reference to a norm capable of directing behaviour in a way such that this corresponds more or less to the propositional content of norms, it would not be possible to explain the maintenance of inter-subjective coordination of actions, of that through which we are enabled to have relations with others, above all language.[18] The concept of "ideology" itself or the use of such concept cannot

---

[17] J. Habermas, *Vorlesungen zu einer sprachtheoretischen Grundlegung der Soziologie*, in Id., *Vorstudien und Ergänzungen zur theorie des kommunikativen Handelns*, Frankfurt am Main 1984, pp. 70–71. English translation mine.

[18] See also above, Chapter 3.

be left to the instrumental decisions of its addresses or of speakers, lest it becomes fully indeterminate and thus useless.

Regarding the conception of law as a set of commands (imperativism) or system of norms (normativism), one cannot claim that the solution to the problem of the relationship between law and morality is limited in one sense or another. When faced with a command or a norm the question of morality immediately rises.

On the other side, the moral justification of the factual regularity or systemic functions can hardly be questioned. Demanding a strongly normative justification for practice or conduct within an institution or for the same institution might thus be excluded. However, even if we assume that this institution offers a kind of the ontological foundation for our subjectivity, when we find ourselves confronted with a command or norm we nonetheless often feel we might ask for a further reason. The question at this point will become whether the issue of a command or norm, in line with the legal order of a certain country or of a given social organization, exempts us from demanding an ulterior justification. A command or norm cannot without further qualification be assumed as an exclusionary reason, something which preempts more normative questions and reasoning.

The concept of law in terms of commands or of norms is subject to a series of defects. These have already been analyzed sufficiently in the first and second part of the book. In particular one should remember that the imperativistic theory obscures the cultural or, if you like, holistic character of legal phenomena that is not reducible to the sum of relations between a *imperator* and an *imperatus*. It thus sometimes lapses into a paradoxical subjectivism.[19] For example, concerning the interpretation of legal norms, it ends up going back to the will of the *imperator* in such a way that the one interpreting is forced to revive an act of will, which has no substance and existence beyond the propositional content of the norm, or to transform a question of rightness in a historical issue referring the former to the original intention of lawgivers. The legislators' statements and acts however have their sense in that they meant a certain ruling to be the right choice and defined it in terms of its material reasonableness, not in terms of a self-referring decision. The normativist in turn, although able to overcome the subjectivism or relativism of the imperativist, or of the "originalist", is not able to explain the social validity (effectiveness, or efficacy) and the legitimacy (the recourse, in the final instance to principles of justice) of law.

I propose therefore – and for the reader I will imagine that it is hardly a surprise – to adopt the normativist version of institutionalism. This has the merit on the one hand of recognizing the fundamental role played by norms in the construction of the law, so long as norms are thought of as possible conditions of the institution of law. On the other hand, it takes seriously the feasibility of legal relationships, in so far as it conceives of the institution of law as the product not only of norms but also fundamentally of norms that are "used" and observed. Normativist institutionalism

---

[19] An attempt to sustain the imperativist theory recognising the "objective" nature of law is that of Karl Olivecrona with his concept of legal norms as "independent imperatives": see K. Olivecrona, *Law as Fact*, 1st ed., Copenhagen 1939. For a criticism, cf. N. Bobbio, *Teoria della norma*, Torino 1958, pp. 134ff.

doesn't overlook – as the previous chapter sought to demonstrate – the problem of "legitimacy", of the justification in a strong sense, of law, as it doesn't conceive of it as a problem that is reducible to the question of effectiveness or validity of norms.

8.4 Connections Between Law and Morality

I will now list some of the principle arguments produced in favour of the idea that there is a connection between law and morality. The first argument to mention is that which maintains that an extremely unjust law cannot be considered a law: *lex iniustissima non est lex.* Ralf Dreier and Robert Alexy call this the *Unrechtsargument*, the "injustice argument". But it was Gustav Radbruch that presented the most influential argument of this type immediately following the fall of the Nazi regime.

According to Radbruch, in cases of conflict between law, especially State law, and moral principles, a judge must always opt for the legal norm, unless the contrast between law and moral principles is so intolerable that it is no longer justifiable to apply law in violation of morality. He writes: "The conflict between justice and legal certainty could be solved in a way such as to give priority to positive law, backed by system and power, even if it is injust and irrational in its contents, except for the case where the contrast between positive law and justice becomes so intolerable that the positive ruling as 'unjust law' has to defer to justice".[20] The position of Martin Kriele, another illustrious German lawyer, can be considered a variation on the theme (*lex iniustissima non est lex*). He affirms a necessary connection between law and morality as a legal norm is seen as morally constrained since it is part of a legal system, which has as a whole to claim to be moral and just. "Indeed, obeying the law is a moral duty, provided law as a whole follows morality".[21]

Similar to Radbuch's theory, but more liberal towards the recognition of the operation of moral principles as arguments for a legal decision, is the argument – which we could label "from strength" – proposed by Carlos Nino. It was presented as a means to judge the legal validity of the laws issued by the Argentine dictatorship installed in 1976 and in power until 1983, which involved the torture and massacre of tens of thousands of citizens: "There is no reason whatever why the rules dictated by a political régime through force should be maintaining their

[20] G. Radbruch, *Gesetzliches Unrecht und übergesetzliches Recht*, in Id., *Rechtsphilosophie*, 8th ed., Stuttgart 1973, p. 345. See also G. Radbruch, *Fünf Minuten Rechtsphilosophie*, in Id., *Rechtsphilosophie*, 8th ed., p. 328: "Es *kann* Gesetze mit einem solchen Maße von Ungerechtigkeit und Gemeinschädlichkeit geben, das ihnen die Geltung, ja der Rechtscharacter abgesprochen werden muß". Cf. W. Ott, *Die Radbruchsche Formel. Pro und Contra*, in *Zeitschrift für Schweizerisches Recht*, 1988, pp. 335–347. Cf. also H. Dreier, *Die Radbruchsche Formel – Erkenntnis oder Bekenntnis*? in *Staatsrecht in Theorie und Praxis. Festschrift für Robert Walter*, ed. by H. Mayer et al., Wien 1991, pp. 117–135.

[21] M. Kriele, *Recht und praktische Vernunft*, Göttingen 1979, p. 117.

original validity. Only whenever their contents is axiologically acceptable, are they nonetheless binding for judges and citizens in general".[22]

The argument establishes a presumption of invalidity for all norms emanating from a political regime that installed itself in an anti-democratic manner and acted in violation of the most elementary human rights. Here the argument tells us what should be generally considered legally *invalid,* not that which should be *prima facie* considered *valid* – as with Radbruch's argument. It holds however, as happens in the case of Radbruch, *exceptions apart,* which are (in the argument that I called "from strength") given when the norm in question is morally tolerable. Obviously the inversion of the argument is not without importance, since it transfers the burden of proof. In Radbruch's argument the burden of proof lies with her who wants to invalidate a norm or a legal act and has thus to demonstrate extreme injustice. In Nino's argument it lies with her who wants to maintain the validity of the norm or the legal act and has to demonstrate that it is acceptable. In virtue of the "argument from strength" – one should remember – the Argentine parliament approved, not the abrogation (with *ex nunc* effects), but rather nullity (with *ex tunc* effects) of the amnesty established by the Videla dictatorship for crimes against humanity.

A recurrent and frequently discussed argument is that which claims that the law as such has an intrinsic moral value. We could call it the "argument of mere existence". There is a moderate, or weak, version and a strong, or extreme, version of this view. According to the former we have a *prima facie* moral obligation to obey the law for one fundamental reason: from the moral point of view it is better to have a law that may in some cases induce us to take decisions that are morally wrong than to have no law at all and thus in any occasion be obliged to trust in the controversial moral will of each individual. Legal certainty (certainty about the rules of law to follow and abide by) is a general, overall moral value that can justify specific immoral legal provisions or rulings.

Thus, we have a moral obligation to observe the law since this is the only way to avoid anarchy, that is, a situation in which there would be no valid inter-subjective rules of conduct, but only those that are produced by individual decisions, therefore no coordination of actions.[23] It would also be too much for the weak and limited intellect of the individual to be charged with the weight of a difficult moral decision when carrying out any important social action. Law thus has the role of relieving individuals from such a titanic effort and rendering it possible for them to act without having to engage in the tiring act of moral reflection. In the absence of objective criteria of moral evaluation moral decisions would lead different individuals to different decisions in similar cases, in such a way that social life would become extremely insecure and in could in the end be ruined.

---

[22] C. S. Nino, *Derecho, moral y política. Una revisión della teoría general del derecho*, Barcelona 1985, p. 67.

[23] See A. Peczenik, *On Law and Reason*, Dordrecht 1989, pp. 243ff. Cf. also A. Peczenik, *Dimensiones morales del Derecho*, in *Doxa*, n. 8, 1990, p. 100.

Somehow close to this thesis is the one according to which law has the function of combating flaws in morality and rendering it certain and efficacious. In particular law is justified through the fact that principles of morality suffer from a high level of cognitive and normative indeterminacy they are thus vague in terms of content and lack a strong capacity for motivating conduct. Law with its public procedures of assessment, deliberation and enactment offers a clear solution to both problems of indeterminacy.[24]

An extreme or radical version of the "argument of mere existence" is that produced by Lord Devlin. Law, he says, reflects positive morality, that is to say, the principles that are actually followed by the majority of the members of the community. Morality (positive morality) is here seen as a type of cement that holds together society. Law, the function of which is to protect life and the continuity of society, has, if it is to remain loyal to itself, to implement, as far as is possible (positive) morality, and leave out of consideration that which critical morality might suggest.[25] Law overlaps quintessentially with positive morality, that which the people follow, not that which is merely speculative and produced by philosophers and other extravagant individuals. Order is a value in itself because it protects the durability of the community, and law, which is the most effective artifice of this order, should be obeyed without batting an eyelid. Here we are close – as the reader will have noticed – to the thesis of communitarian institutionalism.

A third argument in favour of the necessary conceptual connection between law and morality is that which I would call the "transcendental hermeneutic argument". This affirms that any significant or relevant application of a legal norm, especially on the part of a judge, implies or presupposes a moral commitment or assessment. This is the assessment that the legal order in which that norm is valid is in the end just or moral enough to merit our approval and the demand that we observe it and that we ask for its observance. Here at the end of the day an order is legal in so far as it is coherent in accordance with certain strong normative standards, which are then found to be internal or intrinsic to the same order. Following Professors Ralf Dreier and Robert Alexy, we could also call it the "argument from principles". A version of this is the interpretative conception of Ronald Dworkin. According to the American scholar, law mainly is its interpretation.[26] The interpretation is directed or governed by the best interpretative theory that fits the positive morality of a certain community.[27] Here, however, beyond a certain stage (that of "fit" with positive law) the interpretation of the law becomes an openly evaluative, indeed "strongly" normative exercise.

---

[24] See J. Habermas, *Faktizität und Geltung*, Frankfurt am Main 1992.

[25] See Lord Devlin, *The Enforcement of Morals*, Oxford 1965.

[26] This was also the opinion of a brilliant Italian philosopher of law, Giovanni Tarello, whose realist theory, lacking the holistic assumption that lies at the base of the Dworkian conception, led him to a radical normative scepticism. According to this the meaning of a legal norm is only that attributed to it by the one who interprets it with an act of will that is not justifiable in a prior manner. See G. Tarello, *Diritto, enunciati, usi*, Bologna 1974.

[27] See R. Dworkin, *Law's Empire*, Fontana, London 1986.

Connected to the "argument from principles" is the "thesis of the special case" (*Sonderfallthese)* defended by Robert Alexy. According to Alexy the connection between law and morality lies in the peculiarity of legal discourse, which is nothing but a "special case" of general discourse, and in particular of moral discourse. He develops his argument in two moves. The first is represented by the affirmation of a *requirement of correctness* implied in legal practice. "The decisive point – he writes [28] – is rather that a claim to correctness is rooted in the practice of the rulers' system and raised against everyone. This claim to correctness is a necessary element of the concept of law. The connection of law and morality is established by it". The requirement of correctness is raised at two different levels. The first is the constitutional level: "With the act of giving a constitution a claim of correctness is necessarily connected, in this case being mainly a claim to justice".[29] The second level at which the requirement of correctness is made is the juridical, that is to say, as part of the legal process: "A judicial decision always claims to apply the law correctly, no matter how little this may be the case".[30]

The consequent step in Alexy's argument is the so-called *requirement of justifiability* ("the claim to correctness implies a claim to justifiability"[31]) which leads to third and final step: the *requirement of universalizability,* that is, at the end of the day the moral point of view. Once a decision claims to be correct it can be justified, or rather it can be subject to justification, if it contains the demand that whoever raised it has also to justify it. In this context justification is effected through the principle of universalizability: the decision has to be acceptable, ideally speaking, by all those who would be involved in and have their interests affected by that decision. "Whoever justifies something at least pretends that he accepts the other person as an equal partner, at least in discourse and that he neither exercise coercion himself nor is he supported by coercion exercised by others. He furthermore claims to be able to defend his thesis not only against his partner in discourse but against everyone".[32]

8.5 Separation of Law and Morality

In this section I would like to list some of the most significant criteria proposed for distinguishing between law and morality and for denying all conceptual connection between them. Naturally, the conceptual separation of law and morality and the exclusion of a necessary conceptual link does not exclude *every type* of connection. Such a distinction can be traced at the descriptive level, or else from a normative

---

[28] R. Alexy, *On Necessary Relations Between Law and Morality*, in *Ratio Juris*, 1989, p. 177. See also R. Alexy, *Begriff und Geltung des Rechts*, pp. 64ff.

[29] R. Alexy, *On Necessary Relations Between Law and Morality*, p. 179.

[30] Ibid., p. 180.

[31] Ibid.

[32] Ibid. Cf. R. Dreier, *Zur gegenwärtigen Diskussion des Verhältnisses von Recht und Moral in der Bundesrepublik*, in *Archiv für Rechts- und Sozialphilosophie*, Beiheft 44, 1991, pp. 55–67.

perspective. Nevertheless, a *strong* argument in favour of the connection between law and morality, that is to say an argument that seeks to establish a necessary conceptual connection between the two phenomena would in the end almost cancel the dividing line between the two.

A classic argument in favour of the conceptual separation is that which relies on the distinction between conscious conviction and action of conduct. Law – it says – regulates external conduct (action) whilst morality is concerned with the interior attitude of the subjects (their convictions or their conscience). A slightly different way to present the same argument is saying that morality deals with the *ends* of human behaviour whereas law is concerned with the *means* to be used to obtain these ends. Similar is the distinction between *forum externum* and *forum internum* used by some natural law theorists in the seventeenth and eighteenth centuries, although according to this doctrine the two terms don't coincide fully with the area covered by morality and law. Another criterion revolves around the idea of sanction: morality is not guaranteed by any sanctioning mechanism, nor can it be realized through the use of force or other external pressure. Law on the other hand requires sanction and force (institutional punishment) and a coercive apparatus (police, prison, judges). Morality cannot be coerced; law can.

However, it should be remembered that some time ago Ernst Tugendhat, a German philosopher, tried to define moral obligation with reference to the notion of external sanction, that is to say, to a sanction which is not provided for by the conscience of the subject, such as a sense of guilt, embarrassment or even desperation. Rather it would be supplied by other subjects (God or other human beings). Moral norms – according to Tugendhat – are such that "for the case of their not being followed, what happens is that neighbours (or God) apply a sanction".[33] It is obvious that, if one accepts Tugendhat's view, it will no longer be possible to separate law and morality using the criterion of conduct or of external sanction.

When confronted with this theory one can reply by remembering that a sanction is not just any negative consequence, but rather a negative consequence inflicted for the violation of a norm and connected to that violation by another norm. To identify a sanction we thus need a norm that categorizes a certain damaging event as a "sanction". This is as true for legal norms as for the ultimate moral norms that should inflict the sanction. But, if sanctions are such only if there is a norm that qualifies them as such, we can't – without falling into a vicious circle – confirm that norms are such only if they contain (provide for) a sanction. This would require criteria for the identification of sanctions independent of the qualification of sanctions as such by a norm. Such criteria, however, are not given. Should they be then given by a previous norm, then there will be a *regressus ad infinitum* and we'll be again face an argumentative fallacy. Thus, the definition and the identification of norms (both legal and moral) through sanctions is a dead-end street. In addition, one cannot deny the fact that many legal norms don't rest upon sanctions, at least not directly

---

[33] E. Tugendhat, *Fragen der Ethik*, Stuttgart 1984, p. 73.

or immediately, and that – as was discussed in the first part of the book – one cannot maintain that legal order is based on force or violence. Indeed, the legal order, to function in an appropriate and efficient manner, needs widespread approval and more or less convinced support. It is for this reason that even sociology in explaining legal phenomena adopts the notion of legitimacy: power is not sufficient, law needs consensus and a value orientation.

A second criterion is universalizability. While a conceptual characteristic of morality – as the preceding chapter showed – is universal validity, a conceptual element of law is that it is valid only within a certain legal system. Law's claim to validity has precise temporal and spatial limits. On the other hand universalizability is not only a phenomenological element of moral norms (a "concept"), but it is also and most importantly, a justifying or foundational element of the morality of a rule. This is to say that it is the characteristic through which it is possible to ascertain whether or not a certain rule satisfies the conditions posed by morality. This is not the case for legal norms. However, there are scholars (Lon L. Fuller for example and these days Ronald Dworkin) who maintain that the generalizable applicability of a norm is a precondition for it being considered as a legal regulation.[34] The generalizable applicability in question, usually, is meant to have a place only within a certain legal system; this limitation cannot apply to morality.

For a number of reasons linked to the principle of generalizable applicability a new and interesting criterion has been advanced as part of discourse theory of Habermasian origins. Klaus Günther, a pupil of Habermas, contests Alexy's "thesis of the special case" and his idea that there is a necessary connection based on the claim to correctness. Gunther traces a clear distinction in practical discourse (that concerned with norms and principles of action) between *discourse of justification* and *discourse of application.* It is one thing – Gunther says – to justify a rule and an entirely different thing to apply it. In justification the principle of universalizability is valued; application on the other hand, as soon as it involves using an already formed norm in a particular case, is a question of referring back to all the important characteristics of the generic case and thus specifying the general or universalizable norm in such a way as to satisfy the principle of appropriateness or fitting ("Angemessenheit") of the norm to the concrete case. Now, while a legal discourse only involves application of an already given norm, moral discourse primarily involves justification. If this is correct, then one cannot take the principle of universalizability as a basic orientation in legal discourse. But such is the principle necessary in Alexy's opinion in order to establish legal discourse as a "special case" of moral discourse. Thus law and morality can't be said to be conceptually and necessarily connected.[35]

The problem here, however, is first, that Günther admits that morality involves both a discourse of justification and a discourse of application. The clarity of the

---

[34] See for example L. Fuller, *Positivism and Fidelity to Law: A Reply to Professor Hart*, in *Harvard Law Review*, 1958, pp. 630ff.

[35] Cf. K. Günther, *Das Prinzip von Angemessenheit*, Frankfurt am Main 1988.

distinction between law and morality as two distinct types of discourse is thus significantly reduced. The distinction no longer corresponds to and overlaps with that of discourses of justification and application. Thus, one had to say that, whilst moral discourse is composed of a discourse of justification and a discourse of application, law is composed of, or refers to, only a discourse on application. This means however that morality also operates according to the principle of appropriateness that requires that necessary weight be given to all the aspects of the case at hand. If this is true, however, moral discourse is again similar to legal discourse, in so far as it is not possible to isolate legal discourse through identification of a principle that applies to it alone.

One could moreover point out that legal discourse does not only deal with the *application* of a norm but also, at least on the legislative level, or in so far jurisdiction is called to act and decide through general rulings, with the issuing and thus – if one is not decisionistic in the crude manner of Carl Schmitt – with the *justification* of a norm. One could add that justification of the issuing of the norm is not irrelevant to the application of the norm, especially when the case to which the norm applies is *hard* or *difficult* either due to the characteristics of the case itself or due to defects of, or the extreme generality, of the norm itself.

When speaking of law and morality, one can't but also mention the "pure doctrine" of Hans Kelsen. According to the great Viennese legal theorist morality is subjectively normative (it is a "subjective moral ought"), whereas law is objectively normative ("objective moral ought"), as set out in the second edition of *Reine Rechtslehre*.[36] Morality is only the *subjective* sense of an act of will; law alternatively is the *objective* sense of such an act, in so far as this is authorized by a superior norm of jurisdiction. According to Kelsen, furthermore, morality is a "static" normative order (in which norms are connected to each other only through relations of logical inference). Law on the contrary is a "dynamic" order (in which norms are connected to each other through acts of will and establishment of jurisdiction).[37]

The Kelsenian distinction between *dynamic* and *static* normative orders however is not entirely plausible, in so much as a dynamic order cannot but be also a static order. As a matter of fact, it is logically impossible to conceive of a dynamic order that were not at the same time a static order, that is, one in which there weren't some kind of relations of logical inference whereby from a general norm, with the addition of a minor premise along with certain facts, one would be able to arrive at an individual norm as syllogistic conclusion. It is only if we attribute propositional content to the norms and consider them as "general" and "abstract" prescriptions, directed towards certain recipients, for a certain class of situations, that we can claim that a (general) norm authorizes or attributes certain responsibilities to a certain subject. This in fact is possible only in so far as that subject can be subsumed into the class of subjects that the norm refers to as its recipients. This means also that a normative system cannot work only on the basis of mere "acts of will", as Kelsen adds in his

---

36 See H. Kelsen, *Reine Recthslehre*, 2nd ed., Wien 1960.

37 See H. Kelsen, *Reine Rechtslehre*, Wien 1934, pp. 62ff.

last and posthumously published work, *Theorie der Normen*, where he affirms the inapplicability of the principle of non-contradiction, and of the syllogistic inference to all norms.[38] Moreover, it is will itself that doesn't function without logic, at least insofar it is directed to an end and to reach this it chooses the most appropriate means at hand.

For the late Kelsen, who managed a switch of 180 degrees with respect to his original antivoluntaristic doctrine,[39] there will be nothing but single acts of will as determinant or prescription of a specific act. However, if it were like this, it wouldn't be clear why we formulate *abstract* norms (that deal with *classes* of situation not with concrete situations) and general norms (that concern *classes* of recipient and not a determinant recipient with a proper name). According to the phenomenology of acts of will defended by Kelsen, these *classes* obviously cannot be the object of specific willed acts, such that general and abstract norms cannot direct behaviour. The lack of general and abstract norms would mean that, if we wanted to continue to have determinants of action and orientation of conduct, we needed a legislator that could produce a specific act of will for every concrete situation and for every concrete subject. It would have to intimate to the specific subject the specific conduct required. In order to do this, however, the legislator would have to be somewhat omniscient and omnipotent, and permanently issuing its will, a divine or magic entity indeed. The human legislator however is by definition not divine nor magic. Even where one assumes the existence of a divine legislator one can't exclude – as it is held by the overwhelming majority of those that defend natural law of divine origin – *determinatio*, the intervention and the ruling of a human (positive) legislator.[40] Thus, the voluntaristic thesis of Kelsen cannot be considered anything other than a theoretical extravagance or perhaps a *reductio ad absurdum* through an internal radicalization of legal positivism.

On the other hand, a *moral* order can nonetheless "authorize" a particular person, in virtue of her merits, to pronounce important norms or to adopt a certain course of action. For example, a system of (moral) rules (which for Kelsen has to be "static") can authorize parents to pronounce certain norms for their children at least until they reach a certain age. The distinction between law and morality thus does not seem to exactly correspond to that between static and dynamic order and cannot be maintained through recourse to this distinction.

The most common argument used in the defence of the separation of law and morality is, at least in the most recent positivistic legal theory, the so-called "logical thesis". This, used by Jeremy Bentham and John Austin and reformulated by H. L. A. Hart,[41] states that between law such as it "is" (which determines the *legal* point of view) and law such as it "ought to be" (pertinent to the *moral* point of

---

[38]See H. Kelsen, *Theorie der Normen*, ed. by K. Ringhofer and R. Walter, Wien 1978.

[39]One thinks of the radical antivolontarism of the *Hauptprobleme der Staatsrechtslehre* (Wien 1911), his first "dogmatic" monograph, in which the legal norm is reconceptualized as "hypothetical judgment" and not as an imperative or as a command or any other manifestation of will.

[40]Cf. for example J. Finnis, *Natural Law and Natural Rights*, Oxford 1980.

[41]See H. L. A. Hart, *Essays in Jurisprudence and Philosophy*, Oxford 1983, pp. 21ff.

view) there is no logical derivation. The argument centers around a sharp distinction between descriptive and prescriptive sentences.

One could broadly reformulate the argument in the following way: while law at the metalinguistic level can be realized using a series of descriptive sentences, this would not be possible for morality which remains radically normative. ("Critical") morality transferred to the meta-ethical level, and rendered through a series of descriptive sentences, would lose its meaning and be transformed into something else. Hart underlines the difference between knowledge of legal norms and discovery of moral rules. In the first case we find ourselves in front of a descriptive task; in the second it is (strongly) normative. Or rather, while in the case of legal norms it would be possible to distinguish between production and knowledge, in the case of moral norms this would not be possible and the creative element would prevail. Implicit in this argument is the assumption that morality is purely subjective, and cannot be the object of knowledge. Law, meanwhile, as a positivist normative system has a certain, quite high degree of objectivity. The theoretical background to the "logical thesis" is thus provided by meta-ethical non-cognitivism and by a "precomprehension" of the concept of law as "positivistic".[42] Hart thus finishes by establishing a correspondence between legal positivism and non-cognitivism.[43]

Such equivalence is debatable, historically as much as theoretically. Historically, because there have been and there are positivistic doctrines that are also in some way cognitivistic. They begin with Hobbes who many claim to be the father of legal positivism, for whom law as such is morally just and therefore morality is the result of that which is legal.[44] They end with the "Historical School" the ideas of which, even today, constitute at least in the European Continent the "vulgar" philosophy of legal positivism. They connect law to the intrinsic morality of history ("causality is the justice of universal history", as Georg Jellinek says[45]), and normativity with a special "force" of factuality ("die normative Kraft des Faktischen", again in Jellinek's words).

The identification of legal positivism and non-cognitivism is theoretically debatable, since it is possible, that is, not self-contradictory, to be cognitivist in metaethics, believing that values are strongly objective in so far as factual (as did the historicists of the Savigny "Historical School") and yet to maintain that the only law in force is positive law, that is conventions and customs and legal doctrines and precedents, in so far these are a more or less direct outcome of those objective and factual values. Here "law" mainly means either customary or jurisprudential law as created by judges or also "scientific" law produced by scholars. One can distinguish between law "as it is" and law "as it should be", and nonetheless continue to believe that the criteria for determining the latter are fundamentally cognitive and accessible

[42]On this point cf. C. Nino, *Derecho, moral y política*, p. 33.

[43]For a similar position, see N. Hoerster, *Zur Verteidigung der rechtspositivistischen Trennungsthese*, in *Archiv für Rechts- und Sozialphilosophie*, Beiheft 37, 1990, pp. 27–32.

[44]See Th. Hobbes, *Leviathan*, ed. by C. B. Macpherson, Harmondsworth 1982, pp. 120–121.

[45]G. Jellinek, *Ausgewählte Schriften*, vol. 1, ed. by W. Jellinek, Berlin 1911, p. 175.

to acts of consciousness. The fact that they are objective doesn't mean (and certainly not for ethical cognitivism) that they have already been received in the law "as it is".

The "logical thesis" is not convincing because it is founded on too sharp a distinction – not that between descriptive and normative sentences which should be retained, but that between the cognitive nature of the legal point of view (however with the severe limitation that such cognitive character does not apply for hard cases, that is those not covered by the semantic core of legal norms) and the willed or creative or decisionistic nature of morality. The legal universe is actually a little more complicated than that presented by Hart. When law is meant as production of norms it has obviously to a large degree to do with the will or the deliberation to produce norms. On the other hand, morality – as we have seen in the preceding chapter – cannot be reduced to an expression of emotion, sentiment, arbitrary commands, or even fists beating on the table (as Alf Ross says) or to pure nonsense or mysticism (as the early Wittgenstein would like us to believe). Morality (as a combination of judgments and values) is "meaningful", it *makes sense*, at least in so far as it is an *intensional* activity, that is, one directed toward an object that can then become the propositional content of the judgment in question. It is can then be a *rational or reasonable* construct. In moral judgment there is a moderate cognitive element (reducible in various forms to the principle of universalizability). To this should be added the fact that, as shown by Ronald Dworkin,[46] Hart's concept of law, while proclaiming war against so-called *essentialism*, is ontologically compromised. It contains nothing but rules, gone are the "principles" which play a central role in attributing meaning to single norms, within the legal order (thinking, for instance, of everyday democratic constitutions and their norms on fundamental rights). The principles of law (such as that of equality in front of the law, enshrined for instance in Article 3 of the Italian Republican Constitution), even though intended to be purely "legal", due to their extremely general nature cannot but contain elements of and refer to political or moral reasoning.

Hart could object that the separation of law and morality to which he refers is concerned above all with the question of legal reasoning. This would be that which is relevant when a judge or jury can or has to use institutional criteria when carrying out their legal activity. The separation here would be above all an epistemological one. Now, even on this level, the "logical thesis" doesn't work. It doesn't work for the simple fact that neither the "dogmatic" jurist nor the judge limit themselves to ascertaining the law in practice. When they affirm what the law "is", this involves a particular approach to human action, they thus also indicate what law "ought to be". From the point of view of the judge, the lawyer or even the "dogmatic" jurist, ascertaining what legal practice *is* actually serves within an argument as to the conduct that *should be* adopted in a concrete case. Theirs is not an internal *cognitive* point of view neither do they use "detached normative statements". Theirs is an internal *normative* point of view and their statements are "engaged", anything but detached. All this occurs not because of an intrinsic perversity on the part of the

[46] See R. Dworkin, *Taking Rights Seriously*, 2nd ed., London 1978.

jurists, nor because they are lacking in philosophical education and knowledge of the methodological rules of modern epistemology.

The fact is that whenever a sentence directs human conduct it must to some degree make *strong* normative assumptions. In fact, the only perspective producing obligatoriness in human conduct is, in the last instance, the strongly normative one, that which is phenomenologically based on the *autonomy of the will*; every other one is "defeasible" and can always be repealed in part. That which cannot be repealed is the "intensionality" of the act on the part of the subject: the fact that the propositional content of the judgment will be ascribed with a certain validity (here a moral value) through an exercise of reflection. The *logical* priority of the internal aspect of the act (its propositional content that tells us what the act "means") over the external aspect (the context in which the act is executed) becomes in the practical sphere a *deontological* priority. So long as a judgment or an act is normative in a *strong* sense, it will be categorically able to offer the evaluation, orientation and determination of conduct that we expect of it. It is necessary that the judgment or the act is conceived as having a *strong* normative validity, independently of the context in which it takes place (thus of the facts and acts in the world that causally determine the judgment or the act) and of its execution (thus independently of the consequences of its execution). Now – as results from what was said in the preceding chapter –, the *strong* normative point of view coincides with the moral point of view.

The final criterion of separation to mention is connected to the institutional theory defended in these pages. In brief, law is "institutional" and morality isn't. This criterion echoes a "classic" argument, for which morality is *autonomous*, whilst law is *heteronomous.* The validity of a legal rule depends on the state of affairs at the time of its issue and execution, whereas a moral rule is independent of such circumstances. Rules of law are "contextual", those of morality "universal". The rules of morality are primarily "regulative", they deal with conduct that is already possible and with objects for which the rules in question are not (as in the case of "constitutive" rules) conditions of possibility or perception.[47] Legal rules are as "regulative" as "constitutive"; amongst them there are many "regulative" rules, but there are also "constitutive" rules that produce possible spheres for action. Here, obviously, "constitutive" rules are logically and normatively (when the hierarchy of rules in a given order is concerned) superior to the "regulative" ones. This doesn't mean however that the "institution" of law produced by "constitutive" rules is not accessible to moral norms, or that it cannot be "challenged" by these.

One may ask whether *this* institution should be respected and also from *what* should the "regulative" rule be derived. In the end, even the *application* of the rules, be they constitutive or regulative, can be the object of moral deliberation. Moral judgment is "self-referential" in so far as it is presented as a sufficient reason for the justification of a particular action. Empirical facts, such as the good will of the agent or the practicability of the action sustained as morally obligatory, have to give way to this. In this sense, we could say, it is morality, not law, that is "autoopoietic", given

---

[47] For the difference between "constitutive" and "regulative" rules, see *supra*, pp. 146–147.

also that morality needs every time to be *re-constructed* when one finds oneself to deal with a moral issue. There are no "moral books" to look and go though: the ruling and its justification should every time be found through a sort of philosophical invention. Of course, this can be too much of a burden, too time-consuming, and besides too slow to tackle with situations that require a quick reaction. This is a reason why we need *law* that shapes models of right conduct and why we need furthermore education which produces *virtues*, that is a disposition to act in the right way. Remember that moral philosophy traditionally lead to philosophy of law and of education.

A fundamental empirical condition of right conduct is whether the justified action is *possible.* However, realizability of the action (even in the sense of its being perceivable as such) often depends on a sphere of action constituted by the legal norms. This means that moral norms require the law not just for reasons of cognitive or normative indeterminacy but even for *ontological* indeterminacy. Without law constitution of spheres of actions within which moral judgments are made would not be possible. Morality thus is *only* prescriptive, or regulative, law is constitutive *and* prescriptive. The basic normative category of morality is *duty*; the basic category of law is *power* or *competence* and, in the modernity, *rights*.

8.6 "Definitional" and "Derivative" Formulations

In his astute book *Practical Reason and Norms* Joseph Raz identifies two main ways of establishing a necessary relation between law and morality: "definitional", and "derivative" formulation. The "definitional" formulation "consists – he says – in defining law by a set of properties one or more of which are openly moral properties, for example that every law is morally valid, or conforms to the precepts of justice or is laid down by a morally legitimate authority".[48] The "derivative" formulation assumes that law is firstly form of social organization and should be identified as such, but that nonetheless it has a moral value. In other words, according to this second perspective, the moral properties possessed by all legal systems depend on non-moral properties. Whilst for the "definitional" approach to identify a legal order requires reference to moral principles or characteristics, this is not necessary for the "derivative" approach. It can identify legal order solely through reference to factual characteristics of the given phenomenon that are not strongly normative (in this case, the social institution "law")

As one will remember, above I listed three principal arguments in favour of a necessary connection between law and morality: (i) the argument *lex intiustissima non est lex*, or *Unrechtsargument*; (ii) the argument of "mere existence", and (iii) the argument of "principles". Of these three arguments the first and the third can immediately be seen to be variations of the "definitional" approach. Nonetheless, the argument *lex iniustissima non est lex* can also be considered a variant of the

---

[48] J. Raz, *Practical Reason and Norms*, 2nd ed., Oxford 1992, p. 164.

"derivative" perspective. At least until the limit of unjust law is reached. Beyond this limit it is no longer "derivative" and becomes "definitional". As far as the "argument of principles" is concerned, although in this argument law is nothing other than interpretation of law and this interpretation is a moral and political enterprise, there is no reason to deny that we find ourselves in front of a version of the "definitional" approach.

We can raise a number of objections to the "definitional" formulation. Above all there is little doubt that the usual positivistic concept of law allows for a tyrannical or unjust law. It is not logically contradictory, using normal common sense –it is said–, to state "this legal norm is valid (and in use) but is unjust" or to say "this legal order is effective but is unjust". For the definitional formulation it would be impossible to identify law without a previous conception of that which should be considered moral. Legal knowledge would thus be more or less reduced to moral knowledge, or ought to be derived from this.

But – as was seen in the last part of the book – moral knowledge is controversial and fragile, since it presupposes states of affairs or "objects" or a specific moral rationality based on criteria that go beyond factual subjective and inter-subjective approval and acceptance. Are there objects in the world that we can confidently identify as intrinsically moral? Is there a specific moral rationality that can be used only through a cognitive approach? Since a positive response to these questions can only be given "constructively", within a discourse with certain ideal characteristics, it is better to be prudent and remain doubtful with respect to the "definitional" formulation. This is even before considering that different contexts will give rise to different concepts of law.[49] The concepts of law used by King Solomon and by the anthropologist who studied his writing don't have to coincide. The first case is an internal (normative) point of view, and in the second an external point of view or rather a *cognitive* internal point of view.

On the other hand, the "derivative" approach takes it for granted that morality disposes of an already instituted shape of action whithin which and from which human conduct draws its own sense. However, this could only be possible if we had a normative system that is already in force, something that we could equate to law operating as an institution.

To resolve the problem of the relationship between law and morality we can certainly sustain the assumption that in the world there are moral attitudes, praxes and statements *bestowed with meaning*, and that this meaning is not merely emotive or imperative and obviously, much the less, descriptive. However to present them as normative in a strong sense we must adopt or share such attitudes, praxes or statements, that is to say, in some sense to evaluate them, to deliberate on them and not only to know them. Knowing the law is, at least in principles, a question of demonstrable or verifiable statements: to use as Raz' words, "what the law is in force can on occasion be a controversial question, but it is in principle soluble".[50]

[49]Cf. C. S. Nino, *Derecho, moral y política*, Chapter 1.
[50]J. Raz, *Practical Reason and Norms*, p. 165.

If we accept a formulation according to which law and morality are by definition connected we must assume that it is possible that statements are verifiable in virtue of values of moral properties, thus a strongly cognitivist or objectivist view of meta-ethics. It is however advisable to avoid this, considering the uneliminable will-based element of moral judgments and also the burdensome and controversial metaphysical assumptions which – as we saw in the preceding chapter – often constrains us to meta-ethical cognitivism.

Let us now consider some objections to the "derivative" formulation. This – following Raz' reconstruction – consists of two main arguments. The first is based on the argument of "mere existence". This argument assumes a double form. The existence of a legal order is morally positive and good, because in any case it is preferable to have a society with a legal order rather than to have no society (remembering that a legal order is a condition of its existence). It is also preferable to having a (bad) society lacking a legal order (again, this is a condition for a well ordered society). The mere existence of a legal order is good in so far as – according to Raz – "however bad the laws may be, the subjection of human behaviour to the government of rules on the basis of which certain disputes are to be settled is of itself of moral value or ensures the realization of some moral value".[51]

This second argument is also based on that which has been defined the "argument of content" which affirms that every legal system, in order to be truly legal, has to contain at least some just laws and norms. A formulation of this type is for example that which speaks of the "minimum content of natural law". The *minimum content of natural law* set out by H. L. A. Hart and long before him, by Georg Jellinek who spoke of the "ethical minimum", *das ethische Minimum*, of law.[52] According to Hart, a legal order in order to be recognizable as such, has to carry out some morally based functions. For example, every legal system has to contain provisions that protect the human life of its members and their property.[53]

There are two principal objections to the first version of the "derivative" approach. The first is founded on an empirical argument: Are we sure that in every case having a legal order contributes to the life of society? Is it not possible that in some cases a legal order is damaging to the existence of a certain society? Is it not possible that a group of devils need law to fulfill their dastardly plans? Is it not clear that law – as seen in the first part of the book – can organize and render functional the "dominion", non-democratic or indeed tyrannical or totalitarian forms of power and rights, not serve to protect human rights and property but rather lead to their annihilation?

The second objection is founded on a meta-ethical argument. The fact that a legal order contributes to the existence of a certain society is not enough to lead to a positive evaluation, in moral terms, of the law in question. It is enough only if one

---

[51] Ibid., p. 167.

[52] See G. Jellinek, *Die sozialethische Bedeutung von Recht, Unrecht und Strafe*, reprint of the 1st ed. (Vienna 1878), Hildesheim 1967, p. 42.

[53] See H. L. A. Hart, *The Concept of Law*, Oxford 1961, p. 195.

believes that the society in question is good and just, so maintaining that law, which is an instrument for its protection, is equally good and just. The only way to reply to this is through a very general statement: any society as such is just, and law (which is by definition its protector) equally morally positive. However, this thesis (which is at heart a variant of communitarian moral doctrine) is too general to be convincing. *We know* that there have been, and that there are still, unjust societies: we know that members revolted against their own unjust societies because they were judged morally intolerable. We know that at least in certain cases there has been moral progress in the passage from one type of society to another and this was achieved through denying the moral value of the legal order and the laws of society. We know that *disorder* can be preferable to an order whose only purpose is oppression and annihilation.

Two objections can also raised to the second version of the "derivative" perspective. The "argument of content", in particular the thesis of the minimum content of natural law, states that each legal system contains (should contain) at least a few laws that have the moral function of realizing, or helping to realize, some moral values, such as protection of the lives and property of people. But are we sure that these are always good laws? Are we sure that every legal system defends or protects life and property in a *way* that we could consider just or moral? Can we consider the death penalty just when it is introduced to defend the lives and property of citizens? Is it not perhaps the case, when speaking of law, that means are as important as ends? Or that the end justifies the means?

Moreover, the fact that a legal system contains *some* laws that are morally acceptable, or just, doesn't render the entire system moral or just. From the morality of a particular law we cannot infer the morality of the entire body of law. The fact that the Nazi legal system maintained to a large degree the BGB, the German civil code of 1900 and protected the property of the majority of its members, and that in many cases murder continued to be punished as such, does not justify the opinion that the legal system was moral or just. In fact let's adopt the "argument of content" and by "content" we mean some generic function played by the law in all societies (that which would be their moral value). It should follow that every legal system (if it functions and is minimally predictable in its behaviour) is moral. The fact that a citizen is interned in a concentration camp every time he expresses an opinion contrary to that of the ruling party, and that internment is entirely predictable, is no reason to attribute to that predictability, and to that "security" of expectation and prediction on the part of the citizens, a moral value that "security" hardly deserves to be said "legal security". The conclusion that every legal order in so far as it is predictable has a (at least minimal) moral content seems, barely plausible.

8.7 Epilogue

Every law and every legal decision, even those made by the infamous Dr. Ronald Freisler, the president of the *Volksgerichtshof* of Nazi Germany, are implicitly based on a claim to justice, or at least, of not being unjust. We can agree with Robert Alexy who sees a performative contradiction if a law or legal decision, after prescribing certain behaviour of establishing a certain state of affairs, were then to add “and this is unjust”. This doesn’t mean, however, that if a sentence or a law is not just, it is no longer a sentence or a law, but only that we can always subject the law or the sentence to a test of justice or morality.

The application of the theory of “linguistic acts” to legal phenomena is possible if one interprets the “linguistic act” other than in merely empirical or pragmatic terms. It is in fact doubtful that a law or a legal decision are forms of “linguistic acts” in this sense, as they cannot be reduced to forms of such as acts. A “linguistic act” in the purely pragmatic sense is based on a more or less personal relationship between the emitter and the recipient of a linguistic expression. One is thus dealing with an act between people who could be influenced be the behaviour (the “speech act”) of each other. This is, however, not the case for law (to conceive of a law as an empirical “speech act” would somehow imply falling back into a voluntaristic conception of law yet again).

Law is not *pronounced*; rather, it is deliberated and made public. Even in the case of judicial rulings the personal or interpersonal element is not the only or the mainly one. It is true that here there is a direct relationship between the one who issues a series of statements (the judge) and the one who receives them (the parties). However, this personal element is contingent and tangential. For instance, as the study of legal reasoning teaches us, in deciding a case (in both civil and common law) judges take into consideration the effects of their rulings on the whole of the normative system and on future decision, not only on the parties concerned. The performative element of the case ruling, however, as a “speech act” (in the strictly empirical sense), could refer only to concrete subjects, revolving around the pragmatic effect produced by the act of ruling.

It is necessary therefore, even if one wants to maintain the definition of legal ruling as “speech act”, to conceive of this as an act within an institution, as set out in the second part of this book. In this case, however, it is only through presenting the institutional norms within a discourse on justification that one can claim justifiability. Such a presentation assumes the character of a public discussion – especially within the cultural sphere labelled “modernity”. “Modernity” – as Carlos Nino describes well – proposes a *discursive* form of reproduction of positive morality.[54] This is linked in a strict way to “critical” morality and to the “strong” normative viewpoint. It might however be the case that the reflective and deliberative character of a legal institution would reach also beyond the precinct of “modernity”. What has been said and shown in this book renders this latter hypothesis more than plausible.

In order that the presumed justice of the ruling or of the law be the subject of a moral discourse we need to refer firstly to the procedures and the conventions that provide the initial and internal justification of the ruling and the laws. Accordingly we should consider the “institution” of law in its totality and its “meaning”. It is only when we reach this point that it will be possible to begin a *strongly* normative

[54]See C. S. Nino, *Derecho, moral y política*, p. 60.

discourse aimed at justification. In order to do this, however, we need a "liberal" conception of law, a concept that doesn't prejudice in any way the relationship between law and morality. It should neither take as fulfilled the moral character of law nor exclude a connection between the two. Two conditions need to be fulfilled in order to debate the possible injustice of a norm or a legal act: law should not be "definitively" declared deaf to the claims of morality and independently of this; law should not be "derivatively" deduced from morality. The concept of law as "institution" presented in this book satisfies, I believe, these two conditions.

My conclusion then is the following. Although it has not been proven that there is a necessary *conceptual* and *material* connection between law and morality, such that where there is law there would also be a morally satisfying system of norms, in other words, such that it wouldn't be possible to identify a legal system without recourse to moral criteria, it is equally the case however that it cannot be demonstrated that law and morality are separated in such a way that once immorality or injustice has been discovered in a normative system, it would still be possible to describe this system as legal or such that it could be claimed that legal decisions are always morally neutral and morally irrelevant. It is evident, rather, that between law and morality there is a necessary *practical* connection, in the sense that every law and every legal decision are morally relevant in that they have effects on the liberty, dignity and well-being of human beings. "Given that law is what its is – Neil McCormick writes [55] –, it can neither be operated nor fully understood without acceptance that it does and must serve some – doubtless both contestable and not wholly coherent – scheme of values. Thus the law is always and necessarily moral relevant. It is always and necessarily open to moral criticism. It is always and necessarily a topic for practical reasoning".

It is also evident that law has a *functional* connection with morality, if by this is meant positive morality – the dominant ideology of a society. Law doesn't work if its mechanisms and content do not correspond to positive morality. Without a widespread consensus based on shared values and the support of a "dominant ideology" there cannot be either political power or an effective legal order, as demonstrated in the first part of the book. Positive morality, as we know, is not morality in the critical and strongly normative sense that we use when we refer to moral judgments as reasons that justify conduct independently of a concrete state of affairs. Positive morality depends on the circumstances that are socially dominant. As noted above, positive morality does maintain a link with critical morality in that it represent its internal aspect: the propositional content of each judgment in which the given positive morality is made concrete. Such content has a deontological character ("It is just that...", "it is obligatory that...", etc.) that renders it permeable from a strongly normative viewpoint. If one judges the "justice" of an act (with a judgment in positive morality) it is possible to transcend the fact that the judgment is dominant widespread and majoritarian in a certain social group and examine the merits of the same judgment. Positive morality, thus, above all in modernity which

[55] N. MacCormick, *Natural Law Reconsidered*, in *Oxford Journal of Legal Studies*, 1981, p. 109.

is primarily discursive, is "defeasible", can be challenged from a strong normative, that is a critical moral point of view and it sometimes necessitates the categorical justification that this view offers.

If we next consider the three main moments of legal practice, production, application, and the interpretation of norms, we can observe that all these moments imply or presuppose or require some type of moral evaluation.[56] This is evident in the case of production of norms, especially in the sphere of legislation and in the setting out of a constitution. Establishing laws or a constitution requires a *strong* normative point of view. To regulate human conduct cannot but be the result of moral evaluation and deliberation. The same is true of the application of norms and in particular of jurisdiction. To determine what ought to be the rules of conduct for oneself and for others could never be merely an intellectual exercise or neutral enterprise. Moreover it has considerable impact on the lives of interested parties. The process of application has a certain discretionary sphere, the restriction of which remains a moral obligation of the judge. At this point one could advance the idea of a connection that is as based on *justification* as on *interpretation* of law and morality, in that in order to justify the normative value of law and to operationalize this, reference to morally-based criteria is indispensable or useful.

The only case in which the moral relevance or implications of legal practice is not so evident is perhaps that of legal interpretation. This is especially true when it is done *docendi causa*, by teaching in a Law School for instance, or when it assumes features that are doctrinal or based on the so-called legal dogmatics. However, anyone who has some familiarity with legal studies knows perfectly well that doctrine quite often has practical ends in mind as soon as it deals with producing interpretation of a particular law, norm or sentence. It is well-noted, above all by legal scholars, that their work, the self-proclaimed "science" of law, can have a dramatic impact on the legislation and constitution of a country. It is for this reason, in order to influence judges, legislators and constituents, that they often write in legal journals and publish, ponderous "dogmatic" monographs. Thus the "dogmatic" legal "scientists" cannot hide their moral responsibility behind a rather suspect claim to *Wissenschaftlichkeit,* the "scientific" and therefore morally neutral nature of their work.

Nonetheless, we can admit and defend that in principle it is possible to ascribe meaning to a legal norm without entering into any kind of moral reasoning. The contrary thesis relates legal knowledge to morality, in such a way as to render difficult even the task of identifying the individual legal norms and the legal system on which the jurist is called upon to give information without becoming a moralist. I could say that according to Ottoman law a male adult had the right to be married to more than one woman, without having to recognize this moral system or feel myself constrained to obey it or to approve (or disapprove) of it. This is banal and the banality of an argument (very different to its irrelevancy) is not an argument in its disfavour.

[56] Cf. C. S. Nino, *Derecho, moral y política*, Chapter 3.

Anyway, all that does not resolve the true problem, that which is at the heart of the interminable debate about the relationship between law and morality. This is expressed as the following question: Is the law a *strongly* normative reason for an action? The fact that it is possible to establish, or describe, law without recourse to moral criteria does not provide an answer to this question. I can ascertain what is the law in force independently of any moral consideration and still be looking for arguments that demonstrate the law in force should direct my conduct.

As law is a (*strongly*) normative reason for action it requires a (*strongly)* normative premise, a premise that is, which tells me that the law is moral, or rather that I must (in a *strong* sense) obey the law in question. In this regard, Julius Binder is as correct as Carlos Nino. The former, we remember, as a Neo-Kantian, claimed that law as a positive ruling didn't imply an obligation by the law addressees, the latter said that a claim to legal validity that did not refer back to moral justification could be of interest to the sociologist but says nothing to the individual in search of a way of directing her social conduct. For this reason, the argument that moral judgments should be constrained such that critical morality directed towards law would be forbidden, and that an attempt should be made to remove the critical dimension from legal decisions, is not convincing. Only moral rulings are *in the last instance* bestowed with a motivating force of obligation.

Even for a magistrate law is not a *strong* normative reason for acting without ulterior premises, however unexpressed. Even where the judges thinks as "mouthpiece of the law" and acts accordingly a strongly normative principle is needed, that is one that assumes as a moral value that the judge should be rigidly and constantly subordinate to positive law. The separation of law and morality in the sense expressed by the principle "no punishment without a crime, no crime without a prior law" excludes punishment of behaviour just because it is contrary to morality. It is without doubt a *moral principle.* Law cannot but receive from *outside*, from "nowhere", its ultimate claim to constrain the will of human beings. Law can be *prima facie* obligatory if it is imbued with legitimacy – in virtue of constitutional principles of which it is an expression and thus of a particular political theory. It cannot either constitute a surrogate for morality or liberate citizens from the *deliberation* to act and the consequent and inevitable *ethical* responsibility.

My final conclusions are all expressed as a lack of certainty even though that said above implies a more decisive position and sometimes my theses and their tone were rather less moderate. Prudence suggests one to assume a "modest" perspective, in a field that is both difficult and controversial. Thus: It is not proven that morality is purely subjective and permanently because "ontologically" open to disagreement and that law alone can provide a certain degree of objective justification and certainty. It is not clear that law provides "exclusionary reasons" for action, that is to say, reasons that exclude the consideration of prior reasons for action that are conflicting or competing with the legal ones. Said in different terms, it is not at all proven that law is not open to disagreement, and that this makes all the difference with morality. It is not either clear that it is not possible to identify law from an "external" viewpoint (as propositional concept or content that is not part of the actual justification for the action or for the ruling) without recourse to norms or moral principles. But it is no less certain that a possible normative point of view (that justifies behaviour) is the *strong* one (that is, the moral point of view)[57] and that reasons for action are not given only by a "weak" normative viewpoint that is generally prudential, conventional, institutional or even "ontic". As matter of fact, the latter could be overcome or overwhelmed by *strong* normative reasons, especially in an area such as law which refers almost immediately to the ideal of *justice*, whatever its substantive content might be. In law "ontology" could and sometimes should defer to "deontology". However, in the law there wouldn't be any "deontology" without "ontology".

[57]This seems to be the opinion of Carlos Nino for whom the difference between "constative and prescriptive judgments" is thus descriptive and "pure normative judgments" are not an intermediate or spurious or weak form of moral judgment. In contradiction with his conception of "pure normative judgment" as a judgment whose content is independent of the consequences of its execution, Nino includes prudential judgments in "pure" normative judgments (see C. S. Nino, *Derecho, moral y política*, pp. 118–119). The category of "supportive normative judgments" introduced by Nino alongside that of "pure normative judgments" consists in reality of a category in itself with respect to "pure normative judgments", since such supportive judgments are nothing other than conclusions derived logically – with the use of a factual premise represented by "prescriptive constantive judgments" – from pure normative judgments and can thus be classified as *applied* "pure normative judgments".

Name Index

M. La Torre, *Law as Institution,* Law and Philosophy Library 90,
DOI 10.1007/978-1-4020-6607-8, © Springer Science+Business Media B.V. 2010

Subject Index

FSC
www.fsc.org
MIX
Papier | Fördert gute Waldnutzung
FSC® C083411

Kolibri 360 GmbH
Ferdinand-Jühlke-Straße 7
99095 Erfurt, Deutschland
produktsicherheit@kolibri360.de